THE TRAGEDY
OF THE CHINESE
REVOLUTION

THE TRAGEDY
OF THE CHINESE
REVOLUTION

By

HAROLD R. ISAACS

SECOND REVISED EDITION

STANFORD UNIVERSITY PRESS
STANFORD, CALIFORNIA

The first edition of this book was published in 1938 in Great Britain. The revised edition was published in 1951 by Stanford University Press. The present edition was first published in 1961.

Stanford University Press
Stanford, California
Copyright © 1951, 1961 by the Board of Trustees
of the Leland Stanford Junior University
Printed in the United States of America

SECOND REVISED EDITION
First published 1961
Last figure below indicates year of this printing:

88 87 86 85 84 83 82 81 80

M EN fight and lose the battle, and the thing they fought for comes about in spite of their defeat, and when it comes turns out to be not what they meant, and other men have to fight for what they meant under another name.

WILLIAM MORRIS

PREFACE TO THE SECOND REVISED EDITION

IT IS JUST ten years since the first revised edition of this work appeared in 1951, twenty-three years since it was first published in 1938. I can only observe, with as much detachment as I can muster, that this is a book with a grip on life all its own, and I herewith extend my grateful respects to all who continue to find it useful in the effort to study contemporary China.

The body of this book remains unchanged from the 1951 edition. I have made only two changes of any magnitude. One was to reinstate without change, as an appendix, the chapter from the original edition dealing with the Kiangsi Soviet period of the Chinese Communist movement, from 1928 to 1934. This chapter was dropped in the first revision as part of the effort to confine the book's span to the 1925–27 events. It has been strongly urged upon me that despite some interpretations and judgments which are now quite obsolete, there is still considerable reference value in this chapter for students of Chinese Communism. If this is true, it seems right to make this material once more accessible.

To make room for this addition, I have dropped Chapter 19 of the 1951 edition. This was a discussion of the larger historic framework of the China events, an attempt to examine the rise and the challenge of Communist totalitarianism. The book now concludes with Chapter 18, also added in 1951, which attempts to relate the 1925–27 events to the Communist conquest of power in China in 1949. From this chapter I have deleted only the more topical passages (e.g., relating to the Korean War) and some of the details from its summary of the Kiangsi period, now made more fully available in the newly added Appendix. Otherwise this chapter is also left virtually intact. The intent of all this is to leave a book which will carry the reader up to the new thresholds of history established by the Communist takeover in China in 1949.

Of the development of affairs in China since that time we have had only a limited view. There are mountains of Chinese Communist materials, and a shelf of works of reportage by more or less friendly or hostile European and Asian reporters. But American contact with China during this period has been all but totally severed. There has been some secondhand reporting in the American press, and a few serious attempts by scholars to examine and interpret the data available from Communist sources. But none of this overcomes the handicap of our total physical divorce from the new Chinese reality. We have been seeing events in Communist China only from afar. As I have tried to show elsewhere,* our images of China have long been peculiarly distorted, and perhaps hardly ever more so than in these last years, when the elements of distance, exclusion, propaganda, fear, and hostility have shaped our view of actualities lurid enough in themselves without these enlargements. But this time of severed contact must soon come to an end. It is painfully clear that whatever obstacles or limitations may be involved, resumption of direct contact with the Chinese reality is an absolute condition of our better grasp of just what Communist power has meant to China during this past decade, and may mean for the rest of the world in the decades to come.

As far as we can see them here now, many of the particulars of the Communist accomplishment in China in these ten years are tentative and controversial. The regime itself has made and withdrawn various sets of extravagant claims about its economic gains. It has "advanced" and "retreated" behind barrages of Newspeak and smoke-screens of propaganda so effective that its precise location at any point is hard to fix, especially in the field of agriculture. Yet in certain other basic economic areas it seems clear that if it has not always taken the great leaps of which it has boasted, the regime has taken long, long strides, e.g., in steel and coal production, industrial development and manufacturing, road and railway mileage, river control systems, adding up to the beginnings of a remarkably swift and irreversible change-over of the basis of the whole society. But whatever doubts and queries may persist on this score for lack of adequate information and verification, there is at least one matter on which all accounts seem to agree: the totalitarian system laid upon China by the Communists in the first years of their power has outdone anything ever produced by the Russians. The achievement of total control over the entire people

---

* *Scratches on Our Minds, American Images of China and India* (The John Day Company, New York, 1958).

by the combined use of mass persuasion, coercion, and physical terror is plainly one of the regime's truly staggering successes. The Orwellian world of 1984, which had its prototype in the Russia of Stalin, is being reproduced and vastly embellished in the China of Mao Tsê-tung. By these means, the world's largest population has been put to work to transform backward old China into one of the great new powers in the world, and to do it within a single generation.

Just what effect the Chinese emergence will have on the world in the coming decade is not a subject for reasonable prediction. Even now, before it has in fact acquired most of the necessary prerequisites, China is already widely conceded the role and status of great power, is seen as one of the "twin giants" of the totalitarian world empire and is viewed with a mix of fear and respect. It has taken a great leap indeed in a few years from fulfilling the world's image of it as a weakling state to become abruptly a new power casting fearsome shadows on the future. The old stereotype of "Oriental inscrutability" has already been absorbed into the new view of China as one of the world's most imponderable forces of change. The image of the great submissive mass of Chinese people also remains; only in the epoch past it was seen as a kind of inert submission to adverse fate, while now it is submission, though hardly still inert, to a new regime of their own, bent upon regaining China's historic place as the true center of the world.

Even when, by some measure of hardheadedness, the image of the new China is reduced to a more "realistic" size and shape, it is still impressive and formidable. It has already proved its capacity to exert a force of its own in the large arena of the world power struggle. Within the Soviet orbit, it operates as an ally and not as a satellite of the dominant Russia. Nor is it an easy ally. It is a challenger for different kinds of primacy within the Communist world empire. It acts in response to its own profound expansionist drives in dealing with its Asian neighbors. Its contest with India over the Himalayan frontiers is no small matter itself; it is also an omen of things to come. The new China by no means confines itself to Asia. In the great new game of power politics, it operates on its own out to the world's farthest corners. Chinese missions of various kinds—political, commercial, cultural, technical, military—Chinese goods, rice (even in times of need or famine at home) and even Chinese arms, now appear to serve strictly Chinese purposes in such places as Egypt, Algeria, Morocco, in Guinea and Mali and other parts of emergent Africa, in Cuba and elsewhere all over Latin America—indeed at almost every point where societies are in motion and there is a contest for control and influence from the outside, and even, as in Albania, within the Soviet empire itself.

In the larger issues of war and peace, the Chinese remain unavoidably subordinate to the greater power of the Russians. But even here, in a whole range of critical matters affecting the strategy of the Soviet orbit in the world power struggle, the Chinese have more and more intruded their own demands and visibly influenced major policy decisions. Ten years ago American discussion of the China problem often turned on the ways and means of detaching China from its allegiance to Russia. It is a real measure of the change of these years that by now far more commonly the talk is of detaching Russia from China. And indeed, as the issue of disarmament or arms control becomes more and more critical as viewed in the two major capitals of the power struggle, the problem of China intrudes more and more insistently. When Communist China will acquire atomic capacity of its own we do not know; but no one thinks it is a safe distance away. On the contrary, we have to contemplate the possibility that China will become an atomic power even while some of its peasants may still be working their land with wooden plows, carrying their goods across their shoulders, or pushing wheelbarrows along ancient stone paths through countrysides still uncut by road or rail. This speculation, not at all idle, does not lighten the outlook, whether seen from Washington or Moscow.

But far more immediate, far more direct, and far more powerful at this time is the image the Chinese Communists have managed to cast throughout the world as the possessors of a magic key to the swift emergence from backwardness. Possession of such a key was for long, and still is, a principal ingredient in that attractive power that Russia exerts in the underdeveloped areas of the world. But to many newly risen nationalists, in Africa especially, standing raw and uncertain just over the thresholds of political power, the Chinese example in some ways seems to be even more attractive than the Russian. This is partly because the Chinese have seemed to move even more swiftly than the Russians. It may be partly because of a feeling that the Chinese started from a level of backwardness closer to their own. It is partly out of awe, respect, and envy for the greater totality of Chinese totalitarian power. It is also because the Chinese are nonwhite. There is a strong

measure of racism in Chinese hostility to the West and if one is sensi-
tized to read relationships in these terms, it is not difficult to discover
this same element in the tensions between the Chinese and the Russians
as well, and to identify it with the anti-Western, antiwhite black nationalism that runs so strong now among so many Africans. In any case,
the promise of power and speedy development made real by the Chinese
example has an almost hypnotic pull upon many an emergent nationalist who comes now so late into the world's political arena. This is a
man who is impatient for change and hungry for power, but hungry
most of all for that sensation, which he sees the Chinese already enjoying, of commanding the respect and the fear of the Western world that
held them in such base contempt for so long. Whoever among us still
underestimates the power of this emotion is hopelessly and dangerously
blind.

I had this borne in on me again and again in West Africa only a
few months ago. I think most particularly of a young man I met in
Guinea—a land whose new rulers have already shaped their party
and its politics on the Chinese model and where Chinese political and
technical missions are quite busily at work—an ardent young nationalist who passionately, and not without anguish, cried out: "I don't
care if it takes a hundred Stalins, a hundred Mao Tsê-tungs. We'll
have them, if this is the way for us to get out of the dirt and stand up
and be seen in the world. Can you really show us a better way?"

Well, can we? This challenge is a massive one. Imbedded in it
are the issues that will decide the great power struggle over the decades
that lie ahead. The only other way they will be decided will be by the
release of nuclear and missile power. In that case much becomes ir-
relevant. But if we do manage to avoid that ultimate catastrophe,
then the shape of the world will be determined by what paths are taken
by the newly emergent countries of Asia and Africa. At the end of this
work ten years ago, I wrote: "At the end of the blind alley of totalitarianism there is no outlet to greater freedom or peaceful growth.
There is nothing but self-destruction or the darkness of a new barbarian epoch." And finally: "We will either transform our paretic
world and create a global society in which Asia and Africa can thrive
with us, or else they will, out of intolerable frustration, create a new
set of tyrannies, of which Russia's will have been the first, and China's
the second."

This was urgently said in 1951. It is all the more urgently repeated now. This option will not stand indefinitely and will not even stand for long. It does not seem to me unreasonably gloomy to say that if we do not take it up and begin to meet this demand upon us before another ten years go by, the chance to do so will probably pass and not long thereafter no one may even remember that we ever had the choice.

H. R. I.

CAMBRIDGE, MASSACHUSETTS
February 25, 1961

PREFACE TO THE FIRST REVISED EDITION

THIS BOOK is a history of the defeat of the Chinese revolution of 1925–27. It examines the first intervention of the Soviet Union in China and its consequences. This is the story of the initial experiences that molded the Chinese Communist movement. It is also the story of how Chiang Kai-shek came to power. It is offered in this new edition in the hope that it can contribute to an understanding of the events, moods, and attitudes in China today, where the Communists now rule and where Russia is once more able to wield a powerful influence in Chinese affairs.

First published in England in 1938, this book has led an eventful life of its own. The plates and surviving copies of the original edition were destroyed in the Nazi bombing of London in 1940. A pirated edition published in Shanghai had a much wider circulation, copies of it turning up in many different parts of the world in later years. In India in 1944 I came across a condensed version circulating in mimeographed form. It has remained in all this time the only detailed, documented account of the original Kuomintang-Communist alliance, and of the way in which Russian-dictated policies drove the Chinese Communists and the great masses of Chinese who followed them into a tragic debacle. As such, it has been cited in numerous bibliographies and mentioned in many a footnote, while actual copies of the book became increasingly rare. As events again and again brought reminders of the pertinence of early Kuomintang-Communist relations, it became a much-sought-after work, pursued through advertisements in book journals and by direct inquiries, of which many have reached me through the years. It has not been possible for a long time to meet this demand and I am grateful to the Stanford University Press for making this revised edition available now.

Many who are familiar with the original work will want to know whether its "point of view" has changed. The answer is, of course, that no serious student of social movements and international affairs could have lived through these tumultuous years without developing new points of view about the problems of social and political change. But these have not required me to make any substantive changes in the presentation of the facts in this book. This work was undertaken in the first place with too intensive a study of the material and with too great a respect for the graspable truth to be subject to revision of objective facts because of any shift in subjective outlook. It set out to describe, with maximum possible fidelity to the historic record, what happened in the Chinese revolution of 1925–27. That is still its purpose, and whatever its defects, the basic text remains the same, largely as it was originally written.

The revisions that have been made, however, should be clearly described. The purely editorial changes are simple ones. In the first place, the three chapters in the original edition which described the principal developments of the decade 1927–37 have been replaced by two new concluding chapters. In these the attempt is made to trace the imprint of the revolution of 1925–27 on the history of the two subsequent decades and to sketch in this form the later history of the Kuomintang, the Communists, and the new Russian impact on China, carrying the account up to the present. Second, this book was originally undertaken as a history that would refute, by faithful resort to the documentary record, the gross falsifications in which the Communist International tried to bury the facts of what actually happened in the critical years 1925–27. It will, I hope, serve that purpose more effectively in this edition as a result of cuts and stylistic revisions designed to eliminate polemical excesses, subjective comments, and repetitious arguments. These changes, I hope, allow the facts and documents to speak more fully for themselves.

Concerning the changes in "point of view," there is more to be said. "Point of view" is another phrase for interpretation, interpretation is another word for bias, and bias is another word for outlook. Every writer is conditioned by all the individual and social factors that shape his thinking about man's affairs. This is especially true in current history and politics, although the historian's personal involvement in remoter events is often no less marked. All historical and political questions are the products of conflict and are therefore controversial. They all concern unresolved human problems on which all thought is subject to contradiction and revision. The writer's responsibility, it has always seemed to me, is not to claim some unattainable detachment—for which another word is objectivity—but rather first to respect the facts as the record discloses them and, second, to make the nature of his own outlook, or bias, perfectly plain.

Thus the basic approach in this work is one that seeks to contribute to a radical transformation of all social relations and political institutions to bring about the fuller popular acquisition of greater material welfare and political and cultural freedom. For the people of China, and of Asia and Africa in general, this has involved a prolonged struggle against political and economic domination by Western nations. It has required, and in much of the world still tardily requires, an end to the system of Western colonialism. It has involved the need to create new social and economic relations in which the masses of people could begin to free themselves of the fetters of intolerable poverty. It involves, further, the effort to find a way out of the blind alley of national sovereignty into some broader and more inherently cooperative organization of the world in which all peoples can hope to thrive.

These needs and conflicts have been the main content of the great upheavals in China and elsewhere in recent decades. The role of the Communist movement in these events has been a decisive one, both in defeat and in victory. The interaction of the Russian state and the Chinese revolutionary movement was the prime factor in the events in China in 1927. This same interaction, now in 1951, with the Communists in power in China, has become a still greater determining influence in the fate of the whole world. With the collapse of the last remnants of Western colonialism in Asia and the emergence of Russia as an aggressive and powerful contender for world power, the issue of Russia's relationship to China in particular and to Asia in general has become a central one in the great conflicts that mark world affairs in our time.

The subversion of indigenous social revolutionary movements by Russian national policies and strategic interests has been a major facet of all this history. This book was written in the first place as an attempt to show how this process unfolded at an early date in China. It was intended then, and is even more so intended now, to serve as a weapon against the Stalin dictatorship in Russia and to show its cruelly destructive influence on revolutionary movements elsewhere in the world. This influence came into being, however, not mechanically or automatically, but emerged from the evolution of the Russian state itself after 1917 and from the whole course of world events. The terms and tempo of the degeneration of the state which emerged from the Russian revolution has long been a matter of debate among socialists and will be wrestled with by historians for a long time to come. When this book was first written it largely accepted the view of the Russia of 1925–27 as a workers' state that was being deformed by a usurping bureaucracy but which nevertheless still played a progressive role in world affairs. This seems to me now to have been a formula for rationalizing the Russian reality. It eventually served, indeed, as the epitaph of a whole generation of revolutionists in Russia and elsewhere. The precise nature of the bureaucratic state in Russia still awaits adequate description, but from a socialist point of view its "progressive" role in world affairs ceased at a very early date. The "socialist" and "working class" features of this state barely survived the Russian civil war. Their vestigial remains became part of the liturgy with which the new bureaucratic power sanctioned its counterrevolution and hypnotized and corrupted its own tools and supporters.

This process of degeneration was spread over a number of years and the Chinese events of 1925–27 played a crucial role in it. But by 1924 the Russian regime had already cut itself off from its proletarian roots. It had already foregone its socialist premises. It had already choked off the profoundly democratic impulses and aspirations which the revolution had initially expressed. The soviets, or popularly elected councils, had already been deprived of their democratic character, and the bureaucracy had begun to fashion out of the victory of the revolution a regime designed to enable a tight oligarchy to wield absolute power. Lenin's doctrines of uncompromising internationalism had already been replaced by Stalin's theory of "socialism in one country."

Aware of the effects of Russia's isolation and the growth of nationalist tendencies within the new bureaucratic power machine, Lenin as early as 1922 saw an abyss yawning at Russia's feet. Probably neither he nor any of his closest associates, including Trotsky, dreamed how deep that abyss was or how swift the plunge into it would be. By the time Soviet Russia actively intervened in the affairs in China, beginning in 1923 and 1924, the lineaments of the totalitarian dictatorship had already become visible. Under Stalin's leadership, the Kremlin had already subjected the German workers to destructive policies determined not by the circumstances in Germany but by the strategic-military interests of the Russian state. It was already, with complete cynicism, Russifying the Communist parties abroad and turning them into blind tools of Soviet foreign policy.

Aside from the narrower matter of tempo of development, it has also been necessary to draw from the Russian experience conclusions about the concept of the "dictatorship of the proletariat." This concept, never fully explored in the literature of revolutionary Marxism, was seen in theory as a brief, transitional passage on the road to greater freedom. The Russian reality has given it instead a dark and fearful content. This experience has taught us that the contradiction between authoritarianism and democratic socialism is complete. The one-party monopoly of political life, developing into a bureaucratic oligarchy, an outcome that clearly rose out of some of the basic premises of Bolshevism, cannot serve socialist ends. No broader democracy can come from a political system based on force and lacking in institutional safeguards against the corruptions of power and violence.

I cannot now be as categoric as I was in judging what course the Chinese revolution might have pursued of its own momentum two decades ago if it had not suffered the deforming pressure of Russian control and influence. Given the immense popular upsurge and the instinctive drive to create new and fundamentally democratic institutions both in city and country, it still seems possible even now to believe that it might have developed new revolutionary forms capable of preserving both democratic intent and democratic practice. The Stalin dictatorship in Russia was still weak enough to have been incapable of imposing itself with complete success on the emergent revolutionary regime in China and might indeed have found itself modified by the Chinese outcome. But between their defeat in China in 1927 and their victory in 1949, the Chinese Communists grew into a force capable only of imposing a new totalitarian dictatorship upon China. In the same interim, Russia, in that day still an adolescent tyranny, has grown into a totalitarian monster, imposing its great weight not only upon China but upon the whole world.

The tragedy of the Chinese revolution in 1927 was the Russian-made debacle that imposed upon China the heavy burden of the Kuomintang regime. The tragedy of the Chinese revolution now is the victory of the Communists which has laid upon the country the still heavier burden of a new totalitarian tyranny and condemned it to a new and indefinite term of subjection. At both ends of this brief historic cycle, the Chinese people have been deprived of the chance to begin creating an urban-centered democracy through which they might revise the relations between town and country and begin to achieve greater freedom and more dignity. The defeat of two decades ago was but the first act, the interim years of Kuomintang rule the second, and the Communist victory now the beginning of the third act in the unfolding tragedy of the Chinese revolution.

This book has often been identified in bibliographies as "Trotskyist" and one may properly ask now whether it still merits that label. It is difficult to know what the much-abused term "Trotskyist" means today. In the course of the Chinese events of 1925–27, Trotsky, resisting the Stalinist degeneration, was a consistent internationalist. He saw and understood what was happening more clearly than any other Russian leader. He predicted, with startling precision, every turn of events as it took place. His analyses and criticisms of the official course were confirmed again and again by the evidence which this book examined in detail for the first time. This is a fact that is not altered by the passage of time, or, again, by shifts in a writer's outlook. However, while this work still confirms much of Trotsky's analyses of the time, it no longer accepts his conclusions and cannot be characterized as Trotskyist.

Although I reject the Bolshevism of which Trotsky became the most authentic spokesman, I still have great respect for some of Trotsky's conceptions of what the socialist revolution was meant to be. Although he was himself the prisoner of certain Bolshevik prem‐ ises that nourished dictatorship, it was Trotsky, nevertheless, who in the end stood up against the totalitarian bureaucracy and came to symbolize a surviving revolutionary morality that rose above the intrigues, the power machines, the calumny, and the sanguinary repressions of Stalinism in power. It was never necessary to agree with Trotsky to respect him. But I could hardly feel free, because of this, to include in this edition the Introduction in which Trotsky warmly endorsed the original work. Trotsky was murdered by a Kremlin assassin eleven years ago. I cannot know what his views would be today on the nature of the Russian state and the way to achieve a new and more democratically fruitful synthesis of revolutionary thought and action. I cannot assume that he would agree with the views I now hold and which have been written into this book. Nor could I presume to re-print the Introduction with his endorsement deleted. For better or worse, the book must stand by itself. If a label be needed, its bias can be described as democratic socialist, although one feels compelled to add that political labeling nowadays has become virtually a form of abuse, driving one to try to make a political philosophy out of the defense of simple human decency.

A word finally about how this book was put together. Work was begun on it in China in 1934, barely seven years after the events it describes. A year was spent in painstaking study, excerpting, and translation of a large collection of contemporary materials—news-paper files, books, pamphlets, reports, documents—a few of which were found in Peking libraries but most of which came from private collections long hidden from the Kuomintang secret police. I was enormously assisted in this part of the work by my friend J. C. L., who was later arrested and imprisoned by the Kuomintang and whose subsequent fate I never learned. After that in Europe I combed libraries and bookshops for published Comintern material of the period. In Norway I discussed the Chinese events with the exiled Trotsky. In Holland I saw H. Sneevliet, who under the name of Maring was one of the first representatives of the Communist Inter-national in China, and secured from him a memorandum giving his version of the events in which he participated. In France I saw Albert Treint, who in 1927 had served on the Comintern Executive subcom-mittee on China and who gave me extremely valuable notes on the dis-cussions that took place in Moscow. The study, research, and writing of this book consumed, over all, the better part of four years.

In all the original preparation, as well as in the making of this revision, I have had the indispensable assistance and collaboration of Viola Robinson Isaacs.

H. R. I.

CONTENTS

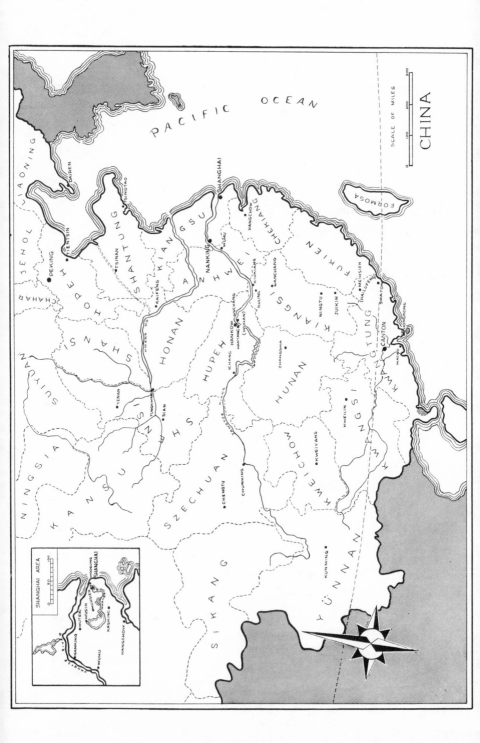

Chapter 1

THE ROOTS

ON THE FRINGES of big Chinese cities the shadows of lofty factory chimneys fall across fields still tilled with wooden plows. On the wharves of seaports modern liners unload goods carried away on the backs of men or shipped inland on primitive barges. In the streets great trucks and jangling trams roar past carts drawn by men harnessed like animals to their loads. Automobiles toot angrily at mandrawn rickshas and barrows which thread their way through the lanes of traffic. Streets are lined with shops where men and women and children still fashion their wares with bare hands and simple tools. On some of these streets are huge mills run by humming dynamos. Airplanes and railroads cut across vast regions linked otherwise only by footpaths and canals a thousand years old. Modern steamers ply the coasts and rivers, churning past junks of ancient design. Throughout the towns and villages and on the tired land of the great river valleys that stretch from the sea to the heart of Asia, these contradictions and contrasts multiply. They embody the struggle of nearly half a billion people for existence and survival.

The pattern of Chinese life is jagged, torn, and irregular. Modern forms of production, transport, and finance are superimposed upon and only partially woven into the worn and threadbare pattern of the past. That ancient fabric was already giving way just over a century ago when the West invaded China with its commodities, its guns, its greed, and its ideas. The result of that impact was catastrophic and revolutionary. Chinese economy was forcibly transformed. Classes of society, for so long stable, entered upon a period of violent change. Forms of government, habits, the entire social equilibrium were upset. China was faced with the immense historical task of finding a new framework in which its productive forces could thrive. The new pressures on the old Chinese society generated conflicts which soon accumulated, gathered momentum, and drove the country and its people convulsively forward in search of new solutions.

1

The backwardness of Chinese economy was determined primarily by the stagnation of productive forces over a prolonged historical period. Introduction of the iron plow led, some two thousand years ago, to an increase in agricultural productivity. Partially as a result of this impetus, land was at that time converted into private property. Land held in fief or cleared by imperial grant became alienable, i.e., it could be bought and sold. Labor thus released and capital thus acquired were in part absorbed by the State in the construction of great public works, dams, canals, palaces, walls, and fortifications. But capitalist modes of production did not develop. Feudal forms of exploitation were perpetuated in the villages. Chinese society remained organized in small agricultural units. Home or local handicraft industries supplied the major supplementary needs of the community. The State took direct part in trade and manufacture. It exercised monopolies, for example, in salt and iron. Both the system of production and the internal market were rigidly controlled by the State bureaucracy and all-embracing guilds of merchants and artisans. Urban centers of production and commerce grew up but seem to have been restricted to luxury products and regional specialties, fine silks, lacquer, chinaware, carvings, ironwork.

The whole structure rested solidly on the mass of peasants who paid rent to the landlords, interest to the merchants and moneylenders, and taxes, in labor, kind, and money, to the State. The latter was represented by a bureaucracy of local officials joined in a hierarchy reaching through the provincial viceroys to the Emperor. These officials joined with the landlords and merchants in exploiting the peasantry. To meet ever increasing tax demands, the landlords multiplied their exactions from the men who worked the soil. Small landholders mortgaged themselves to the moneylenders and were gradually reduced to the status of tenants or agricultural laborers. As each succeeding dynasty passed its peak and went into decline, its financial demands increased and the corruption of its officials deepened. When the burden of accumulated rent, debts, and taxes became intolerable and the prevailing hardships were, as often happened, multiplied by natural disasters, local revolts against rent and tax collectors would often begin to take place and frequently broadened into great peasant wars.

Military cliques, headed by ambitious landholding nobles, took the field at the head of scattered peasant bands and provincial soldiery, overthrew the dynasty, and fought for primacy among themselves.

Attempts at social and agrarian reforms usually featured the period of civil war and confusion which often lasted decades and at one time several centuries. The most famous of these were the attempted reforms of Wang Mang after the fall of the Han Dynasty at the beginning of the first century of the Christian era, and those advocated by Wang An-shih after the collapse of the T'ang Dynasty and the rise of the Sung at the end of the tenth century. Some of their proposals went as far as abolition of private property rights in the land and its reversion to its original owner, the State. Others provided for the establishment of an embryonic state capitalism. None of these reforms matured. The peasant wars which provoked them invariably exhausted themselves. One of the warring cliques would finally assert its supremacy and erect a new dynasty. While the new Emperor and his immediate descendants consolidated their power and gradually suppressed all rival claimants to the throne, the original social forms in the village were reproduced and the same gradual process of expropriation resumed.[1]

In the middle of the seventeenth century, the Manchus came to power by taking advantage of one of these peasant rebellions. Once established as alien rulers, they had a natural interest in preserving China from any other external contact while they completed the subjugation of the country. During this period Europe was locked in the bitter wars which accompanied the birth of Western capitalism and the modern national states. European contacts with Cathay were occasional and episodic. The early Manchu emperors were able to enjoy the period of their ascendancy. With the passing of another two centuries, however, a remarkable growth of population brought renewed pressure on the land. The Manchu Dynasty had already entered upon its decline. Its power was beginning to disintegrate and it had been compelled to make severe levies on the population to meet repeated revolts in different parts of its domain. Chinese society was on the brink of a new era of political breakdown and chaos when the first waves of expanding Western capitalism broke against China's shores. The advent of the new barbarians who came from across the seas deepened, transformed, and complicated the inner divisions in the classes of Chinese society. Their coming meant that the old solutions, arrived at in the old manner, would no longer suffice.

Driving forward irresistibly toward the expansion of trade and the accumulation of capital resources, the Western nations smashed the barriers that had until now divided the Celestial Empire from the rest of the world. Out of this impact profound economic, social, and political changes had at last to come. Capitalist economy had begun to draw the whole world into its orbit. China's isolation was irretrievably at an end. For Capital was a new type of conqueror, hitherto unknown in Chinese history. Invading hordes which had swept down across the northern frontiers had in the past been assimilated with little difficulty into the more highly organized framework of the older Chinese civilization. These new barbarians possessed technical equipment and a material superiority which nothing in China could match. Mere traditions could not cope with cannon, any more than the hand could cope with the machine or the palanquin with the railroad. Against the driving force and weapons of the Western barbarians, China could pit only the sheer weight of its age, its size, its numbers. These could determine the length and agony of this uneven conflict, not its outcome.

The Chinese economic and social structure, already in crisis, reacted swiftly at top and at bottom to the corrosive influence of the foreign invasion. Economically, China was laid prostrate. With the help of opium, the foreign traders established a balance of trade permanently in their favor. Silver, heavily imported during the first period of the foreign trade, began draining away as early as 1826. Ten years later opium replaced silver as the medium of payment for Chinese tea and silk.[2] Through the breach made by the drug and widened by British and French cannon in the Opium Wars of 1842 and 1858, manufactured commodities made their way. As British cotton goods came in, the export of Chinese woven cloth (nankeens) began to fall off and disappeared almost entirely by 1833. The curve of Chinese exports dropped sharply with the corresponding spectacular rise of opium imports during the first quarter of the nineteenth century. Cotton imports rose steadily, and by 1870 cotton goods accounted for 31 percent of China's imports and a few years later replaced opium at the top of the list. The rapid strides in industrial organization and technique in the West, the opening of the Suez Canal, and the development of steam navigation stimulated the China trade, which doubled between 1885 and 1894. The flow of commodities was soon followed by capital investment and loans. Foreign shipping companies, cotton mills, railways, and telegraph lines occupied by the end of the century all the commanding positions in Chinese economic life.

This economic conquest was accompanied by the establishment of foreign political control. The Manchu regime was reduced to impotence. Its early attempts to check the silver drain by restricting the opium trade were beaten down in a series of wars in which it suffered humiliating defeats and for which it had to pay heavy penalties. Humbled by the Westerners, the Manchu court lost immeasurably in prestige and authority over the Chinese. Treaties exacted by the foreigners at the cannon's mouth provided for the free propagation of Christianity and legalized the trade in opium. To the Chinese, the Gospel and the drug, in the words of a British historian, "came together, have been fought for together, and were finally legalized together."[3] These treaties also opened coastal and river ports to trade, limited the Chinese tariff to a nominal 5 percent, granted territorial footholds and concessions whence later came the different foreign "spheres of influence," and set up the system of extraterritoriality which exempted foreigners from the jurisdiction of Chinese law and the payment of Chinese taxes. China became in all but name a subject land, saved from outright dismemberment or colonization only by the acute rivalries among the imperialist freebooters.

The spread of opium, the drain of silver, and the influx of machine-made commodities greatly aggravated the crisis in the countryside, which arose primarily from the rapid growth of population and the shortage of cultivable land.[4] The widespread use of opium caused a flow of wealth from the countryside to the towns and led to an alarming contraction of the internal market.[5] The silver shortage caused by the drain resulted in a 20 to 30 percent depreciation of the copper currency in common use and a sharp rise in the cost of living. Debased coinage came into use.[6] Foreign cotton goods and other commodities drove Chinese handicrafts to the wall, especially in the southern provinces. The weavers who had produced the 3,359,000 pieces of cloth exported in 1819 lost their means of livelihood when the exports dropped to 30,600 pieces in 1833 and almost to zero in the next three decades.[7] Finally, as if man and his works were not sufficiently malignant, nature joined in the physical destruction of the old order of things. Scarcely a year passed in the middle decades of the nineteenth century without its quota of floods and famines, droughts and plagues, in the great river valleys and beyond.

The accumulative result of all these agencies of dissolution was mass pauperization and the creation of a large floating population.

Sporadic revolts among the minority Miao tribes in the Southwest and the Moslems in the Northwest heralded the beginning of a new period of civil war. In the traditional course of events it would have confirmed the exhaustion of Heaven's mandate to the ruling dynasty and led to the rise of a new reigning house. But while agrarian revolt was brewing in the provinces, the Chinese ruling class was finding resources for renewing itself by participating, directly and indirectly, in the profits of the foreign trade.

Merchants and officials in the seaports had begun to acquire large fortunes through their dealings with the foreigners. Prior to 1830, when foreign ships still arrived at Canton laden with silver dollars to pay for the tea and silk carried back to Europe and the United States,[8] little of this wealth had found its way back to the ultimate producers. Most of it remained in the hands of the port merchants and mandarins. Members of the co-hongs, special merchant monopolies officially established to deal with the foreigners, and local officials who had a free hand in levying special taxes and "contributions" profited handsomely from all the new dealings, especially in the contraband opium trade. Membership in the co-hong was often worth as much as 200,000 taels, then equivalent to about 250,000 American silver dollars.

Among these merchants and officials, a new class took shape, the class of compradores, brokers for foreign capital on the Chinese market. This was one of the first direct effects of the imperialist invasion on the fabric of Chinese society. The commanding economic positions the foreigners occupied blocked the channel of indigenous, independent capitalist development. The wealth accumulated by these Chinese merchants and officials went not into capitalist enterprise but back into land. Most of these individuals stemmed to begin with from the landed gentry and they used their money to increase their family holdings. This process visibly hastened the growth of large landed estates and the expropriation of smaller landholders.[9] Landlords sent their sons into the cities to join the lucrative business of compradoring. It was the rare compradore who was not also an absentee landlord. The profits went back not only into land purchase but into loans at usurious rates to the peasants, who increasingly had to borrow to bridge the gap between their decreasing incomes and their rising costs and taxes. Because they were unable to compete with the superior force and material technique of the foreigners, the old landlord-merchant ruling class was transformed, in significant degree, into a class of brokers, moneylenders, and speculators, with interests divided between town and country and directly tied to foreign interests.

This process helped hasten the disintegration of the State structure. The Manchus had been defeated by the British in the Opium Wars "with an ease that shook their own confidence in the prowess and destiny of their race and completely dispelled its prestige of military power in the eyes of the subject Chinese."[10] Broken by military defeats, the Manchu bureaucracy was soon undermined by bribery and the attractive profits from opium smuggling. Edicts from Peking often remained inoperative. Peking was far away, its authority was reduced, and the clink of foreign silver was near and enticing. Chinese officialdom, theoretically virtuous, already had an ancient tradition of corruption. The dependence of officials on tax revenues for their own sustenance had from time immemorial placed a premium on official honesty. The riches of the foreign trade crowned this tradition with a new source of illegitimate income. With the decline of the dynasty, the falling off of revenue to the center, and growing financial stringency, all pretense at virtue was thrown to the winds and official position became an object of open barter. The plums of power were acquired not by the learned but by those who had the price. Naturally it was the wealthy merchant or compradore who could buy his son or brother a mandarin's button. As the practice became common, the merchants, landlords, and officials became even more indistinguishably the branches of the same class tree. This class, vitally concerned with preserving all the inequalities on the land from which it profited, became one of the chief instruments of foreign penetration and control.

The imperialists, on their part, having battered the Manchu court into submission and adapted the upper strata of Chinese society to their own uses, became the protectors of the Chinese rulers against the wrath of the people. This was to become the basic formula of imperialist control in semicolonial China. The whole Chinese economic, social, and political structure had been thrown into solution by the impact of the Westerners; but new elements had barely begun to form when the Westerners found it necessary to join with everything conservative, oppressive, and backward in the nation to resist agencies of revolutionary change.

This relationship crystallized during the Taiping rebellion, which threatened to overthrow the Manchu Dynasty in the middle of the nineteenth century. Repeated revolts, brought on by insupportable economic hardships, culminated in 1850 in a mighty antidynastic peasant rebellion. It swept northward from Kwangsi and established its power for a period of eleven years in the Yangtze Valley. Beginning as a tiny religious sect of neo-Christian "God worshipers" who came into conflict with local authority in the south, the Taiping movement developed swiftly into a social upheaval of the first magnitude. All the discontented and rebellious of the land flocked to its standard. Ancient anti-Manchu secret societies, never entirely extinguished, came once more to life. Chinese intellectuals and members of the lesser gentry, dispossessed from their land, weary of Manchu exactions, and angered by Manchu racial discrimination, joined its leading ranks. In the flush of anti-Manchu feeling, the queue, badge of subjection, was abolished, and the old Ming costume restored. But above all and primarily, the great masses of pauperized peasants, migrating artisans and seekers of land, rebels against the authority of local officials, landlords, and tax collectors, gave the movement its flesh and blood and stamped it with the traditional features of the peasant uprisings which in the past had led to dynastic changes.

Taiping military successes were rapid and spectacular. Manchu authority was swept from the provinces of the south and the Yangtze Valley. Taiping armies reached almost to the gates of Peking itself. Hung Hsiu-ch'üan, the fanatically religious leader of the movement, assumed the title of T'ien Wang, or Heavenly King, and established his capital at Nanking. At its height, the rebellion was marked by the seizure of land by the peasants in many places. This fundamental agrarian radical tendency was not supported at the top, although its pressure produced unenforced decrees for the destruction of land titles and plans for a collective sharing of landed property.[11] It is also a significant fact that wherever the Taiping regime was relatively stabilized, partially successful efforts were made to suppress the opium trade, check the silver drain, stimulate the internal market, standardize taxation, and increase agricultural productivity. It is a fact of the utmost interest, for example, that during the Taiping period the export of silk from Kiangsu districts to the coast reached new high levels. The Taipings, according to some accounts, made repeated efforts to conciliate the foreigners on a basis of a free exchange of goods and suppression of the ruinous opium trade. Thus the Taiping rebellion, primarily a peasant war of the primitive or traditional variety, also revealed tendencies, neither too directly nor clearly, but unmistakably, toward "normal" bourgeois development. The Taiping movement came into collision with all the forces of privilege on the land and in the cities. The rebellion destroyed the authority and position of the old official class. The radical actions of the peasants brought them into direct conflict with the landlords and with the compradores and merchants who were so heavily involved in landed property as owners, and as holders of mortgages at high rates of interest. "The destructiveness of the Taipings," says a standard history, "antagonized the influential classes."[12] The "influential" Chinese classes were ranged solidly on the side of the Manchus.

To the imperialists the Taipings first appeared as possibly desirable successors to the Manchus as the rulers of China. The Christian character of the movement aroused a certain sympathy among some missionaries. The Taipings, moreover, gave some promise of stimulating trade and restoring the tranquillity which the Manchus were unable to preserve. Nevertheless, the foreigners soon threw their full weight to the side of the Manchus. The opium trade, it must be remembered, was still the most lucrative part of the China trade for the dominant foreign interests. It supplied wealth for accumulation and for development which only at a later date would make the marketing of more legitimate commodities more profitable. The fact that the Taipings opposed the trade in the drug placed them in opposition to the immediate interests of the foreigners.[13]

The civil war gave the imperialists an excellent opportunity to strengthen their grip and extend their economic and political positions. In 1854 foreign guns prevented the anti-Manchu Triads from capturing Shanghai. The foreigners took advantage of the complete collapse of local authority to assume control of the customs administration[14] and extend the domain of the foreign settlement. In 1858, French and British guns hammered away at the weakened Manchu forces in the north and forced the signature of new treaties fully satisfactory to foreign interests. The opium trade was legalized and the entire country was thrown open to foreign penetration. With the signing of these treaties, the foreigners had a definite stake in the preservation of the existing regime. The subjugation of the government was completed by the campaign of 1860 with its brutal sacking of the Summer Palace near Peking. Now a fully pliable instrument, the dynasty became an asset definitely worth protecting. The Taipings were transformed in the eyes of the foreigners "from possibly friendly successors to the Manchus into mere rebels who interfered with the carrying out of the new agreement."[15] The Taiping version of Christianity, hitherto looked upon with a certain curious interest, was promptly perceived to be the rankest blasphemy. The Christian General Gordon took the field with the fervor of a crusader and stopped at nothing, treachery included, to deal with the Taipings as Jehovah's Chosen People dealt with the Amalekites and all the worshipers of Baal. British and French forces, throwing aside all formal pretense at "neutrality," intervened actively in the conflict with decisive results.

The battle for the preservation of the Manchu Dynasty was fought and won by two Chinese statesmen, Tsêng Kuo-fan, representative of the landed interests, and Li Hung-chang, spokesman and leader of the new compradore class. They organized and led the defense of the Dragon Throne, and they succeeded mainly because foreign military and naval forces swamped the ill-armed Taipings before whom the Manchu troops were helpless.

Final defeat and dispersal of the Taipings in 1865 took place when the movement was already itself internally exhausted. The ravages of the civil war, which cost heavily in lives and laid waste large sections of the land, dissipated the resources of the peasant war. The leaders of the Taiping movement were unable to give a consistent lead to the agrarian revolt which degenerated, inevitably, into sporadic partisan warfare and banditry. The leadership split into warring cliques of hopeless adventurers. The great Taiping rebellion failed and the status quo was preserved because none of the older classes in Chinese society was capable of leading the country out of its impasse and because the new factor of imperialist pressure choked off the growth of new and more progressive forces. The weight of imperialism at the same time made forever impossible a repetition of the old cycle of peasant war, dissolution, and dynastic change.

Such were the terms of the central contradiction around which the history of China was doomed to revolve for nearly a century to come. The advent of Western imperialism, the end of Chinese isolation, and the appearance of the machine-made commodity on the Chinese market inexorably decreed the revolutionary transformation of Chinese society. But, once entrenched, Western imperialism defended itself by supporting all that was archaic, conservative, and backward in that society. To put agricultural production on a new and more fruitful basis, China obviously had to do away with the old system of land-holding and give its farmers a greater stake in the product of their toil. The imperialists, however, joined in propping up the sway of the landlords, merchants, and officials who kept the mass of peasants in bondage. To relieve population pressure and to create a new rela-tionship between town and country, successful industrialization by indigenous capital was needed. But the commanding position of for-eign interests, the enforcement by treaty of the superior competitive position of foreign products and foreign enterprise, blocked this road for decades and forced a subordinate and dependent role upon Chi-nese capital. To meet its problems, the country obviously had to be unified to ensure maximum use of its resources. But the rivalries of the different Western powers fed on separatist conflicts which under-mined the central authority and encouraged provincial and regional satrapies which corresponded roughly to the "spheres of influence" carved out by the contending Western interests. Effective social and economic progress was contingent, in short, on the national inde-pendence of the country while the maintenance of imperialist privilege demanded continued subjection. Such were the terms of Chinese history for nearly a hundred years.

The Taiping rebellion was the last attempt to respond to the need for change in the traditional Chinese manner. It failed because the path to that solution was cut off by the new conditions created by the imperialist invasion. Exhausted by twenty years of revolt and defeat, the masses of Chinese people had to await renewal in a new generation in entirely new circumstances before they could again intervene in affairs. At the base of Chinese society in the ensuing decades all the causes of chronic poverty were profoundly aggravated. The concen-tration of land continued. The flow of commodities and commercial capital into the villages broadened and governed the lives of the people, while denying them any chance to increase their own produc-tivity in any significant degree. Meanwhile, at the top of the social structure and in the developing urban centers, other changes were taking place, giving new form and new content to the struggle for China's future.

From the fight against the Taipings and other outbreaks which lasted until 1880, the Manchu Dynasty emerged a spent force. Having barely sustained the shocks of internal rebellion, famines, and repeated natural disasters, it had again to face blows from without. Confronted by a new imperialist offensive on the fringes of the Empire, it was helpless. France occupied Cambodia and Annam in the late 'sixties and "legalized" its acquisitions by a brief war against China in 1884–85. The next year Britain added Burma to its Indian Empire. These countries in the south had, loosely speaking, recognized Chinese suzerainty. Across Asia on the northern frontier Czarist Russia laid the course of a new railroad and established its "sphere of influence" in northern Manchuria. In these same years Japan, responding more unifiedly and more quickly to the imperialist impact, had modified its feudal structure and with the Meiji Restoration in 1868 had embarked upon its remarkable course of adaptation to Western modes of production and organization and international relations. It quickly joined in the expansionist scramble, reaching across the narrow Sea of Japan in search of a continental foothold. In 1894 the new island power inflicted a humiliating defeat upon its aged and hitherto venerated neighbor. The amputation of Korea and the establishment of Japanese influence in South Manchuria signaled a new scrimmage among the Great Powers for territories and concessions. Buffeted and helpless, the Imperial Court signed treaty after treaty. The dismemberment of China and the absorption of its several parts into the colonial empires of the Western nations seemed imminent as the nineteenth century came to a close.

Renewed imperialist pressure, however, brought to life new movements of reform and revolution quite different in character and class origin from the great mass revolts of the mid-century years. These new agencies of change developed in the upper strata of Chinese society. Foreign political and economic pressure had molded the Chinese ruling class into a shape fitting imperialist requirements, and foreign privilege closed most doors to native capitalist development. Nevertheless, the accumulation of wealth by this class could not fail in the nature of things to stimulate efforts to compete with the foreigners on their own ground. Imperialism had destroyed the old economic base. It could hinder but not entirely prevent the erection of a new one. Li Hung-chang, compradore-in-chief, himself initiated the first independent Chinese capitalist enterprises. The first rice-cleaning mill was built in Shanghai in 1863. The Kiangnan shipyard was established in 1865. Seven years later the China Merchants Steam Navigation Company was organized to compete with the foreign monopoly in coastal and river shipping. The next year the first modern silk filature was built, and in 1876 the first railroad, a twelve-mile span from Shanghai to Woosung, came to confound the spirits of the ancestors of frightened peasants. A modern coal mine began operations at Kaiping in 1878, and in 1890 the first cotton-spinning and -weaving mill was built at Shanghai and the first ironworks at Wuchang. Match factories and flour mills had followed by 1896. The industrialization of China had begun.[16]

China's trade position, especially in cotton and cotton goods, visibly improved during this same period. An unfavorable balance in raw cotton was transformed into an export excess in 1888. The export of locally woven cotton cloth, which had dropped almost to zero after 1833, recovered ground after 1868, rising from 238 piculs* that year to 30,100 piculs in 1900, the sharpest rise occurring after 1883, although the import of manufactured cotton goods enjoyed at the same time an uninterrupted growth.[17] Alongside these gains in industry and trade came development in transport, communications, and banking facilities. A modern postal system came into existence in 1878. A telegraph line was laid between Shanghai and Tientsin in 1881. The Commercial Bank of China was organized in 1896 with all-Chinese capital. Other lines, other banks, soon followed in increasing numbers.

From the outset, however, Chinese capital fought a losing battle against foreign competition. The Treaty of Shimonoseki, which concluded the Sino-Japanese War in 1895, established the right of foreigners to build industrial plants in China. Enterprises quickly sprang up to enjoy the benefits of cheap and plentiful Chinese labor. The superior technical equipment and knowledge of the foreigners, together with the special economic and political privileges they enjoyed, placed their Chinese rivals at an immediate disadvantage. In addition to being subject to technical limitations and tax burdens from which the foreigners were free, the Chinese were dependent upon the foreign market for credit facilities, machinery, and the great variety of manufactured products which China could not yet produce. The budding Chinese industrialists tried to overcome these handicaps by exploiting their labor more intensively. But it was not long before the desire to create more favorable conditions for the operations of Chinese capital also forced its way into the political arena, taking the form of agitation for changes in a regime that no longer corresponded to the needs of the newly growing economic interests.

* One picul equals 133⅓ lbs.

In the years following the defeat of the Taiping rebellion, Li Hung-chang sponsored a series of limited attempts to modernize the regime. Initiating new industrial enterprises on the one hand, Li also introduced the beginnings of a modern army and navy, urged changes in the schools, and sent student groups abroad to acquire for China the secrets of Western economic and political power. These efforts were cut short by the Japanese attack in 1894. The defeat, the new loss of territory, and the new drive of the Powers which followed brought new political tendencies to the surface. Quicker and more drastic changes were sought.

Two distinct currents dominated Chinese political life after 1895. The first hoped to reform the Imperial Court and adapt it to the new requirements. It dreamed of an emperor who would play the role of Peter the Great and of a government that would resemble England's constitutional monarchy. The second advocated the overthrow of the Manchu Dynasty and the establishment of a Chinese Republic along American or French lines. Entering upon the final period of its decline, the Manchu rulers gradually gave way before the reformers and brought closer the day of its abdication in favor of the revolutionists.

The reformers began by revising Confucius. They daringly represented him not as the classic defender of the status quo, but as a progressive liberal. Into the old molds of Chinese social, political, and economic thought, they tried to pour the ideas of Adam Smith, John Stuart Mill, Herbert Spencer, and Thomas Huxley, whose works began to appear in Chinese translations. They believed the nation could be transformed by imperial rescript and thought their cause won when in 1898 they gained the ear of the young Emperor Kuang Hsü and launched the famous "Hundred Days" of reform. A series of sweeping decrees were issued to transform the archaic government of the Manchus into a modern state instrument. They called for the establishment of schools, election machinery, the elimination of tax abuses and official corruption. They ordered state aid to industry and agriculture and the democratization of the regime.

Unhappily for the reformers, the stream of new ideas that flowed out of the austere gates of the Forbidden City swirled into the moat and there stagnated. To the old mandarins and magistrates, it appeared that the Emperor had gone mad, for his orders seemed designed to strip them of all the perquisites of office and to destroy all the insti-

tutions canonized by centuries of usage. Edict after edict begged that
the Imperial will be obeyed, but the officials who received them now
doubted strongly whether the Imperial will any longer enjoyed the
necessary sanction of Heaven. These doubts were soon confirmed at
the Imperial Court itself where resistance to the reforms crystallized
around the Empress Dowager. In September 1898, she imprisoned
her nephew and with a few strokes of her brush effaced all the reforms
he had sponsored. Some of his advisers she executed. Others, including the leaders K'ang Yu-wei and Liang Ch'i-ch'ao, barely
escaped into exile with their lives. These intellectuals had attempted
during the "Hundred Days" to adapt the Manchu regime to Western
ideas by working from the top down. They hoped to find, in an enlightened monarch, a substitute for a class in society capable of carrying out the necessary changes. Unfortunately, the "Imperial will"
proved impotent as an instrument of social change. The Emperor,
after all, only personified his own State apparatus. When he commanded it to destroy itself, it is not strange that it stolidly resisted.
Against the inertia of the mandarinate, the reformers were helpless.[18]

The conservative Manchu bureaucracy could check the thin trickle
of reforms supported only by a few individuals, but it could not resist
the powerful and varied factors that were encompassing its doom.
It was staggered by blow after blow from the Western imperialists.
The closing years of the century were marked by the predatory exac-
tion of territorial, trade, and railway concessions by one power after
another.[19] Within the country, the destruction of the old handicraft
economy, the high cost of living, new floods and droughts had upset
all the normal conditions of life and led to widespread mass discontent.
Out of these conditions and moods rose another primitive mass revolt,
this time in the Northern provinces, where ancient secret societies
revived and flourished and turned the wrath of the people against all
the foreign barbarians, Manchu and Western alike. Recoiling from
the reform movement, the Manchu bureaucracy, headed by the
Empress Dowager, fell back on the dangerous expedient of turning
this anti-Manchu revolt into a weapon against the hated foreigners.
Open official support was given to the I Ho Ch'üan (Fists for the
Protection of Public Peace), the insurgent society that became known
to the foreigners as "Boxers." The rebels changed their slogan from
"Down with the Manchus! Protect the Chinese!" to "Down with the
Foreigners! Long Live the Imperial Dynasty!"[20] The result was a

new disaster. The fierce, primitive local uprisings were crushed by allied foreign arms. Heavy penalties were imposed upon China by the victors, including an indemnity of $350,000,000 (U.S.) and the exaction of new military advantages for foreign forces under the Boxer Protocol of 1901.

In ensuing years, China became the helpless spectator and victim of the rivalries and conflicts and demands of the Powers. The fate of railways, of concessions, and of whole Chinese provinces was decided in European chancelleries. Control of Manchuria and Korea was determined by a war fought across Chinese territory by Russia and Japan in 1904–5 and settled by a treaty which freely bartered Chinese possessions without consulting the Chinese government. The Manchu Court no longer effectively represented any section of the Chinese population, nor could it offer any resistance to the gradual destruction of its power and its sovereignty.

From hopes in reform, the Chinese intelligentsia turned to propaganda for revolution. The realization that the dynasty had outlived itself took firm root. Students and intellectuals turned their backs on the reformer K'ang Yu-wei and began to listen more closely to the voice of another exile, Sun Yat-sen. Sun had been among those who in 1895 had addressed reform memorials to the Emperor. His political development, however, differed radically from that of the more prominent reformers of that day. Born in a village near Canton the year after the final suppression of the Taiping rebellion, Sun in his youth and early manhood came into contact with unreconstructed radicals steeped in the Taiping tradition of armed revolt. Sent as a youth to Honolulu, Sun became a Christian. He returned to China to begin a long career as a revolutionary conspirator who aimed at the overthrow of the dynasty. His first attempt in 1895 failed and Sun went into foreign exile, seeking and winning support among overseas Chinese for his revolutionary program.

The overseas Chinese played a key role in the development of the Chinese revolution. Most of the Chinese who had emigrated abroad lived out hard lives as contract laborers, some of them eventually returning to China with small savings. Others rose to wealth in trade in the Indies, the South Seas, Europe, and the United States. The strong protection afforded foreign nationals in China contrasted sharply with the defenselessness of overseas Chinese in the face of economic and racial discrimination and abuse. Among them strong nationalist feeling grew long before it developed in China itself, where the same factors that hindered the growth of Chinese capitalism also hindered the rise of an effective bourgeois national revolutionary movement. Powerful racial, family, and traditional ties bound the overseas emigrants to their native land and from them came the first financial and moral support for the revolutionary movement. It is interesting that only a few of the more wealthy overseas Chinese joined in the struggle for a strong and independent Chinese republic. Most of the money Sun raised came in small sums from contract workers and petty merchants who proved ready before anyone else to support his program.

This was a program for the overthrow of the monarchy by military insurrection. It began to attract many of the disillusioned reformers and most of the new generation of students, especially those who flocked to Japan after 1895 and in much greater numbers after 1900. In China, the movement forged links with the old secret societies. The new elements from the intelligentsia of town and country gave these ancient organizations a nationalist and democratic coloration they had never before possessed. Students who went abroad and returned bulging with new ideas and radical fervor found ready listeners everywhere. Discontent with the existing order of things grew. Japan's victory over Russia in 1905 had made the West seem less invincible. The 1905 revolution in Russia made an impression on the Chinese intellectuals and had a specific influence in driving the Court toward concessions.[21] Chinese merchants and capitalists began to assert themselves more boldly. Nothing showed this more clearly than the boycotts against the United States in 1905 and against Japan in 1908.

These boycotts took on a broad, popular character. They were supported by the merchant guilds and the newly grown popular press. The anti-American boycott began in reaction to the abusive attitude toward Chinese immigrants in the United States. It revealed the rise of a new spirit of confidence and solidarity among the merchants and petty capitalists along the China coast. The boycott campaign tightened the bonds between the Chinese in the United States and those at home. It helped break down sectional barriers. The boycott was strongest in Canton, most of the Chinese in America having come from that area, but it was also notably successful in Shanghai and Tientsin, as well as overseas in Singapore. Perhaps most significant was the open defiance of imperial authority which had, in response to American diplomatic pressure, issued an edict against the boycott. The anti-Japanese boycott in 1908 was even more specifically antigovernmental in character. It arose from the Chinese authorities' cringing submission to Japan in connection with a shipping incident. Merchants burned Japanese merchandise and workers at the docks refused to unload from Japanese vessels, marking perhaps the first direct participation of Chinese workers in the anti-imperialist struggle of the present century.[22]

One of the demands that arose in connection with the anti-American boycott had been for the cancellation of the concession granted to an American firm for construction of the Canton-Hankow railway. It was around the issue of railway concessions that opposition to the Imperial Court now developed among the wealthy provincial merchants and gentry. Plans to build railways linking Canton, Hankow, Changsha, and Chengtu had already been drawn up and companies had been established with Chinese capital to carry the plans through. The Peking government, now little more than a band of venal officials battening on the profits derived from granting concessions to foreign interests, used foreign money to buy up Chinese holdings already invested in various railway schemes in order to turn the projects over to the foreigners. Resistance to this flared among the incipient Chinese railroad magnates, especially in Hunan, Hupeh, and Szechwan. The underground revolutionary societies[23] made a great deal out of the issue, which helped identify the Manchu regime with the hated foreign rivals. This drew new strata of the upper classes into the fight against the monarchy. It was an outbreak over precisely this issue, in Szechwan, which finally provoked open rebellion.

The threat of total collapse was present during the whole last decade of the dynasty's existence. It was put off only by surrender to the pressure for reforms. The Empress Dowager and her advisers were forced to compromise with the critical unrest that grew after the Boxer episode. It was a matter of giving in or going down. In 1906, the Manchu Court, absolute ruler of the Celestial Empire for nearly two hundred fifty years, grudgingly recognized the "principle" of constitutional government. The dynasty's last vigorous representative, the Empress Dowager, died at the end of 1908. She took with her to the grave the imprisoned Emperor Kuang Hsü.

Her oldest advisers soon followed. On the Dragon Throne sat the three-year-old Emperor Hsüan T'ung.* A foolish and incompetent man reigned as regent. The court degenerated into a swamp of petty nepotism and clique rivalries. Paper reforms, more numerous but also more niggardly and unreal, were granted. In 1910, provincial viceregal assemblies, resembling the zemstvos under the Czar in Russia, came into existence as a result of rigorously limited "popular" elections.[24] These had only the right to debate, and to debate only the topics prescribed by the Throne. But even these carefully picked "long-gowned" assemblies came into conflict with the Court. They urged that broader, more responsible government could alone preserve the monarchy. Delegates of the provincial assemblies joined in a national body at Peking and over Court resistance tried desperately to hasten parliamentary reform. Some changes were introduced, but the hand of the old regime, still heavy upon the new bodies, reduced them to hopeless fictions. The assembly, composed of imperial appointees and eminently safe friends of the viceroys, argued over the amount of parliamentarism that could save the monarchy. While they wrangled, revolution overtook them and the Court they hoped to save.

A local outbreak against the Imperial officials in Szechwan in September 1911 was followed in October by the revolt of the garrison at Wuchang. When Imperial troops stationed at Lanchow refused to march against the rebels, the days of Manchu rule were at long last numbered. While the revolt spread, the Court abjectly offered to surrender all claims to authority in return for the semblance of rule. But it was too late. The Empire fell apart. With it went the "national assembly" whose banner it had tried feebly to wave in the face of its oncoming fate.

Internal corrosion had already reduced the dynasty to a cipher. Only a tiny push was needed to erase it. The revolution of 1911 generated enough energy to produce this tiny push, no more. No class or group emerged from it capable of directing the transformation of the country, of solving the agrarian crisis, of regaining national independence and building strength to resist the pressure and incursions of the imperialist Powers. In the earlier classic bourgeois revolutions of the West, the nascent capitalist class had been able to

* Otherwise known as Henry Pu Yi, destined to rise again and fall again as Emperor K'ang Tê of Japan's puppet state of Manchukuo.

win and consolidate power by terminating feudal relations on the land. But in China this class was too closely identified with these relations to lead the impoverished peasantry out of its difficulties. None of the revolutionists of 1911 even tried to do so. The masses of the peasantry played no role in the overthrow of the dynasty. Their passivity made it possible for the old provincial military and civilian apparatus to continue in power on a local basis, minus only the dynastic sanction, which had in any case long since lost its authority. One of the few popular manifestations of the change was the gradual disappearance of the queue, imposed on the people centuries earlier as a badge of subjection by the Manchu conquerors.

With the disappearance of nominal central authority, power passed into the hands of provincial or regional satraps committed to the preservation of the existing social system. Through them, the squeeze on the peasants was not loosened but tightened. The foreign stranglehold on the country's political and economic life was made even stronger. The regional powers that came into existence corresponded in the main to the respective "spheres of influence" of the Great Powers. Militarists in Yunnan and southern Kwangsi were subject to the influence and control of France. The river valleys economically controlled by Hongkong and Shanghai passed more definitely under British influence. The provinces of Manchuria were divided, by secret treaties, between Russia and Japan. The civil wars that soon began to take place among these rival militarists and rival governments came to reflect in considerable measure the conflicts among the principal imperialist Powers jockeying for key economic positions. It is this fact which distinguishes the post-1911 period from similar periods of division, civil wars, and confusion following the collapse of earlier dynasties.

The revolutionary intellectuals who had conspired so fervidly to bring the monarchy down were helplessly sidetracked in the developments that followed. There had been no authentic popular movement from which they might have drawn strength. The revolution had occurred almost independently of their efforts. Afterward they became mere appendages of the militarists who seized power. The parliaments and constitutions they now elaborated were not organs of any actual political power but window dressing tolerated or utilized at will by the militarists they depended upon for protection. Thus Sun Yat-sen, who had returned from exile in triumph and had been named first president of the Chinese Republic, was quickly compelled to give way to Yüan Shih-k'ai, a general of the old regime who took command in Peking and who soon began to see himself as the founder of a new dynasty. Those intellectuals who did not become secretaries or jobholders under illiterate generals fell away from politics into passive despair. Sun Yat-sen and the remains of his party, the Kuomintang, wrote on their party banner the slogan: "Protect the Constitution." But the only protection they sought was in the camp of one set of generals pitted against another. At this game they lost with consistent regularity. Only the generals won.

The downfall of the monarchy seemed to have brought the country from bad to worse. The civil wars and the reign of the generals deepened the misery in the countryside. Exactions increased. Land was laid waste. Agricultural production declined. China was compelled to begin importing rice and wheat. Famines and unchecked floods took heavy tolls in human life. Millions of peasants, driven off the land, swelled the hordes of the militarist armies or took to banditry, often much the same thing. Harsh taxation and militarist requisitions hastened the destruction of Chinese rural economy and condemned the majority of the population to chronic starvation. It seemed as though domestic industry would never be able to absorb the large labor surplus that crowded into the cities. But it was precisely in this sphere that spectacular changes began to take place as a direct result of the outbreak of the first World War.

That war absorbed the attention and full industrial output of the Western nations. Chinese producers suddenly found themselves with a great market open before them in their own country in circumstances temporarily relieved of the constant pressure of foreign competition. Thanks to the war's demands, China's unfavorable trade balance dropped abruptly to record lows, amounting to only 16,000,000 taels in 1919, mainly as a result of a sharp increase in exports. Taking 1913 as 100, imports were 91.6 in 1914 and 105.9 in 1919. Exports rose from 83.8 in 1914 to 140.1 in 1919.[25] Even more significant was the spurt of industrial growth. Imports of industrial machinery rose from 4,380,749 taels in 1915 to 56,578,535 taels in 1921. Cotton mills increased from 42 in 1916 to 120 in 1923, spindles from 1,145,000 to 3,550,000. Silk filatures rose from 56 in 1915 to 93 in 1927. Four cigarette factories in 1915 grew to 182 by 1927.[26] Again with 1913 as 100, we have the following figures for

1923: coal production, 183.5; iron ore production, 180.6; silk exports, 152.3; bean oil exports, 432.5; cotton spindles, 403.9. At the same time there were smaller but significant increases in land transport and shipping facilities.

Along with this growth came extensive alterations in the Chinese business structure. Corporate forms were more widely adopted. Banks multiplied. As machines replaced handicraft production in steadily increasing measure, the old master-journeyman-apprentice relationship began to give way in decisive economic sectors to the stockholder-manager-worker relationship.

This rise of productive forces brought on a new contest between aspiring Chinese capital and entrenched foreign interests and the existing structure of foreign economic and political privilege. It also brought the new class of industrial workers into conflict with their employers, foreign and Chinese alike. From these new springs flowed fresh nationalist currents which swept China into the upheavals of the next decade.

Chapter 2

CHINA'S CRISIS: THE CLASS PATTERN

SOCIAL CHANGE came belatedly to China. That is why it is today a land of such deeply chiseled contrasts. It is forced by the pull of a whole world system to make the leap from wooden plow to tractor, from palanquin to airplane. Western imperialism forced the Celestial Empire to find its place in a terrestrial world that had already advanced materially beyond it. For China there was no chance of a gradual ascent nor the opportunity to pass through the stages of development that the dominant Western world had already left behind. Tardily forced to find a place in the main stream of world history, China had to make a mighty leap forward. It had to try to make in decades the changes the West had accomplished in centuries. This wrench could not occur without the most profound convulsions. Hence the turmoil, the speed, the scope, the depth, the explosive character of events in China during the last forty years.

To make the necessary changes, China had not only to break sharply with its past; it had to transform its present. Old and new fetters both had to be sundered. Imperialist penetration had introduced the most modern techniques in production, transport, communications, and finance, the tools of modern capitalism. Yet, by adapting to its own uses the merchants, landlords, officials, and militarists, imperialism helped perpetuate the precapitalist forms of Chinese social organization. Foreign-built factories and railroads were used to extract profits out of the backwardness that survived in China as a whole. By occupying all the strategic positions in Chinese economy and drawing off tribute for the benefit of principals abroad, the imperialist system stifled the "normal" or independent development of China's resources that might have raised the standard of living of the Chinese people and secured for China a less unequal competitive position in relation to the advanced West. The existence of the foreign "spheres of influence" prevented China from achieving any reasonable degree of internal coherence and unification. If the Chi-

nese people were to raise themselves from intolerable poverty, productive forces had to be freed to grow. To begin with, the farmer had
to regain a stake in his land and his toil; industrialization had to begin
to provide a new and more mutually fruitful relationship between
town and country; and the foreign grip on Chinese economic and
political life had to be broken. These were the inseparable elements
of the crisis in modern Chinese society. These were, and amid all the
changes still are, the problems of the Chinese revolution.

The heaving events of the last two decades, the world economic
crisis, the Japanese invasion, the Pacific war, the collapse of Japan,
the civil war in China, and the onset of ruinous inflation brought the
crisis in China to the climax that ended with Communist conquest
of power in 1949. These events altered the foreign relationship to
China, both politically and economically. Extraterritoriality and the
other special privileges acquired in the last century were finally yielded
in treaties signed during the war. The foreign economic role in China
was likewise transformed by the wartime dislocations and the subsequent political changes. But the root problem is still the same one
that drove China into revolutionary upheaval two decades ago. China
has suffered from being a vast, overpopulated, backward country in a
world that has stubbornly refused it an opportunity to come abreast.
The intense pressure of the swollen population in the crowded river
valleys has been a product not merely of technical backwardness but
of a whole encrusted system of social relations in which that backwardness was preserved. The events of 1925–27, as well as all the
more recent events, have their roots in the struggle of the Chinese
peasant for survival.

As China entered upon its new period of revolutionary conflict
after 1919, it was plain that any radical revision in Chinese life had
to begin with restoring to the peasant his land and the product of
his toil. Only in this way would the old landholding system be abolished. It was the indispensable first step in the eventual transformation of the whole rural economy and the increase of agricultural
productivity in new forms and by new methods. More than three-
quarters of China's population, or more than 300,000,000 people,
depend upon the land for their livelihood. The problems of these
millions are the problem of China. Their poverty is China's poverty.
All of China's hopes for the future depend on releasing the productive energies of this great mass of people. Up to now they have been
drained by a system which has taken away from them the fruits of

their infinite toil as well as the land itself, and has given them nothing in return.

Chinese rural economy has been characterized by the following main features: (1) The increasingly swift concentration of land ownership in the hands of a constantly narrowing section of the population; (2) the passage of title in much of the land to absentee landlords, government officials, banks, and urban capitalists, who controlled the commercial capital penetrating to the remotest villages via the local merchants and usurers, and who were in turn dominated by foreign finance capital and the regime of the world market; (3) the dislocation and decline of agricultural production as a result of the uneconomic use of increasingly parcelized land, preservation of the most backward farming methods, the harsh impositions of the landlord, the usurer, and the state, exposure to the ravages of famine, flood, and drought, and civil wars fought by armies swollen by hordes of dispossessed peasants.

Scientific surveys made in recent years have destroyed the illusion, once so common, that China was a land of relatively comfortable small landholders. From sectional studies made under his direction, Professor Chen Han-seng estimated in 1936 that no less than 65 percent of the peasant population was either entirely landless or land-hungry, i.e., possessing land in parcels too small and too burdened by all the adverse conditions of the regime to provide a living even on the barest subsistence level.[1] Differences in land owned and tilled and in the labor applied or exploited on the land disclosed the deep cleavages within the peasant population.*

* Professor Chen defined these categories as follows: "When a peasant family is barely capable of self-support from the land, and in its agricultural labor is not directly exploited by, nor exploiting, others, we may say that such a family belongs to the class of *middle peasants*. The status of the middle peasants helps us to determine that of the other two classes of peasantry. When a peasant family hires one or more agricultural laborers by the day or by the season during busy times, to an extent exceeding in its total consumption of labor power that required by the average middle peasant family for self-support, or when the land which it cultivates surpasses in area the average of the land used by the middle peasant, we shall then classify this family as that of a *rich peasant*. Where we see families cultivating twice as much land as the middle peasants in their village, we safely classify them as those of rich peasants without further considering the labor relations. The *poor peasants* are comparatively easy to recognize. All peasant families whose number of cultivated *mow* (one *mow* is one-sixth of an English acre) falls below that of the middle peasants and whose members, besides living on the fruits of their own cultivation have to rely upon a wage income or some income of an auxiliary nature, belong to the poor peasants in general. Those poor peasants who do not cultivate any land, either of their own or leased, but hire themselves out, or who cultivate a mere patch of land but have to support themselves chiefly by selling their labor power in agriculture, are called *hired agricultural laborers*, but still belong to the peasantry." *Agrarian Problems in Southernmost China* (Shanghai, 1936), p. 8.

Conditions of land tenure provide the clearest mirror of class relations in agriculture. One official estimate made in 1927 held that 55 percent of the Chinese peasantry was entirely landless and 20 percent holders of inadequate land. It was calculated that 81 percent of the cultivable land was concentrated in the hands of 13 percent of the rural population.[2] These figures have been in the main substantiated by later investigators. In the north, where individual landholders predominated, study of a sample district showed that although only 5 percent of the farming population consisted of landless tenants, 70 percent of the total held less than 30 percent of the cultivated land in average plots of 10.9 mow, or less than two acres. In another district, it was found that 65.2 percent of the population held 25.9 percent of the land in parcels of less than seven mow, or a fraction above an acre. Landlords and rich peasants, together comprising 11.7 percent of the farming population, held 43 percent of the land, and middle peasants held the rest.

In the far more densely populated Yangtze Valley and in the south, where foreign influence had first been felt and where the commercialization of agriculture was more advanced, the disproportions were found to be much greater. In one district of Chekiang province, investigators found that 3 percent of the population owned 80 percent of the land. In Wusih, another district of Central China, 68.9 percent of the farming families owned only 14.2 percent of the land in individual average parcels of 1.4 mow, or less than a quarter of an acre. Landlords and rich peasants, 11.3 percent of the families, owned 65 percent of the land.[3] A separate survey made in the southern province of Kwantung[4] revealed that landowners in different sections of the province comprised 12 to 32 percent of the population, and tenants and agricultural laborers 68 to 88 percent. Of the poor peasants representing 64.3 percent of the population in one area, investigators found that 60.4 percent were landless. An average of all the districts studied showed that more than half the farming population owned no land. Of all the land tilled by the poor peasants, only 17.2 percent was owned and 82.8 was leased. The average area owned by a poor peasant family was found to be 0.87 mow and the average area cultivated, including leased land, 5.7 mow. The number of mow necessary to provide the barest subsistence for a peasant family was found, in different districts, to vary between six and ten, and twice that many for tenant farmers.

This extreme concentration of land came about partially through the gradual alienation of the once considerable state, temple, or community lands and the conversion of the large collective holdings of the rural clans into the virtual private property of small groups of powerful clan leaders. The steady decline in agricultural production and the increasing weight of the burden placed on the peasant's shoulders soon lost him what land he had left. His skill in coaxing growth out of his tiny plot of ground could not match the results of scientific advances made elsewhere in agriculture or enable him to halt the decrease in the productivity of his land. China's chief commercial crops, tea and silk, surrendered their positions in the world market because better products were more efficiently grown by more modern competitors.[5]

The invasion of the village by commercial capital and cheap manufactured commodities put an end to the peasant's old self-sufficiency. But because the country remained backward in communications and production techniques, the peasant could not adapt himself to the change. He was simply ruined by it. He had to produce for sale in order to exist, yet the smallness of his land and the primitive character of his farming made it difficult, if not impossible, for him to do this with much success. He not only could not produce enough to provide him with a surplus, but had to go into debt for fertilizer, for food to tide him over until harvesttime, for seed, for the rental and use of implements. For these he mortgaged away not only his crop but his land, at rates of interest never lower than 30 percent and more often 60, 70, 80 percent and even higher. The crushing burden of taxes and the rapacious extortions of the militarists who came to rule over him drove the peasant more deeply into debt each successive year and placed him and his land at the mercy of the usurer and the tax collector.[6] He was fleeced at will by the merchant because he could not ship his tiny crop to more distant markets and hope for a return. Crops were freely cornered and prices manipulated at the village level by the merchants. Invariably, new debts were all the peasant had to show at the end of a season's toil. They followed him into the next year and into the next generation. Losing his land, he became a tenant. To the landlord he had to surrender 40 to 70 percent of his crop and a substantial additional percentage, often in special dues, gifts, and obligations preserved from the dim feudal past, including the duty of free labor on special occasions fixed by ancient tradition.

Famines, floods, and droughts, against which he was defenseless, often cost him his crop, his land if he had any, and frequently his life. Even in the best years, however, he and his family lived on the edge of starvation. He was little better than a bonded slave to the landlord, the tax collector, the merchant, and the usurer.

This process, in its manifold aspects, plunged the great mass of the peasantry into chronic, unrelieved pauperism. Millions driven off the land begged, starved, took to banditry, or swelled the armies of the war lords. From the south they had streamed abroad, to the Americas, to Malaya, and to the Indies. From the north, they emigrated to the undeveloped lands of Manchuria. Millions of them clogged the cities and towns on the rivers and on the seaboard, an inexhaustible source of cheap manpower that the new infant industries could not absorb. Their labor was still cheaper than that of animals, and throughout the length and breadth of China men did the work of beasts of burden. More and more land was left untilled. China, one of the greatest agricultural countries, was compelled to begin importing foodstuffs in steadily increasing measure.' The internal and external markets entered upon a disastrous decline. The whole economic structure rotted at its core.

Over the years these conditions erupted in violence that became chronic but remained localized. Such was the banditry that became epidemic in China in the years following the 1911 revolution. It was obvious that the rise of any new revolutionary banner would bring the peasants to their feet and marshal them, almost at a word, in any new effort to revise the conditions of their life. It was also obvious that any new political force which undertook to lead the peasant masses toward a new dispensation would have to undertake in the first place to relieve the peasants of their worst burdens and restore them to their land.

This did not mean that mere redivision and redistribution of the land was the final answer to peasant well-being. Parcelization of the land was already one of the basic ills of Chinese agrarian economy. Any revolutionary transformation of Chinese society would have to include a long-term and far-reaching program for increasing the efficiency of agricultural production in economically larger units making full use of modern farming methods and industrial organization. This is why in the most fundamental sense a peasant economy, with all it contains of the narrow and limited outlook of the small and isolated producer, comes into conflict with the demands of a more rationalized system of urban and rural production. This is why the process of change must necessarily be one of patient education, of experiment and example, and of gradual transformation based upon proved results. It is also the reason why, in the first instance, the conditions for such changes cannot be established until the peasant himself has overthrown the old system that keeps him in thrall. In a backward peasant society, it is impossible to think in terms of rational planning and modernization before the peasant has been helped to free himself from all the older bonds of social subjection and ignorance which hold him down. This is why, above all, these changes have to take place not in rural isolation but as part of a fundamental revision of the economy as a whole.

In China this meant, as we have stated, that the economy of the country as a whole had to be freed to develop in accordance with its own needs. Here it ran into the formidable barrier of foreign capital functioning not as fuel for the general welfare of the people but as a sluice for draining away the country's wealth. In the 1920's, foreign capital owned nearly half of the Chinese cotton industry, the largest industry in the country. It owned a third of the railways outright and held mortgages on the rest. It owned and operated more than half the shipping in Chinese waters and carried in its own bottoms nearly 80 percent of China's foreign and coastal trade. The drain of wealth was a steady one. China's adverse trade balance accumulated between 1912 and 1924 to a total of $1,500,000,000* and to twice that sum in the next ten years. Between 1902 and 1914, foreign investments in China doubled and in the next fifteen years doubled again, reaching an estimated total of $3,300,000,000 (U.S.). More than four-fifths of this sum was directly invested in transport and industrial enterprises and the rest in loans which converted the various Chinese governments into docile tools and preserved the foreign grip on internal and external revenues.[8]

To regain control of its own productive forces, then, China had to recapture this lost ground; it had to free itself from the political and economic control of the Western powers and Japan. It had to unify itself by cutting across the sectional rivalries perpetuated by rival militarist satrapies in the different foreign spheres of influence. Only in this way could internal peace be restored, the incubus of

* Calculated in United States dollars at the then par rate, two to one.

militarism removed, and the internal market freed to develop by its own momentum. To gain the strength needed to do this, China needed a political leadership that would galvanize the peasantry by opening the way to release from its burdens. The Chinese revolution, in short, had to be an anti-imperialist movement that inscribed the slogans of the agrarian revolt on its banners.

How and by whom could this be done? The answer to this key question involves an estimate of the class forces and relationships as they existed at the time—and we speak now of the first years after the first World War—for each section of the population obviously stood in distinct and different relations to the land and to the foreign interests and each would enter the political arena with different objects in view. The peasantry itself, as history has abundantly proved, cannot function independently in the political arena. It is deeply cleft into layers with sharply conflicting economic interests. It is the most numerous, but also the most scattered and most backward section of the population. It is localized and limited, economically and psychologically. For these reasons the village has, in China as elsewhere, always been subject to the town. The peasantry has always been at the command of the urban class able to centralize, weld, control, whether in the economic process or in politics. Without the centripetal force of the city, around which rural economy must inevitably revolve, the peasant is helpless, especially the poorest peasant, the most exploited and the nearest to the soil. His own attempts to better his own lot, without the aid of or in defiance of the dominant city class, have almost invariably taken the form of isolated acts of violence without permanent issue.

This has been especially true in China, a land of impoverished millions, darkened by illiteracy and superstition, so divided sectionally that customs, habits, and the spoken language differ sharply from province to province, town to town, and even from village to village. China's great peasant wars, rising and falling at intervals through the centuries, had always ended in a restratification within the peasantry. The rebelling masses were usually taken in tow by a section of the ruling group which sought not a new society but a new dynasty. When the fighting was done, a new emperor sat on the Dragon Throne and the landlords rose anew. Only an urban ally capable of transforming all social relations could release the peasantry from this vicious historical circle, free it from its own exploiting minority in the countryside, and help it bridge the cultural gap separating town and country.

In Europe the bourgeois revolutions of two and three centuries before had played this historic role. The pattern had many variations, but in essence the rising capitalists of that time had to extend the rights of bourgeois property to the land and free labor from serfdom on the land in order to place it at the disposal of the newly rising industrial system. In France, England, and Holland, the most radical sections of the petty bourgeoisie came forward to help the peasantry break the bonds with which feudalism kept it chained to the soil and thus laid the foundations of the strong national bourgeois states. In twentieth-century China, however, a different social pattern in a different historic context imposed different solutions. The Chinese ruling class could not liberate the peasantry because, as a result of the peculiar conditions and belatedness of its growth, it was too organically tied to the exploitation of the peasantry. It has already been shown how this class rose, not as a distinctly urban grouping with a new economic stake, but out of the old ruling classes. Unlike the European burghers of the past, the urban men of property in China remained bound by a thousand links to the precapitalist or semifeudal system of exploitation on the land. The peasant was subject to the depredations of landlord, usurer, merchant, banker, war lord, tax collector, and local official. The interests of these groups fused and became the interlaced interests of the ruling class as a whole. Not uncommonly, the collector of rent, interest, feudal dues, and taxes, was one and the same person.

"Quite unlike the landlords in France *sous l'ancien régime,* the landlords in China are often quadrilateral beings," wrote Professor Chen Han-seng in a striking summary passage. "They are rent collectors, merchants, usurers, and administrative officers. Many landlord-usurers are becoming landlord-merchants; many landlord-merchants are turning themselves into landlord-merchant-politicians. At the same time many merchants and politicians become also landlords. Landlords often possess breweries, oil mills and grain magazines. On the other hand, the owners of warehouses and groceries are mortgagees of land, and eventually its lords. It is a well-known fact that pawnshops and business stores of the landlords are in one way or another affiliated with banks of military and civil authorities. . . . While some big landlords practice usury as their chief profession, nearly all of them have something to do with it. Again, many landlords are military and civil officers."[9]

This was the real physiognomy of the Chinese ruling class and of the system through which it bore down upon the peasant. The fundamental relations that governed it were bourgeois in character. Feudalism in its classic form disappeared from China many centuries ago when land, the basic means of production, became alienable. The penetration of commercial capital into the village established there a predominantly capitalist economic structure which continued to bear many precapitalist features. Thus the landlord-merchant-banker-politician-tax collector derived his wealth from usury, market speculation, land mortgages, state taxes, industrial profits, and ground rent. At the same time, from the older sources of revenue imbedded in the social structure, he extracted tolls strongly feudal in character and origin: dues to the landlord in free labor and gifts, rent in kind, forced labor, military service, and "likin" or local customs taxes.

Under the molding pressure of imperialism, as we have seen, the most important section of the Chinese ruling class had also become brokers, once, twice, or thrice removed, for the operations of foreign or foreign-controlled capital, just as the war lords and their governments had been converted into pawns on the chessboard of inter-imperialist rivalries. Now aspiring Chinese industrialists looked forward, certainly, to developing their own wealth. They began to seek a loosening of the foreign grip on the country. But the fact was that they still leaned heavily on their foreign rivals and derived much of their revenue from them. The gulf which separated them from the great mass of the people was far wider and less bridgeable than the antagonism between them and the foreigners. From the foreigners they could and would try to exact concessions, to demand and secure a larger share of the spoils. But they could not hope to satisfy the masses of the people without undermining themselves. Land could not be restored to the peasants without upsetting all existing property relations and destroying the economic foundations of the ruling class itself in town and country alike. This fundamental and inescapable fact predetermined the limits to which the propertied classes of China would go in the national-revolutionary movement that rose in the years following 1919.

But these were by no means the limits of the perspectives of the revolution in China. The same economic growth and circumstances

which had stirred nationalist feeling among nascent Chinese industrialists after the first World War had also brought into being an
urban working class which now also entered the political arena as a
major participant. This section of the population was estimated in
1927 to consist of about 1,500,000 factory workers, about 1,750,000
other industrial workers (miners, seamen, railroad workers) still
closely linked, socially and economically, to the mass of urban shop-
workers and handicraftsmen, numbering more than 11,000,000.[10]
This new urban class was still raw and young. The first modern labor
unions, as distinct from the older craft guilds, appeared in China only
in 1918. Yet, barely a year later, workers were already intervening
in the political life of the country, striking in support of nationalist
students. Six years later, 1,000,000 Chinese workers participated
in strikes, many of them directly political in character. Two years
after that, Chinese unions counted 3,000,000 members and in Shanghai the workers carried out a victorious insurrection which placed
political power within their grasp.

The existence of this class in Chinese society introduced a wholly
new element and opened entirely new perspectives for the nationalist
revolution. Unlike the city banker, industrialist, official, or money-
lender, the Chinese worker had no stake in preserving the existing
system of rural exploitation. On the contrary, he was a victim of that
same system. In some ways, his close ties to the village represented
a liability rather than an asset in a political sense. The typical Chinese worker was fresh from the ranks of the peasantry. His family
was still possibly on the land somewhere, trying desperately to survive.
He himself had come to the city because rural hardship had driven
him there. The Chinese industrial worker had been physically severed from the land but he was psychologically still bound to it. His
own dearest hope, usually, was to return to it. It was not impossible
that the landlord who owned his family's land was his urban employer's father or uncle or cousin. But the Chinese worker, on the
other hand, found himself able to come to grips with his problems
in an entirely new way and with far greater power. Feeble as Chinese
industry was, the specific gravity of the worker in it was still greater
than that of the propertied class. The worker proved this by plunging
swiftly and even decisively into political life. He became the newest
and most significant among the political forces taking shape and getting into motion in the China of the early 1920's. He was not mature,

either in the political or economic sense, but the situation into which he was thrust was maturely ripe for his intervention. The whole course of the oncoming revolution would be determined by the ability of the urban working class to assert its leadership over the mass of peasants in the countryside.

But this was not left to the interplay of Chinese social forces alone. The Chinese worker became the object—and ultimately the victim—of a whole new set of influences that had been set in motion far from China itself. In Russia a revolution had taken place only a few years before. Its leaders had proclaimed it to be a workers' revolution that marked the beginning of the end of world capitalism. The influence of that revolution moved eastward. The invasion of its ideas, its spokesmen, its representatives was the most fateful invasion of China since the arrival of Western merchants and warriors nearly a century before.

Chapter 3

WORLD CRISIS: THE RUSSIAN IMPACT

THE CHINESE revolution rose out of the soil of Chinese social conditions and historic circumstance. Its course was shaped largely by the interplay and friction of different class interests within the country. But the time had long since passed when events in China could be purely "Chinese" in content. A nationalist revolution in China, by definition, meant a collision between Chinese and foreign interests. The seeds of nationalism had been sown in the first place by the invading imperialism of the West, which had shaken China out of its stagnation and forced profound and belated changes upon it. Ultimately, the stimulus that touched off the revolutionary impulses in Chinese cities and villages came from the war of 1914–18, fought by Western powers on battlefields half a world away. China was inextricably enmeshed in world events and directly affected by the course of world power politics. In turn, China itself exerted an influence on the outcome of great struggles waged beyond its borders and, often, beyond its ken. It was not merely that China was now entering upon a crisis in its own history. Its travail was part of the crisis of world society in our century.

China had been brought face to face with the need to break with its precapitalist past and to establish and define itself as a nation. This same purpose had been achieved in the West by the revolutions of the eighteenth and nineteenth centuries. Since then a whole historic epoch had intervened. Capitalism had established the division of labor on a world scale. Great technological advances and the automatic expansion of capital wealth were now straining against the national barriers originally erected to help organize the internal market and the productive system that fed it. For two centuries, rival national groups fought for markets, for fresh sources of raw materials, for cheap labor, and for higher profits. Out of these conflicts, colonial empires grew. By the end of the ninteenth century all the economically undeveloped areas of the world had been more or less forcibly subjected to the more advanced countries and drawn irresistibly into the orbit of world capitalist economy. Asia and Africa became the theaters of large-scale economic, political, and military conflicts. Out of the ruthless competition that lay at the heart of this swiftly unfolding process emerged the movement toward concentration of capital wealth and the division of the world into a decreasing number of increasingly mighty economic and political groups which warred incessantly with one another by economic or military means. Industrial control was transformed into financial control, crossing seas and the highest mountains and reaching into the remotest African jungles and Asian villages.

By the beginning of this century, the productive power generated by this system had already outstripped the national-economic structure through which it functioned. Concentrated economic power within the nations developed into international and world-wide monopolies and cartels. These, in their own way, demonstrated the need to enlarge the economic units of the world and produced the greater inter-nation conflicts which finally exploded into the first World War of 1914–18. The scope of that war proved that the globe itself had become the smallest possible unit of necessary change. National states, each jealously seeking to retain or increase its share of a contracting world economy, could no longer fruitfully or peaceably coexist but were doomed to constant conflict with one another. The great system of national political economies had nourished the growth of productive forces on a spectacular scale for more than two hundred years. But it had now outlived its usefulness. This is the root of the crisis in world society in our time. All the convulsions of our century are the symptoms of this crisis, and the Chinese revolution was subject to all its terms and all its pressures. China, like the rest of the subjected East, had to try to become a nation at a time when the nation, as such, had ceased to be the instrument of fruitful human progress. China's revolution had to be part of the effort to replace international anarchy by a new system that would embrace the entire globe in some kind of more rational social and economic order; or else it had to suffer, with the rest of the world, the agony of prolonged frustration. Such was the issue that emerged in all its full global dimensions at the end of the World War in 1918 and has been with us ever since.

Woodrow Wilson's conception of a League of Nations based

upon the peaceful co-operation of all peoples was aimed to meet this fundamental historical problem, but it was doomed by the failure to break through the established framework of national political, social, and economic interests. These had to be successfully assaulted and transformed if men were really going to begin to find the way to fashion some better system under which to live. This the League of Nations never undertook to do. Instead—and this is perhaps the cruelest paradox of our era—the first really vigorous attempt in this direction came not from among the more advanced industrialized countries of the West but in backward, peasant Russia. Wilson's ringing phrases had made a profound impression, even in remote Asia. But the cynical horse trading at the Versailles conference soon made it plain that they signified nothing. This was especially plain to the Chinese, who were asked at Versailles to accept Japan's wartime encroachments in China. In China in particular, as the wave of hope aroused by Wilson receded, the tide of the Russian revolutionary influence began to roll in. It came upon China as a set of ideas and soon as an actively intervening political force.

Russia played a decisive role in the whole course of events in China between 1924 and 1927. Conversely, the events in China formed a critical episode in the evolution of Russia itself. The history of this period, which is the subject matter of this book, can be made intelligible only in terms of the interaction of the Chinese and Russian revolutions. This relationship, in its own time and place, was extremely complex. Its main features tend to be obscured for us now, moreover, by the many events and transformations that have taken place since, especially in the position of Russia as a factor in world affairs. We know the Soviet Union in 1951 as a supernationalist totalitarian state which rules by brute force and police terror and cynically manipulates other peoples to further its own national-strategic ends. An oligarchic bureaucracy rules the people and the economy of Russia under conditions of total tyranny. It is, along with the mortally sick but stubbornly surviving system of Western capitalism, a huge and formidable obstacle in the path of human advance toward freer institutions. But this Russia by no means sprang full-grown from the brow of Lenin and his Bolshevik party in 1917. It grew, over a period of years, out of the backwardness of Russia itself and the frustration of revolutionary impulses elsewhere, especially in Europe immediately after the end of the first World

War. In conception and purpose, the Bolshevik revolution was not nationalist but daringly internationalist. Bolshevism certainly bore within it the seeds of totalitarianism, particularly in the system of one-party rule that rose out of it. This system certainly provided no adequate safeguards against the consequences of power won and held by violence. But it is certainly equally true that the men who made that revolution were convinced that they were overthrowing tyranny and opening the door of history upon a new era of expanding freedom. That was the conviction that communicated itself to millions of people in Asia and elsewhere and became an objective political fact of the first magnitude.

For Lenin and Trotsky the revolution did not merely signalize the end of Czarism in Russia. It heralded the downfall of the capitalist system throughout the world. It was, as they saw it, the beginning of a new world order based on the social ownership of the means of production. The Bolsheviks did not in the least consider that they were engaged in building a new national power in Russia. They were seeking an end to all national power. They were interested in building not a new Russia but a new world. Theirs, they believed, was the first in a series of socialist revolutions soon to reverberate around the world. They looked upon their own as merely a prelude. The break in Russia, as they saw it, was only the snapping of the weakest link in the chains of world capitalism. Lenin said, and repeated a thousand times in 1917 and afterward, that socialist Russia could not survive alone in a hostile capitalist world. "World revolution" was neither catch phrase, by-product, nor afterthought. It was a necessity, the core of their hopes and expectations. It was, they believed, the only way to break out of the mortal crisis in human society, to end the cycle of wars over colonies, markets, raw materials, and strategic position in the world by reorganizing the globe for the more rational use of its physical and human resources.

They believed they were launching this great effort by establishing in Russia the "dictatorship of the proletariat."' This is a term and an idea that was never very precisely defined by Marxists from the time Marx first used it in 1852. There was never any clear development in Marxist thought about the nature of the state that would emerge from the proletarian revolution. It was always clouded by Marx's utopian notion about the withering away of the state. Among the Russian Marxists, and particularly between Lenin and Trotsky,

there were bitter polemics for years over Lenin's conception of what
he called "the democratic dictatorship of the proletariat and the
peasantry." These disputes in theory had their own considerable
importance, and they were summoned up later to play a role, both in
the Chinese events and in the internal political struggle in Russia.
But in the first years of Bolshevik power, the new Russian state was
molded not so much by theories as by the harsh circumstances of civil
war and intervention. In later years, the evolution of the Russian
state under Stalin provided its own definition of the term "dictatorship of the proletariat." The historic reality usurped the claims of the
theoretical concept, and despite the possible appeal to the real democratic content of many other aspects of Marxist thought, no restoration on this score seems possible.

Neither Lenin nor Trotsky could be described as liberal democrats. But neither were they authoritarian monsters. The fact is that,
to consolidate his power, Stalin had to replace Lenin's uncompromis-
ingly internationalist ideas with a Russian nationalist doctrine of his
own. He had to exile Trotsky and imprison and ultimately annihilate
the whole leadership of the Bolshevik party which actually made the
revolution of 1917. Stalin did not take this path until Lenin died, but
it is not difficult to believe the bitter remark made by Lenin's widow,
Krupskaya, in 1927, that had he lived Lenin would by then have been
rotting in a Stalinist prison. There is evidence that in his failing last
years Lenin was aware of the abyss into which the Russian revolution
was falling as a result of its isolation. The police state that emerged
from his handiwork signalized the failure, not the victory, of his ideas
and his leadership.[1]

From the whole record of his written and spoken words, it is
abundantly plain that Lenin looked upon the revolution in Russia as
the opening skirmish of a world struggle that would soon shift to
other, more important theaters. He saw the civil war in Russia as a
holding operation which would enable the Bolsheviks to cling to
power until the workers' revolutions in Central Europe took over the
leadership of the anticapitalist struggle. To the interests of the revolution elsewhere, above all in Germany, Lenin was ready to make the
utmost sacrifices. At the Second Congress of the Communist International in Moscow in 1920, Lenin defined internationalism as "the
subordination of the interests of the proletarian struggle in one nation
to the interests of that struggle on an international scale, and the

capability and readiness on the part of one nation which has gained a victory over the bourgeoisie of making the greatest national sacrifices for the overthrow of international capitalism."[2]

The Russian revolution was like an option on world socialism, valid for only a short period. It had to extend or else retreat upon itself. It had to become in fact international or else reassume, in some new form, its purely national identity. It could not survive, as Lenin foresaw, as a socialist revolution. But it could and did transform itself into something else. Internationalism was a tender plant that had to grow strong rapidly or else be choked in the weeds of renewed nationalism. First subtly, then headlong, this choking process began to take place within the Russian Bolshevik regime. It began the shift now slowly, now perceptibly, now swiftly, from the radical world view to the conservative national view. Instead of making "the greatest national sacrifices for the overthrow of international capitalism," the regime began to seek from elsewhere the greatest international sacrifices for the preservation of Russian national "socialism."

The Bolsheviks triumphed in their own country. They were victorious in the civil war and fought off the military intervention of the Great Powers which lasted until 1922. But the successful revolutions in Central Europe upon which Lenin had so desperately counted did not materialize. They rose and fell. They were dammed and diverted. Russia was isolated. It had to adapt itself to lone existence within a bristling rim of hostility. Its people war-weary, its land ravaged, its revolutionary vitality ebbing, Russia turned in upon itself. The economic structure inherited from Czarism had been strained to its meager limits by the drain of war communism. To win a breathing space, Lenin retreated to the New Economic Policy, re-establishing the free market. Lenin was fully aware of the new dangers that bore down on the infant state as the revolutionary wave in Europe receded and the high tension of the Russian people began to give way to fatigue and disillusionment. He could hope for a new conjuncture of events that would alter the external prospect, but he could not hope to freeze the Russian state in a posture of waiting for it to come about. In these conditions of isolation and the retreat of the people from the political arena, especially after the last great battles of the civil war were fought, bureaucratic reaction within the Bolshevik regime grasped at the machinery of power. It began to entrench itself long before the young and green revolutionary parties in Europe could find their way once more to opportunities for political conquest.

This bureaucratic stratum which began to solidify on the outer crust of the Soviet state took Russia's national isolation as its starting point. Under its influence, Soviet policy began to shift from the premise of the international socialist revolution to the need for consolidating and extending the privileges of the new bureaucracy. This bureaucracy identified itself with the workers' power even while it took all power into its own hands. Lenin opposed this shift, but it was stronger than he was. When he died, the representatives of the new bureaucratic caste, personified and led by Joseph Stalin, took over. Stalin's party machine already reigned, but it was not until after Lenin's death in 1924 that Stalin formalized the new orientation by advancing, for the first time, his theory of "socialism in one country" —the idea that socialism could triumph and maintain itself indefinitely within a single national state. This represented a complete ideological break with the internationalism of Lenin. It rationalized the isolation of the Russian state and provided new theoretical justification for the gradual abandonment of the original ideas and perspectives of the Bolshevik revolution.

This transformation in the character and emphasis of the Soviet regime took place over a period of several years. The impulse to subordinate revolutionary movements abroad to Russian national interests appeared almost from the beginning. It began to play its role in some of the earliest maneuvers of Soviet diplomacy. It was reflected in Russian domination of the Communist International and the "Russification" of Communist parties abroad, in organizational structure, attitude, and policy. This had become so evident, even in 1922, that at the Fourth Congress of the Communist International, the last Lenin attended, he criticized the Congress for imposing Russian terms and Russian ideas on the other parties and warned, perhaps more pregnantly than he knew, that this would in the end lead to defeats.[8] National interest already dominated the policies dictated by the Kremlin leaders to the German Communists in the critical year of 1923. The tactics of the party were determined not by the conditions of the social crisis among the German people but by the shifts in the foreign policy orientation of the Stresemann government. In the spring of the year, when German-Russian relations were apparently prospering, especially in the military sphere, the German Communists were instructed to stand back from the immense revolutionary surge that sent great masses of the German workers out into the streets in a leaderless and vain attempt to grasp political power. When that summer Stresemann began to seek a rapprochement with England, the Kremlin abruptly turned about face and drove the German Communists into a hopeless insurrection.[4] The defeat and dispersion of that uprising in Germany in October 1923 dissipated the last Russian hopes in the European revolution. The Russian retreat from Europe was turned into a rout.

The next three years, 1924 to 1927, the new bureaucratic leadership in Russia devoted to consolidating itself. It did not go unchallenged. To settle itself in power, Stalin's party machine had to wage a bitter struggle against the surviving members of the original leadership of the revolution and against its original ideas and impulses. Tendencies within Bolshevism toward nationalism and oligarchic dictatorship had been vainly challenged by obscure oppositions and small factional groups ever since 1918. Resistance now belatedly took form in the top leadership of the party itself. Zinoviev and Kamenev, who had joined hands with Stalin in the "triumvirate" of 1923, made a bloc with Leon Trotsky against Stalin in 1925. This united opposition attempted in the next two years to speak against Stalin in the accents of the international socialist revolution. It had wide support among members of the Bolshevik party, but this support was already muted under the control of the bureaucratic machine and the opposition itself was laced tight within the rigid party regime that Bolshevism had created and which Stalin already had under his control. Beyond the council chambers of the party, the Russian workers and the people generally were already too tired and too passive to respond to the new conflict. The opposition's fight was ineffectual and unsuccessful. The headlong plunge toward the creation of a monolithic police state inspired by nationalist motives was already under way. It was precisely during this three-year period of transition that the Russian influence came to bear in China. The climactic events of the Chinese revolution in 1926–27 took place while Stalin, in Russia, was riding roughshod over the opposition in his final conquest of power. The struggle, in which debate over the Chinese events played a large part, decided the course of Russia for a whole historic epoch. It also, tragically, determined the fate of the Chinese revolution.

* riding roughshod

The defeat in Germany in 1923 led the Kremlin to look with new interest and calculation on developments in Asia. In the rising tide of national and colonial revolt in that part of the world, it hoped to find new sources of diplomatic, political, and military support for Russia against the pressure of the Western powers under the leadership of Great Britain. The colonial powers were being challenged in the years after 1918 in almost all the countries of Asia. Russian influence was present, if only as an idea, in many of these movements. But circumstances of geography and time fixed China as the main theater of active Russian intervention. Here the opportunity for action at both the diplomatic and political levels was obviously the most promising: Russian Bolshevism and nascent Chinese nationalism had a common enemy in England. The first Soviet approaches to China were, strikingly enough, efforts to establish contact with any group, with any clique of militarists or politicians, which might prove usefully ready to join hands with the Russians against the British.

It might be worth reminding the reader at this point that in the time of which we speak, a bare thirty years ago, Great Britain was to all appearances still the world's paramount Great Power. It was still the master of the world's greatest empire, still the mistress of the seas. The decline of Britain was already a fact, but an unacknowledged or at least a stubbornly resisted fact. The passage of the center of gravity in world affairs across the Atlantic to the United States was already under way, but the United States had not yet recognized, much less welcomed, this new immigrant to its shores. It was going to take another world war to complete the rearrangement of strength and weakness among the nations that had by then already begun. In the 1920's, however, it was England who led the Western world in its hostility to Bolshevik Russia. It was also England, great imperial England, who was the prime target of the major national revolutionary movements in Asia. In China, Britain held the largest capital stake, the premier positions of privilege. The burgeoning Chinese revolution was directed in the first place, against the British. The identity of purpose on this score was the primary basis for the co-operation that soon developed between the intervening Russians and the Chinese nationalists.

But this was by no means a mere repetition of the old pattern in which Chinese political interests would seek to jockey between contending powers, or by which a foreign power tried to utilize a Chinese political faction to further its own interests against a foreign rival. The Russian influence that came to bear in China also contained other, newer ingredients that gave it an entirely different and unique historical significance. There was the prestige of the October Revolution itself as an historic fact; the ideas underlying the Russian revolution and their theoretical significance for China; the grotesque deformation of these ideas filtered through the minds of the new leaders in the Kremlin and translated by the agents and advisers and military specialists who came to China from Russia; finally, the conflict between the unfolding dynamics of the revolution within China and the purposes and prospects of that revolution as viewed by the Kremlin.

To begin with, there was the fact of the Russian revolution. Russia, like China, was a huge backward country. It was more Asian than European in the quality of its despotism and in the nature of its economy. The Russian peasants had risen in a gigantic *Jacquerie* that had fused with revolutionary currents in the army and in the cities, had overthrown the Czar, rejected the moderate leaders, embraced the Bolsheviks, and fought off the united forces of the Western powers for four years. This was something the Chinese could translate directly into their own terms, whether it was the Chinese peasant suffering the exactions of landlords and autocratic militarists, or the Chinese intellectual smarting under the subjection of his land to the control of the same Western powers and the same Japan who had tried so hard to smash the Russian revolution. This new Russia, in 1919 and 1920, had in startlingly new language abrogated all the unequal treaties imposed by the Czarist government on China in the past. It had offered China friendship based on complete political equality.

The contrast between this attitude and that of the Western powers was extremely compelling. Belief in the good intentions of the World War victors was quickly dispelled by events. The discovery that the Powers had no intention of applying the idea of self-determination to China led Chinese of all classes to look with receptive interest toward Russia, either through the misty eyes of inspired revolutionists or with the calculating eyes of men in search of a makeweight against Western pressure. The first great swell of the Chinese revolution had come in 1919 when nationalist students, supported by workers in the cities, rose in protest against the Versailles settlement and against the corrupt Peking politicians who wanted to capitulate to Japan.

This new current in Chinese life and the new revolutionary impulses radiating out of Russia quickly found a common path, generated a high political amperage, and sent powerful shocks coursing through the entire political structure of China and, for that matter, the whole East.

The October Revolution offered more than an example to the Chinese people. It appeared to be a successful test, on a huge scale, of a whole set of ideas that had peculiar relevance in China. Marxist thought had already begun to make its way among Chinese intellectuals, following the path opened into Chinese libraries and universities a generation earlier by Huxley, Spencer, and Mill. As a political-economic analysis of Western industrial society, these ideas seemed to have at best only an indirect application to China. Marx's few allusions to Asia were never fully developed and were little understood. But now they had been sifted through the experience of Russia, which was at least a semi-Asian nation with a backward peasant economy in the main and governed by a system of entwined capitalist and precapitalist economic relations not too different from those existing in China. The ideas stemming from Marx, developed in polemics between Lenin and Trotsky, and tested in Russia in 1905 and 1917, came down in essence to this: that in a world ripe for socialism, a backward country had to make the leap from its precapitalist past to the threshold of the socialist future; that the bourgeois or nascent capitalist class was not capable of leading the country through these changes; that it was both possible and necessary now to skip over the stage of capitalism and the bourgeois-democratic order; that this could be done if the urban working class shouldered aside the would-be builders of a national capitalist system, took over the leadership of the peasantry, and assured the breakup of the old system of land relations. This achieved, the workers in power could set out to make over the economy and political institutions of the country on the new basis of socialist property relations, i.e., social ownership of the principal means of production. Large-scale urban industrialization would bring on, in due course, industrialization of agriculture as well and bring rural and urban workers into a new and more harmonious relationship nourished by an elevated standard of living. But—and this was the crucial qualification—this all was going to be possible only in a world engaged in building socialism. It could be accomplished not in one country, particularly a backward country, but only through the co-operation of the backward countries with at least some of the more advanced countries of the world and "through the creation of a unified world economy based on one general plan and regulated by the proletariat of all the nations of the world."[5]

In more precise Marxist terms, it can be put this way: With the world as a whole maturing for socialism, an entirely new political perspective opens up for those backward countries which have not yet fulfilled the tasks of the bourgeois revolution, i.e., achievement of national independence and unification, and breakup of precapitalist forms of rural economy. These tasks can now be carried through to completion only by a proletarian revolution, taking place in a context in which the more advanced countries of the world are converting themselves from capitalist into socialist states. In these circumstances, the purely national or anticolonial revolutions in the backward countries would tend to "grow over" into socialist revolutions. The process would be a fusing or telescoping of stages, the bourgeois into proletarian into world revolution. This was, in essence, the theory of "permanent revolution" developed by Trotsky. In the time of the revolution itself, it fused with the ideas of Lenin, bringing to an end years of harsh polemics between them.[6] It formed the root conception of the Communist International and was immediately applied to the broad strategy of world events, as the Bolsheviks saw it, after their victory in Russia. The struggle to overthrow capitalism in the advanced West, sparked by the overturn in Russia, would go hand in hand with the struggle for national liberation in the subject countries of Asia and Africa. Guided and helped by the advanced countries, the Asians and Africans would be able to emerge from their varying stages of backwardness and join directly in the socialized reorganization of the world's productive forces, skipping entirely the intermediate stage of capitalism.

For China these ideas had unique and overwhelming significance. They opened a way through what was otherwise a blank wall. The world had no place to offer it as a new and free national state based upon a freely functioning capitalist economy. The hope of budding Chinese capitalists for national sovereignty collided with the political and economic and territorial positions of the foreign Powers. China's hope for expansion on a capitalist basis collided with the superior competitive position of foreign capital, which was far more interested in extracting immediate profit from Chinese raw materials and cheap labor, in the classic manner of colonial exploitation, than it was in the systematic development of a new and productive economy for the Chinese people as a whole. Finally, the ruling class in China could not by its own efforts revitalize the internal Chinese market without solving the agrarian problem; and it could not solve the agrarian problem, as we have seen, without destroying itself. With the rise in China of an urban working class of substantial proportions and weight in the society, the underlying ideas of the Russian revolution offered a radically new point of departure.

At the Second Congress of the Communist International, Lenin worked out in considerable detail the application of these ideas to the colonial and semicolonial countries. He laid it out in terms of the strategy to be followed by the Comintern and by the Communist parties which were even then just coming into existence in the various countries of Asia. The Congress resolution stressed the distinction to be made between bourgeois-nationalist movements which, it warned, would try to compromise with imperialism, and revolutionary-nationalist movements which would fight imperialism to the bitter end on the basis of solving the most pressing internal social and economic problems.[7] In a group of theses written for the Congress, Lenin defined the relationship between these two tendencies in colonial nationalism and suggested the strategy and tactics to be followed by the Communist parties in colonial struggles. Since this was the crux of the problems that developed in China in the ensuing years, it is important here to quote them at length:

It is of special importance to support the peasant movements in backward countries against the landowners and all feudal survivals. Above all we must strive as far as possible to give the peasant movement a revolutionary character, to organize the peasants and all the exploited into Soviets. . . .

It is the duty of the Communist International to support the revolutionary movement in the colonies and in the backward countries for the exclusive purpose of uniting the various units of the future proletarian parties—such as are Communist not only in name—in all backward countries, and educate them to the consciousness of their specific task, i.e., to the tasks of the struggle against the bourgeois democratic tendencies within their respective nationalities. The Communist International must establish temporary relations and even unions with the revolutionary movements in the colonies and backward countries, without, however, amalgamating with them, but preserving the independent character of the proletarian movement, even though it be still in its embryonic form.[8]

To guard against being "taken in tow" by national bourgeois movements seeking to exploit the prestige of the Russian revolution, Lenin injected a specific warning "to wage determined war against the attempt of quasi-Communist revolutionists to cloak the liberation movement in the backward countries with a Communist garb." In a supplementary document drafted by M. N. Roy under Lenin's eye and presented by Lenin at the same Congress, this warning was elaborated as follows:

There are to be found in the dependent countries two distinct movements which every day grow farther apart from each other. One is the bourgeois democratic nationalist movement, with a program of political independence under the bourgeois order, and the other is the mass action of the poor and ignorant peasants and workers for their liberation from all sorts of exploitation. The former endeavor to control the latter, and often succeed to a certain extent, but the Communist International and the parties affected must struggle against such control and help develop class consciousness in the working masses of the colonies. For the overthrow of foreign capitalists, which is the first step toward revolution in the colonies, the cooperation of the bourgeois nationalist revolutionary elements is useful. But the foremost and necessary task is the formation of Communist parties which will organize the peasants and workers and lead them to the revolution and to the establishment of soviet republics. Thus the masses in the backward countries may reach Communism, not through capitalist development, but led by the class conscious proletariat of the advanced capitalist countries. . . .

The real strength of the liberation movements in the colonies is no longer confined to the narrow circle of bourgeois democratic nationalists. In most of the colonies there already exist organized revolutionary parties which strive to be in close connection with the working masses. (The relation of the Communist International with the revolutionary movement in the colonies should be realized through the mediums of these parties or groups, because they are the vanguard of the working class in their respective countries.) They are not very large today, but they reflect the aspirations of the masses and the latter will follow them to the revolution. . . .

The revolution in the colonies is not going to be a Communist revolution in its first stages. But if from the outset the leadership is in the hands of a Communist vanguard, the revolutionary masses will not be led astray, but will go ahead through the successive periods of development of revolutionary experience. . . . In the first stages the revolution in the colonies must be carried on with a program which will include many petty bourgeois reform clauses, such as division of land, etc. But from this it does not follow at all that the leadership of the revolution will have to be surrendered to the bourgeois democrats. On the contrary, the proletarian parties must carry on vigorous and systematic propaganda for the Soviet idea and organize the peasants' and workers' Soviets as soon as possible. These Soviets will work in cooperation with the Soviet Republics in the advanced capitalistic countries for the ultimate overthrow of the capitalist order throughout the world.[9]

In sum, Lenin was proposing to Communists in the colonies that they concentrate on building workers' parties, however embryonic. These parties had to aim at giving the most radical kind of leadership to the peasantry. They had at all costs to preserve their political independence, even while they co-operated with bourgeois nationalist groups. They had to resist being swallowed up by these groups, whose object was not the transformation of society but a better bargain with the foreign masters.

These were potent ideas and this was potent advice. Translated into the Chinese political terms and circumstances of 1923, they would have had results that no one can measure now. But the fact is that while the Russian revolution came to enjoy in China immense authority and prestige, its basic ideas were never communicated, never translated into Chinese terms, never independently applied. They were tested in China only by negation. The Communists, under Russian direction, not only did not follow any of Lenin's prescriptions, but they fell into every pitfall against which he warned. They were caught fast by the fact that by the time Russia actively intervened in China, the revolution in Russia itself was in full retreat and the new nationalist Russia had begun to emerge. The Soviet bureaucracy, thrust back, as we have seen, from the frontiers of Europe by the collapse of the German uprising of 1923, did not come to the East in search of new proletarian conquests. It came looking for new allies, new bulwarks, new fronts on which to blunt the hostile pressure of the Western powers and of England in particular. To accomplish this, it still freely borrowed all the terms of the international socialist revolution, twisting them grotesquely in the process to serve the national ends of the Russian state.

It would be difficult to try to measure in this the degree of conscious cynicism which was certainly present at the top. But it was in any case a simple matter for the Soviet bureaucracy to begin to identify international revolutionary aspirations with its own narrow interests. Russia was the vanguard of the world revolution: anything that helped Russia helped the world revolution; the bureaucracy represented Russia; ergo, anything that helped the bureaucracy helped Russia. By an almost natural and inevitable shift of emphasis, the Kremlin bureaucracy had begun to view popular movements abroad as tools to be manipulated for its purposes. It came to regard the prime function of Communists abroad as the servicing of Russian diplomacy. Similarly, as they retreated from the original premises of Bolshevism, Stalin and the other new leaders lost sight of the ideas which had brought them into power. They had only dimly understood what had happened in the revolution of 1917. Lenin had come back from abroad and practically bludgeoned them into following his course.[10] Once the civil war was won, they were able with comparative ease to establish first their power over the Bolshevik party and then, in an increasingly absolutist manner, over the people and the nation. To the business of intervening in popular movements abroad, they brought little more than the pseudo-cunning psychology of manipulators who believed that great social forces in motion would respond mechanically to their pedantic and self-interested notions.

It has to be stressed, however, that while this shift in power and emphasis was taking place, it had by no means taken on the brutally cynical character which Soviet policy and action acquired in later years. For one thing, Russia was much weaker. It still, in 1924, had to depend more on the attractive power of ideas than on its own brute strength, and when it came to ideas and revolutionary strategy, Stalin was on uncertain ground. In 1924, the Kremlin's approach to events in China was in a way more myopic than malignant. It was eclectic, scholastic, and remarkably self-deceiving. Russian leaders like Joseph Stalin and Nikolai Bukharin, who had never understood how in Russia the bourgeois and proletarian revolutions had fused, reverted for Chinese purposes a few years later to the notion of rigidly separated stages in the revolutionary process. Because they desperately wanted to convert the Chinese bourgeoisie into an ally of Russia, they proceeded to endow it with infinite revolutionary capacity. Out of a profound ignorance of the real social physiology of China, they convinced themselves that there was irrevocable conflict between the Chinese bourgeois nationalists and the Western imperialists. They cloaked this conviction in lawyerlike briefs that reduced people to robots and ideas to lifeless dogmas. They were certain that all they had to do was to place a powerful mass movement at the disposal of the Chinese nationalist leaders, and to this end they were ready to sacrifice anything that stood in the way, including the Chinese Communists.

Both the Chinese Communist party and the Kremlin have come a long way since the events of 1925–27. Both have shed the naïveté of those early days. Both have been hardened by war and shaped by the successful exercise of power. The Chinese Communists remain ritualistically faithful to the Kremlin, but the well-preserved memory of past defeats due primarily to Russian dictation must always be subtly present in their mutual relations now. The Kremlin, for its part, has transformed Russia into a world Power of the first magnitude. It has hardened itself in the mold of a totalitarian state, with pervasive police terror and military strength as the prime tools of its authority. Abroad it subverts and perverts popular movements to its own ends and has grown far more cynically accustomed to juggling foreign Communists on the international checkerboard, using them as spies, puppets, or pawns for purely Russian purposes. This Russia evolved out of a history in which the Chinese revolution of 1925–27 was an important episode. But that evolution had, at that time, only just begun. These events took place less than ten years after the October Revolution in Russia. The supernationalist totalitarian state we know today had then only begun to take shape out of the ashes of the October dream. By the measure of history, the span of time has been short and the tendency to flatten the jagged path of development into a straight line is not easy to resist. Yet in this case, to endow the evolving Russia of 1924 with all the characteristics of the developed Russia of 1951 would be to obscure the real history of the intervening period almost entirely and make great and decisive events virtually impossible to understand. The tragedy of the Chinese revolution of 1925–27 lay precisely in the fact that it took place within the same period of years during which the Russian national dictatorship was coming into being. Had it occurred a few years earlier, the whole course of history would have been different.

Thus it is necessary to see that if even today hosts of people are still drawn into the Russian political orbit by the pull of the mummified remains of the revolutionary ideas of 1917, the attraction was far more legitimate in 1924–27, when these ideas and impulses had not yet been extinguished and when the real lineaments of the so-called "dictatorship of the proletariat" in Russia were still not visible. Some of the Russian and Comintern advisers and specialists who swarmed into China in 1924 undoubtedly still thought of themselves as social-ists and revolutionists, although they were already little more than Soviet diplomatic agents. In the name of serving the Chinese revolu-tion, they came to serve Russian national interests and in doing so they led the Chinese people to a catastrophe.

The Chinese workers had already embarked spontaneously on the revolutionary path. The impulses they radiated from the cities were already beginning to stir great layers of the peasantry into action. Chinese industrialists and businessmen, their hopes for expansion fluttering, were already reaching out to control this incipient move-ment and were already attempting to cloak themselves, as Lenin fore-saw they would, with the authority of communism. In a few short, swift years, a stupendous mass movement rose from the streets of Chinese cities and the tired land of Chinese fields. It threatened to destroy all that was corrupt and rotten in Chinese society. Russia intervened in this movement and, blindly defeating its own purposes, prevented this movement from breaking clear of the hold of the ex-ploiting classes. As a result, the Chinese revolution was halted in its forward surge, the new organizations of the people were shattered, their leaders cut down. Such was the cruel irony, such was the tragedy of the Chinese revolution.

Chapter 4

THE NEW AWAKENING

CHINA'S economic spurt during the first World War opened all the sluices of change. Along a thousand channels new ideas, new thoughts, new aspirations found their way into the country and crashed against the dead weight of the past like mighty waves against a grounded hulk. Among the intellectuals the mood of despair and discouragement engendered by the failure of the 1911 revolution gave way to the beginnings of a vigorous cultural renaissance which rapidly drew a whole new generation into its orbit. New leaders, new forces came to the fore. Out of the thinned ranks of the revolutionary intellectuals of 1911 emerged the figure of Ch'ên Tu-hsiu, scion of an Anhwei mandarin family, who began posing the tasks of revolt more boldly, more clearly, more courageously than anyone who had preceded him. To his side rallied the men who with him were going to make over the life of a whole generation and who in later years would enter and lead opposing armies on the battlefields of social conflict.

The task of the new generation, proclaimed Ch'ên Tu-hsiu, was "to fight Confucianism, the old tradition of virtue and rituals, the old ethics and the old politics . . . the old learning and the old literature." In their place he would put the fresh materials of modern democratic political thought and natural science.

We must break down the old prejudices, the old way of believing in things as they are, before we can begin to hope for social progress [wrote Ch'ên in 1915 in his magazine, *New Youth*]. We must discard our old ways. We must merge the ideas of the great thinkers of history, old and new, with our own experience, build up new ideas in politics, morality, and economic life. We must build the spirit of the new age to fit it to new environmental conditions and a new society. Our ideal society is honest, progressive, positive, free, equalitarian, creative, beautiful, good, peaceful, cooperative, toilsome, but happy for the many. We look for the world that is false, conservative, negative, restricted, inequitable, hidebound, ugly, evil, war-torn, cruel, indolent, miserable for the many and felicitous for the few, to crumble until it disappears from sight. . . .

I hope those of you who are young will be self-conscious and that you will struggle. By self-consciousness I mean that you are to be conscious of the power and responsibility of your youth and that you are to respect it. Why do I think you should struggle? Because it is necessary for you to use all the intelligence you have to get rid of those who are decaying, who have lost their youth. Regard them as enemies and beasts; do not be influenced by them, do not associate with them.

Oh, young men of China! Will you be able to understand me? Five out of every ten whom I see are young in age, but old in spirit. . . . When this happens to a body, the body is dying. When it happens to a society, the society is perishing. Such a sickness cannot be cured by sighing in words; it can only be cured by those who are young, and in addition to being young, are courageous. . . . We must have youth if we are to survive, we must have youth if we are to get rid of corruption. Here lies the hope for our society.

This memorable call was really the opening manifesto of the era of the second Chinese revolution. Ch'ên Tu-hsiu was a professor at the time at Peking National University, where new ideas and new impulses were stirring and where a new spirit was germinating. Ch'ên's magazine was eagerly snatched up by students in every school and college in the country. When it was published, wrote one student, "it came to us like a clap of thunder which awakened us in the midst of a restless dream. . . . Orders for more copies were sent posthaste to Peking. I do not know how many times this first issue was reprinted, but I am sure that more than 200,000 copies were sold."[1] It nourished the impulsive iconoclasm of the young people. It gave direction to the mood of unease and unsettlement that pervaded all classes in the population. It was a call to action that awakened immediate response. An outlet was not long in offering itself.

Japan had taken advantage of the wartime circumstances in 1915 to impose upon China its Twenty-one Demands, which would have reduced China to a virtual Japanese colony. Japanese troops had also occupied the province of Shantung. Woodrow Wilson's promises of self-determination and social justice for all peoples had bred the hope that in the general postwar settlement, China would be relieved of Japanese and Western overlordship. When, at Versailles, these illusions were cynically spiked by horse-trading politicians,[2] the student youth in China rose in fury against the treachery of the Japanophile

Peking Government. On May 4, 1919, huge student demonstrations took place in the old capital. The homes of pro-Japanese ministers were attacked and wrecked. The movement spread across the country. In it a new note sounded when workers in factories struck in support of the student demands for a new regime.

At the end of 1916 there were already nearly 1,000,000 industrial workers in China and their number nearly doubled by 1922. An army of nearly 200,000 Chinese laborers had been sent to Europe during the war. Many of them learned to read and write and, even more significantly, came in contact with European workers and the higher European standard of living. They returned with new ideas about man's struggle to better his estate. Nationalist sentiment had taken strong hold among them. Many on their way back from Europe had refused to step ashore at Japanese ports during the furor over Shantung. When strikes in factories began to deepen the roar of the May 4 movement, the returned laborer was already regarded as "the stormy petrel of the Chinese labor world."[3] These workers played a key role in the creation of new labor organizations, in which they formed a solid and energetic nucleus. Just as old family firms and partnerships were beginning to give way to modern corporations, the guilds were beginning to break up and to divide into labor unions and chambers of commerce. Chinese workers, new to their machines and new to the ideas and techniques of labor organization, were thrust at once into the political turmoil that rose around them. Their strikes in Shanghai and other cities in 1919 more than anything else forced the release of student demonstrators arrested in Peking and hastened the resignation of the offending government officials.

The tide of May 4 engulfed the entire country. It ushered in the second Chinese revolution. It seemed to touch off waiting impulses of astonishing vigor. Traditional ideas and modes of conduct were crumbling and the echo of their fall sounded from one end of the country to the other. Young men and women in towns and villages began to break with the old authority of the family and the village elders. A fissure opened between the generations that was never again closed. The old ways of doing and thinking still governed much of Chinese life but they were now being mortally assailed. In the colleges and universities there was a great churning. The disillusionment with the West after the Versailles Conference turned popular attention among the students to the Russian revolution. This new current brought with it to China belated tributaries of all the main streams of European social thought, democracy, anarchism, syndicalism, and Marxism, opening up new horizons and stimulating a veritable revolution in thought, morals, and literature, and rapidly deepening the channels of political change and social conflict. All classes of society entered the political arena. Old political organizations took on fresh life. New organizations came into being.

When these fresh political currents began to flow in 1919, the Kuomintang, heir to the party of the 1911 revolution, had fallen into sterile impotence. Its "right" elements, conservative bourgeois intellectuals, had become helpless dependents of the war lords. Sun Yatsen, leader of the more radical wing of the intelligentsia, was pursuing his schemes for revolution by military conspiracy, by attempting to use the lesser against the greater militarists. He had evolved his own political philosophy, summed up in his "Three People's Principles." These were not distinguished by their clarity or boldness, or even by any consistent radicalism. His principle of Nationalism, which concerned the liberation of China from foreign control, was heavily diluted by Sun's own naïve illusions. As first president of the Republic, Sun had promised the Powers that their perquisites and privileges, extracted by force from the overthrown dynasty, would remain intact and that payments due them on their loans would be assumed by the Republic.[4] After the war of 1914–18, he counted on the benevolent co-operation of the Powers. He submitted to the various foreign offices a plan for "sincere" collaboration among the different nations in the development of China's resources. He envisaged an idyll in which the foreign holders of privilege would join with the Chinese in a "socialistic scheme" from which all would benefit. "It is my hope," he wrote, "that as a result of this, the present spheres of influence can be abolished, international and commercial war done away with, internecine capitalistic competition can be got rid of, and last but not least, the class struggle between capital and labor can be avoided." Sun's "nationalism" also included the prospect of Chinese domination over minority nationalities within the former Empire. He looked for the "assimilation" of the Manchus, Mongols, Mohammedans, and Tibetans, in a Greater China ruled by the Han. The idea of the self-determination of nations, like that of a vigorous struggle against imperialism, entered his thinking somewhat later.

Sun's second principle, Democracy, provided mainly for a period of "political tutelage" during which enlightened leaders would gradually guide the dark and miserable masses toward self-government. Conceived by Sun as a kind of benevolent paternalism, this doctrine became in the hands of his heirs and successors a justification for the most despotic kind of tyranny. There was, in fact, little in common between Sun Yat-sen's concept of democracy and the idea of the direct conquest of political rights and liberties by the people.

The third principle of the People's Livelihood expressed Sun's thinking on future Chinese economic organization and the all-pervading question of the land and the peasantry. He advocated "restriction of capital" and "equalization of rights in the land," two formulas broadly and variously interpreted by Sun himself and by his disciples in subsequent years. By "restriction of capital" Sun hoped to save China from the blights of capitalism, although it was never clearly shown how this was to be done. By "equalization of rights in the land," Sun meant a plan to correct inequalities in such a way that "those who have had property in the past will not suffer by it."[6] His plan was to have land values fixed by agreement with the landlords and for all future increment in these values to revert to the State. By the power of purchase, the State would then proceed to create better conditions for the landless or land-hungry peasant population. Sun Yat-sen never ventured for years, however, to propagate even these plans for fear of alienating his military allies and many of his own followers. Sun totally rejected the idea of a class struggle, and the participation of the masses in political life was quite outside his ken. His hope was to bring about the peaceful and benevolent transformation of Chinese society after first securing power for himself and his followers by purely military means. This was the aim of his long series of invariably fruitless military adventures and alliances.[7]

The renewal of political activity in the country in 1919, however, energized Sun Yat-sen's declining party. Sun himself began appearing before student gatherings, and when General Ch'ên Ch'iung-ming permitted him the next year to establish a government in Canton, he made contact there with the newly organized trade-unions. The labor movement had already begun to make headway. Railroad workers had established a union at Ch'anghsintien, near Peking, and students went there nightly to teach the union members. Unions had also begun to spring up along the seaboard and in Canton and Hongkong in the south. Marxist journals appeared in the schools and universities. Marxist study groups formed in 1918 and 1919 expanded into Socialist societies and from these it was but a step, in 1920, to the foundation of the Chinese Communist party. Its founders included some of the leading figures of the May 4 movement, chief among them Ch'ên Tu-hsiu. The party's first national conference took place in Shanghai in July 1921. Most of the delegates were young intellectuals. It was a mixed group destined to break into many parts. Some, drawn by adolescent sentiment or quickly stifled anarchist leanings, soon dropped away into obscurity or found their way to opposing political camps. Among the founders, for example, was Tai Chi-t'ao, who in a short time became the leading ideologist and spokesman for the Right Wing of the Kuomintang. Others who began their careers as Communists included Ch'ên Kung-po, Shao Li-tzǔ, and Chou Fu-hai, all later luminaries in the Kuomintang regime. Ch'ên Kung-po ended up as a puppet of the Japanese. Others, like the famous Li Ta-chao, librarian of Peking National University, were destined to lose their lives in the coming battles. Also among the founders was Li's young assistant, a Hunanese named Mao Tsê-tung.

The new Communist party soon had to face the problem of its relation to other burgeoning political groups. At its second national conference, in 1922, it was decided to propose a two-party alliance to the Kuomintang. When this plan was laid before Sun Yat-sen, he rejected it. He said he might permit Communists to join the Kuomintang but would countenance no two-party alliance. Shortly afterward, Maring, the first delegate of the Comintern in China who had already been in contact with Sun in the south, met with the Communist Central Committee at West Lake, Hangchow. He proposed that the Communists simply enter the Kuomintang and use its loose organizational structure as a means for developing their own propaganda and contacts among the masses.* Maring based his proposal in the first place on his own prewar experience in Java. There he had been associated with Left-Wing Social Democrats who joined the Saraket Islam, a mixed political-religious movement opposing Dutch colonial rule. Within the Saraket Islam this group had begun to organize workers' groups and during the war had succeeded in developing a

* This information is based on notes of a conversation with Maring in Amsterdam in 1935. Maring, whose real name was Sneevliet, was a Dutch Communist who later broke with the Comintern and headed a Left-Wing Socialist group in Holland. He was killed by the Nazis during the second World War.

substantial Left-Wing political movement in the colony. Maring also was convinced that in Sun Yat-sen's group in Canton there was the nucleus of the kind of national-revolutionary movement to which Lenin had referred at the Second Congress of the Comintern. He cited Sun's connections with the growing labor movement in the south.

According to Maring, the majority of the Chinese Communist Central Committee accepted his views. Those who opposed his plan did so on the grounds that they doubted the weight of the Kuomintang as a political force and did not believe it would or could develop into a mass movement. Ch'ên Tu-hsiu, listed by Maring as among those who agreed readily to enter the Kuomintang, has written an account of the Hangchow conference which differs on this point.[8] He says that all the Central Committee members opposed Maring, claiming that even at that time the Chinese Communist leaders believed such a step "would confuse class organizations and curb our independent policy." This was written, however, after the event. In 1922, Ch'ên had written: "Co-operation with the revolutionary bourgeoisie is the necessary road for the Chinese proletariat"[9] and it was obviously in this spirit that he approached the Kuomintang issue when it arose. It seems fairer to assume that the opposition to Maring was based on the belief that the Kuomintang was defunct and not worth considering, a view which he remembers was most strongly expressed by Chang Kuo-t'ao, another of the founding leaders of the Communist organization. In the end the proposal was adopted, although there was considerable doubt whether the Kuomintang, and especially Sun himself, would welcome it.*

The Communists entered the Kuomintang as individuals in hopes of winning over to their influence the Southern workers who had already affiliated with the Kuomintang.[10] At the same time they pressed Sun Yat-sen to reorganize his party on the basis of a new program

* According to Ch'ên Tu-hsiu, the entry was voted when Maring invoked the discipline of the Comintern. Maring denied this, pointing out that the Chinese Communists could have appealed to higher organs of the Comintern. "Moreover, I possessed no specific instructions," he added. "I had no document in my hand." Further light on this point may exist in the unpublished and unavailable archives of the Comintern. According to P. Mif, of the Far Eastern Bureau of the Comintern, the first formal instructions "to co-ordinate the activities of the Kuomintang and the young Communist Party of China" were issued in a special communication of the Executive Committee of the Comintern dated January 12, 1923. By that time the Communists had already entered the Kuomintang as individuals although the formal decision to do so was not taken until the Third Conference of the Chinese Communist Party in June 1923. Cf. P. Mif, Heroic China (New York, 1937), pp. 21-22.

capable of attracting popular support. Sun remained cool to these proposals. Only when he was forced once more to flee for his life, following a revolt by General Ch'ên Ch'iung-ming in Canton in June 1922, did he grow more receptive to the arguments of Maring, supported by Liao Chung-k'ai, the most radical of Sun's immediate entourage. Sun was still unattracted by the role of a mass movement as a political weapon, but he had begun to be attracted by the prospects of direct and concrete aid from Russia.

Several factors combined to start Sun thinking about a Russian alliance. His plan for the international development of China had been rebuffed by all the foreign governments who received it.[11] The Powers had set about regulating their relations in the Far East at the Washington Conference of 1921–22. But while that conference produced the Nine Power Treaty guaranteeing the territorial integrity of China, the main issue settled there had more to do with Anglo-American relations with Japan than with the needs of China. That conference, to borrow Wang Ching-wei's summary, "freed China from the Japanese policy of independent violent encroachment" only to leave it victim "to the cooperative slow encroachment" of all the Powers.[12] Sun and his followers began to lose some of their faith in Western good intentions. Simultaneously, they began to see in Russia not only a source of material aid but a lever for extracting concessions from the Western Powers.

The Moscow government had already indicated its readiness to put Chinese-Russian relations on a radically new basis. On July 4, 1918, Chicherin, then Commissar for Foreign Affairs, declared that Bolshevik Russia had unilaterally renounced all Czarist "unequal" treaties with China and its agreements with Japan and other countries relating to China. This policy was again set forth in a manifesto issued on July 25, 1919, over the signature of Leo Karakhan, deputy commissar for foreign affairs. This manifesto said that the Soviet government annulled and repudiated "all the secret treaties concluded with Japan, China, and the former Allies; treaties by which the Czar's government, together with its allies, through force and corruption, enslaved the peoples of the Orient, and especially the Chinese nation, in order to profit the Russian capitalists, the Russian landlords, and the Russian generals." Again, on September 27, 1920, in a formal note to China, the Soviet government reiterated its denunciation of all previous treaties, renounced all Czarist annexations

of Chinese territory, and returned to China "free of charge and forever all that was ravenously taken from her by the Czar's government
and by the Russian bourgeoisie."[13] Early Soviet missions to Peking,
under M. I. Yurin and A. K. Paikes, tried from 1920 to 1922 to
negotiate a new treaty on this basis but were blocked, mainly by Western and Japanese pressure on the Peking government.

These first contacts between Bolshevik Russia and China illus-
trate how, even at this early date, contradictions arose between Russian national purposes and Communist international revolutionary
purposes. The declarations from Moscow in 1919 and 1920 had
breathed a note of change new in the annals of international diplomacy. The offer of this new revolutionary government to deal with
China on a basis of equality nettled the Western Powers and won a
delighted and sympathetic hearing for Russia among all classes of
Chinese. But there were some significant equivocations, relating to
the Chinese Eastern Railway in particular, which strongly suggested
second thinking by at least some Russians in policy-making positions
at the time.*

But even more striking is the fact that the first Soviet agents to
reach China, sent by the Chita government and by the Irkutsk Bureau of the Comintern, came looking not for new revolutionary currents to swim in but for a deal with any likely looking band of militarists and politicians who might serve Russian diplomatic interests. The
government at Peking was then in the hands of the notoriously pro-
Japanese Anfu clique and the Russians scanned the field for promising opponents. The puny nationalist movement led by Sun Yat-sen
in the south did not impress them as a point of support for Soviet
interests. They were more attracted by the military strength of the
war lord Wu P'ei-fu, who was interested in overthrowing and replacing the Anfu regime in power. When Wu did seize the government
in Peking in 1920 and set up a puppet civilian cabinet of his own, the
Far Eastern expert V. Vilensky wrote in *Izvestia*: "Wu P'ei-fu has
hung out his flag over the events which are taking place in China

---

* There is evidence, for example, that the Manifesto of July 25, 1919, originally
contained a specific Russian offer to return the Chinese Eastern Railway to China
without compensation. This sentence appeared in one version published in Moscow,
was deleted in other published versions, and then was left in by mistake in a text
officially communicated to Peking the following March. It was the source of much
dispute in subsequent Soviet-Chinese negotiations. The history of this interestingly
elusive sentence is traced in a graduate thesis prepared at Columbia University in
1950 by Allen S. Whiting, "Sino-Soviet Relations, 1917–1924."

and it is clear that under this flag the new Chinese cabinet must take an orientation in favor of Soviet Russia."[14] But Wu's orientation was toward the British; the Rising Sun had merely been replaced by the Union Jack at the back door of the Peking government. That was why, in the final analysis, the 1921 negotiations were without result.

When Maring came to China in the spring of 1921 and established connections with Sun Yat-sen, whom he first visited in Kwangsi, he decided that the main stream of Chinese nationalism flowed through Sun's Kuomintang. This belief was strengthened when in Canton and Hongkong in January 1922 a major seaman's strike took place and Maring found that the Kuomintang already had substantial links to the young Chinese labor movement. Maring's proposal to the Chinese Communists to enter the Kuomintang marked a reversal of the so-called "Irkutsk line" of the Comintern. When Sun Yat-sen, expelled from Canton by the militarist Ch'ên Ch'iung-ming, arrived in Shanghai in August 1922, Maring met him again and urged him to substitute a campaign of mass propaganda and organization for any attempt to recapture Canton by purely military means. This time he found his views more welcome. Sun, dismayed by the outcome of the Washington Conference, had begun to think in terms of seeking Soviet assistance. This was the report that Maring took back with him to Moscow the next month. On the basis of his findings, the Comintern abandoned the "Irkutsk line" of trying to establish links with Northern militarists and turned its attention instead to Sun Yat-sen. Maring's views were published in the Communist press and became the starting point of an entirely new orientation of Soviet policy.[15] The Soviet government sent Adolph Joffe, one of its top diplomats, to establish formal contact with Sun Yat-sen.

Joffe met Sun in Shanghai. On January 26, 1923, they issued a joint statement in which Joffe agreed that "conditions do not exist here for the successful establishment of Communism or Socialism," that "the chief and immediate aim of China is the achievement of national union and national independence." Joffe assured Sun that, in seeking these aims, the nationalist movement "could depend on the aid of Russia."[16] This diplomatic formula inaugurated the formal entente with Sun. The Russians at the same time pressed their treaty negotiations in Peking and the next year Leo Karakhan, as Soviet envoy, triumphantly concluded the Sino-Soviet Treaty of May 1924. By that time, however, the whole emphasis had shifted to the south. Arms, money, and advisers were beginning to move in to implement the deal with Sun and the Kuomintang.

From the outset, it was automatically assumed that the Chinese Communists would henceforth devote themselves solely to the job of helping to make the Kuomintang a worthy ally. All the elaborate formulations and explanations came later. In the beginning it was a "practical" and obvious outcome of the new turn in Soviet policy. The Russians had entered into an arrangement with the Kuomintang. It became the duty of the Chinese Communists to facilitate and fructify that arrangement. When Michael Borodin took his post as adviser to Sun Yat-sen in the fall of 1923, he came not as a delegate of the Communist International to the Chinese Communist party, but as adviser to the Kuomintang delegated by the Politbureau of the Communist party of the Soviet Union. This distinction was far from purely formal. It reflected the underlying political realities. Borodin's job was to reorganize and pump new life into the Kuomintang. All efforts, especially those of the Chinese Communists, had to be concentrated now to that end. The Executive Committee of the Comintern had ruled, on January 12, 1923: "Insofar as the working class . . . is not yet sufficiently differentiated as an absolutely independent force, the E.C.C.I. considers that it is necessary to co-ordinate the activities of the Kuomintang and of the young Communist Party of China."[17] The party was "not to merge" with the Kuomintang nor "furl its own banner" but, on the other hand, the "central task" became co-ordination with the Kuomintang and recognition that it could not be an "absolutely independent force." Some of the members of the Chinese party may have found these formulas a little tricky but the third conference of the Chinese Communist party in June 1923 silenced all internal opposition to the Kuomintang entry and raised the slogan: "All work to the Kuomintang!" The conference manifesto declared that "the Kuomintang should be the central force of the national revolution and should stand in the leading position."[18]

Borodin set out to convince Sun Yat-sen that what the Kuomintang needed was a disciplined party organization with a powerful mass movement behind it. Sun had managed to re-establish himself in Canton and in November was again threatened there by Ch'ên Ch'iung-ming's army. Borodin, with the help of the Chinese Communists, managed to demonstrate that the militarist forces could be easily repelled by a show of popular strength. The ease with which this was done finally convinced the Kuomintang leader. With his support, Borodin drafted a new program for the Kuomintang. It was based upon co-operation between the Kuomintang and Soviet Russia as well as the Chinese Communist party, the idea of a militant anti-imperialist struggle mounted on a mass basis, and a platform of liberal reforms for the workers and peasants. Borodin took over Sun's formulas, "restriction of capital" and "equalization of rights in the land." He translated them into planks for a 25 percent reduction in land rents and a promise of a labor code.[19] This new program was adopted and the reorganization of the Kuomintang approved at the first national congress of the party, which met in Canton in January 1924, on the day that Lenin died.

The Kuomintang was transformed into a rough copy of the Russian Bolshevik party. Bolshevik methods of agitation and propaganda were introduced. To create the basis of an army imbued with Kuomintang ideas and to put an end to the previous dependence on old-style militarists, the Russians in May 1924 founded the Whampoa Military Academy. This academy was supplied and operated with Russian funds, staffed by Russian military advisers. Before long, shiploads of Russian arms were coming into Canton harbor to supply the armies which rallied to the new banner as soon as the Kuomintang began to display the new strength with which all these activities endowed it. The Chinese Communist party, chief organizer of the new movement, confined itself religiously to building the Kuomintang and propagating its program. Its members were the most indefatigable party workers, but they never appeared as Communists nor presented any program of their own. The Communist party became in fact and in essence, in its work and in the manner in which it educated its own members, the Left-Wing appendage of the Kuomintang. In the initial stages, however, the ultimate significance of this fact was overshadowed by the spectacular growth of the mass movement. For neither the tactics of the Communists nor the requirements of the Kuomintang brought the mass movement into being. Its sources were imbedded, like ore in rock, in the conditions of Chinese life.

In foreign-owned and Chinese factories in Canton, Shanghai, Hankow, Tientsin, and other cities, factory workers lived and toiled in conditions comparable only to the worst helotry of the early stages of the industrial revolution in England. Men, women, and children worked, as they still do, for twelve, fourteen, and sixteen hours a day for wages as low as eight cents a day, without the most elementary provisions for their safety or hygiene. An apprentice system provided small producers and shopkeepers with an inexhaustible supply of child labor working daily up to eighteen and twenty hours in return for a bowl of rice and a board to sleep on. What these conditions cost in poverty was visible to the eye. What they cost in human life no one could know because no one knows the mortality rate in China.[20] Against these conditions of chronic hunger, the workers, their ranks swelling with the growth of industry, began to rebel as soon as they realized that they did not have to submit docilely to their fate. Small strikes had begun to occur even before the political events of 1919. In 1920 the Mechanics' Union in Canton won a major strike and in 1922 the Hongkong seamen wrote a historic first chapter in the new-style fight against imperialism by winning a strike victory over the British, securing recognition of their union and sizable wage increases.[21] These strikes stimulated the rapid flow of workers into unions. In May 1922 the first national labor conference met in Canton under the leadership of the triumphant seamen. The conference was attended by delegates of 230,000 union members. Under the direct pressure of this strong new group, Sun Yat-sen's Kwangtung government revised the penal code to legalize union organization and the path was cleared for further growth.[22]

In Central and North China the fight for higher wages, the right to organize and to bargain collectively, was also getting under way. Chief of these struggles affected the Peking-Hankow Railway workers. An organization conference of the union was called at Chengchow, in Honan. Wu P'ei-fu ordered his troops to break up the meeting. The result was the massacre of sixty workers on February 7, 1923. This repression only briefly checked the organization of the railway workers. A year later almost to the day, the National Conference of Railway Workers was held and a national committee formed to carry on the fight for "improvement of our conditions, respect for our fate, education for us and our children, the right to form individual unions, to forge solidarity among all railway workers."[23] In Shanghai, by the beginning of 1923, there were already 40,000 workers organized into twenty-four unions.

In 1918, according to incomplete records, there were twenty-five recorded strikes in the country, involving fewer than 10,000 workers. In 1922 there were ninety-one strikes, involving 150,000 workers.[24]

The labor movement grew with astonishing speed and militancy. On May Day 1924, in Shanghai, 100,000 workers marched through the streets and twice that number marched in Canton. Contemporary reports describe how in Wuchang, Hanyang, and Hankow, despite rigid martial law, red flags appeared over working-class quarters. The traditional May Day slogan, the eight-hour day, must have sounded millennial to workers who had just begun to dream of working fourteen instead of sixteen, twelve instead of fourteen, ten instead of twelve hours a day.

"Eight hours of work, eight hours of education and recreation, eight hours of rest—how reasonable this program is!" ran the leaflets of the day. "For forty years the working class has poured out its blood for its realization. The time is past when the workers are but fodder for the bosses. They will not cede but to revolution? Then they shall have it!"

"Remember today, fellow workers, that you are men, just as the bosses are. Demand then that you be treated as men. Organize! Numbers give strength. Comrades will extend to you their hand!" They marched through the streets singing new songs: "Work shall be a pleasure, our offering to brotherhood. We shall be called to it by the bells of liberty!"[25]

It is obvious that by the time the Kuomintang was reorganized in 1924, workers in China had already begun to organize themselves in a movement marked by its independent spirit and militancy. There is also evidence that they were skeptical and suspicious of the new "allies" who were springing up in Canton. There on May Day, Sun Yat-sen told a workers' audience: "The difference between the Chinese workers and foreign workers lies in the fact that the latter are oppressed only by their own capitalists and not by those of other countries. . . . The Chinese workers are as yet not oppressed by Chinese capitalists. . . . They are oppressed by foreign capitalists."[26] Similar statements were made by a Kuomintang speaker at the first conference of transport workers, held at Canton the next month. G. Voitinsky, a Comintern representative who was destined to play a large role in overcoming this skepticism, reported at the time that the delegates "gave a cold and dubious reception to the declaration of the responsible representative of the Kuomintang, who called upon the workers to form a united front with the peasants and intellectuals, but not under the hegemony of the proletariat."[27] This mood and this impulse were soon submerged by the demands of the Kuomintang-Communist alliance.

Similarly, the peasants had also begun to stir and group themselves into organizations before the revived Kuomintang made its appearance in 1924. The modern Chinese peasant movement was cradled in Haifeng, in the East River districts of Kwangtung, by P'êng Pai, one of the most appealing figures of the Chinese revolution. Son of a wealthy Haifeng landlord, P'êng Pai became a schoolteacher in his native village. He was one of the first in the district to join the Communist party and he was soon engaged in trying to organize the peasants. Dismissed from his school job for leading a May Day demonstration of his pupils in 1921, P'êng went out into the countryside to devote himself entirely to the business of rousing the peasants. The story of his early rebuffs, his first successes, and the initial successes of the Haifeng Peasant Association, he has himself left behind in a small pamphlet of personal notes and reminiscences.[28] As a landlord's son he was first received with mistrust and hostility. He finally fired the imagination of a few peasant lads. With conjuring tricks and a gramophone, he drew village audiences and was soon convincing them that they had to form an organization to fight for their own interests. The first Peasant Association was formed, grew swiftly, and was almost immediately baptized under the fire of Ch'ên Ch'iung-ming's soldiers.

Thus begun, the organization spread rapidly to neighboring districts and the framework of a Kwangtung Provincial Peasant Association was already in existence before the middle of 1923. "It is not true," said one of the manifestoes of the new body, "that the landowners' land was acquired by purchase. The fathers and grandfathers of the present landowners took it by force from the peasants. Even supposing that it was bought, it was paid for only once, while the landlords have received rent for it annually for hundreds and thousands of years. . . . The landowners receive the greater part of the harvest without doing any work. How much money and sweat have we and our peasant forefathers expended on this land!" These were simple phrases. They dealt with a situation which the peasants had been taught was immutable and sanctioned by Heaven. When the peasant unionists suggested that it could be changed by their own efforts, and proceeded to prove that it could be, it was as though the world had changed its face. Heaven discovered an interest in peasants as well as in landlords. These ideas seeped quickly through the countryside like rain into the earth. Rapidly they bore fruit. Peasant struggles against the landlords, against the magistrates, police, and soldiery, multiplied throughout the East River districts and ignited similar conflicts in the west and north of the province. Demands for reduction of land rent passed over almost immediately to demands for its total abolition. As early as 1923, in Kaoyao district, according to a documented Chinese account, "some of the unionist farmers had the courage to refuse to pay rentals to the landowners and the latter had to resort to the army and police to make collections."[29] Sharp skirmishes were fought in every case. The peasant movement was already taking shape when the Kuomintang moved into the picture in 1924.

The Kuomintang had still to make itself the governing power not only in the province of Kwangtung but in the city of Canton itself. In the summer of 1924, the Kuomintang in Canton was challenged by the Merchants' Volunteers, an armed organization supplied and financed by the British and by the wealthy compradores of Hongkong and Canton. It was organized by Ch'ên Lien-po, chief compradore for the Hongkong and Shanghai Banking Corporation, leading British financial institution in the Far East. On August 10, Sun Yat-sen seized a boatload of arms consigned to Ch'ên and prepared, after considerable vacillation and delay, to suppress the armed corps that threatened his rule in the city. On August 26, the British Consul General issued a virtual ultimatum, threatening British naval intervention in case of an attack on the Merchants' Volunteers. Sun protested, vainly, to Britain's Labour Prime Minister, Ramsay MacDonald. Sun also appealed to the League of Nations but received no reply. Finally, in October, a force composed of Whampoa cadets, workers' battalions, and peasant guards descended on the Merchants' Volunteers and after a brief but sharp battle defeated and disarmed them. The British river gunboats did not intervene after all.[30]

Four months later, in February 1925, Canton was again threatened by Ch'ên Ch'iung-ming, Sun Yat-sen's former militarist ally who still enjoyed military control over most of the province. The Kuomintang forces attacked him in his own strongholds on the East River. But the new and decisive thing was the intervention of the peasants. In Haifeng, Lufeng, Waiyeung, and Wuhua, they attacked his rear, cut his communications, and seized his supplies. Peasants of Tungkwan, Siapen, and other districts fought alongside the Kuomintang troops and served as guides, spies, and carriers. Against this attack, which seemed to rise against him from all sides in his own territory, Ch'ên was impotent. He fell back and gave up his plan for an attack on Canton.[31]

On May Day 1925, the Second National Labor Conference and the First Provincial Assembly of the Peasant Association took place simultaneously in Canton. It was an impressive demonstration of the Kuomintang's new sources of strength. The labor conference brought together 230 delegates of 570,000 union workers in all the principal cities of the country.[32] The peasant associations were still confined to twenty-two hsien (districts) in Kwangtung, with 117 representatives attending for 180,000 peasant unionists.[33] The delegates paraded jointly, together with thousands of Canton workers and farmers who poured into the city from the countryside. It was, perhaps, the first formal worker-peasant solidarity demonstration in Chinese history. They marched to the assembly halls of various Canton schools which were thrown open to them for the ten-day sessions. Students and political workers addressed their meetings. They heard for the first time of some of the new mechanical implements that could lighten their toil. They wandered through classrooms and libraries. They glimpsed the world from which a life of unremitting labor relentlessly cut them off.

A few weeks later, the budding Kuomintang regime finally established its own power in the city of Canton. The city had been under the military control of two Yunnanese generals, Yang Hsi-min, and Liu Chên-huan, who hoped, like so many others, to benefit from cooperating with the Kuomintang. But a struggle for power in the city was inevitable. Once more the Whampoa cadets and armed workers fought side by side. The result was a foregone conclusion. The Yunnanese troops were demoralized, scattered, and expelled from the city. Peasants in the West River districts completed the job by cutting off the retreating remnants and destroying them after a brief but sharp engagement at Kiangtun.[34] Meanwhile a new wave was sweeping out of Shanghai. The high tide of the new mass movement was only just coming in.

Shanghai workers had begun their own drive against the prevailing slave-labor conditions, particularly in the cotton mills. A series of strikes took place in the early months of 1925, for wage

increases and in protest against the brutality of foremen, especially
in the Japanese-owned mills. The shooting down of striking workers
in Tsingtao and the murder of a Chinese worker by a Japanese fore-
man in Shanghai aroused the anger and resentment of the awakening
mass. A protest parade was held in Shanghai, with students and
workers marching together. Several of them were arrested and the
demonstrators marched to the police station to demand the release of
their comrades. A panic-stricken British officer shouted orders to fire.
Twelve students were killed. It was the afternoon of May 30.

The effect was swift and tumultuous. Shanghai, the great foreign
stronghold with its Western banks and mills and its foreign areas,
was paralyzed by a general strike. Even servants left foreign homes.
The foreigners, accustomed for decades to regarding the Chinese as
so many dirty but docile and necessary pack animals, were appalled
when this unrecognizable mass rose and shook its fist in their faces.
The tie-up was so complete, said the *China Weekly Review*, that "it
was difficult for foreigners to do anything except serve as part of the
local defence units."[35] The rising was not confined to Shanghai. It
soon spread across the country. Incomplete statistics gathered by a
Chinese labor investigator recorded 135 strikes arising directly out
of the May 30 shootings, involving nearly 400,000 workers from
Canton and Hongkong in the south to Peking in the north.[36] At
Hankow on June 11, a landing party of British sailors fired on a
demonstration, killing eight and wounding twelve.[37] In Canton, Chinese seamen employed by British shipping companies walked out on
June 18 and three days later were joined by practically all the Chinese
workers employed by foreign companies in Hongkong and Shameen,
the Canton foreign concession area. On June 23, a demonstration of
students, workers, and military cadets paraded in Canton. As they
passed the Shakee Road Bridge, British and French machine gunners
on the concession side of the creek opened fire on the marchers. Fifty-
two students and workers were killed and 117 wounded.

A boycott of British goods and a general strike were immediately
declared. Hongkong, fortress of Britain in China, was totally im-
mobilized. Not a wheel turned. Not a bale of cargo moved. Not a
ship left anchorage. More than 100,000 Hongkong workers took
the unprecedented action of evacuating the city. They moved en masse
to Canton. The strike halted all foreign commercial and industrial
activity. It drew 250,000 workers out of all principal trades and in-

dustries in Hongkong and Shameen.[38] In Canton workers cleaned out gambling and opium dens and converted them into strikers' dormitories and kitchens. An army of 2,000 pickets was recruited from among the strikers and a solid barrier was thrown around Hongkong and Shameen. The movement was, by all accounts, superbly organized. Every fifty strikers named a representative to a Strikers' Delegates' Conference, which in turn named thirteen men to serve as an executive committee. Under the auspices of this body, actually the first embryo of workers' power in China, a hospital and seventeen schools for men and women workers and for their children were established and maintained. Special committees handled funds and contributions, the auctioning of confiscated goods, and the keeping of records. A strikers' court was set up which tried violators of the boycott and other offenders against the public order.[39]

Police functions were almost wholly assumed by the striker-pickets. The picketing was thorough. "The boycott against British goods in Canton," wrote a foreign observer, "is controlled by a strike committee which operates through pickets, whose work it is to prevent breaches. . . . Wherever in Kwangtung there is a highway for the transfer of goods, the pickets are present, ready to examine cargo, to open packages, to search individuals. . . . Foreigners as well as Chinese are subject to search. . . . The strikers' rule is that no goods, not even foodstuffs, are to be taken to and from the Shameen. . . . If there is an infraction of the boycott, the guilty person is brought before the strikers' tribunal for punishment. . . . The boycott is complete . . . [and it] must be regarded as a war on Hongkong and Great Britain and the pickets as the soldiers in that war. There is no other possible interpretation of the completeness and ruthlessness with which it is carried out."[40] The task of covering all lines of communications along the Kwangtung coast and at all ports was carried out in co-operation with the peasant associations. Peasant pickets patrolled the coast at Swatow, Haifeng, P'ingshan, and other points, to make the blockade complete.

Shameen, with its marooned little colony of bitter and fuming foreigners, was cut off from all contact with the rest of Canton. All entrances to the concessions were guarded. Only occasional ships coming up from Hongkong, mainly warships or British vessels manned by volunteer foreign crews, kept it supplied with the bare necessities of life. British communities in other cities suffered the same fate. "More food must come from Hongkong—no fresh milk here. The Club is empty, servants gone," complained a Swatow Briton in a communication to the *North China Daily News*. The strike in Hongkong also affected the removal of refuse. Among themselves, the strikers changed the Chinese name of Hongkong from Hsiangkang (fragrant harbor) to Ch'oukang (stinking harbor) and finally, as the strike throttled the rich British colony, to Szŭkang (dead harbor).[41]

"An attack has been made upon us, as representing the existing standards of civilization, by the agents of disorder and anarchy!" cried the governor of Hongkong. The strike was costing the standard-bearers of civilization about £250,000 a day. "The number of British steamers which entered the harbor of Canton . . . from August to December, 1924, varied between 240 and 160 each month," reported an official of the British Chamber of Commerce. "During the corresponding period of 1925, the number varied between 27 and 2."[42] Demands for armed intervention in defense of civilization in Hongkong were raised from the city's forsaken housetops. "Responsible British and Chinese residents of Hongkong are convinced that intervention by the British government and local action is imperative. . . ." Otherwise "it is hopeless to expect the Canton anti-Reds to succeed without British assistance." Prompt military action, it was urged, could "easily place alternative and friendly Chinese authorities in power at Canton."[43] But Whitehall saw more wisely than the frantic gentlemen in Hongkong and other ports that "alternative and friendly Chinese" would not be won in these circumstances by direct use of military force. Every effort was made to harry the Canton regime. There was probably not a militarist or bandit leader in Kwangtung province who did not in this period get his price for raids on the picket lines or promises to organize military opposition to the Canton government. But the more astute Britons probably realized that the best hope for the rise of alternative and friendly Chinese lay within the new Kuomintang movement itself.

The strike and boycott enabled the Kuomintang to consolidate its power in Kwangtung. At the end of June 1925 it organized and proclaimed a new National Government of China. In September its troops finally cleared hostile militarists' forces from the East River districts and by the end of the year all enemy forces in the province had been dispersed or defeated. With Kwangtung unified and under its control, the Kuomintang could begin to look northward toward the sources of real national power in Central and North China. It had achieved this position as a direct result of the mass movement that had risen so spectacularly in less than two years' time. A weapon of immense power had been forged. How it was to be wielded and *who* would wield it were the questions that now pushed themselves forward onto the order of the day.

Chapter 5

CANTON: TO WHOM THE POWER?

SUN YAT-SEN used to be fond of saying that there were neither rich nor poor in China—only the poor and less poor. Had he lived a little longer (he died in March 1925) he would have seen what happens when circumstances force into the open the underlying conflict between the "poor" and the "less poor." He would have seen how the "anti-imperialist united front" within the Kuomintang began to divide along class lines. As the mass movement rose and grew, it created new social and political alignments. The factory worker could not be expected long to continue making a formal distinction between the Chinese employer and the foreign employer. If anything, the conditions imposed upon him by the former were worse. Nor could the peasant be expected to remain satisfied with limited promises or to refrain from taking the logical road of action in his own interest as he saw it. The limits so glibly and formally set by the leaders and organizers of the Kuomintang were soon exceeded. A mass movement on such a scale as that which swept China in 1925 developed a momentum all its own. Against its pressure, the propertied classes, the employers of labor and owners of land, began to pit themselves.

The propertied classes obviously preferred compromise with the foreigners to the alternative that the mass movement seemed to suggest. But this did not mean that they would react uniformly to events. The whole social process had been too suddenly shaken, the normal social balances too crudely broken by the intervention of the masses of people in the cities and in the countryside. Crystallization of class forces and of political groupings was taking place simultaneously with the development of the struggle itself. The Chinese ruling class in general wanted the revolution to create a new, stronger, bourgeois power, more stable, more amenable to control than the regime of the war lords, and more capable of commanding better terms from the imperialists who held the real reins of power. But this class was itself divided in sections, ranging from ultraconservative to radical. Their

fundamental community of interest would eventually drive them into
a common front and a common effort. But this was going to take
time. There were groupings which differed on the best way to accomplish the common purpose. There were personalities striving with and
mauling one another in the struggle for place and position and power.
The common motive, however, was mutually recognized. There was
nothing blind about the way that foreign representatives, compradores, Chinese industrialists and bankers, landlords, and their political
hangers-on reached out for means with which to control the new
political forces in motion. There was a remarkable degree of self-
consciousness and definition. They knew what they wanted and set
about getting it with the utmost deliberation.

The compradores, the brokers for foreign capital, were one of the
most powerful of these groups. Merchant princes, bankers, and commission men, their interests collided most directly with the Nationalist
aims of the budding Chinese industrialists who dreamed of competing
with the foreigners in industry and trade. The compradores fought
the new nationalism from the start. They used the old militarists and
provided the channel along which the imperialists backed the militarist defense of the status quo. Through them were supplied the money,
the arms, and the encouragement which kept the old militarist provincial forces in the field. In some cases, as in Canton in 1924, they
organized their own fighting detachments. But that was when the
new Nationalist power had barely established itself in one city. As
the movement spread, it became a question of strengthening and using
the old militarist armies. This group also had its political representatives in the Kuomintang. These were the oldest, the most conservative, usually the most corrupt, and always the most nearsighted
politicians of the old Kuomintang. Most of them had long since
become the ministers and clerks and appendages of the war lords.
They were utterly opposed to the course that Sun Yat-sen took in
1924, the turn to co-operation with Russia and the Chinese Communists and the program for mobilizing the masses to fight imperialism. When the Kuomintang congress in 1924 adopted these policies,
they immediately organized an opposition whose avowed purpose was
to save the Kuomintang from the perdition which they believed
threatened it. They argued that the path to effective compromise
with the foreign Powers was being hopelessly blocked.

"Since the admission of the Communists into the Kuomintang," said one of their manifestoes, "their propaganda about overthrowing the imperialists of Great Britain, France, the United States, and Japan is aimed at the destruction of the international good will of the Kuomintang. . . . Their intention is to obliterate the Kuomintang."[1] Various organizations for "saving the party" sprang up. Their members attached themselves to the entourages of the various local militarists in North China and Manchuria. They scurried between Peking, Tientsin, Shanghai, and Hongkong, organizing, propagandizing, intriguing, and conspiring. After Sun Yat-sen died, they raised the slogan of rescuing "pure" Sun Yat-senism from the "Bolshevism" of the epigones. One of these groups, which became the most important one, took the name "Sun Yat-senist Society." It met in November 1925 for a conference in the Western Hills just outside of Peking and from that meeting took the name by which it was subsequently known: the Western Hills Conference group. These groups considered themselves the guardians of the policy of compromise with the Powers. In practice, they played the role of keeping open the path to such a compromise until the time when it would become propitious. _beneficial_

The foreigners, on their part, were driven off balance by the impact of the mass movement. In the beginning they seemed to think that the freebooting methods of the Opium Wars and the Boxer days would suffice. But the more intelligent among them soon realized, with no small sense of shock, that the times had changed. The British threat to use force in support of the Merchants' Volunteers in Canton had availed them nothing. Foreign gunfire the next year at Shanghai, Tsingtao, Hankow, and Canton, far from cowing the Chinese, had only aggravated the revolt. Foreign bullets sown in Chinese soil brought a swift harvest of tens of thousands of new revolutionary recruits. Without forsaking their own strong-arm policy, the Powers began to give the most active possible support to every available anti-Nationalist force. During the East River wars in 1925, Hongkong vainly fed Ch'ên Ch'iung-ming with munitions and cash. When the pro-Nationalist Kuominchün ("People's Army") of Fêng Yü-hsiang in the north attacked the Manchurian war lord Chang Tso-lin late in 1925, Japanese arms and money bolstered Chang's defenses. When the revolt of Kuo Sung-ling, one of Chang's subordinates, threatened to bring about Chang's collapse, Japanese military forces were thrown into the battle[2] and the threat to Chang was smashed, checking for the time being the further spread of Nationalist influence in North China. But this too, it was understood, was but a temporary respite.

Out of the growing awareness of the new political realities, a whole new orientation in the policies of the leading foreigners in the treaty ports began to make itself felt. It developed into the careful and conscious attempt to establish a common front of foreign and Chinese property owners. "We know by long years of friendly association with you that you do not sympathize with rioters and strikers," said the British-owned *North China Daily News* to Shanghai's Chinese men of property at the height of the Shanghai general strike. The paper, virtually the official British mouthpiece in the country, called upon wealthy Chinese to show that they had "no fellowship with the unfruitful workers of anarchy and ruin. . . . How long this threat to your peace, your welfare, and your safety is to last depends largely on you."[3] At the same time the Powers hastened to show that they were prepared to discuss compromises of a concrete nature to bolster the puppet Peking government against the Nationalist threat. Arrangements made at the Washington Conference in 1922 to take up the questions of Chinese tariff rights and extraterritoriality had not been implemented. Now they were hastily revived. In October 1925, a tariff conference opened at Peking, and it ended by promising to restore tariff autonomy to China by January 1, 1930. At the end of the year an international commission on extraterritoriality was formed to assist in bringing about legislative and judicial reforms which, in the terms of the Washington resolution, "would warrant the several Powers in relinquishing, either progressively or otherwise, their respective rights of extraterritoriality." Early in 1926, Britain sent out a mission to decide on the allotment in China of the British share of the Boxer Indemnity Funds. Thus from several strings, hopes and promises were dangled before the increasingly eager noses of Chinese leaders.[4]

Strikes had not been confined to foreign enterprises. Even Chinese liberals who agreed that the labor movement had "created a nation-wide social consciousness which is essential toward the building of a new and vigorous Republic" were uneasy about the movement's "foolish excesses, like the rapid increase of strikes in China's industries."[5] The feeling was growing, a Chinese observer reported, "that it is one thing to utilize the workers . . . but quite another to let them bite off more than they can chew." It was a good thing to

enjoy "the benefits of strong organized labor" but on the other hand
"too much of a good thing is often harmful."[6] The deplorable lack
of discrimination shown by the workers soon made the Chinese fac-
tory-owner realize that he was in the same boat with his foreign rival.
Every new event brought this into sharper relief. Moreover, his
dependence on the foreigner was only too painfully apparent. When
the workers walked out of foreign plants in Shanghai on June 1, the
American-owned city power plant cut off all power and wheels stopped
in Chinese factories as well. This brought the gentlemen of the Chinese Chamber of Commerce flocking to the council chambers of the
foreigners, offering to support drastic reductions in the sweeping
demands initially put forth by the striking workers. Rich Chinese
began to cut off the flow of contributions into the strike-bound city.
Respectable leaders began to put heavy pressure on the unions.
Mutual profit dictated an entente with the foreigners and this soon
found expression in open attempts to force the labor organizations
into line. Gradually the back of the strike was broken. At summer's
end the Fengtien military, who had assumed control of Shanghai, in
co-operation with the foreign settlement authorities and with full
sanction and support of the Chinese Chamber of Commerce, closed
down the Shanghai General Labor Union, and raided and sealed some
120 workers' clubs and other organizations. The strike wave in
Shanghai was temporarily halted and remained so during the winter
months of 1925–26.

During this period the flirtation between foreign and Chinese men
of property became more audacious. There was no difficulty about
the preliminaries. Both sides organized their own anti-Communist
leagues, published violent anti-Communist propaganda. British businessmen developed a new and rather touching concern for the fragile
structure of Chinese culture. "I appeal to you," pleaded one of them
at a Shanghai meeting, "to save for China the priceless heritage of
its ancient civilization." As the end of the fiscal year drew near, board
chairmen counted up fading earnings. "It is to be hoped," said one
company report, "that the authorities will in future take drastic steps
to curb the activities of professional agitators."[7] What was apparently meant by "drastic steps" was demonstrated on March 18, 1926,
in Peking, when troops of Tuan Ch'i-jui, head of the Peking government, fired on a student demonstration, killing scores of boys and
girls who were protesting Tuan's readiness to submit to a foreign

ultimatum concerning demilitarization of Tientsin harbor.[8] That same night an unusual affair took place in Shanghai.

At the Majestic Hotel, the members of the foreign Municipal Council sat down to dine with the pillars of Shanghai Chinese society. The event was called a "milestone in the history of Shanghai." It was "the first time in the history of this municipality when any such gathering has taken place."[9] The foreign official or taipan (business leader) present at this dinner was the type that was accustomed to sending Chinese of all classes to the back doors of the exclusively foreign clubs. For the Chinese present, bankers, brokers, merchants, and officials, this dinner was exactly the kind of social revolution they wanted.

"We, your hosts," began the American chairman, Stirling Fessenden, speaking for his British and Japanese colleagues on the council, "count ourselves fortunate in having been able to secure the attendance of so distinguished a company of Chinese gentlemen. . . . We have with us a representative gathering of the men who mold and guide that vast and wonderful force known as public opinion." He then came directly to the point. Trouble lay ahead and it was necessary "to devise countermeasures." Force might have to be used but had its drawbacks because it might "quickly lead to an international situation of extreme gravity." Attempts at arbitration would "probably end in failure." The workers of Shanghai were gullible victims of agitators who lured them from the security of their factories. Why not, then, take advantage of the "extreme credulousness of the Chinese working classes . . . why not take advantage of it for their good and for ours? Why not set up a different kind of leadership from that to which they have been accustomed, a leadership they would be inclined to follow at least as readily as any other? . . . It needs, I suggest, men like some of whom we have with us here tonight."

Yü Ya-ch'ing, leading Chinese banker and compradore, rose to reply. "We are all fully aware of the exceedingly tense situation," he said. "It is no exaggeration to say that spontaneous combustion is apt to take place at the slightest provocation which may quickly lead to a worse conflagration than that of last year. For our respective and common interests we must by all means prevent it." Time was short and drifting dangerous, he went on. "It is most important for us, through combination of local initiative and concerted action on a national and international scale to provide the earliest and most satisfactory settlement of our outstanding problems." Peace was desirable, Yü then said bluntly, "but speaking frankly, we do not care to have it at 'any price.'" The foreigners had to give some recognition to the principles of "racial equality" and "sovereign rights." More specifically for the moment, they had to give the Chinese property-owners a hand in the administration of Shanghai.[10]

Three weeks later the annual meeting of foreign ratepayers approved the admission, for the first time, of three Chinese members to the Shanghai Municipal Council, governing body of the International Settlement. This bargain, the first of many, was a plain example of the new relationship established between Chinese and foreign property interests. It was a frank and deliberate alliance against the revolutionary mass movement. It became increasingly conscious, alert, and planful in all its moves. Its influence was by no means confined to Shanghai and the North but reached down into the heart of the nationalist movement in Canton itself. The more simple-minded moneyed men, Chinese and foreign, were prone to see Canton in the single hue of red. Others began to learn that it was not that simple. The foreigners, particularly, had to learn a great deal in those harried months and the sharpest of them learned quickly. They had to discover that their end would be gained not by use of their brute force but by class differentiation inside the movement that threatened their interests. "The serious mistake made by foreigners," wrote one of them at the time, "was to emphasize Communism as the cause of all the troubles in 1925. . . . As long as anti-Communism was in any way identified with pro-foreignism, there was little hope of the better elements among the Chinese really opposing the Communists."[11] The Chinese politicians and businessmen with whom these foreign leaders were rapidly cementing new contacts had to teach their less intelligent colleagues that Canton, far from being of a single hue, in reality reflected all the colors in the class spectrum. It had to be broken down with the utmost care if the red was to be crowded from the screen.

At Canton, class antagonisms smoldered and grew. The old-guard "Rights" of the Kuomintang had broken away in opposition to the 1924 Reorganization, which they believed shut the door on compromise with the Powers. But the so-called "Left" at Canton consisted of men whose primary calculation was that a powerful mass movement would extract concessions from the imperialists. Events so far had justified them. The great mass strikes of 1925 had brought from the foreign Powers and interests substantial offers to concede and to compromise, although still on a limited scale. But the rise of this mass movement at the same time sharply raised the question of leadership. The Right Wing of the Kuomintang had to assert, establish, and consolidate its control. Thanks to the acquiescent policy of the Communists this was duly accomplished. To follow the process by which it was done, we need to reach into the maze of intrigues and clash of individual wills that composed the political life of Canton, and find and trace a single thread, the career of a young officer named Chiang Kai-shek, a man whose ambition, fathered by ruthless cunning and a total lack of scruple, brought him now to the center of the Chinese political scene.

Scion of a moderately well-to-do Chekiang merchant family, Chiang Kai-shek was at military school in Toyko when the first revolution took place in 1911. He hurried back to Shanghai where he joined the staff of a general named Ch'ên Ch'i-mei. Under Ch'ên's patronage, Chiang met Sun Yat-sen. He also came into contact with Yü Ya-ch'ing, then already a powerful compradore, and Chang Ching-chiang, a millionaire banker and dealer in bean curd and curios. Chiang also associated with Huang Ching-yung, one of Shanghai's notorious underworld leaders, and is generally believed to have become a member at this time of the most powerful secret society in Shanghai, known as the Green Circle. Gangsters, bankers, military men, murderers, thieves, smugglers, and brothel-keepers helped draw the original lines of the portrait the world was to come to recognize as Chiang Kai-shek. Far from being effaced as time passed, they deepened. In the years to come Chiang was destined to lean upon and be leaned upon by these early mentors. Curiously little is said about this period in the official biographies of Chiang Kai-shek. Details vary widely in different accounts and the dates are vague. It is clear, however, that Chiang for a time abandoned his military career and became a petty broker on the Shanghai Stock Exchange under the tutelage of some of his wealthy sponsors. For reasons on which the available records are not clear, he was soon in trouble. Chang Ching-chiang and his other sponsors bailed him out of a difficult situation.

They made good some questionable losses, lined his pockets, and shipped him off to Canton to link his fortunes with those of Sun Yat-sen. Few investments have ever paid greater dividends.

In Canton, Chiang Kai-shek joined Sun Yat-sen's military staff. After Sun made contact with the Soviet government, he sent Chiang to Moscow to study Red Army methods. Chiang left China in July 1923 and remained in Russia for six months. There is no credible record of his impressions of that visit, but from his own subsequent conduct it seems plain that he must have been impressed by the effectiveness of centralized political power and party discipline. He certainly had the opportunity to observe the power of a popular movement as a political and military weapon. He returned to China, at any rate, with an enormous advantage over his fellow militarists. For as long as it suited him, he could now cry "Long live the world revolution!" and reap the benefits of association with that slogan. He used it crudely and deliberately to build up his own power. Chiang undoubtedly understood the risks involved, but his boldness and readiness to gamble, which had undone him on the Stock Exchange, paid off when power became the stake. On his return to Canton at the end of the year, Chiang became the dark-haired darling of Borodin and the Russian military advisers. In May 1924 they set up the Whampoa Military Academy. Chiang Kai-shek, the only military man who had been to Russia and studied Russian military methods at first hand, and what is more, a man who made himself sound reliably radical, was the logical choice for director. Whampoa set out to breed a new type of soldier for China. It became the breeding ground of Chiang Kai-shek's power in the land.

Whampoa's cadets distinguished themselves in all the early battles —in the suppression of the Merchants' Volunteers, the expeditions to the East River, the short war against the Yunnanese generals, and the clean-up of the rest of southern Kwangtung. Chiang was their military leader and each of these campaigns heightened his prestige, power, and influence, especially after Whampoa cadets began to take their places as officers in regular military units. But the young men who flocked to Whampoa were all involved in or affected by the surrounding political atmosphere. All their military successes had been won in joint fighting with worker and peasant detachments. Some cadets were actually drawn from these forces. Many regarded themselves as Kuomintang radicals. Many were Communists. On the other hand, many of those who entered the first classes at Whampoa from bourgeois and landlord families reacted to events in accordance with their family backgrounds. The Whampoa student body, like every other group in Canton, split into opposing camps. The Sun Yat-senist Society, already active in Central and North China, organized a Whampoa branch. The Communist cadets and their more or less radical Kuomintang allies formed into what they called the League of Military Youth. During the campaigns of 1925 these two groups openly clashed on several occasions. Chiang Kai-shek tried to keep balanced between them, a role he was already trying to play on the broader stages of Canton politics. When the armies got back to Canton after their second successful expedition to the East River in October 1925, Chiang gathered his young officers at a banquet. A guest at the dinner has described how "he pounded the table and scolded them" and demanded that they keep the peace between them.[12] It was the time, he knew, for "unity."

Chiang was still some distance from power. He still needed the Communists, the mass movement, and the Russians—their advice and their arms and ammunition. Politically, he was still several rungs down the ladder, below the Kuomintang party leaders, Hu Han-min and Wang Ching-wei, and even below Liao Chung-k'ai, political director of the Whampoa Military Academy. In the military domain, he had many rivals among the generals who had hitched their fortunes to the rising Kuomintang star. Chiang Kai-shek counted on the momentum of the mass movement to sweep him to a point of vantage from which he could command. His position coincided almost mathematically with that of the property-owning class; it, too, wanted to reach the point at which its control of this immense movement was assured. Chiang Kai-shek, in full and deliberate consciousness of what he was about, intended to be the wielder-in-chief of that control.

Borodin, for his part, saw in Chiang the most reliable kind of "ally" in the Kuomintang leadership. He and the Kremlin leaders from whom he took his cue were convinced that the Chinese liberal bourgeoisie would have to lead the anti-imperialist revolution to a successful conclusion. He thought he saw in Chiang Kai-shek the best possible confirmation of this belief. The movement needed military leadership and all the other militarists in Canton were products of the war-lord system. Borodin accordingly employed every possible stratagem to drive Chiang to the top of the heap. Chiang, of course, did nothing to discourage him. On the contrary, he wrapped himself in radical phrases and offered himself as the red hope of the revolutionary army. It has been recorded that Chiang "often quoted a saying of Dr. Sun to him that in taking Borodin's advice, he [Chiang] would be taking his [Dr. Sun's] advice. Borodin reciprocated by exhorting that 'no matter whether Communist or Kuomintang, all must obey General Chiang.' "[13] Obviously, when Borodin "advised" the enhancement of Chiang's power, Chiang had no difficulty hearing the ghostly voice of the late leader issuing from the lips of his Russian counsellor.

A murder provided the opportunity for Chiang's next step toward power. Liao Chung-k'ai, who had been close to Sun Yat-sen but had become the real leader of the extreme Left Wing of the Kuomintang, was assassinated in August 1925. The plot was traced to a Right-Wing conspiracy. Hu Han-min, senior leader of the Kuomintang, and General Hsü Ch'ung-chih, commander of the Cantonese army, were involved. By skillful maneuvering, of which he was evidently very proud, Borodin succeeded in forcing Hu Han-min to go abroad. General Hsü and a number of others linked to the plot likewise left Canton.[14] Canton awoke one day with a new set of leaders. Wang Ching-wei, also a leader of the "Left," became head of the party and the government and civilian chairman of the Military Council. Chiang Kai-shek succeeded to the command of the Cantonese army.

These new combinations were being dealt out at the top at a time when the mass movement below had assumed great proportions. The Canton-Hongkong strike, country-wide economic and political strikes involving nearly one million workers, the phenomenal growth of the peasant associations, the beginnings of the war against the landlords in the countryside,[15] all marked the sharply rising curve of popular struggle. These forces had been primarily responsible for the victory of the Kuomintang in Kwangtung. Only by grace of them did the Canton government exist at all, a fact which even Chiang Kai-shek publicly acknowledged. Yet the government was not required to respond in any concrete manner to the interests of the workers and peasants. A few minor tax burdens were lifted. A few of the more glaring official abuses were eliminated. The rest was in the realm of promise.

The Communists, who occupied the positions of field leadership in the mass movement, never dreamed of giving it any political orientation of its own. That impulse had dropped away under the pressure of the new dicta that came from Moscow. Their political education, and in turn the education they brought to the people, consisted of developing delusions about the Kuomintang. In Moscow, the band of politicians riding the crest of the revolutionary wave in China had begun to look more and more like the creators and leaders of a future Chinese government that would be tied, by every circumstance of obligation and international position, to the Russian diplomatic wheel. They began, accordingly, to see the Kuomintang as the prime revolutionary force in Asia. In January 1926, Stalin and the presidium of the Fourteenth Party Conference of the Communist Party of the Soviet Union sent the following telegram to the presidium of the Second Congress of the Kuomintang: "To our party has fallen the proud and historical role of leading the first victorious proletarian revolution in the world. . . . We are convinced that the Kuomintang will succeed in *playing the same role in the East and thereby destroy the foundation of the rule of the imperialists in Asia* . . . if the Kuomintang strengthens the alliance of the working class and the peasantry in the present struggle and allows itself to be guided by the interests of these fundamental forces of the revolution."[16] (Italics in original.)

The nature of the Kuomintang was being redefined in various ways. In the beginning it had been viewed as the party of the liberal bourgeoisie with whom the Communists were in a temporary alliance. Then it began to appear that it was the party of the workers and peasants. In a speech to a group of students on May 18, 1925, Stalin said that in colonial or semicolonial countries the nationalist bloc "could assume the form of a single party of workers and peasants, like the Kuomintang."[17] The Sixth Plenum of the Executive Committee of the Communist International continued the process of redefinition. In March 1926, the plenum described the Kuomintang as "a revolutionary bloc of the workers, peasants, intellectuals, and urban democracy [i.e., the bourgeoisie] on the basis of a community of class interests of these strata in the struggle against the imperialists and the whole militarist-feudal order."[18]

The question of "proletarian hegemony" in the revolution was mentioned in some Comintern accounts of events in China, but the central organ of the Comintern informed its sections that "a Kuomin (people's) government closely resembling the Soviet system, was formed in Canton on July 1, 1925." It proudly quoted the speeches of Chiang Kai-shek and Wang Ching-wei at a Kuomintang congress. Said Chiang: "Our alliance with the Soviet Union, with the world revolution, is actually an alliance with all the revolutionary parties which are fighting in common against the world imperialists to carry through the world revolution." Said Wang Ching-wei: "If we wish to fight against the imperialists, we must not turn against the Communists. (Loud applause). If we are against the Communists, we cannot at the same time describe ourselves as antagonists of imperialism. (Loud applause)." The report concluded: "The work and struggles of the Kuomintang prove that Sun Yat-sen's disciples have remained true to his fundamental idea."[19]

The Sixth Plenum of the E.C.C.I. said in its resolution that it was glad to see that the Kuomintang in Canton had dealt blows to its Right Wing. It was referring to the statements made when Wang Ching-wei and Chiang Kai-shek assumed the leadership following the murder of Liao Chung-k'ai. Yet at this same plenum an episode occurred which demonstrated the cynicism, the ignorance, or the hopeless self-delusion of the Comintern leaders. The honored guest of the plenum was Hu Han-min, the Right-Wing leader who had been exiled from Canton because he was implicated in the murder of Liao. He had gone to Moscow, where he was promptly elected to the ruling body of the so-called Krestintern, the Peasants' International, as "a representative of the Chinese farmers."[20] At the Sixth Plenum, he was invited to bring the fraternal greetings of the Kuomintang.

Andreyev Hall, the former throne room of the Czars, "presented an unforgettable picture," said the official record:

when the Generalissimo of the Canton Army* stepped up to the tribune in military uniform. For several minutes the speaker was unable to commence speaking on account of the continually renewed applause. The solidarity between the revolutionary proletariat of the West and the oppressed peoples of the East was expressed here with striking clearness. . . . These demonstrations of enthusiasm lasted several minutes and punctuated nearly every sentence of the speaker.

"On behalf of the Chinese people," said Hu, "of the Chinese workers and peasants, of the oppressed Chinese masses, I express gratitude for being able to attend personally this international session. There is only one world revolution and the Chinese revolution is part of this world

* In Moscow Hu made full use of the honorary title of "Generalissimo" which he inherited from Sun Yat-sen.

revolution. The slogan of our great leader Sun Yat-sen is identical with the slogan of Marxism and Leninism. No one has faith any longer in the Second International. The influence of the Third International has considerably increased in China of late. The movement embraces intellectuals as well as large sections of workers and peasants, the entire proletariat.

"The Kuomintang slogan is: for the masses, i.e., seizure of political power together with the workers and peasants! All these slogans coincide with the policy of the Third International. . . . I feel I am one of the fighters for the world revolution and I greet the session of the Communist International. Long live the solidarity of the proletariat of the world! Long live the victory of the world revolution! Long live the Third International! Long live all the Communist Parties of the world! Long live the comrades here!"[21]

Hu Han-min's political identity could hardly have been unknown, at least to Stalin and his principal lieutenants in the Comintern, but they were convinced that even Hu and the political forces back of him had no choice but to go along with Russia. After all, even the Canton Chamber of Commerce in those days was signing its manifestoes with the slogan: "Long live the World Revolution!" After listening to Hu, the plenum passed its resolution declaring that "the Canton Government is the vanguard in the liberation struggle of the Chinese people [and] serves as a model for the future revolutionary-democratic order of the whole country." It urged unity within "a single national revolutionary front of the widest strata of the population [workers, peasants, bourgeoisie] under the leadership of the revolutionary democratic organizations."[22]

Because it was necessary to preserve this "front" at all costs, Borodin in Canton was seriously disturbed by the prominent role of the Communists in the organization of the popular movement. A Chinese account, written from the left Kuomintang point of view, says:

The prominent position which the Communist members occupied in the new revolutionary system . . . not unnaturally caused anxiety among the leaders of the Kuomintang and the Communist Party. Borodin, too, was greatly concerned about it and often during 1925 he discussed the question with Wang [Ching-wei], Liao [Chung-k'ai], Hu [Han-min] and Chiang [Kai-shek]. "Every since the Reorganization in 1924 the Kuomintang was divided into two parties, those supporting and those opposing the Reorganization. This division, however, is not serious, for the Leftists are bound to be victorious. What would be serious, however, is that there might be a division in the Left itself," he said, foreseeing a split between the Kuomintang and the Communist Party. "The only way to surmount future difficulties is, therefore, for the leaders of the Left to present a united opinion."[23]

This meant, as Borodin later explained, that radical reforms, especially in agrarian matters, could not be introduced at Canton because the Kuomintang, "in view of its mixed class composition" could not "undertake the confiscation of private property."[24] This meant, in turn, that the Kuomintang was not, as Stalin said, a "worker-peasant party" and did not really operate, as the Comintern said, on "the basis of a community of class interests." In practice, it was a party whose program was limited by the economic requirements of the bourgeoisie. The other class interests had to be subordinated. The task of the Communists was to see that this was done. This was not an easy matter. In Canton in the winter of 1925–26, the Canton-Hongkong Strike Committee, the Canton Workers' Delegates' Council, the peasant associations, and the Left-Wing groups in the army were the real sources of power. They had raised the Kuomintang nationalist leaders on their shoulders. The Communists were now required to hold this mass movement in check in order to keep it within the social and economic limits acceptable to these leaders. In subsequent analyses of the situation in Canton at the end of 1925, Borodin said that any attempt to take an independent course toward political power "would have gone down in a sea of blood."[25] Trotsky challenged this view, arguing that all the preconditions of a successful proletarian movement in the Soviet manner were present, and that in any case the Comintern bureaucracy defeated itself by teaching the mass organizations to remain servile in their relation to the bourgeois leaders.[26] But the arguments came later when the facts were more commonly known and understood. At the time, on the spot in Canton, the policy dictated by Stalin in Moscow was unquestioningly applied. It was to appease the Kuomintang leadership at any price.

What actually existed at Canton was a power vacuum in which all the elements were defined but their mutual relationships were still undetermined. While a wholly passive strategy dominated the thinking and the actions of the Communists, it was quite otherwise among the Kuomintang leaders. The strongest among them, Chiang Kaishek, was feeling his way toward a decisive assertion of authority.

Chapter 6

CANTON: THE COUP OF MARCH 20, 1926

IN THOSE DAYS at Canton, Chiang Kai-shek was like Cerberus, the three-headed guardian at the gates of Hell.

One head faced right and bore the face of Tai Chi-t'ao, who had become the chief organizer and propagandist for the conservative wing of the Kuomintang in Canton. Tai served as the link between the open Right Wing in Shanghai and the covert Right Wing in Canton. According to the simplified view of Kuomintang politics held by Borodin, the party was divided between those who supported the 1924 Reorganization and those who opposed it. The opponents were the Right, scurrying about their plots and intrigues in Shanghai and Peking. The supporters were the Left, the leaders of the Kuomintang in Canton. But Tai Chi-t'ao's presence in the Kuomintang capital and the scope of his activities there were proof enough that Canton already had its own well-developed Right Wing. Its connections with the conservative politicians in the North were well-established. As early as July 1925, when the National government was formed in Canton, Tai Chi-t'ao had already begun his activities under the tacit protection of Chiang Kai-shek. He began to issue anti-Communist and anti-Marxist pamphlets. He proclaimed the inalienable right of the "conscious" sections of the population to guide and govern the "unconscious." Communism, he said, had nothing in common with the doctrines of Sun Yat-sen, which had to be protected from the threat of Communist adulteration. Tai openly organized in behalf of the Sun Yat-senist Society, which at this time tried to distinguish itself carefully from its parent organization, the Western Hills Conference group. The Sun Yat-senists "declared that they differed from the Western Hills people on three points: 1. The Western Hills group was against the Reorganization of 1924, while they supported it. 2. The former consisted only of corrupt and reactionary bureaucrats and anarchists, while they were active revolutionaries. 3. The object . . . [of the Western Hills group] . . .

was the overthrow of Wang and Chiang, while they accepted them as their leaders. But while belonging to the Left, they were as actively and energetically opposed to the Communists as were the Western Hills people. They also desired to break with the Communist Party."[1]

The second head of Cerberus faced left. It bore Chiang's own face. From its lips dripped fealty to the cause of the revolution. "I, too, am willing," it said, "to lie beside the graves of those who have already fallen martyrs to the National Revolution, the Three People's Principles, and Communism. The revolution cannot do without Dr. Sun's Three People's Principles. Neither can the international revolution neglect Communism. We cannot deny that the Chinese Revolution is part of the World Revolution. The realization of the Three People's Principles means the realization of Communism. Knowing that we cannot separate the Chinese Revolution from the World Revolution, why should there be any quarrel amongst us about the Three People's Principles and Communism?"[2]

Cerberus' third head held the center and looked forward, the jealous guardian of sprouting ambition. To his left, Chiang heard himself establishing an identity between communism and Sun Yat-senism. To his right, he heard his man Tai Chi-t'ao proclaiming an ineradicable contradiction between them. From the left he drew sustenance, prestige before the masses, and Russian arms, money, and counsel. From the right he drew his basic political orientation and the people out of whom he fashioned his own power machine. In appointments to key posts, Chiang carefully chose only non-Communists. In these matters, it was easy for him to influence the party leader, Wang Ching-wei, a handsome, weak man who always believed himself to be in one camp and invariably ended up in the other, and who was destined to finish his career ignobly as a puppet of the Japanese.

In the Kuomintang organization, several Communists were members of the large Central Executive Committee, but no Communists were allowed posts in the party secretariat. The Military Council employed Russian technical advisers and the Political Department of the army was in most places dominated by individual Communists, but Communists were excluded from the general staff and the army's financial bureau. In the National government itself there were no Communists, only Borodin in an advisory capacity. On the other hand, in all the mass organizations, in the lower layers of the government and party machinery, Communists and their sympathizers carried on all the daily work and exerted the greatest personal influence. From them, the Canton Left Wing drew the strength which enabled it to reign supreme over the second National Congress of the Kuomintang which met in January 1926.

This Congress met under the glow of the great victories over local militarists and the sweep of popular mass organization. The number of organized workers in the country had reached 800,000. Peasant associations in Kwangtung alone had grown to a membership of 600,000. Hongkong was paralyzed by the strike and in Canton the pickets patrolled the streets and wharves of the city. The lessons of the unification of Kwangtung were still fresh in Kuomintang minds. There was still the rest of the country to win. So the Congress passed with acclaim resolutions which repeated the vague promises and phrases of the Kuomintang's "worker-peasant policy." It frowned on Cerberus No. 1 by mildly censuring Tai Chi-t'ao for his anti-Communist propaganda. It welcomed Cerberus No. 2 by electing Chiang Kai-shek, for the first time, to the Central Executive Committee of the Kuomintang. He was present to accept and dutifully to hail "the alliance with the Soviet Union, with the World Revolution."[3] But Cerberus No. 3, the jealous, ambitious, calculating Chiang, chafed with impatient dissatisfaction, for at this Congress the supreme figure was Wang Ching-wei, head of the party and government, chairman of the Military Council, holder of all the high posts to which Chiang aspired.

Chiang Kai-shek had early come to regard himself as chief among the disciples of Sun Yat-sen. The murder of Liao Chung-k'ai and the removel of Hu Han-min left only Wang, Sun's longtime personal favorite, to rival his claim. Chiang was still only head of the Whampoa Academy and commander of the First Army, while Wang, as leader of party and government, not only exercised the leading civil power but, as chairman of the Military Council, represented civilian control over the military apparatus. Other military commanders who had joined the Kuomintang enjoyed an intolerable equality in the distribution of political and material advantages, especially in arms. In February, when the Soviet military delegation banqueted the Kuomintang leaders, a Russian officer made a toast in which he placed Wang's name before Chiang's. A fellow guest says he saw Chiang go white and tight-lipped. Chiang "did not utter a word for the rest of the evening."[4] Chiang was fiercely jealous of Wang's manifold prerogatives, and the politicians of the Right Wing knew very well how to play on the keyboard of Chiang's vanity. The Kuomintang old guard had early realized that through Chiang Kai-shek they had their best hope of regaining mastery. At the Western Hills Conference, which Tai Chi-t'ao helped organize, they had adopted the slogan: "Ally with Chiang to overthrow Wang." At the time Chiang publicly repudiated any such idea but in private he undoubtedly cherished it. When a rump congress of the Right Wing met in Shanghai, also in January 1926, and insistently repeated its overtures, Chiang proved more receptive. Although the "Left" had seemingly triumphed and from Moscow the Comintern had hailed "the transformation of the Kuomintang into a resolute fighting force, into a real party of the Chinese revolution,"[5] deep fissures were already beginning to show and the influence of the Right Wing was plainly discernible in Canton.

"The Right or anti-Red wing of the Kuomintang, with headquarters at Peking and Shanghai . . . has no small backing on the part of the less radical Kuomintangites in the southern capital. This has been felt by General Chiang and other comrades," wrote a perspicacious Chinese correspondent from Canton.[6] This influence was no longer indirectly communicated. It was no longer a matter of emissaries and private parleys. Chang Ching-chiang, the Shanghai millionaire and the young Chiang's early benefactor, had personally come down to nurse his investment. He became Chiang Kai-shek's mentor, chief political aide, and counselor. Chiang's drive for power quickened. The object was to establish hegemony over the growing mass movement, to ensure that it would not exceed bourgeois interests. For this, concretely, it was necessary to whip the Communists into line, to regularize and define their position as auxiliaries to the Kuomintang. It was time, in short, to cut the political wages of the Communists, to increase the political profits of the bourgeoisie, and to place at the latter's disposal the immense and still untapped capital reserves of the mass movement. It was a question of stabilizing the leadership at the top by taking it out of the hands of vacillating liberals. For this a sharp blow had to be struck, damaging but not fatal, to the Communists and their petty bourgeois radical allies. If Canton's cliques of politicians and generals were rift and rent by crisscrossing intrigues, it was only because many strove to strike this blow first. Thanks to Borodin, Chiang was in the favored position and it was he who decided to act.

The influence of the imperialists acted on the Right Wing, and through Chang Ching-chiang and the Sun Yat-senist Society, it reacted on Chiang Kai-shek. Their desires fused with his intense personal ambition, his cunning, his envy of political and military rivals, his flair for intrigue, his unmistakable lust for power. To level the Communists was to assure bourgeois hegemony over the masses. To subdue his rivals was to win for himself the leading place in the exercise of that hegemony. All the varicolored threads in this pattern were drawn swiftly into a knot. He became what Karl Marx, referring to Louis Napoleon, once called "a man who did not decide at night and act during the day but decided during the day and acted at night."

Several hours before dawn on the morning of March 20, 1926, Chiang's troops moved. The pretext was the allegedly threatening attitude of the gunboat *Chungshan*, which had anchored off Whampoa during the night. The incidents of that night cut across the lines of many complicated intrigues far too devious to be traced here, for the clashing wills of many ambitious individuals were involved. Chiang was not the only one who wanted to become master of the Kuomintang. But by this blow, he brushed all his rivals aside or took them into his camp. His detachments systematically carried out his orders. All political workers attached to units under his command, some fifty men, most of them Communists, were arrested. The headquarters of the Canton-Hongkong Strike Committee were raided and all arms found there were seized. All Soviet advisers in the city were placed under house arrest. Têng Yen-ta, a pro-Communist Kuomintang figure who had succeeded Liao Chung-k'ai as political director of the Whampoa Military Academy, was detained. Chiang had caught all his victims quite literally napping. Li Chih-lung, the Communist head of the Naval Bureau, was one of those dragged from their beds and carted off to the military prison.* Morning found Chiang Kai-shek master of Canton. It also found the other leaders of the Kuomintang in a state of panic and confusion. They were all "utterly unprepared and did not even dream the coup was coming,"

* Li, who all unwittingly became the chief nominal object of the night's operations, has left behind the fullest account of the night's events in a pamphlet, *The Resignation of Chairman Wang Ching-wei*, which was published in 1927 at Wuhan.

according to Hua Kang, a Communist historian.[7] They were all badly frightened.

Members of the Kuomintang Central Executive Committee hurriedly gathered. "Since Chiang Kai-shek has always struggled for the revolution, it is hoped that he will realize his mistake in this event," they ventured in a resolution. "But in view of the present situation, the comrades of the Left should temporarily retreat."[8] For Wang Ching-wei this meant his departure from the scene. He fell conveniently ill. His biographer relates that he "considered the best way to solve the situation was for him to retreat and to allow Chiang to take charge of affairs for the time being."[9] After an ignominious scene at the Mint, during which he handed over the seals of his authority to Chiang, he withdrew, first to a village near Canton and a few days later to European exile. Before leaving he wrote Chiang imploring him to keep to the "revolutionary" path. "If he would only do so, Wang did not mind sacrificing himself."[10]

The Kuomintang "Lefts" weakly capitulated because Chiang's sudden descent upon them brought no corresponding pressure from the real Left, from the organized masses who were confused and completely uninformed as to what was taking place at the top.[11] One foreign observer who arrived at Canton a few days later was delighted to discover that the Communists were in hiding and that the Russian advisers were packing to leave.[12] It was not Chiang's intention as yet, however, to strike directly at the mass movement. He sought only to bring that movement under the assured control of the bourgeoisie and to concentrate that control in his own hands. Having successfully put the leaders of the "Left" to flight, he came forward with explanations to the workers. The events of March 20 and, in particular, the raid on the strike headquarters, were due to a "misunderstanding," he told them, and promised to reprimand the officers responsible. The Communists themselves were so completely confused that they did not know whether to believe him or not.[13]

Meanwhile Right-Wing politicians, until now on the outside looking in, poured into Canton from their Hongkong and Shanghai refuges. A plenary session of the Kuomintang Central Executive Committee was called for May 15, and, as the date for that meeting approached, a deliberately manufactured pogrom atmosphere enveloped the city. Walls were covered with posters warning against mysterious "provocations," and rumors of an impending Communist coup against the government were set in circulation. A run was staged on the Central Bank. On the eve of the conference martial law was suddenly clamped down on the city. No one outside of Chiang's immediate entourage had the faintest notion of what to expect.

At the opening session Chiang introduced and put through a special resolution "for the readjustment of party affairs." It was framed to limit and define within the closest possible bounds the organizational activity of the Communist members of the Kuomintang. Communists were required "not to entertain any doubt on or criticise Dr. Sun or his principles." The Communist party was required to hand over to the standing committee of the Kuomintang Executive a list of its membership inside the Kuomintang. Communist members of municipal, provincial, and central party committees were limited to one-third of the committee membership. Communists were banned from serving as heads of any party or government department. Kuomintang members, on the other hand, were enjoined "not to engage in any other political organization or activity." That is, Communists could join the Kuomintang, but members of the Kuomintang could not join the Communist party without forfeiting their Kuomintang cards. All instructions henceforth issued by the Communist Central Committee to its own members were to be submitted first to a special joint committee of the two parties for approval.[14]

Thoroughly lacing the Communists into this political strait jacket, Chiang at the same time took all power in his own hands. The coup of March 20 had destroyed the authority of the civilian Military Council and the removal of Wang Ching-wei had left Chiang in undisputed control of all party and government affairs. The May 15 plenary session regularized these changes. Chiang was formally put at the head of the party and he promptly deputized Chang Ching-chiang to act for him as chairman of the Central Executive Committee. Plans for launching a northern military expedition were also approved and Chiang Kai-shek was appointed commander-in-chief of all the expeditionary armies. Subsequently a set of special decrees conferred emergency powers upon Chiang for the duration of the campaign. All government and party offices were subordinated to the headquarters of the commander-in-chief. The Military Council, originally conceived as a civilian check on militarist ambitions, passed entirely into Chiang's hands. He became arbiter of the government's finances. He controlled the Political Department, the arsenal, the general staff, the military and naval schools. The Canton government was transformed into a military dictatorship. Chiang's victory was complete.

It would seem reasonable to expect that this bloodless seizure of power by Chiang Kai-shek in Canton would have set the warning bells ringing for the Chinese Communists and their mentors in the Kremlin at Moscow. They had before them the remarkably accurate prediction made by Lenin in 1920 that in the colonial revolutionary movements every effort would be made by the bourgeois nationalists to seize and keep control of the movement in order to facilitate a compromise with the imperialist Powers. He had even warned that in this process the bourgeois nationalists would try to cloak themselves in the mantle of Communism. He had warned that the Communists would have to preserve their own independence, preserve their own leadership, and prevent the national revolution from being derailed.[15] Lenin had since died and his ideas had been embalmed along with his corpse. But now Stalin had before him, on a grand scale in China, a test and a confirmation of the analysis Lenin had made. If, unlike Lenin, the Kremlin strategists could not forsee the event, they were at least now confronted with the accomplished fact. Unlike Lenin, however, the new leaders were not concerned with the dynamics of the revolutionary struggle, which remained a closed book to them. They were concerned with winning a strong ally in a new nationalist China. They were convinced that the Chinese bourgeoisie was, and would have to remain, such an ally. They were quite ready to accept the fact of its hegemony in the national revolution, whatever the cost to the Chinese Communists or the masses of the Chinese people. Lenin had warned against surrendering leadership to "bourgeois democrats." Stalin was quite ready to have the Chinese Communists surrender leadership to a military dictator. Stalin and his colleagues still had to justify their policies in revolutionary terms, however, and Chiang's coup in Canton was on this score not easy to explain. So they chose the interesting alternative of not explaining it at all. They simply denied that it had taken place. They suppressed all news of its occurrence.

The facts were kept out of the Russian press and the international Communist press. They were concealed from the members of the Executive Committee of the Comintern and even from the presidium of the Executive Committee. For this there is the testimony of members of both these bodies.[16] When news of the coup was published in China and abroad, with specific facts often garbled but containing the essentially true assertion that power in Canton had passed into the hands of Chiang Kai-shek, the centrally geared machinery of the Comintern began turning out vehement denials. The central organ of the Comintern on April 8, 1926, said:

> Reuter's Telegraphic Agency . . . recently issued the statement that in Canton, Chiang Kai-shek, the supreme commander of the revolutionary troops (whom Reuter had hitherto described as a red), had carried out a coup d'état. But this *lying report* had soon to be denied. . . . The Kuomintang is not a tiny group with a few members but is a mass party in the true sense of the word and the revolutionary Canton troops and the revolutionary Canton government are founded on this basis. It is, of course, impossible there to carry out a coup d'état overnight.

Far from being converted into an instrument of bourgeois policy, the Canton government was more than ever "aiming at world revolution" and extending its power into the neighboring provinces as a "Soviet government." The prospects

> were never so favorable as they are now. . . . The province of Kwangsi will shortly form a Soviet government. . . . *The power of the generals, as a result of the national revolutionary movement, is beginning to disappear.* The Kuomin government is now proceeding to organize all district and town administrations within the province of Kwangtung *according to the Soviet system.*[17] [All italics in the original.]

A Moscow dispatch to the New York *Daily Worker* in April said:

> The reactionary British press at Hongkong and in London have spread sensational stories of disruption within the Nationalist government in an effort to further their imperialist propaganda. These reports have no real basis. They are nothing but provocative maneuvers of British imperialism. There has been no insurrection in Canton. The basis of the reports seems to be certain differences between a general of the Canton army, Chiang Kai-shek, and the Canton government. These differences were not concerned with matters of principle and had no connection with an armed struggle for power. The differences have since been abolished and Canton remains the stronghold of the movement for the emancipation of the Chinese people. The attempt of British imperialism to utilize the unimportant differences in Canton in its own interests has failed. . . . The Moscow press regards this provocative maneuver of the British reactionary press as an exposure of the real plans of British imperialism with regard to Canton. *Izvestia* writes: "The wish was the father of the thought and the British imperialists presented their real intentions as a fait accompli."[18]

If it were conceivable that these denials arose out of genuine ignorance of the facts, the same could hardly be said of the report of the Comintern representative, G. Voitinsky, writing from Canton:

The British imperialists . . . were vainly attempting to provoke an insurrection in Canton and at the same time trumpeting forth to the whole world that the Canton government had already fallen, that the Right Wing of the Kuomintang had seized power and formed a government which had agreed to a compromise with the British and was arresting partisans of the Left Kuomintang as well as the Communists. All this proved to be an invention of the imperialists. . . . The Canton government, which was "overthrown" by the imperialist press is now actually stronger than ever.[19]

As late as the end of 1926, the highest body of the Comintern deliberated on the situation in China and produced a resolution which, as we shall have occasion to show, made no mention whatever of the March events in Canton or their sequel.

Borodin, who had been on a trip to the north, returned to Canton after the coup but before the Kuomintang plenary session of May 15. An American observer, who was already in connection with some of Chiang Kai-shek's closest advisers (and who later entered the service of Chiang's government), arrived in Canton a few days later. According to his account:

The Russians seemed to believe the game was up. Most of the Chinese Communists were in hiding. . . . The anti-Communists were jubilant. . . . Borodin had it out with Chiang. Chiang wanted to know how far Russia would support him in a military expedition against the North. Borodin had heretofore opposed the Northern Expedition. Chiang's attitude toward the continuance of the Russian alliance depended upon Borodin's attitude toward the Northern Expedition. They came to an agreement. The Russians would support the Northern Expedition. The Russian alliance was continued. The Communists were reinstated.[20]

Subsequently, according to other accounts, "Chiang's relations with Borodin became more cordial than ever"[21] and all the decisions of the Kuomintang session of May 15 "were fully endorsed by M. Borodin."[22] It is further recorded that all the emergency powers delegated to Chiang after his appointment as commander-in-chief were delegated "at the advice of Borodin."[23] It is in any case a fact that Borodin, and after him the leaders of the Chinese Communist party, submitted without question to the military dictatorship established as a result of the March 20 coup. Borodin even saw to it that the Russian military advisers who had incurred Chiang's displeasure were dismissed and replaced by more amenable colleagues. In most cases this involved Russian officers who had worked with Chinese army formations not under Chiang's direct control. Chiang could hardly have asked for more. Having secured all these gains with far less difficulty than he himself must have imagined possible, he dispensed with some of the Right-Wing conspirators who had helped him execute his coup. He sent them out of Canton. He needed more than ever now to reappear as a "Leftist." His Right-Wing associates could wait for him in Shanghai.

In his account of these events, which unqualifiedly gives Borodin's version and apologia, Louis Fischer describes the sequel to March 20 as follows: "But Chiang, whose distinguishing characteristic was not courage, apparently had been frightened by his own action and sent . . . a humble letter begging Borodin to return south without delay." When Borodin got back, Chiang "overflowed with apologies. . . . What, he asked of Borodin, must he do? 'Prepare for the Northern Expedition,' Borodin replied." Then, it was "because Borodin wished to repair some of the damage done by the coup of March 20" that Chiang "engineered a second coup . . . this time against the Right."

"But why did not Borodin, the Left Kuomintang, and the Chinese Communist Party eliminate Chiang Kai-shek?" Fischer continues. "Because they were too weak," he replies, after Borodin. . . . They had wide mass sympathy but in Canton they wielded insufficient forces to overcome Chiang and the bourgeoisie which supported him. . . . Both sides knew that the struggle between them was inevitable. But rather than engage now in bloodletting from which only the Cantonese militarists could gain, they tacitly agreed to postpone the issue until they reached the Yangtze. The resolution to commence the Northern Expedition was adopted by the Kuomintang Central Committee on May 15. At that meeting the expressed sentiments of each faction amounted to this: "Gentlemen, we know we must fight one another. But we need a wider area. Let us delay the day of reckoning and meanwhile go forward to a common goal."[24]

Fischer's account omits all mention of the other resolutions adopted on May 15, which all but hog-tied the Communist party. It was correct that the bloodletting was postponed, but if, as Fischer avers, Borodin was preparing to give future battle to Chiang Kai-shek, one might ask why all weapons and all power were surrendered in advance. Contrary to Borodin's *post factum* version, the facts on the record show that it was Chiang Kai-shek who acted with boldness and Stalin-Borodin & Company who retreated in panic. Acting under their orders, the Chinese Communists now had to capitulate, even to grovel, before the new master of the Nationalist movement.

Chiang Kai-shek had carried out his coup and put through the May decisions on the pretext that the Communists were plotting a coup d'état of their own. There were, to be sure, rival conspiracies in Canton directed against Chiang Kai-shek. But these were all mounted by competitors among the generals and politicians who aspired to play the role which he finally assumed. The only role played in any of them by the Chinese Communist party was that of intended victim. Nothing was further from the calculations of the Chinese Communist leaders in March 1926 than an attempt to assert their power. Chiang Kai-shek and his Right-Wing conspirators manufactured the rumors of Communist "plots" out of the material which the logic of the situation itself presented to them. It was they, and not the Communists, who saw that the workers, with their growing organizations, their armed picket forces, their militancy and strength, were capable of seizing and holding the hegemony of the revolutionary movement. It was they, therefore, and not the Communists, who realized the time had come to act. When they acted forthwith, no one was more shocked, more pained, more aggrieved, and more frightened than the Chinese Communist leaders.

First of all [wrote Ch'ên Tu-hsiu, general secretary of the Chinese Communist party], unless the Communist Party is a party of madmen, certainly it does not want to establish a workers' and peasants' government in Canton. Secondly, Chiang Kai-shek is one of the pillars of the national revolutionary movement. Unless the Communist Party were the tool of the imperialists, it would surely not adopt such a policy of disrupting the unity of the Chinese revolutionary forces! . . . The policy of the Communist Party, contrary to the declarations of the Rights, is not only that the revolutionary forces in Kwangtung should not be split, but that the revolutionary forces of the whole country shall be united. Otherwise one cannot fight the enemy.[25]

In an open letter addressed to Chiang Kai-shek on June 4, Ch'ên Tu-hsiu protested further:

At this time to conspire for the overthrow of Chiang Kai-shek in Canton—what a help to the reactionary forces this would be! If the Chinese Communist Party is such a counter-revolutionary party, it should be got rid of. . . . If among the comrades of the Communist Party there are any who harbor ideas of such a counter-revolutionary conspiracy, you should shoot them without the least ceremony. But I know, I am convinced, that in our party nobody has any such idea in mind.[26]

As evidence that such ideas did exist in the minds of Communists, Chiang Kai-shek, in a speech at Canton shortly after March 20, had recalled the remark of a certain Communist who had said: "In our organization there is a Tuan Ch'i-jui* and in order to overthrow the northern Tuan Ch'i-jui we must first overthrow the Tuan Ch'i-jui in our midst." The Communist who had made the offending speech hastened into print with an open letter to Chiang explaining that he had meant "Tuan Ch'i-jui ideology," that is, old feudal ideas, and that since he spoke Anhwei dialect and not Cantonese, there had been a mistake made by the interpreter.

I never slandered you in my words and it is everywhere open and clear that what I said was to love and protect you for the sake of the national revolution. . . . I remember that after March 20 I met you . . . and earnestly expressed to you my attitude of everlasting confidence in you. If you truly regarded me as a comrade, you should have taught me; or if you saw anything wrong in me, you should have severely blamed me or chastised me and made me correct my error. But you only mildly and indifferently replied, "Never mind, never mind, nothing, nothing. . . ." So now why do you charge me with slander and ulterior motives?[27]

The man who wrote this letter, Kao Yu-han, was not an obscure individual but a leading member of the Communist party who also held office on the Supervisory Committee of the Kuomintang.

While the March 20 coup was met with denials and reproaches, the resolutions of the May 15 plenary session were unquestioningly accepted, the Communists seeking every devious means of rationalizing and justifying them. "When the imperialists saw it [the resolution on the readjustment of party affairs], they may have suspected that your party had fallen into their trap and had voluntarily broken the revolutionary front in order to turn to the Right. . . ." said an official letter from the Central Committee of the Communist party to the Kuomintang, "but it *may be* that your party did this because the form of cooperation between our party and yours has for several years aroused suspicion and jealousy in certain quarters. . . . Therefore you tried to make several changes in the form of cooperation in order to do away with unnecessary suspicion and jealousy, and later to

---

* Tuan Ch'i-jui was head of the notoriously corrupt government at Peking.

purify the ranks, deal blows against the reactionaries, consolidate the revolutionary front and proceed to fight against the imperialist and militarist rule and oppression with all your might. If this is the case, then there is no fundamental conflict in the policy of cooperation with our party. The principal thing is to consolidate the revolutionary forces against imperialism, no matter what the form of consolidation and cooperation is. If such is the case, the spirit of alliance between our two parties will not be dampened. . . . Your resolution . . . is a question for your own party and no matter what you decide in connection therewith, [we] have not the right to accept or reject."[28]

On May 28, the Canton correspondent of the Communist *Guide Weekly* wrote that in view of the fact that the May 15 plenary session had adopted "a declaration for the consolidation of all revolutionary elements against the reaction, no fundamental change in the policy of cooperation had taken place," and that

a mere resolution on party affairs is not sufficient to indicate a Rightward development of the Kuomintang Central Executive Committee. The Communists clearly recognize that the present situation of the revolution demands a strong and consistent revolutionary front. Their attitude toward the new resolution of the Kuomintang Central Executive Committee is guided by this criterion. The Communist fraction in the Kuomintang plenary session did not dispute in the least . . . the internal organization of the Kuomintang.*

This complete capitulation at Borodin's orders did not take place without some protest inside the ranks of the Communist party. A group of members in Shanghai opposed the course of surrender and demanded the immediate withdrawal of the party from the Kuomintang, declaring that it was impossible for Communists to work under the conditions laid down by the May 15 Kuomintang resolutions. Both the Central Committee in Shanghai and the Kwangtung party vigorously opposed this demand. The Kwangtung committee considered that

to withdraw from the Kuomintang would mean to abandon the toiling masses, to abandon the banner of the revolutionary Kuomintang to the bourgeoisie. This would be an irretrievable loss. At this time, a policy of temporary retreat must be pursued in order to remáin in the Kuomintang.[29]

---

* The author of this report, Ts'ao Szŭ-yüan, paid with his life for not having "disputed in the least" the new state of affairs in the Kuomintang. He was murdered a year later by Chiang Kai-shek's executioners.

Despite this, signs appeared that even the leadership had accepted Borodin's decisions with some reluctance. There were second thoughts. The pressure to regain some measure of party independence was so strong that in June the Central Committee of the Communist party decided to propose that the Communist party resume its own existence and replace its current submersion inside the Kuomintang with a formal two-party bloc.[30] This decision was sent to the Comintern in Moscow where it was immediately and drastically condemned and rejected. In Moscow, the Opposition led by Trotsky had already begun to demand the liberation of the Chinese Communists from the strait jacket of the Kuomintang and the proposal that arrived from China much too uncomfortably suggested that the Chinese party, which had no connection with nor any knowledge of the internal fight in Russia, was coming to the same conclusion as the Opposition. This could not be permitted, or even considered. The same official Comintern article which nearly one year later revealed for the first time that the March 20 coup had placed the Kuomintang under the control of its Right Wing also disclosed, likewise for the first time, that the Communists in China had demanded their freedom and that this demand had been ordered "revised." Even the Chinese Communist proposal to organize Left-Wing fractions within the Kuomintang—a remarkable confession that the so-called Left did not even have a fractional organization of its own—was condemned in favor of a policy of "directing the entire Kuomintang to the Left and guaranteeing it a stable Left policy."[31]

In China, Borodin and the other agents of Russia and the Comintern clamped down on the impulse of the Chinese Communists to try an independent political policy of their own. Ch'ên Tu-hsiu quotes Borodin as saying at this time: "The present period is one in which the Communists should do coolie service for the Kuomintang!"[32] Proposals to withdraw from the Kuomintang had been squelched because they meant "abandoning the banner of the revolutionary Kuomintang to the bourgeoisie." The only difficulty was that this banner was already abandoned to the bourgeoisie. It was firmly in the hands of the aspiring dictator, Chiang Kai-shek, and the Right Wing. The masses generally were never informed of this fact but were left to learn it suddenly and catastrophically. The coup of March 20, 1926, presents the remarkable spectacle of a huge mass movement, led by Communists, being painlessly deflected from the course of its own interests and placed under the direct control of its worst enemies, and being kept in total ignorance of this change by its own leaders.

As a result of this, the men who now fully controlled the nationalist movement could still appear before the people as "revolutionary leaders" between whom and the Communists there was little discernible difference. In May 1926, Chiang Kai-shek came as an honored guest to the Third National Labor Conference, which had swelled to a body of 500 delegates, representing 400 unions and 1,240,000 workers, of whom 800,000 had participated in more than 200 political and economic strikes since the previous May.[83] With becoming modesty, Chiang referred to himself as *shun ti*—"your younger brother." He coolly paid tribute to the decisive role played by the workers and peasants in the East River and southern campaigns during 1925. "In this period," he said, "the worker-peasant masses . . . hastened the unification of Kwangtung, swept away all the counter-revolutionaries and consolidated the basis of the National Government. From this one can see that the workers and peasants are already able to fight imperialism with their own forces, without reliance upon the forces of the army."[84] Having told the Chinese workers what the Communists never dared to tell them, Chiang Kai-shek clenched his fist, cried "Long live the World Revolution!" and stepped down from the rostrum amid loud cheers.

Thanks to the Communist policy of retreat and acquiescence, Chiang could go ahead with the Northern Expedition secure in the knowledge that he would have the mass movement at his disposal and the power to act against it at the time of his own choosing. The great mass organizations, geared by the Communists, were now thrown into the battle for the conquest of the North. The armies of the expedition set out in July and were soon sweeping from victory to victory on the crest of a new revolutionary wave that surged torrentlike across the provinces of Kiangsi, Hunan, and Hupeh, drawing fresh millions into the struggle and, before long, engulfing the great metropolitan centers of Wuhan and Shanghai. But the fruit of these triumphs had been guaranteed to Chiang Kai-shek in advance. As the Nationalist movement moved out toward the conquest of new provinces, the reality of the pattern fixed by the coup of March 20 made itself evident in what now became the Nationalist rear, the city of Canton and the province of Kwangtung.

The Northern Expedition was hardly under way before covert

maneuvers of the leadership against the mass movment gave way to overt repression. The "temporary retreat" of the Communists in Canton was turned into a permanent rout. On July 29, Chiang Kai-shek's headquarters proclaimed martial law. Public organizations, assemblies, the press, workers' and peasants' volunteer corps, strikes, all came into the orbit of military authority. Three days later an order was issued "forbidding all labor disturbances for the duration of the Northern Expedition." While the Canton authorities nominally stood aside, the gangsters of Canton were mobilized into a "Central Labor Union" and were turned loose in armed attacks on the regular union organizations. Startled out of the calm into which their leaders had lulled them, the workers grabbed up clubs, bamboo sticks, knives, an occasional revolver and rifle, and defended themselves as best they could. In six days' street fighting, more than fifty workers were killed. On August 9 the authorities stepped in with regulations for the compulsory arbitration of all labor disputes under government auspices. Workers were forbidden to bear arms of any description, to assemble, and to parade. "Any attempt during the period of the war against the North to make trouble at home will be considered an act of counter-revolution and treason against the Kuomintang," read a police order. Military patrols took over in the streets. Members of the "Central Labor Union" were called in to break a printers' strike which had paralyzed the city's press. The Workers' Delegates' Conference, representing 170,000 Canton workers and shop employees, now threatened a general strike, but the threat came months too late. The strike never materialized. The few small gains which the workers of Canton had wrested from their employers after years of struggle were now wiped out. The contract system, which had made workers the helpless dependents of their employers and which had been partially abolished in Canton, was restored. Public abuses such as licensed gambling and opium dens, which had been suppressed, resumed a flourishing existence with the rates of official "squeeze" boosted far above those of pre-Nationalist days.[35]

In the Kwangtung countryside, the March 20 coup was the signal for a brutal counteroffensive of the landlords against the rebelling peasants. A report of the Kwangtung Provincial Peasant Association in February 1927 listed scores of attacks, murders of peasant leaders, and breakups of peasant associations which began in June 1926 and continued until the revolutionary peasant movement was all but destroyed. Even in this report, prepared by Communist leaders in the peasant movement, the attempt was made to conceal the identity of the real authors of this counteroffensive in the countryside. The March 20 affair, it said,

really had no influence upon the policy of our Kuomintang, but avaricious officials, corrupt gentry, and rowdies took advantage of it to spread rumors such as "the peasant associations are to be dissolved," and "the Kuomintang is discontinuing the worker and peasant policy," . . . The resolution passed on May 15 by the Central Executive Committee plenary session was merely to deal adequately with the problems of the Kuomintang's internal affairs, but it was taken by the unprincipled landlords, the corrupt gentry, and the avaricious officials to indicate that the government was about to dissolve the peasant associations and that the Kuomintang had abandoned the worker and peasant policy.[36]

The landlords and their minions had, in fact, correctly taken their cue from Chiang Kai-shek's coup. The peasants never understood that the attacks on them were entirely "lawful" and that the March 20 coup had, in fact, put the peasant revolt beyond the pale of Kuomintang "legality." The changes it brought about also resulted in the the fruitless termination of the strike of the Canton-Hongkong workers.

Negotiations for a settlement of the great strike were resumed shortly after the March coup. They had been suspended in January when the British categorically rejected the demands of the Hongkong strikers. The Canton government at that time still insisted that it could negotiate only as an intermediary between the Hongkong authorities and the strikers. When the strike began, in June 1925, the newly established National government had demanded retrocession of the Shameen concessions and the withdrawal of all foreign naval vessels from Kwangtung waters. The workers of Hongkong had demanded freedom of speech and press, the right to vote in the selection of Chinese representatives in the government of the Crown Colony, improvement in working conditions, prohibition of child labor, enforcement of an eight-hour day, and cancellation of the general house rent increases scheduled to go into effect on July 1 that year. The British refused to negotiate and sat isolated on their Hongkong rock while the strike and boycott continued. "Only the unlawful activities of the Canton Strike Committee, instigated by Bolshevik intrigue, prevent the resumption of normal relations between Canton and Hongkong on the old, familiar footing," said the governor of Hongkong on February 4, 1926. "We expect and require the Canton government to put an end to these illegalities. I also wish it to be clearly understood that the Hongkong government will never agree in principle to strike pay or to compensation for non-reinstatement of laborers."[37] What His Excellency expected and required came to pass a few weeks later. The changes in Canton resulting from Chiang Kai-shek's March coup made possible a resumption of relations on the "old, familiar footing."

Unofficial contact between Hongkong and Canton was resumed on April 9 when a Mr. Kemp, attorney general of the Hongkong government, conferred with C. C. Wu, the Canton Foreign Minister, in what was officially described as a "hearty talk."[38] A few days after the adjournment of the May plenary session of the Central Executive Committee of the Kuomintang, the Canton government officially approached Hongkong to reopen negotiations. The British readily agreed. The delegates met in July. The original demands of the Canton-Hongkong workers were mutually deprecated. "These demands," said Eugene Ch'ên, who now headed the Foreign Office, "were conceived and formulated in the unusual circumstances immediately following the shooting of June 23 and they included terms which my government, actuated by a sincere desire to arrive at a satisfactory settlement, is prepared to review in order that nothing incompatible with the real dignity and interest of Great Britain as a trading power in China shall continue to obstruct the path of settlement."[39] It was no longer a question of strike pay for the workers. It became instead a matter of a $10,000,000 loan from the British to the Canton government, conditional upon "the complete cessation of the boycott and of all other anti-British manifestations throughout the territory controlled by the Canton government."[40] The Chinese delegates no longer even pretended to represent the interests of the strikers. When the Strike Committee demanded a voice in the parleys, Chiang Kai-shek issued an order "instructing the Canton chief of police to prevent any interference by labor unions with the Canton-Hongkong Conference now in progress."[41]

During the negotiations squads of soldiers and police patrolled the main streets and a close check was kept on labor union leaders "to prevent any movement among the workers which will create an opinion that the Kuomintang is unable to command the Canton situation and that any arrangement with the Kuomintang relative to the strike settlement . . . will be futile," reported the *China Weekly Review*. "The Canton Strike Committee is still clamoring that it should be heard, if not admitted to the negotiations now in progress in which the workers are chiefly concerned; and it is understood that should there be no objection from either side, in certain matters a subcommittee or the whole conference may hear representatives of the workers. In Canton Chinese opinion has been that the whole matter had been straightened out among the Kuomintang leaders and General Chiang Kai-shek before the meeting of the . . . delegations of July 15, and they cannot see how any agitation among the workers will change the policy already formulated. Any attention to the Strike Committee will be more a matter of courtesy than anything else."[42]

But even the proposal to buy out of the strike for $10,000,000 soon fell through. The bargaining position of the Canton government had collapsed as soon as it became apparent to the British that Canton's rulers no longer spoke for the workers and, in fact, were as anxious as the British to end the strike. The parleys were dropped. On September 3, a British naval landing party cleared the wharves of the Canton West Bund of worker-pickets. In protest against this act, Eugene Ch'ên asked for the "retirement of the British gunboats now moored along the jetties to their usual anchorage off the Shameen."[43] This was a far cry from the demand for the removal of all British vessels from Kwangtung waters. But the back of the strike movement was already broken. On October 10, 1926, the Canton government unconditionally called off both strike and boycott. The Kuomintang and the Strike Committee explained that this step was required "by the change in the national situation brought about by the extension of Nationalist power and influence to the Yangtze." The termination of a historic fifteen months' struggle without a single concession to the demands of the workers who conducted it was termed in this statement "not a defeat but a great victory."[44]

"Imperialism either had to capitulate to China," explained Borodin later, ". . . or China acknowledge defeat. Since, however, defeat could not be countenanced, it became necessary to terminate the battle in this corner in order to start out with greater vigor to fight imperialism throughout China—on the wider base."[45] Defeat could not be "countenanced" and therefore had to be rationalized into a victory. It was necessary to conceal the fact that the strategic moment had long since passed and the decisive positions had long since been yielded to the enemy without a struggle. The Hongkong strike and boycott had opened wide the door to an independent working-class initiative and had demonstrated the ability of the workers to function independently in their own interests. Under the mentorship of the Comintern and Borodin, the Chinese Communists had let the opportunity slip by without ever having recognized it. The workers of Canton and Hongkong had to pay dearly for this "victory."

Following the voluntary liquidation of the strike and boycott, the Governor of Hongkong happily declared that "we may reasonably hope that a determined effort will now be made by the Cantonese authorities to re-establish law and order." Hongkong desired to see in Kwangtung and Kwangsi "a strong, stable, and enlightened government; of such a government we should gladly be close friends and staunch supporters."[46] With the departure of the National government to the Yangtze in December, the task of re-establishing "law and order" in Kwangtung passed to the Kwangsi militarist, Li Chi-shên, who took over full control. Strict police measures were enforced against the workers. A set of stringent regulations was issued ordering arbitration of all disputes and forbidding workers to possess or carry arms, to make arrests, to picket shops or factories. In the face of these measures, the pickets and other workers' volunteer groups were "instructed by the Workers' Delegates Conference, acting under the auspices of the Communist Party, to remain indoors for the present pending readjustment of their standing." Anxious only to propitiate Li Chi-shên, the Communists hastily ended their agitation for a popular re-election of delegates to the various provincial Kuomintang organizations. They made no protest when Li Chi-shên reorganized the party, filling all posts with his own appointees. There was no resistance. Canton was tight in the militarist grip. The capitulation of the Communists was complete.[47]

This was Canton when a delegation of the Communist International arrived for a visit on February 17, 1927. The delegation consisted of Earl Browder, the American Communist leader, Tom Mann, the British Communist trade-union figure, and Jacques Doriot of the French Communist party. They inspected the outer shell of the mass movement that still remained and were feted by the local dictator, Li Chi-shên, who told them that "never, never would the Nationalist government proceed against the interests of the working class."[48] They sent their greetings to Chiang Kai-shek, who wired back his welcome.[49] Their first reports to the international Communist press glowed with pride in "revolutionary Canton" and were unmarred by any suggestion of the presence of discord.[50] At the graves of the Hongkong pickets killed in action during the strike they laid wreaths with this inscription: "The martyred Hongkong pickets symbolize the great contribution of the Chinese working class to the Chinese revolution and the world revolution."[51]

Six months later, when events had long since taken their course, the delegation wrote of its visit to Canton:

The Northern Expedition was in full swing and the Canton merchants cleverly utilized the slogan of the united revolutionary front in order to free themselves of all obligations to the working class. . . . Some of the leaders of the Canton proletariat were far from clear in their policy in the face of this clever and demagogic tactic of the bourgeoisie. . . . [They] neglected . . . the fundamental class interests of the proletariat for fear of breaking the united front with the bourgeoisie. . . . The only class, it seems, which took the slogan of the "united front" of all anti-imperialist forces seriously was the proletariat and its revolutionary leaders. . . . This was undoubtedly a mistake which later cost the Chinese working class much sacrifice and good blood.[52]

Chapter 7

FROM CANTON TO THE YANGTZE

THE KUOMINTANG marched its forces northward to replace the power of the older militarists with its own. It marched not to fight imperialism but to compromise with it. Deluded by their own leaders into believing that a Kuomintang victory would bring about a great improvement in their conditions of life and livelihood, the masses of ordinary people rose in a veritable tidal wave that swept the expeditionary armies to the banks of the Yangtze.

The spontaneous rising of the people gave the Kuomintang armies little more to do, often, than occupy territory that had already been secured for them. The bands of political workers which went out in advance of the troops were able, with the slightest touch, to unleash forces which leveled all opposition. Before this onslaught, the mercenary armies of the Northern war lord, Wu P'ei-fu, were demoralized and helpless. They either fell back in confusion or, with their local commanders, sought the safety of an alliance with the Nationalists. A foreign eyewitness tells how "an indigenous intelligence service . . . was ready waiting to assist the incoming army, reliable guides were available to serve whenever wanted; in some cases days before the army arrived, towns and cities were taken possession of by little groups of enthusiasts . . . in the name of the National government."[1] Peasant detachments took part in the actual fighting. Railway and telegraph workers cut the enemy's communications. Peasant intelligence made every move of the enemy almost instantly known to the advancing Nationalists.

T'ang Shêng-chih, a Hunan militarist who was among the first to jump on the Nationalist band wagon, occupied the Hunan provincial capital, Changsha, on July 12. A few weeks later the expeditionary forces reached the Northern defenses at Yochow, strategic port on the Yangtze. The way had been cleared by the action of the peasants at Pingkiang and of the workers of the Canton-Hankow and Chuchow-Pingsiang railways. Peasant guides led the Nationalists to a crossing unknown to the Northern commander which enabled the attackers to ford one of the adjacent tributaries of the Yangtze and to fall upon Yochow's defenders from the rear. "The enemy thought the army had come from heaven," gleefully reported a front dispatch to a Canton newspaper. Twelve hours later, on the morning of August 22, Nationalist troops entered Yochow. Soon they were converging on Wuhan, the collective name of the three great cities of Hanyang, Hankow, and Wuchang, located at the confluence of the Han and Yangtze rivers. The arsenal workers in Hanyang struck. The Northern garrison retreated and the Nationalists occupied Hanyang on September 6 and Hankow two days later. Wuchang's defenders held out behind the city's great walls for nearly a month, however, before the assaults of the famous "Ironsides" army battered the gates in. By mid-October the flag of the Kuomintang was firmly established over the heart of the Yangtze Valley.

Farther east, the advance of Chiang Kai-shek through Kiangsi had been less spectacular and less successful. Chiang had restricted the activities of the propagandists and had along the line of march already adopted repressive measures against the mass movement. This enabled Sun Ch'uan-fang, militarist overlord of the five eastern provinces, to put up stiffer resistance. Nanchang was finally taken, and on November 5, Chiang's forces reached Kiukiang, on the south bank of the Yangtze.

The victories of the Northern Expedition coincided with the mushrooming growth of the mass movement. In Hunan labor unions spread from five to forty hsien, or districts, and their membership rose from 60,000 to 150,000 by the end of November. In Wuhan, within two months of the Nationalist occupation, more than 300,000 workers and shop employes were organized in more than two hundred unions under the banner of the Hupeh General Labor Union. These organizations were hasty and often rickety structures. They were the products of an inspirational mood more than of solid work at the base. The use of compulsion by the more advanced groups over the more backward was not unknown. There was more blind following of leaders than action based on democratic procedures among the masses. But the readiness of the mass to act was the prime factor. The people believed that an opportunity had come to better themselves and they threw all their strength into the new struggle. Wuhan was rocked by a terrific series of strikes.

Even more spectacular was the growth of the peasant movement. According to organizational reports published in the *Guide Weekly*, by the end of November in Hunan there were fifty-four organized hsien, with a total registered membership in the peasant associations of 1,071,137. By January 1927, this number passed 2,000,000.[2] The peasants first rallied to the demand for rent reduction and abolition of the worst miscellaneous taxes, and asked for arms to fight the village gentry. Village authority fell largely to the peasant associations, and in Hunan, as elsewhere, the logic of the situation asserted itself: before long the peasants began first to refuse to pay rent and then to seize the land outright.

This was the picture when the National government moved in December from Canton to the Yangtze. The flush of victory and the powerful glow of the mass movement gave new life to the little band of liberal Kuomintang politicians who came up from the south. These men of the "Left" were able temporarily to shed the inferiority complex which Chiang Kai-shek's show of power had thrust upon them. Chiang himself was in the east, and around Wuhan great new forces of the revolution were gathering. In their shadow, the Kuomintang "radicals" strutted back and forth, gushing a torrent of revolutionary phrases. But as the popular movement rose, especially in the countryside, they quickly shrank to size and the traditional cry of the petty bourgeois radical sounded like a wail in the meeting chambers of government committees: "The masses are going too far!"

After their first disarray, the owners of the Wuhan factories stiffened. On December 3, the General Chamber of Commerce threatened a general strike of capital unless steps were immediately taken to restrain the workers. Borodin, the Communist leaders, and their Kuomintang associates hastened to comply. A Board of Arbitration was set up to recognize "reasonable" wage increases, to advise different trades "to follow traditions in fixing working hours," and "to leave the power of employing and dismissing laborers entirely in the hands of the employers." The personnel of the board included representatives of the Kuomintang, the General Labor Union, and the Chamber of Commerce. Its decisions were to be "binding on both employer and employees." An attempt was made to introduce legislation fixing a minimum wage of $13 a month, but this "improve-ment" never became effective.[3]

The approach to the peasants was much the same. Borodin and the Kuomintang radicals who now established themselves in Wuhan simply avoided any concrete program to meet peasant demands. The 25 percent reduction of rent promised by the Kuomintang program was not enforced by any act of the government. The leaders confined themselves to deploring peasant "excesses" which they feared might prejudice the united front of all classes.

The Chinese Communists acted no differently. The period of the Northern Expedition, with its widening of the political arena and the entry of new millions of people into active political life, offered the Communists a chance to break from the policy of capitulation they pursued in Canton. But this would have brought them into conflict not only with Chiang Kai-shek, but with the politicians of the "Left Kuomintang" as well. It would have threatened the "unity" with which the Chinese Communists, Borodin, and the chief Comintern representatives were hypnotically obsessed. The mass movement came to be regarded as not so much a source of strength as a constant menace, in its "excesses," to the preservation of political unity at the top. This notion pervaded the entire Communist leadership, of which an extraordinary picture was painted by three younger Comintern representatives in Shanghai. At considerable political risk to them-selves, they wrote a special report to Moscow, dated at Shanghai on March 17, 1927, from which we quote here at length:

Up to October, 1926, the question of the peasantry . . . was never raised in a more or less serious form either by the representative of the E.C.C.I. [Executive Committee of the Communist International] or by the C.C. [Central Committee] of the Chinese Communist Party, except for the deci-sions of the June Plenum of the C.C., which completely hushed up the peasants' struggle and appealed for a bloc with the "good gentry." . . . In October a program of peasants' demands was worked out, but the repre-sentative of the E.C.C.I. as well as the party leaders considered it only as a program for the party congress. For a period of three to four months the program did not pass beyond the walls of the C.C. and only in January was it sent out to the local organizations. But up until now, nothing has been essentially changed in the tactics of the party on the peasant question. The old policy of curbing the struggle in the village and applying the brakes to the peasants' movement as a whole still prevails. . . . The fear of the peasants' movement has existed and still remains in the party. The realiza-tion of peasant possession of land (that is, the occupation of the land by the peasants) is called by the C.C. "a dangerous infantile disease of Leftism." It continues to speak of the "united front with the good gentry and the small and middle landlords against the bad gentry and the blackguards." (Report from Hunan of December 30.) The expression "good gentry" is found to this day in all party documents, in articles by leading comrades. This replacement of social categories by moral categories is essentially a suspension of the revolutionary movement in the village.

At the December plenum of the C.C. a resolution on the peasant question was adopted with the participation of the representative of the E.C.C.I. Not a word is to be found in this resolution on an agrarian program and on the struggle of the peasantry. The resolution does not answer a single one of the most burning questions of the day; the question of the peasants' power is answered negatively. It says, the slogan of a peasants' power must not be raised so as not to frighten away the petty bourgeoisie. From the neglect of the peasants' revolution springs the suspension by the leading party organs of the arming of the peasantry. . . .

The tactic of the party in the workers' movement is no different from its tactic in the peasants' movement. Above all, there is an absolute underestimation and lack of attention to it. The C.C. has no trade union department. More than a million organized workers have no guiding center. The trade unions are separated from the masses and remain to a large degree organizations at the top. The political and organizational work is replaced everywhere by compulsion, but the main thing is that reformist tendencies are growing inside as well as outside the revolutionary trade union movement. . . . there occur refusals to support and defend the economic demands of the workers. Out of fear of the elementary growth of the labor movement, the party in Canton consented to compulsory arbitration, then it did the same thing in Hankow (the idea of compulsory arbitration itself comes from Borodin). Especially great is the fear of the party leaders of the movement of the non-industrial workers. . . .

The report of the C.C. at the December plenum says: "It is unusually difficult for us to decide our tactics in relation to the middle and petty bourgeoisie, since the strikes of non-industrial and office workers are only conflicts within the petty bourgeoisie themselves. Both sides (i.e., the employers and the workers) being necessary for the national united front, we can support neither of the two sides, neither can we be neutral. . . . The employees in concerns producing vital necessities (rice, salt, coal, fuel, etc.) must never resort to strikes if there is the slightest possibility of attaining concessions in a peaceful manner."

Thus the party abandons the defense and support of the non-industrial workers, i.e., the majority of the Chinese working class, and covers it up with the necessity of the united front with the petty bourgeoisie. Incidentally, it is quite clear that it is not so much a question of the petty bourgeoisie, especially of the artisans, as of the commercial middle bourgeoisie. . . . The party leadership also fears the arming of the workers. . . .

A characterization of the party attitude towards the army was given by comrade Chou Ên-lai in his report. He said to the party members: "Go into this national revolutionary army, strengthen it, raise its fighting ability, but do not carry on any independent work there." Up to recently there were no nuclei in the army. Our comrades who were political advisers occupied themselves exclusively with military and political work for the Kuomintang. . . .

With the aid of all sorts of combinations, oppositions, etc., our comrades hoped to maintain a balance of forces in the army, but it never occurred to them to capture it. . . . With particular ardor does the representative of the E.C.C.I. deny the possibility of political work in the army. The December plenum of the C.C. adopted a decision to build nuclei in the army (only of commanders, to be sure, with the prohibition against taking in soldiers), and in January of this year, when the other Russian comrades (not for the first time) raised the question of work in the army, comrade V.* already expressed himself sharply against the organization of nuclei. First he told comrade M.† that Moscow had decided not to form nuclei and then he showed the impossibility of organizing them; first, because the military commanders, especially Chiang Kai-shek, would see in it the machinations of the Communists, which would strain relations; second, because the Cantonese army was not susceptible to influence from below. When it was proposed to draw workers and Communists into the army on a mass scale . . . as well as peasants and members of the Peasant Associations, he laid it aside with pretexts, declaring that nobody would take them into the army anyway, nothing would ever come of it, there is no recruiting going on now, etc. And since he did not dare to appear as an opponent in principle in the question of arming the workers, he discovered a thousand difficulties, and showed that the arming of the workers is absolutely unthinkable, that we cannot get weapons anywhere, etc.

Besides, there are dozens of company commanders and a few regiment commanders who are Communists and have a colossal influence; there is a Communist regiment, and through all these channels an enormous work could be conducted. But out of fear of revolutionizing the army which pervades some party leaders, isolated comrades working in the army became detached from the party, were transformed into "individual" Communist commanders. . . . Despite the fact that the representative of the E.C.C.I. after a long resistance admitted to us that the work of the party in the army must be reorganized, he subsequently did nothing to carry through this reorganization. We do not even know if he spoke of it to the C.C.[4]

The Comintern representatives who wrote this letter were naturally careful not to say that Borodin, Voitinsky, and the Chinese Communist leaders were simply carrying out the policies laid down

* Voitinsky.   † Mandalyan.

in Moscow. But this was the case and the proof requires a fairly extended analysis of the directives that did come from Moscow in this period. They are worth the space and the reader's close attention, for they contain the real explanation of what happened to the Chinese revolution.

In March 1926, as we have seen, the Sixth Plenum of the Comintern Executive Committee had sanctified the policy of the "bloc of classes" in China. Chiang's coup had exploded the notion of "community of class interest" on which that policy was based. But the Kremlin leaders, intent upon winning a strong ally in China, overcame this difficulty by ignoring it and concealing the fact that power in Canton had passed into the hands of the extreme Right Wing of the Kuomintang under the leadership of Chiang Kai-shek. Shortly afterward, the Political Bureau of the Communist Party of the Soviet Union, against one adverse vote—Trotsky's—approved the admission of Chiang's Kuomintang as a "sympathizing party" into the Communist International. "In preparing himself for the role of an executioner," wrote Trotsky, Chiang Kai-shek "wanted to have the cover of world Communism—and he got it."[5] In October 1926, the Stalin-Bukharin leadership in Moscow wired the Chinese Communists to keep the peasant movement in check in order not to drive away the generals leading the victorious northward march. When confronted with it,[6] Stalin later admitted that such a telegram had been sent and, more notably still, confessed that it had been a "mistake," hastily adding that it had been "canceled" a few weeks after it was sent.[7] The cancellation consisted of the directives of the Seventh Plenum of the Executive Committee of the Comintern, which met in Moscow in November 1926.

The theses on China adopted by this plenum[8] were drafted by Stalin and Bukharin and they provide an instructive example of the kind of double-entry bookkeeping that had by now become standard practice in the Comintern. Lawyerlike, they provided for all contingencies. They enabled the Comintern to profess "independence of the proletariat" while it practiced capitulation to the bourgeoisie, and to stress, in general terms, the importance of the Chinese agrarian revolution while requiring the Chinese Communists more than ever to check the tumultuous uprising of the peasant millions. Technically, it was a matter of uniting antithetical elements and presenting them

as a synthetic whole. Thus, when events required it, the drafters of
the resolution could always justify themselves by citing their professions and blame the practices on others.

The theses, for example, observed that "the progressive abandonment of the revolution by the big bourgeoisie is historically inevitable." This phrase was later worn thin when quotations were needed
to prove that the Comintern "foresaw" and "predicted" everything.
The resolution, however, also said: "This does not signify that the
bourgeoisie is totally eliminated, as a class, from the struggle for
national independence, since side by side with the small and middle
bourgeoisie, even a certain section of the big bourgeoisie can for a
certain time still march with the revolution. . . . The proletariat
must, of course, broadly utilize those strata of the bourgeoisie which
at present are actively cooperating in the revolutionary struggle
against imperialism and militarism."

The document warned that the "bourgeoisie" was trying to
"smash the revolution." But it omitted to say which bourgeoisie,
what persons, what events, what places, names, dates, were involved.
"Smashing the revolution" implied an activity of an extremely concrete nature. The Chinese Communist might ask: Who was smashing
it? Where, when, how? To these natural questions, the document
provided no answer. It said nothing of Chiang Kai-shek's March
coup, of the repression of the workers in Canton, the killing of peasants and party workers in Kwangtung and in Kiangsi in the wake of
Chiang's advancing army. There was a single reference, unexplained
and unelaborated, to the fact that "the labor and peasant movement,
even in Kwangtung province, has had to surmount many difficulties."
In his report to the plenum, T'an P'ing-shan, delegate of the Chinese
Communist party, referred cryptically to "the March affair this year
in Canton" as "an attempt on the part of the bourgeoisie to take the
leadership of the revolution away from the proletariat" but he never
mentioned it again, nor, according to the official published record,
did anyone else.[9] Stalin himself, in a speech on November 30, gave
the assurance that "the big national bourgeoisie is weak . . . the role
of leader of the Chinese peasantry must inevitably fall into the hands
of the Chinese proletariat, which is better organized and more active
than the Chinese bourgeoisie."[10]

From all this, the attentive reader or listener could conclude that
while the "bourgeoisie" might be trying to "smash" the revolution,

Chiang Kai-shek, for his part, was doughtily leading the revolution from victory to victory. When Chiang's personal representative, Shao Li-tzǔ, appeared on the rostrum as the fraternal delegate of the Kuomintang, the delegates gave him a stormy ovation and rose to sing the "International" in his honor. The record says the enthusiasm was indescribable when "in the name of the Kuomintang," Shao ("comrade Shao" in the record) declared: "We expect the support of the Comintern and all its affiliated parties. . . . Long live the Comintern! Long live the world revolution!"[11]

Albert Treint, a French member of the Executive Committee of the Comintern and a member of the subcommittee on China who a year later broke away as an opponent of both Stalin and Trotsky, has recorded that the Moscow leaders were well aware of the bloody suppression of the mass organizations in Canton and in the rear of Chiang's armies.[12] Nevertheless, in his speech before the Chinese Commission of the plenum, Stalin spoke of Chiang Kai-shek's Northern Expedition in these terms:

> The advance of the Canton troops meant a blow aimed at imperialism, a blow aimed at its agents in China. It meant the freedom of assembly, freedom to strike, freedom of the press, freedom of coalition for all the revolutionary elements in China and for the workers in particular. . . . In China it is not the unarmed people against the troops of their own government, but the armed people in the form of its revolutionary army. In China armed revolution is fighting against armed counter-revolution. This is one of the peculiarities and one of the advantages of the Chinese revolution. . . . What is important is not the bourgeois-democratic character of the Canton government, which forms the nucleus of the future all-Chinese revolutionary power. The most important thing is that this power is an anti-militarist power, and can be nothing else, that every advance of this power is a blow aimed at world imperialism and is therefore a stroke in favor of the world revolutionary movement.[13]

In sum, the "bourgeoisie" would "inevitably abandon" the revolution, but its chief agent, Chiang Kai-shek, was the leader of an "armed revolution," and its chief agency, the Canton government, was the shining spearhead of the struggle against the militarists and against imperialism, and could be nothing else. The Communist who reasonably wanted to know the identity of the evil forces of the bourgeoisie who were "smashing" the revolution had somehow to figure it out for himself.

On the crucial subject of the agrarian revolution, the Communist who carefully studied Stalin's speeches and the theses of the plenum was left in the same bewildered state. The plenum theses, at one point, were bold:

Not to deal boldly with the agrarian question, not to support in their entirety the political and economic aims of the peasant masses would be a real danger for the revolution. It would be false not to place the program of the peasant movement first in the program of national liberation for fear of alienating the uncertain and perfidious cooperation of a part of the capitalist class.

This was, presumably, the "cancellation" of the October telegram that ordered a restraining hand on the peasants precisely in order not to upset the other groups in the coalition. Taken thus far, it seemed explicit enough. But the inquiring Communist had to read on to the next passages of the resolution:

While recognizing that the Communist Party must proclaim the nationalization of the land as the fundamental demand of the agrarian program of the proletariat, it must nevertheless for the present differentiate its agrarian tactic according to the economic and political peculiarities of the different sections of China territory.

It then went on to specify the program for the Chinese Communists to follow. It repeated the oft-cited but unimplemented program of the Kuomintang for rent reduction, tax adjustment, credit aids, government support of peasant organization, and asked for arms and "confiscation of church and convent land and of *land belonging to the reactionary militarists.*"[14] This was the real nub of the "differentiation" proposed by Stalin. It was akin to his proposal that in industry a program of nationalization be considered only for the property of those owners who "have distinguished themselves by special hostility and special aggressiveness toward the Chinese people."[15] The resolution, on the one hand, ordered the Chinese Communists to support peasant demands "in their entirety." The peasants were demanding the land. On the other hand, the resolution limited Communists to seeking confiscation only of the land of "reactionary" militarists. In China, every local satrap joined the Kuomintang as soon as it reached his territory. He thus became part of the "armed revolution" and his land became theoretically inviolate, along with the land of his satellites, his relatives, his supporters, i.e., all the local owners of land for whom he ruled. Peasants in Kwangtung, Hunan, and Kiangsi were already discovering this as they reached out to take the land for their own. Protection of "officers' land," sanctified by the Comintern and enforced by the Communists, became a noose for the revolution on the land. It meant in effect defense of the landlords against the peasants.

This was the kind of "agrarian revolution" that even Chiang Kai-shek was glad to support. As Shao Li-tzŭ said to the Plenum: "Comrade Chiang Kai-shek declared in his speech before the members of the Kuomintang that the Chinese revolution would be unthinkable if it were unable to solve correctly the agrarian, i.e., the peasant question. . . . We are convinced that the Kuomintang, under the leadership of the Communist Party and the Comintern, will fulfill its historic role!"[16] There was a grim validity in "Comrade" Chiang Kai-shek's conviction that the Kuomintang would fulfill its role "under the leadership of the Comintern" so long as this leadership firmly bound the Chinese Communists to a policy of subservience to bourgeois interests. The theses were most emphatic in their insistence that the program of revolution had to be achieved through and by the Kuomintang government. Suddenly but casually admitting that "since its creation, this government has really been in the hands of the Right wing of the Kuomintang," they added: "The task of the Communist Party is to see that the Canton government carries out these measures as a transition toward a further development of the agrarian revolution. . . . Recent events indicate that the Communists must enter the National government to support the Left wing in its struggle against the feeble and wavering policy of the Right." Actually, recent events, again unspecified in the resolution, had really proved that the "Left" was the feeble and wavering prisoner of an aggressive and powerful Right. To order the Communists into this government therefore only ensured that they in turn would become the obedient prisoners of the "Left."

Stalin and Bukharin created the image of a Kuomintang regime which was easy enough to set down on paper in a Moscow resolution but which the Chinese Communist, look as hard as he could, could not find anywhere in China. Repeating Stalin's formula, Bukharin told a Leningrad party conference:

What is essentially new and original is that now the Chinese revolution already possesses a center organized into a state power. This fact has enormous significance. The Chinese revolution has already passed the stage of evolution in which the popular masses struggle against the ruling regime. The present stage of the Chinese revolution is characterized by the fact that the forces of the revolution are already organized into a state power with a regular, disciplined army. . . . The advance of the armies, their brilliant victories . . . are a special form of the revolutionary process.[17]

If this meant anything at all to the Chinese Communist, it meant that there was no conflict between him or the popular masses and the Kuomintang government. But everywhere he looked around him, this government appeared to represent the exploiters in town and country and its generals were already beginning to repress the mass movement. This was a "special form of the revolutionary process" which it was difficult for him to understand. T'an P'ing-shan, the Chinese delegate, who had timidly ventured to say that he feared the Communists had "sacrificed the interests of the workers and peasants," unconsciously summed up the dilemma:

We must safeguard the interests of the peasantry, but on the other hand we must maintain and solidify the united front of the national revolutionary movement. In so contradictory a situation, it is not easy to maintain a correct tactical line.[18]

It was not only "not easy," it was impossible; for it required the Chinese Communists to reconcile the irreconcilable, to safeguard the interests of peasants and landlords at the same time when they were already in open conflict, to maintain the unity of "all strata of the population" when these strata were obviously pulling in opposite directions. Any suggestion that the Chinese Communists pursue an independent course of their own was quickly muffled. Stalin and other speakers at the plenum strongly condemned the idea of withdrawal from the Kuomintang. "It would be the greatest mistake," Stalin said.[19] When P. Mif suggested that the time had perhaps come to call upon the Chinese peasants to form "soviets" or popular councils in their towns and villages, Stalin called him brusquely to order and he quickly subsided. In sum, the resolution of the Seventh Plenum spoke about "the path of noncapitalist development" and the "agrarian revolution" but it laid down a policy that made both these goals impossible to achieve. It sacrificed both of them for the sake of a get-rich-quick bloc with the Chinese bourgeoisie. Preservation of this bloc at all costs was the task assigned to Borodin in Hankow, to Voitinsky in Shanghai, to the Chinese Communists who were never allowed to go out into the factories and the fields and tell the workers and peasants to have faith in themselves.

The spectacular growth of the peasant movement coincided with a strike wave of unparalleled intensity in all major industrial centers throughout the year 1926. Incomplete records show a total of 535 strikes for the year, compared with 318 in 1925. More than one million workers were directly involved. Most of the strikes were fought for wage increases and improvement in working conditions. More than half of them were wholly or partially successful. Counting only those strikes for which full data were available, one investigator calculated that 49.7 percent were wholly successful, 29.01 percent were partially successful, while 22.29 percent failed.[20] These statistics are eloquent enough, but they are only part of the story. By the end of the year, the strike wave was passing the bounds of economic struggle and becoming, as it had to become, a political movement. In Hankow this happened on a spectacular scale when, at a single blow, the workers took the fight against imperialism into their own hands.

On the afternoon of January 3, 1927, a great demonstration took place at the boundaries of the Hankow British Concession. The British, with memories of the shootings in Shanghai on May 30, 1925, still fresh in their minds, voluntarily withdrew their naval landing party the next day. The leaders of the Nationalist government were even more frightened than the British by the demonstrations in the streets, but they agreed to take over responsibility for policing the British area after the marines and volunteer guards were withdrawn. In midafternoon on January 4, great crowds again gathered at the concession boundary. "Finding that the concession was merely being policed by their own men and that it had not actually been taken away from the British, the cry went up to 'Take it now!'" reported the *Hankow Herald*. "Squads of coolies then started a round of the concession removing the barricades. Sandbags which had been stacked up at the entrances to all concession roads were torn open, the sand scattered in the street, and the sacks taken away. Barbed-wire barricades were removed bodily as were all other obstructions. . . . The foreigners' day was done on the streets of the British Concession."[21] Press dispatches to Shanghai and the world outside spoke of "mobs" and of looting and pillage. But as a British resident of the Concession later acknowledged, the victors "were riotously excited and jubilant in the Concession thoroughfares for a day or two and there were some instances of insolence and threats toward foreigners; but no personal violence was done and no houses entered."[22]

Down river at Kiukiang two days later the British Concession was similarly recovered when the British hurriedly evacuated from the city under the threat of mass action. Similar stories of vandalism were circulated. Six weeks later, the well-known British journalist Arthur Ransome visited Kiukiang and inspected some of the "violated" premises which had been especially sealed for investigators. "The looting seemed to me to have been very inefficient," he wrote, "floors covered with torn-up papers which must have been left by foreigners while preparing to leave; corners of sofas and mattresses ripped up. . . . Very little furniture was broken and no windows, not even a very ugly ostentatious hanging lamp which I should have liked to smash myself. . . . It is curious to observe that at 6 P.M. of that day (January 7) a party of fifteen, two men and the rest women who had come down . . . from Kuling, came through the Chinese streets into the Concession and down to the ships without molestation."[23]

The seizure of the British Concession in Hankow was a spontaneous act of the Hankow workers. "Nobody foresaw the events of January 3," reported the three Comintern officials in their letter from Shanghai. "The occupation of the Concession by the Hankow workers took place spontaneously, without any leadership, either from the government, from the Kuomintang, or from our party. They were all confronted by an accomplished fact, by a spontaneous act of the masses and all of them had to reckon with it."[24]

For the foreigners, and for the British in particular, the Hankow events spurred the policy of retreat before the mass movement which had already begun to take effect in the course of the previous year. This policy combined cajolery with threats. It consisted on the one hand of making concessions sufficiently attractive to the top layers of the Chinese leadership to establish a new basis for united action against the mass movement, and, on the other, the continued display and use of force. Thus, for example, on August 31, 1926, the Powers had signed an agreement for the rendition of the Shanghai Mixed Court to become effective on January 1, 1927. A few days later, British gunboats shelled the Yangtze town of Wanhsien, far upriver, inflicting heavy casualties on the civilian population in retaliation for a minor shipping scuffle. It was a reminder that "gunboat policy" still held good.

Early in December 1926, when the Nationalist government moved to Hankow, the British minister, Sir Miles Lampson,* was sent there on an official mission to explore possible channels of compromise. The Japanese and United States governments likewise sent special diplomatic representatives to treat with the Wuhan regime. On December 18, 1926, to the angry dismay of the British community in China, the British government circulated a memorandum to the other signatories of the Washington Treaties of 1922 proposing progressive relinquishment of foreign treaty privileges in China. On January 27, 1927, the British followed this up with similar proposals addressed impartially to the Peking and Wuhan governments. The same week, the United States Secretary of State announced his government's readiness to join in a compromise arrangement. In line with this general policy, the British government accepted the *fait accompli* at Hankow. It opened negotiations which ended with the signature of the Ch'ên-O'Malley notes of February 19 and March 2, 1927, which returned the Hankow and Kiukiang concessions to Chinese jurisdiction.[25] To the British residents of other treaty ports, it seemed to be a surrender that heralded the end of their world. They could take solace, however, from the continuous arrival at treaty ports of more troops and warships. The strategy was, in fact, to divide the Nationalist movement by making concessions, while at the same time by no means abandoning the threat of armed intervention.

When the liberal politicians of Hankow recovered from their fright at the audacity of the workers who had seized the Concession, the spectacle of a retreating and conciliatory Britain gave them new heart. They readily stepped in to negotiate and emerged dazzled with the Ch'ên-O'Malley accord. It was greeted as a great diplomatic victory for Eugene Ch'ên, although it was the humble Hankow coolie who had brought the mighty Britain to heel. The Communist leaders, on their part, had been dazed by what happened. According to the three Comintern delegates: "How did the Central Committee of the Communist Party react to the events in Hankow? At first it did not want to react at all. . . . The C.C. was of the opinion that the foreigners and the petty bourgeoisie need not have been irritated."[26]

* In later years Lord Killearn.

Again, according to Ch'ên Tu-hsiu: "The seizure of the British concession by the Wuhan workers . . . was not only carried out without the knowledge of the party leadership, but afterward the Central Committee regarded it as having been incorrect."[27]

The seizure of the British concession, however, gave the Left Kuomintang leaders a temporarily enhanced view of their own power and stiffened their attitude toward Chiang Kai-shek. Chiang had established himself at Nanchang, capital of Kiangsi, where the politicians of the Right Wing gathered about him. Go-betweens like Huang Fu and C. T. Wang scurried to and fro, seeking ententes with the Japanese and with the Manchurian war lord Chang Tso-lin, through his emissary, Yang Yü-t'ing. Chiang's eyes were fixed on Shanghai, the chief economic and political base of compradorism, the stronghold of foreign and Chinese capital. Pending conquest of that vital center, with its ready funds and direct access to the foreigners and the wealthiest Chinese, Chiang maneuvered to keep control of the party in his own hands. He demanded that the seat of the government be established at Nanchang. He wanted the Central Executive Committee of the Kuomintang to meet there under his auspices. He even made a quick trip to Wuhan on January 10 to press his demands, but there the Left Kuomintang radicals and Borodin, momentarily exhilarated by the victory over the British and the strength of the movement behind them, were bold enough to give Chiang a cold reception. At a banquet attended by Chiang, Borodin made a few pointed sallies about power-seeking militarists, a bit of audacity from which he himself "immediately recoiled in fright," saying: "I am afraid I made a mistake. . . . Our intervention against Chiang Kai-shek was provoked by the pressure of the general opinion and I do not know whether I acted correctly."[28]

Chiang left Wuhan. Back in Nanchang, he openly announced his intention to crush the Communists. "If the T'ung Mêng Hui [the predecessor of the Kuomintang in Chinese party politics] failed to construct an ordered Republic," he said in a speech on February 19, "it was because in its ranks there were too many disparate elements who did not march together. There were . . . reactionaries and counter-revolutionaries who compromised the work. Of these people there are still now too many. The time has come to expel them since they are not true comrades. . . . No more differences or tendencies among us! Being known as a faithful believer in the doctrines of

Sun Wên [Sun Yat-sen], I have the right to say that every true member of the party must be just that and nothing else. Whoever goes against the aims and methods indicated by Sun Wên will not be a comrade but an enemy who must not remain among us."[29] Again on March 7 Chiang delivered a broadside, directed this time against Borodin and the other Russian advisers. He insisted, however, on his continued friendship for the Soviet Union. "It is not [Russia's] policy to tyrannize over us," he said, "and though her representatives have acted otherwise, insulting our every movement, I am convinced that it has naught to do with Russia but are the individual actions of these representatives."[30] As for the rumors of his negotiations with Mukden and Japan, Chiang said that "one or two individuals" were maliciously trying to injure his reputation for revolutionary purity.

The bold mood of the Wuhan radicals during these weeks was reflected in the decisions of the third plenary session of the Kuomintang Central Executive Committee convened by them, in defiance of Chiang, at Hankow on March 10. Here Borodin and his colleagues put through a series of resolutions which, on paper, restored to the regular party organs the powers assumed by Chiang Kai-shek just a year before. The emergency powers delegated to Chiang at that time were revoked and the Military Council re-established. Chiang Kai-shek "resigned" from the chairmanship of the Central Executive Committee and the plenary session abolished the post itself as a gesture against the concentration of too much power in the hands of a single individual. At the same time, resolutions were passed concerning "cooperation" between the Kuomintang and the Communist party, calling upon the latter to share responsibility by sending "responsible comrades to join in the Nationalist and provincial governments." It was also resolved that "the press organs of the Third International, of the Chinese Communist Party, and of the Kuomintang shall not violate the spirit of cooperation in their reports and criticisms of one another."[31]

The decisions regarding the Communist party were implemented at once by the nomination of two Communist ministers to the newly created portfolios of Labor and Agriculture. This move was made specifically and consciously to tighten the bonds that already strapped the Communists to the Kuomintang. On this point the Kuomintang leaders were quite clear. "The present cooperative plan is important," it was explained in the official *People's Tribune*, "because it signifies greater control by the Kuomintang over all the forces participating in the national revolution. . . . the Communist Party will have to fulfill its obligations to enable the party [the Kuomintang] and the government to exercise full control over the mass movement."[32]

While these resolutions took effect, the decisions concerning Chiang Kai-shek remained mere words on paper. The Communists accepted the authority of the Wuhan leaders. Chiang did not and Wuhan did not dare try to bring him to book. While the press throughout China buzzed with rumors and reports of the growing schism in the Kuomintang, the Wuhan radicals and their Communist allies tried desperately to deny that there was any rift in the Nationalist lute. "The military organs are willingly and gladly turning over all political functions to the party . . . " the Wuhan leaders declared. "The party and the army are in agreement." Asked about the rumors of a split, they said it was "a pure fabrication."[33] The changes in the party high command were made by general agreement, it was asserted. "In all these changes there is now complete concurrence," said the Nationalist News Agency on March 19. "The very individuals and groups which seemed directly aimed at . . . have now signified their concurrence."[34]

This whistling in the dark harmonized perfectly with the tune Chiang Kai-shek wanted to play. He had yet to reach Shanghai. He had yet to conclude and consolidate his new alliances. He wanted no open break so long as he remained in Nanchang. He would break with Wuhan on his own terms once he was established in the Whangpoo metropolis. In Kiangsi he had already loosed the terror against the labor and peasant leaders and against the Communists. Press reports almost daily told of his negotiations with Mukden for "a reconciliation of North and South to fight the Reds." Chiang's course toward a split was clear. For Wuhan, however, the "crisis was over" and the national revolutionary movement was declared to be "in a position to move on unhampered by the slightest suggestion of inner conflict."[35]

"What did the C.C. of [the Communist] Party do . . . ?" demanded the Comintern trio in their letter from Shanghai:

One would think that it should have conducted a broad campaign among the masses . . . baring the secret motives behind this conflict and exposing the right-wing intriguers, encircling Chiang Kai-shek, and bringing strong pressure to bear on the government and on Borodin to stop camouflaging the conflict as a personal one and to move among the masses on the basis of a political platform of social reforms, and above all agrarian reforms, so that Chiang Kai-shek would have been forced to accept battle (if he wanted it) on the basis of a determined program—a fact which would have created grave difficulties for him. But the Central Committee of the Chinese Communist Party and the representative of the E.C.C.I. for a long time "did not notice" this conflict and took no position with regard to it. . . . We repeat: the leading nucleus of the party took no position and did nothing for two months in the Nanchang-Wuhan conflict. . . . The Central Committee only hid itself and evaded answering the questions that the situation placed before it. The local organizations of the party in Hupeh developed, at their own risk and peril, a campaign around this question without awaiting the decisions of the Central Committee.[36]

When he finally took public notice of the situation on March 18, Ch'ên Tu-hsiu simply addressed himself reproachfully to Chiang Kai-shek. He quoted a headline from a Shanghai Japanese newspaper of March 17: "Nanchang openly proclaims a pro-Japanese policy; Refuses to recognize the results of the Central Executive Committee Conference; Decides to get rid of Borodin." Chiang should repudiate these Japanese rumors, said Ch'ên Tu-hsiu, and not "abuse his own associates." He went on: "Our duty, therefore . . . is earnestly to persuade the Nationalist revolutionary leader, General Chiang Kai-shek, to prove immediately in words and actions that the so-called reconciliation between North and South to oppose the Reds is but the scheming of imperialist Japan."[37]

The advance to the Yangtze and the gigantic upsurge of the mass movement had brought the class contradictions within the nationalist movement to the breaking point. Chiang Kai-shek was openly steering for Shanghai to come to terms there with the imperialists. It was obvious he could succeed only if he undertook to decapitate the mass movement. This was what really lay behind the so-called Nanchang-Wuhan conflict and the climax was obviously just ahead. Yet the Wuhan radicals, flattered by the boldness of their own paper resolutions, considered the crisis over. The Communists tried only "earnestly to persuade" the erring general. The issues were kept carefully screened from the people, and especially from the Shanghai workers who all unknowingly held the key to the crisis in their hands. Unwarned, unprepared, they became first Chiang's pawns and then his victims.

Chapter 8

THE SHANGHAI INSURRECTION

In Shanghai the factory workers had responded to the victorious advance of the Northern Expedition with a strike wave of unexampled militancy. During 1926 in Shanghai there were, according to one official survey, 169 strikes affecting 165 factories and companies involving 202,297 workers. Of these, 82, or just under half, were listed as wholly or partially successful. Another survey listed for the same period 257 strikes, of which more than half were recorded as wholly or partially successful.[1] A steady depreciation in the value of copper coins during the year had caused a sharp rise in the cost of living which was felt most acutely by the lowest strata of the population. In most cases of strike action, demands centered on wage increases; recall of discharged employes; dismissal of offensive foremen; payment or increase of food allowances; reduction or limitation of working hours; improvements in factory equipment, living quarters, eating rooms, and general working conditions; abolition of corporal punishment of workers; release of arrested workers; and compensation for injuries suffered while at work. Other recurring demands, reflecting conditions prevailing in Shanghai industry, were for medical service, sick-leave pay, wages for apprentices, six-day week, prompt payment of wages, one month's salary for women workers during confinement, and nonreplacement of adults by children. These strikes were carried on in the face of repressive measures by local Chinese and foreign authorities. The Shanghai General Labor Union functioned illegally. Few strikes were unmarked by arrests and the use of force against the workers. These measures made little impression on the strike wave, however, which gathered force and began to assume an increasingly political character after the Nationalists occupied Wuhan and Kiukiang on the Yangtze.

The first attempt to overthrow the rule of Sun Ch'uan-fang, the local militarist, arose out of plans for the defection of one of his subordinates in near-by Chekiang in October 1926. An uprising was planned to take place in Shanghai on the 24th to follow immediately upon the open announcement of the revolt in Chekiang. The plans were under the direction of one Niu Yung-chien, chairman of the local Kuomintang committee in Shanghai. No attempt was made to organize a general strike or to involve any large groups of people. The Communists were called upon to supply small bands for action against police stations. Niu, an adherent of Chiang Kai-shek, was concerned with weakening Sun Ch'uan-fang but was equally intent upon limiting the activities of the Communists as far as possible. On the night of October 23, he was informed that the Chekiang plans had misfired. He did not bother to inform the Communists, and the next day when small bands attacked several police stations they were quickly overpowered. The incident passed almost unnoticed on the fringe of events, as uncertainties in Shanghai grew and popular feeling, expressed in two huge mass demonstrations on November 28 and December 12, began to assert itself more insistently.

In these months the political situation in Shanghai became extremely complex. It revolved around a movement which first sought to establish the "autonomy'" of Shanghai itself and then widened to include the province of Kiangsu, Chekiang, and Anhwei. It became the focus for the intrigues and political maneuvers of all groups and classes: for the bankers and compradores led by Yü Ya-ch'ing and the Chekiang-Kiangsu banking group; the Right-Wing Kuomintang politicians led by Wu Chih-hui, Chang Chi, and others; professional intriguers like Huang Fu and C. T. Wang; the criminal underworld under the triumvirate of Huang Ching-yung, Tu Yüeh-shêng, and Chang Hsiao-lin; the Kuomintang committee headed by Niu Yung-chien; and a host of smaller fry, hangers-on, go-betweens, jobholders, and jobseekers. Even Sun Ch'uan-fang himself, the nominal target of the autonomy movement, began poking his finger into the pie. Hovering in the vicinity was Yang Yü-t'ing, the special envoy of Mukden, fishing for a deal between the Manchurian war lord Chang Tso-lin and the Kuomintang. Dragging at the tail of all these politicians and manipulators were the Chinese Communist party and the Communist-led Shanghai General Labor Union.[2]

The worsening of Sun's military position in December helped precipitate this curiously mixed solution. Sun turned in desperation to an erstwhile ally, Chang Tsung-ch'ang, war lord of Shantung and the most notoriously rapacious of his kind. Chang's troops began moving south along the Tientsin-Pukow railway. Shanghai capitalists heard with consternation that Chang was going to force on them ten millions in worthless military paper with a demand for specie payment. The prospect of occupation of Shanghai by Chang's Fengtien-Shantung troops was a frightening one. It helped focus the attention of the city's big business interests on Chiang Kai-shek, who began to look increasingly like a man capable of rescuing them from the attacks of the masses from below and the depredations of the Shantung war lord from above.

The foreign authorities, the British and American more so than the Japanese, seemed to have found the complexities of the situation somewhat beyond them for the moment. The prevailing attitude among them during those early weeks of 1927 seemed to be to bear and protect the evils they had rather than fly to others they knew not of. For—to the foreign businessman, banker, soldier, consul, and missionary—this incomprehensible unrest, these endless slings and arrows for which they were the quivering targets, seemed indeed to be the blows of a universally outrageous fortune. They could not be sure who were the hares and who the hounds. So they barricaded their settlements behind gates and barbed wire. From overseas came regiment after regiment and whole fleets to protect them against all contingencies. Only the keenest among them* understood from the beginning that their interests coincided with those of the Shanghai bankers and oriented themselves accordingly. They knew Chiang Kai-shek as a politically minded militarist who wore a coat of many colors. If the Shanghai bankers were ready to back him, they knew they could follow suit. Only the Shanghai workers stood between them and the consummation of the deal. Chiang's coming would remove this obstacle. Thus by February, when Chiang's troops advanced into Chekiang, the situation had been greatly clarified for all concerned except the workers and the Communist leaders, for whom Chiang was still, for all public purposes, the hero-general of the revolution.

Nationalist troops occupied Hangchow on February 17 and next day advanced to Kashing, less than fifty miles from Shanghai. Vanguard units moved up the railroad as far as Sungkiang, only twenty-five miles away. In Shanghai all grew taut. Expecting an immediate further Nationalist advance, the General Labor Union issued a call

* Men like Ferral, the banker in André Malraux's *Man's Fate*.

for a general strike effective on the morning of the 19th. Within forty-eight hours upwards of 350,000 workers had left their jobs.[3] "Pompous Shanghai became like a graveyard," runs one account. "The tramcars stopped running. Steamships were unable to leave the port. The Post Office closed down. The department stores ceased business and all the big factories were silent. The sirens could not call a single worker back to work."[4] Clashes with the police began to occur. The strike was effective but its leadership had no goals of its own. The slogans announced by the Communists were confined to: "Support the Northern Expeditionary Army!" "Overthrow Sun Ch'uan-fang!" "Hail Chiang Kai-shek!" The Central Committee of the Communist party simply waited on events and orders from the outside. According to Ch'ü Ch'iu-po, one of its leading members in Shanghai at the time:

. . . The proclamation of the strike was not an official decision of the party. After the strike broke, it was not regarded as the first step toward an uprising. Not only among the petty bourgeois masses was there no kind of political propaganda but even among the workers few were clear on the aims and purposes of the general strike. . . .

Although the slogan "For a Citizen's Delegates' Assembly!" was decided upon, it was not looked upon as a slogan of action which required calling upon all the workers in the factories and unions to elect delegates and inviting the small merchants to send their own representatives. There was no attempt to make this assembly a sort of Soviet of the national revolution, to transform it into an organ of action where issues of the workers' strike, the merchants' strike, and the passage from armed defense to armed uprising could be discussed. In other words, there was no effort to turn it into a *de facto* provisional revolutionary government.

The party simply organized a provisional revolutionary committee composed of top delegates of the workers and representatives of the big bourgeoisie. Consequently the masses out on the streets had no chance to join in the "class struggle" between the workers' delegates and the bourgeois representatives. . . . The natural result was that the workers' delegates yielded to the big bourgeoisie on every question. . . . Our party sent the masses out into the streets and left them there for three days without paying any attention to them. We did not lead them forward, ordering an offensive along the path of the uprising. We did not even put up any defensive struggle. The workers' capture of rifles and the executions of traitors were mostly spontaneous acts. . . .

What we did was to bend all our efforts to negotiate with Niu Yung-chien, Yang Hsin-fu, Yü Ya-ch'ing, Wang Hsiao-lai—simply to negotiate, trying to use the conflicts among these various [bourgeois] groups. Such tactics amounted to this: the workers were on strike but were waiting for the permission of the big bourgeoisie before going any further. The petty bourgeoisie was left out in the cold, without leadership, without directives. We hoped that after conditions guaranteeing the victory were created [i.e., the successful outcome of negotiations between Niu Yung-chien and Li Pao-chang, the Shanghai garrison commander, on the one hand and the big merchants on the other], we hoped after all this to begin preparations for an uprising. This amounted objectively to betraying the working class.[5]

Li Pao-chang, the garrison commander, and the police of the International Settlement and French Concession did not wait for the outcome of all these talks to begin acting against the strikers. Students and strikers caught distributing leaflets in the streets were beheaded or shot on the spot. On the very first day of the strike, Li sent his execution squads into the streets with their great broadswords. Persons arrested by the foreign police were sent out into Chinese territory for execution. In the concessions and in Chinese territory alike police squads searched pedestrians and shops and created such a reign of terror that most shops, especially in crowded Chapei and Nantao, were closed and boarded up. Hua Kang tells of a peddler in Pootung, the industrial area across the Whangpoo River, who cried his wares: "Mai ta ping!" (I sell big cakes.) Soldiers shot him dead, claiming he had cried: "Ta pai ping!" (Beat a retreat.) Two metalworkers and a tram conductor distributing leaflets were beheaded where they stood near the West Gate. The dread squads also seized people reading some of the small colored sheets and executed them. Three students caught speaking to crowds in Jessfield, a town on the edge of the Settlement, were similarly done to death. The exact number killed was never known. Estimates ran up to two hundred. On February 20, the correspondent of the *New York Herald Tribune* watched the killings:

After the heads of the victims were severed by swordsmen, they were displayed on the top of poles or placed upon platters and carried through the streets. This sight in a parade through crowded thoroughfares had the effect of creating a veritable reign of terror, because the victims were denied the semblance of a trial. The executions occurred in the densest quarters. The executioners bearing broadswords and accompanied by a squad of soldiers, marched their victims to a prominent corner where the strike leaders were forced to bend over while their heads were cut off. Thousands fled in horror when the heads were stuck on sharp-pointed bamboo poles and were hoisted aloft and carried to the scene of the next execution.[6]

Street fighting between the workers and the soldiers and police began on the 21st. The workers had already begun to take arms wherever they found them to put up a defense against the terror in the streets. Skirmishing was already under way when the Communist leaders finally fixed 6:00 P.M. on February 22 as the time for an uprising. It was supposed to coincide with the arrival of the Nationalist troops who, everyone believed, were advancing upon the city along the Shanghai-Hangchow railway. Three days of the general strike had already passed. Workers' heads were falling and blood was flowing freely in the streets. The Communist leaders were negotiating with Niu Yung-chien and other representatives of the propertied class. But all this time the Nationalist forces never budged from Sungkiang. There was no military obstacle in the way of their advance on Shanghai. Between them and the metropolis, only twenty-five miles distant, there were only small bands of demoralized Northern soldiers, looting the villages as they fell back in disorder toward the city.

The failure of the Nationalist troops to march was no accident. Following receipt of a wire from Niu Yung-chien advising "cessation of the advance for the time being,"[7] Chiang Kai-shek had issued sudden orders for suspension of all operations along the Kashing-Sungkiang front pending the drive on Nanking and the Shanghai-Nanking railway. Military conditions entirely favored the occupation of Shanghai but it had evidently been agreed to give Li Pao-chang time to kill as many active strike leaders as he could. "General Li has been trying to get into the Nationalist Party," said the well-informed *China Weekly Review*, "and, according to report, General Chiang Kai-shek has agreed to take him in. . . . It is even rumored that conservative Kuomintangists were not altogether displeased at General Li's bloody rampage because it struck at the power, as well as the heads, of the radical Communist wing of the party."[8] Confirmation of this came a few weeks later when Li was rewarded with command of the Eighth Nationalist Army.[9]

The uprising that began on the evening of February 22 was put down with great slaughter. Fighting continued in the streets until the 24th, growing more sporadic and finally dying out altogether. Meanwhile the strike had dissolved. Most of the workers, bewildered by the turn of events, had gone back to work. Arrests and executions continued. To these the foreign eyewitness already quoted adds a final ironic touch: "Many persons were arrested because they carried handbills which read: 'Welcome Chiang Kai-shek, gallant commander of the Cantonese.' These were found guilty and executed on the spot.''[10]

Despite the savage repression and the continued confusion and vacillation of the Communist leadership, the events of February 19–24 proved to be only a prelude to greater events still to come. The workers' organizations, despite the heavy casualties, were still intact. The workers had learned how to fight. The question was whether their leaders had learned to lead. The strike of February 19 had posed the issue of power. The Communist leadership, under the guidance of the Comintern representative G. Voitinsky, had "debated whether or not to make an insurrection while the insurrection was already taking place," and, while the workers fought, continued to seek combinations at the top with those who were suppressing the insurrection. Voitinsky's three subordinates, in their letter to the Comintern dated March 17, went on: "The result was that we passed up an exceptionally favorable historic moment, an exceptional combination of circumstances. When the power was there in the streets, the party did not know how to take it. Worse, it did not want to take it, it feared to take it." The writers compared these events to the failure of the German insurrection in 1923, adding: "Only there was this difference, that at Shanghai the proletariat had notably greater forces at its disposal and chances on its side. Had it intervened in a determined manner, it could have conquered Shanghai for the revolution and transformed the relationship of forces within the Kuomintang."[11] But, as the events of the next few days were to show, the exceptionally favorable circumstances had not yet been exhausted.

During the two weeks following the crushing of the insurrection on February 24, Chang Tsung-ch'ang's Fengtien-Shantung troops came down the Shanghai-Nanking railway and took over the Shanghai area, Sun Ch'uan-fang retiring northward out of the picture. In the foreign settlements, garrisons were increased, gates were fortified, and sandbag barricades thrown up. By the end of February there were 7,000 British troops, 1,500 American marines, 600 Japanese marines, in addition to landing parties from the growing fleet of foreign warships at anchor in the Whangpoo. Still more troops were on the way. On February 25, the Shanghai diplomatic body issued a bristling statement in which it proclaimed "the necessary steps to ensure the safety of the Settlement and the protection of its nationals."[12]

Meanwhile military operations spread along three fronts. Nationalist forces moved down the Yangtze, occupying Anking and Wuhu and preparing to march on Nanking. A second force faced the Shanghai-Nanking railway along a Chinkiang-Soochow line. The third point of Nationalist concentration was at Sungkiang, southwest of Shanghai on the Shanghai-Hangchow railway. This front, quiet after the initial advance that had inspired the uprising of February 19–24, came to life again in March. Pai Ch'ung-hsi, a Kwangsi general subordinate to Chiang Kai-shek, moved slowly down the line toward Shanghai. On the night of March 20 he reached Lunghua on the outskirts of the city. There he stopped. Negotiations were begun with Pi Shu-ch'êng, the new garrison commander, for the "peaceful occupation" of the city by the Nationalists. The Fengtien-Shantung troops were completely demoralized and many were already in flight. Their main body, several thousand strong, reinforced by White Russian mercenaries, still held key positions, however, within the city.

Lunghua became the new focal point of a thousand intrigues. Niu Yung-chien called on General Pai. "Delay your entry a day," he advised. "Pi Shu-ch'êng will surrender." Orders came down the line from Chiang Kai-shek: "Do not attack Shanghai. Do not come into conflict with the imperialists. Wait."[13] In the city, however, the General Labor Union issued a call for a general strike and insurrection to break simultaneously at noon on March 21. Delegates sped to Lunghua to ask Pai Ch'ung-hsi to march his troops in to help the workers. He refused to move. They were still trying to persuade him when the workers struck out for themselves. The echoes of the noon whistles had barely died away when the shooting began.[14] The strike was complete. Practically every worker in Shanghai answered the call. The ranks of strikers were joined by shop employees and the masses of the city poor. Between 500,000 and 800,000 were directly involved.[15] This time there were carefully laid plans for an insurrection based upon a workers' militia composed of 5,000 picked and trained men, broken up into squads of twenty and thirty. According to one account, their total initial supply of arms consisted of 150 Mauser pistols.[16] That meant less than one to a squad. The attack on the police and Shantung soldiery was made in the beginning only with clubs, axes, and knives.

Fighting began simultaneously in six parts of the city: Nantao, including the whole area south of the French concession; Hongkew, the narrow strip surrounded on three sides by the International Settlement; Woosung, the fortified area near the confluence of the Whangpoo and Yangtze rivers; East Shanghai, including the industrial district known as Yangtzepoo; West Shanghai, another industrial area adjacent to the Settlement; and Chapei, the most densely populated proletarian district in Shanghai.

The fight for control of police stations and local military posts was won by the workers by nightfall in all sections except Chapei. Many soldiers and policemen tore off their uniforms and surrendered arms and ammunition. Weapons were taken everywhere and by evening the attacking forces were comparatively well supplied. To build barricades around the police stations, furniture, boxes, and benches were pulled out into the streets and doors were torn off hinges. Hundreds of tiny smoking restaurants prepared food which women carried in steaming bowls up to the fighting areas. The insurrectionists bound strips of red rag around their right arms for identification. By dark all police stations were occupied and telephone and telegraph offices taken. Electric power lines were cut.

"In Nantao . . ." records Hua Kang, "the uprising began with an attack on the police station, which was entered shortly after 2:00 P.M. The telephone building and all the branch police stations were taken over in short order. Policemen were all disarmed. Arms were also taken at all the occupied stations. Shortly before four o'clock, the workers believed themselves strongly enough armed to march on the arsenal at Kiangnan, at the south end of the city. There the soldiers surrendered without a fight. Exactly at four o'clock the workers came into possession of the rich stock of rifles and machine guns. By that time the soldiers guarding South Station had fled so it was a simple matter for the railroad workers to take over and use the locomotives for the purposes of the battle. At five o'clock, less than five hours after the attack began, the workers massed in the yards of the Chinese Tramway Company. All Nantao was in their hands.

"In Hongkew no soldiers had been stationed. The workers had simply to deal with the police. Almost immediately after the uprising had begun, the police station surrendered and Hongkew belonged to the workers. But after the police had been driven out, they instigated gangsters to attack the labor unions and the occupied police stations. . . . The workers not only had to fight the organized enemy but they had to use their armed power to suppress the gangsters too."[17] Ho Shên gives another version of this particular incident in Hongkew: "The dispersed police discovered that the attackers were Communists, not members of the Kuomintang. They reassembled and under the leadership of Niu Yung-chien they counter-attacked. . . . But the workers eventually won."[18]

In Pootung the workers formed ranks in military fashion and marched on the Third Branch police station. It fell into their hands almost at once. Soldiers and police caught in flight were disarmed. Many of them joined the pickets in setting up a Provisional Workers' Bureau of Public Safety and in taking over the municipal offices of the whole district. Kuomintang representatives, accompanied by armed gangsters, crossed the river from Shanghai and tried to assume control of the district. They were forcibly put back on their launches and ordered to return to Shanghai.

In Woosung, the soldiery had broken and fled when the attack began. One detachment, not knowing the situation in the city, headed for town along the narrow-gauge railway that links Woosung to Shanghai. At Kiangwan they found the rails torn up. The soldiers thereupon entrenched themselves in and around Tientungan Station, which was located at the point where the Kiangwan, Hongkew, and Chapei districts met along a contiguous boundary. Picket detachments coming from conquered Yangtzepoo joined with units from Chapei in an attack on Tientungan Station. In West Shanghai the workers occupied police stations and seized arms, then crossed the creek and joined the attackers at the Pootoo Road police station, forcing its surrender after a brush in which the picket leader and several policemen were killed. Then the workers gathered their forces and from all directions marched toward North Station in the heart of Chapei where the fighting was heaviest.

Resistance everywhere had crumpled quickly except in Chapei where into nightfall the battle was still going on along and across the main thoroughfares. Chang Tsung-ch'ang's Russian mercenaries cruised these streets in armored cars, raking the houses on both sides with their machine guns. An armored train just back of North Station, also manned by White Russians, dropped shells into the fighting area. From behind the North Chekiang Road gate of the Settlement, which commanded a full view of Paoshan Road across which the workers moved to attack the station, British troops occasionally fired in "defense" of the Settlement, which was not under attack at all. Hundreds of Shantung soldiers were admitted to refuge behind the gates and were later repatriated to Shantung.

With their ranks swelling during the afternoon as workers poured into Chapei from east and west, the pickets settled down to a siege of the six remaining strongholds of the enemy—North Station, the Huchow Guild, the Commercial Press, the Fifth Police Station, and the branch police stations on Canton and Chung Hwa Roads. The seventh and last enemy position was at the other end of Paoshan Road, at Tientungan Station. By late afternoon all the police stations and the Huchow Guild had fallen. The remaining three centers, North Station, the Commercial Press, and Tientungan Station, were strung out along a single line bisecting Chapei. The armed pickets massed between them. Hua Kang's account of the last stages follows:

Fiercest fighting of all took place at North Station. Here, in order to drive back the workers, the enemy set fire to nearby houses, over a hundred of which were razed to the ground before the fire could be brought under control. . . . Pickets left the lines to get water and to haul in disabled fire engines. The people were so enraged at the soldiers and so grateful to the workers that they joined in the uprising on their own. Old and young, working together, emptied their houses to build up the barricades. . . . The soldiers cooped up in the station did not dare to sally out but satisfied themselves with random volleys at the workers. The White Russians opened fire again and once in a while a British shot would come whistling from across the Settlement border.[19]

The battle continued through that night but by the next morning the end was obviously near. At noon the soldiers at Tientungan surrendered. At half-past four in the afternoon some of the soldiers at the Commercial Press tried to escape and were captured. The rest then surrendered. An hour later, under the cover of flames, the White Russian mercenaries fled into the Settlement and the Shantung soldiers dispersed in disorder. A white flag fluttered over North Station at six o'clock.

Such was the position when Nationalist troops of the First Division arrived at Markham Road after coming down from Lunghua. Their orders had been to remain where they were, but the soldiers had insisted and their commander, Hsüeh Yüeh, decided to go along with them. By the time he arrived, however, the battle was over. All of Shanghai, with the exception of the International Settlement and

French Concession, was in the hands of the workers. Along Paoshan, Paotung, and Chingyung Roads, the sound of rifle fire gave way to the crackle of fireworks as the victory celebration began. The railway union ordered the repair of destroyed rail sections. The team of three hundred workers organized to carry out these orders was the first in all Shanghai to resume work after the victory of the insurrection.

Chapter 9

THE PRODIGAL'S RETURN

When Chiang Kai-shek landed at Shanghai early in the afternoon of Saturday, March 26, he had at long last arrived home. Here were his first haunts and his early benefactors, his former fellow brokers and his friends of the underworld. A native of Ningpo, he could here join hands with his fellow provincials—the powerful Chekiang bankers, the Ningpo merchants and industrialists—who shared with the foreigners economic control of China's metropolis.

The bankers and merchants had watched strikes grow into the general strike and the general strike grow into insurrection. The workers' conquest of Shanghai had given them the lever they needed to extract terms of greater equality from the foreigners, but it also served notice that the time had come to disembarrass themselves of the dangerous weapon of mass power. Their own interests were now at stake no less than those of the foreign capitalists. An essential condition of the impending deal between Chinese and foreign capital was the smashing of the mass movement. They had long known that they could look to Chiang Kai-shek, the prodigal now back in their midst, to carry out this task.

To this end Chiang had already resumed contact in the Yangtze Valley with the secret societies that had flourished there from the earliest days of the Ch'ing Dynasty, now known as the Green and the Red societies. Varying in origin and initial purpose, these organizations had become criminal gangs. They traded in opium and slaves. They kidnaped for ransom. They trafficked in blackmail and murder. Rare was the shopkeeper or trader or boatman, big or small, from the Yangtze's mouth to the Szechwan gorges, who did not pay them tribute.

The Green Gang operated out of Shanghai. Its leader, Huang Ching-yung, known everywhere as Huang Ma-p'i (Pockmarked Huang), was chief of detectives of the French Concession police. In a ruling triumvirate with him were Chang Hsiao-lin and Tu Yüeh-

142

shêng, the latter of whom in later years became the undisputed leader of the Shanghai underworld enjoying great public repute as a "philanthropist." It was generally believed that Huang Ma-p'i himself had many years before introduced Chiang, as a stripling officer of the Shanghai garrison, into the inner ranks of the society.[1] When Chiang the Nationalist general arrived at Kiukiang in November 1926, it was Huang Ma-p'i who came upriver from Shanghai to re-establish direct contact with him in behalf of the Shanghai bankers and merchants. Following that conference, the Green Gang was mobilized for the express purpose of breaking up the trade-unions. What had been an organization of common criminals now assumed the combined features of the Russian Black Hundred groups and Louis Napoleon's Society of December the Tenth. Yang Hu, one of Chiang's staff officers, was put in charge of operations.[2] Plans were made to set up rival "labor unions." All the scum and riffraff of the treaty ports were quickly recruited as "members." Arms were plentifully provided. Huang returned to Shanghai. Chiang turned back to Nanchang where he had set up his headquarters.

The campaign of open repression against the mass organizations began in February 1927. Early that month Ch'ên Tsan-hsien, chairman of the General Labor Union of Kanchow, a southern Kiangsi city, was murdered by Chiang Kai-shek's soldiers. The union was driven underground. In Nanchang on March 17, Chiang ordered the dissolution of the city *tangpu* (Kuomintang branch), arrested its Communist and Left-Wing leaders, closed down the unions and the students' association, and suppressed the local Kuomintang daily. The same day an attack was launched on the mass organizations in Kiukiang. Several hundred gangsters, described as "moderate unionists," raided the quarters of the General Labor Union, the city Kuomintang, the Peasant Association, the student and women's groups, and the Political Department of the Sixth Army. Resistance was offered. Four were killed and ten wounded. A Chinese account described how the workers held their own against the gangsters until a company of Chiang's own troops appeared, stormed the building, and released several gangsters who had been captured. A British correspondent in Kiukiang said that

when the raiders appeared to be getting the worst of the battle, the soldiers stepped in and finished off the work they had begun by wrecking the labor union's headquarters. Since then the heads of the labor union have disappeared and it is said the union is to be reorganized on more conservative lines. Martial law was immediately declared and an order issued forbidding persons to collect in groups. Civilians may not . . . carry weapons. . . . The streets are patrolled by soldiers. . . . It is said that Chiang Kai-shek, who was himself in Kiukiang at the time of the rioting but has now left for downriver, instigated . . . the attack. At the time of the trouble he placed a large armed guard in the Concession to protect it. . . . The new magistrate has returned from Nanchang whither he retired after the labor extremists had wrecked his yamen and has brought with him a personal bodyguard of 150 of Chiang Kai-shek's picked troops. . . . The influence of the moderate party represented by Chiang Kai-shek is commencing to be felt throughout the province. . . . The tide has definitely turned.[3]

Similar events took place wherever Chiang Kai-shek touched port on his way down river. Organized gangs attacked and occupied union premises at Anking on March 23 and at Wuhu a day later. Union leaders were killed or driven into hiding. The unions were rapidly "reorganized." Chiang was to have stopped at Nanking, which was occupied by Nationalist troops on March 24, but whatever plans may have been afoot for that city were upset by looting and attacks on foreigners on the day the city changed hands. Several consular officials and missionaries were killed. In retaliation, British and American gunboats anchored in the river shelled the city, killing twelve and wounding nineteen Chinese civilians. The remaining foreigners were evacuated.

The foreign press quickly developed the theory that the "Nanking outrages" were part of a Machiavellian plot concocted by the Communists and the Left-Wingers at Wuhan to "embarrass" Chiang and to embroil him with the foreigners. But the fact was that the Communists and Kuomintang liberals at Wuhan were far more concerned with propitiating Chiang than embarrassing him. It was, moreover, a striking fact that the vast movement which had swept South China had been marked by practically no cases of violence against foreigners. In hundreds of towns mission property had been seized and foreigners forced to leave, but "only in a few isolated instances," wrote one of them, "did a foreigner get even a scratch or a bruise."[4] It has also been suggested that the Nanking incident had been organized by Chiang himself as an act of deliberate provocation against the Communists. This version has equally little to support it. Some of Chiang's troops, especially those who had recently "come over" to

the Nationalist side, were undoubtedly quite capable of running amok
on their own. An American investigator, on the scene a few days
after the events occurred, was able, however, to assemble evidence to
show that the demoralized, retreating Fengtien soldiers were the
actual perpetrators of the attacks.[5] The foreign community, at any
rate, whipped itself into a violent anti-Nationalist passion over this
issue and it contributed heavily to the already heavily overcharged
moods of the time.

Because of these events, in any case, Chiang Kai-shek did not
land at Nanking but continued down the river to Shanghai. Upon his
arrival he was driven from the wharf through the foreign barricades
to the old Foreign Ministry bureau on Route Ghisi, just outside the
French Concession. There his first caller was Pockmarked Huang.
Next to see him was T. Patrick Givens of the Political Branch of the
Shanghai Municipal Police, who presented Chiang with a pass for
entering the foreign areas and accorded him the privilege of traveling
in those sacred precincts with an armed guard. Chiang was, incidentally, the only Nationalist commander thus honored. Chiang, no
less magnanimous, gave assurances that he would "co-operate with
the foreign police in Shanghai" and forthwith plunged into conferences with his own aides and supporters to see how "law and order"
could be established and maintained.

He met with the Right-Wing Kuomintang elders, led by Wu Chih-
hui, Ts'ai Yüan-p'ei, and Chang Ching-chiang. He saw visitors representing the bankers and the Chamber of Commerce, led by Yü Ya-
ch'ing, his first benefactor, Wang Hsiao-lai, and others. He discussed
the military situation with his subordinates, Pai Ch'ung-hsi, who had
occupied the city for him, and Chou Fêng-ch'i, a new recruit who only
yesterday had deserted the Northerners. He again saw Pockmarked
Huang and his chief aides, Tu Yüeh-shêng and Chang Hsiao-lin, and
the usual host of lesser lights and satellites. Their problem was plain:
how were they going to wrest control of Shanghai from the workers'
organizations and establish their own government at Nanking? There
was ample financial support at hand for this purpose, but when they
looked around them those last gray days of March, Chiang and his
friends saw many formidable obstacles in their path. "It was not at
all improbable," wrote one well-informed foreigner, "that he would
be unable to stem the tide of Communist activity on the morrow."[6]
Indeed, for those who did not or could not perceive the gap between

the mass of the workers and the Communist leadership, it was difficult to see how victory could fail to remain with the workers.

Shanghai was in their hands. To be sure, the workers' pickets,
who now patrolled the city instead of the police, numbered only 2,700
men with 1,700 rifles, some machine guns, and a large stock of ammunition captured from Northern troops.[7] But there appeared to be
no serious obstacle to the swift expansion of the numbers and armament of this force. The entire working population, flushed with their
recent victory, was ready to follow the orders of the General Labor
Union, now set up in headquarters at the Commercial Press and in
the building of the Huchow Guild. There was a Provisional Government set up under what appeared to be full Communist control, and it
seemed quite capable of establishing its effective power throughout
the city. Finally, there was no visible reason to suppose that the city
workers would not make common cause with the Nationalist soldiers
now in occupation.

Chiang Kai-shek had only 3,000 troops in the city, of whom only
a few were reliable from his point of view. The nearest reinforce-
ments were at Hangchow, five hours away, where Ho Ying-ch'in sat
with an army of barely 10,000 men. It seemed doubtful if many
of these would have turned their arms against the workers if the issue
had been made perfectly plain to them by the workers' organizations
which they regarded as their main allies. In effect, Chiang did not
know whether he dared order his own men to march against the
workers.[8] In Chapei, the working-class stronghold, was the First
Division, which was enthusiastically sympathetic toward the unions.
Its commander, Hsüeh Yüeh, had already reflected the temper and
pressure of his troops when he marched them into Chapei against Pai
Ch'ung-hsi's orders on March 22.

Across the barbed-wire barricades the foreigners were generally
convinced, as one of them put it, that they were going to be murdered
in their own beds by their own servants. The British and American
communities were quite certain that their fair little islet of foreign
justice and rectitude was about to be overrun by insane mobs thirst-
ing for the white man's blood. They were suffering badly from what
one writer aptly termed "highly accented funk." They had all heard
highly colored stories of the seizures of the Hankow and Kiukiang
concessions in January and the more recent incidents at Nanking.
The tales of fleeing missionaries, which grew taller with every mile

traveled nearer Shanghai, made churchgoing pillars of society shriek hysterically for blood. "Better a thousand times take a strong line of action now and call a halt to this outrageous villainy that is being perpetrated in the name of freedom, even if it does involve the shedding of a little blood. . . ." cried one of the leading members of the British community.[9] Foreign women palpitatingly organized entertainments for the troops pouring off transports for defense of the Settlement. They expected a mob, foaming and frothing, to rush upon them momentarily. The Shanghai Municipal Council, governing body of the Settlement, had declared a state of emergency on March 21, establishing rigid martial law. It followed this on March 24 with a manifesto declaring "it realizes the gravity of the local situation and its possible repercussions throughout the civilized world and will use all the resources at its disposal to retain control of the situation."[10]

These resources were already considerable. Garrisoning the foreign areas were 30,000 foreign troops, nearly one per foreign inhabitant, excluding the White Russians. Counting the British alone, there were two British soldiers for every British civilian in the city. Thirty foreign warships, British, Japanese, American, French, Italian, and even Portuguese, rode at anchor in the Whangpoo River cleared for action. Squadrons of British planes were making regular patrol flights over the city and the surrounding territory, a treaty violation which did not appear to worry the British authorities. Other warships en route would in a few days increase the fleets of all nationalities to a total of forty-five vessels, ranging from gunboats to 10,000-ton cruisers. Yet the cry went up for more troops, more ships. The local foreigners wanted all Shanghai taken over. They wanted Nanking occupied. They demanded an international force to repeat the massacres with which allied foreign troops crushed the Boxers in 1900. Their newspapers, notably the *North China Daily News*, carried on in a frenzy of alarms, threats, and slanders. They showered abuse most of all on politicians in the chancelleries at home who deemed it wiser to move more slowly in dealing with the developments in China.[11]

Any foreigner who by word or deed showed any sympathy for the mildest features of the Nationalist program or was even critical of the prevailing hysteria was looked upon as a traitor and, worse, a renegade from the race. J. B. Powell, publisher of the *China Weekly*

Review in Shanghai, who ventured to doubt that armed intervention would bring the desired results and who perspicaciously urged concessions to the Nationalists, was read out of the American Chamber of Commerce. A lone foreign missionary who joined a handful of Chinese Christians in advocating the peaceful rendition of the Settlement was denounced in the columns of the *North China Daily News* as a betrayer of the faith and a revolutionary agitator. An article by a Chinese Christian which attempted, under the title "Jesus and the Three People's Principles," to draw a parallel between the teachings of Sun Yat-sen and Jesus was denounced by high and low churchmen as "a blasphemous outburst." The National Christian Council, a Sino-foreign body which took a pro-Nationalist stand, was caustically renamed the "Bolshevist Aid Society" and was formally repudiated by a group of thirty-two British and American missionaries "as dangerous to and subversive of the best interests of the Churches in China." Its appeals in behalf of the Christian spirit were declared to be "a direct violation of the Shanghai Municipal Council's prohibition of documents calculated to stir up animosities, foment trouble, cause public alarm, or incite to a breach of the peace." Diatribes filled the press daily in the manner and spirit of one American journalist who defined a labor union as "an organization of filthy coolies who had never worked and never would." In these outpourings, not only the "filthy coolies" but bankers like Yü Ya-ch'ing and politicians like C. T. Wang, even then working feverishly for an entente with the foreigners against the "filthy coolies," were generally described as "rabid anti-foreignists." The moods of the time can be recaptured by these random samples from the press:

Rabid: "The big port of Shanghai is a purely foreign creation. . . . Now the Chinese want it 'returned' and sympathetic understanders run about discussing terms under which all the fruits of several generations of foreign effort can be yielded up to anarchic cooliedom. This strikes me as the exaltation of folly, the apotheosis of imbecility."[12]

Irritated: "The first thought that comes to one is the bother of it. To have one's home turned upside down, to have to hastily lump a few belongings into a trunk or two and a suitcase and leave the rest behind to be looted or whatnot, is an unadulterated bother."[13]

Unctuous: "Coastwards from all directions foreigners are hastening whose only crime is that they are willing to do China good. I say this intending to include not only missionaries but the many splendid businessmen who wish China much better than her present behavior would seem to deserve. We must, however, be merciful. China has some real grievances; many of her present ones of course are of her own making, but the innocent have to suffer and are often deceived into thinking that the foreigner is entirely responsible."[14]

Selfless: "Peaceful foreign residents have been driven from their homes, their property destroyed. . . . Many foreign firms . . . are now facing ruin. But these are really trivial matters. . . . What is important is the struggle against a political idea whose avowed aim is to destroy present world civilization . . . hampered by no scruples of conscience."[15]

Spiritual: "In my capacity as a missionary and thinking primarily of the consequences to the Church of Christ throughout the world if the mad dog of Bolshevism is not checked in China, but is allowed to jump across the seas to our own beloved America, I have no hesitation in asserting my conviction that a Bolshevised China would be the world's greatest peril."[16]

Chaste: (Quoting a widely published but quite false report that the Women's Association in Hankow had staged a "naked body procession" of selected women "having snow-white bodies and perfect breasts") : "Those who are familiar with the modesty of Chinese women during the past centuries require no further or more conclusive proof of the pernicious influence of Russian Communism."[17]

Chivalrous: "The average American gives only passing thought to the vested interests in a foreign country but he can rise to a high emotional pitch over danger to innocent American women and children at the hands of mobs or soldiers."[18]

Innocent: "In China the communist appeal is to class hatreds, social antipathies, greed, and envy."[19]

Mocking: "If the present 'barbed-wire' hysteria continues much longer we would not be surprised to wake up some morning to find that our diligent and energetic Municipal government had constructed a canopy of barbed-wire overhead in order to keep out the rays of the sun on the grounds that our chief Heavenly body was suspected of spreading red propaganda."[20]

Forthright: "In times such as these, fine distinctions and legal quibblings lead to nothing. There can be no room for the C. P. [Communist Party] in Shanghai and it must be fought as the Council would fight bubonic plague. . . . Chinese and Russian C. P.'s should be treated with equal severity—both are enemies of civilization."[21]

Perspicacious: "The Nationalist opportunity—All sympathies with the Kuomintang—But Opposition for the Communists."[22]

Clear-cut: "Chiang Kai-shek . . . stands at the dividing of the ways. . . . It is no exaggeration to say that he and Generals Ho Ying-ch'in and Pai Ch'ung-hsi remain now the only protection of China south of the Yangtze from being submerged by the Communist Party. . . . But if General Chiang is to save his fellow-countrymen from the Reds, he must act swiftly and relentlessly. Will he prove himself the man of action and decision, the champion of the true principles of Dr. Sun Yat-sen, the defender of his country? Or will he too go down with China in the Red flood?"[23]

South of the city at Lunghua, Chiang, too, was pondering this question. In a series of interviews with foreign journalists, he did his best to placate and reassure the foreign community. He deplored the Nanking incidents, promising a thorough investigation and punishment for those responsible. "The Nationalist leaders have always wished to maintain friendly relations with the foreign powers," he said in one interview March 31. "It is the settled policy of the Nationalist government not to use force or mass violence in any form to effect a change in the status of the foreign settlements." He concluded with a further promise which he hoped the foreigners would not fail to understand: "In spite of the present obstacles to a clearer and better understanding, we hope to remove these so that there will be a clearer and better relationship between China and the foreign powers which will be based upon a mutual friendship and understanding."[24]

A few foreigners were able to appreciate this unmistakable offer of collaboration in removing "obstacles." But most of them were still angered more by the protestations Chiang had to make as a "Nationalist" than appeased by his promises to defend foreign interests. The editor of the *North China Daily News* combined both views. He called the interview "an extraordinary farrago of assertion . . . and of brazen pretences contradicted by all experience," but then added: "Apparently General Chiang spoke sincerely, and to do him justice . . . in the districts under his purview [he] seems to have tried to keep order." A few days later General Duncan, commander of the British troops, felt reassured enough to tell a Chinese newspaperman that Chiang had won his respect "because he not only speaks that way but really puts it into practice."[25]

The Chinese bankers and industrialists of the city were readier with faith and trust. Their understanding with Chiang, long in the making, was already sealed. On March 29 more than fifty leading banks and firms and commercial associations banded together into a federation under the leadership of Yü Ya-ch'ing and Wang I-t'ing, the latter a compradore for one of the big Japanese steamship companies and one of Chiang's old Shanghai friends. United in this federation were the various district chambers of commerce, the Bankers' Association, the Native Banks Guild, the Stock Exchange Association, the Cotton Mill Owners Association, the Flour Merchants' Guild, Tea Merchants' Guild, Silk Merchants' Guild—virtually all the organized property interests of Shanghai. A delegation of the new body waited the same day on General Chiang, "who very cordially received them." Their spokesman "conveyed the greetings of the Chinese merchants of Shanghai and emphasized the importance of immediately restoring peace and order in this city. They assured him of the wholehearted support of the merchants. General Chiang responded in a few fitting remarks and took full responsibility upon himself for the protection of life and property, both Chinese and foreign, in Shanghai. He also assured the delegation that the relation between capital and labor will soon be regulated. . . . At the end of the visit, the delegation left in good cheer, fully satisfied that they had found in General Chiang a man of sound principles and a leader of singular power."[26]

Several days later all the merchant guilds issued separate declarations of hearty support for Chiang and sent delegations to express hopes for an early amelioration of the situation. On April 9, representatives of more than twenty commercial organizations met and resolved: "For the Kuomintang San Min Principles and for Commander-in-Chief Chiang! Down with all counter-revolutionary elements!"

But the situation demanded more than faith and support. The men with money had to be more than vociferous. They had to be generous. The first installment paid over to Chiang was a "loan" of $3,000,000 (Shanghai currency) on April 4. An additional $7,000,000 was reportedly paid over a few days later "Chinese bankers and merchants," reported a foreign correspondent, ". . .

sent a delegation to Chiang Kai-shek . . . offering him a fund of 15,000,000 Shanghai dollars on condition that he suppress Communist and labor activities."[27] These advances were quite distinct from the $30,000,000 "loan" floated two weeks later to help launch the new government at Nanking.

Chiang began taking steps to assure his control of the city. He installed one of his staff officers as commissioner of police. One of his political henchmen became magistrate of the Shanghai district. He set up a special finance committee, drafting a number of prominent bankers for the purpose, to raise the funds he required. One of his appointees took over the managing directorship of the Shanghai-Nanking and Shanghai-Hangchow railways. He opened official contact with the foreign authorities by naming Quo T'ai-ch'i Commissioner for Foreign Affairs. Martial law was proclaimed on March 28 making all civilian administration organs in the city responsible to military headquarters at Lunghua. "Unauthorized persons" were forbidden to possess or carry arms of any description. At the same time there came into being the "Workers' Trade Alliance," sponsored by Huang Ma-p'i, Tu Yüeh-shêng, and Chang Hsiao-lin and presented as a new "moderate" labor union. Preparations went ahead swiftly to repeat in Shanghai the tactics already applied in Nanchang, Kiukiang, Anking, and Wuhu. Coming almost as a dress rehearsal for the impending events in Shanghai, they were again successfully carried out in Hangchow on March 30 and 31.

Here, too, Chiang had seen to the organization of a "Workers' Trade Alliance" in opposition to the Communist-led General Labor Union. On the night of March 30 the armed gangsters broke into the headquarters of the union. Several union workers were killed and many wounded in the fight that took place there. Next day, according to a wire from the General Labor Union published in the *Sin Wen Pao* on April 5, a general strike was called. Only the telephone and postal workers responded. A protest meeting was held and a parade formed which marched down Chin Chiao Road. Soldiers, who had been told that the union was trying to sabotage the Nationalist army's advance, were stationed at a main crossing. When the workers approached, the soldiers opened fire. Half a dozen marchers fell. More than one hundred were arrested. The Hangchow pickets, one thousand in number, armed only with clubs and staves, were disarmed and dispersed. The premises of the General Labor

Union were smashed. Union workers were arrested. Nobody ever listed the final number killed. The G.L.U. was closed down "pending reorganization" along the now familiar "more moderate lines." The Hangchow events foreshadowed precisely the events about to occur on a far larger scale in Shanghai. This was true not only of Chiang's moves but of the Communist reactions to them.

When Chiang put his own appointees into posts in the civil administration of Hangchow and repressive steps were begun against the workers, the G.L.U. wired to Chiang a respectful request to remove the offending officials. "During the military period I have the power to appoint the chiefs of the Bureau of Public Safety," he curtly replied. To this they acquiesced in silence. After the arrests and shootings of March 30–31, the union issued a circular telegram which concluded with a request to General Chiang Kai-shek "to come to Hangchow to punish the guilty parties and fight against the reaction."[28] Unfortunately, Chiang happened to be too busy inaugurating the reaction in Shanghai to journey down to Hangchow to suppress it there. The Shanghai General Labor Union, for its part, was too busy trying to placate Chiang to learn anything from the fate that had befallen its Hangchow counterpart.

Nevertheless, Chiang Kai-shek did not approach the task of breaking up the organizations of the Shanghai workers without an awareness of the magnitude of the task. The mass movement had assumed such proportions that he was compelled to begin a series of maneuvers designed to put him into a more favorable position for striking at it. For every step he took toward his goal he made a gesture in the opposite direction. He set out deliberately and with great skill to befuddle his enemies, confuse the issue, and paralyze all potential opposition to the coup already in view. He did this so well that even some of his friends were confused. Just as at Canton, where on the eve of the March 20 coup a year earlier some of his allies "were antagonistic toward him on account of their inability to fathom the real aim behind his actions,"[29] similarly at Shanghai there were many, especially among the foreigners, who were impatient over the apparent contradictions in his behavior. "If General Chiang, it is suggested in Chinese political circles, initiated a frankly anti-Communist movement, he would crystallize support for himself," complained the *North China Daily News* on April 8, "but his half-hearted, apologetic attacks on the Communists leave uncertainty that the rift is irrevocable."

But Chiang was not temporizing. He was preparing to move and needed only a few more days to complete his arrangements. Soldiers sympathetic to the workers had to be removed from Chapei and replaced by units least touched politically by contact with the mass movement. The mobilization of the gangsters for the anti-Communist coup was already under way. While this was being accomplished, Chiang continued to do everything possible to spread the belief that no conflict impended. This took the form of persistent denials, from the very day of his arrival, of reports that he intended to break with the Nationalist government at Wuhan.

On March 27 he told interviewers "that there was no split, that the members of the Kuomintang were united . . . that there were no signs or prospects of serious dissension."[30] To a representative of the Japanese Toho Agency two days later he declared that he unreservedly recognized the authority of the Wuhan Central Executive Committee. He made sure to have Moscow reassured along the same lines. "We know the imperialists hope for a rupture between the Nationalist army and the popular masses," said Pai Ch'ung-hsi to the Shanghai correspondent of *Pravda*, "but that is impossible. Our basic principle is the union of the armed force with the popular masses. . . . The Chinese revolution forms part of the front of the world revolution. The imperialists are trying to break that front by lies and slander. Sun Yat-sen instructed us to co-operate with the Communists who form part of the Kuomintang and we shall not break the alliance with them. The English press in China is spreading all kinds of lies on this subject. It ought to be suppressed."[31]

The arrival of Wang Ching-wei from Europe on April 1 gave Chiang an opportunity to make his words seem even more concrete and convincing. Wang, who had found no sources of new strength within himself during his stay abroad, became again the tool of the man who had forced him to flee so ignominiously from Canton a year earlier. After two days of conferences, Chiang on April 3 issued a circular telegram proclaiming his "explicit obedience" to the Central Executive Committee of the Kuomintang at Wuhan. "I strongly believe that [Wang's] return will result in the real centralization of the party so that we may attain without a split the ultimate success of the Nationalist movement. . . . Hereafter all matters relating to the welfare of the country and the Kuomintang . . . will be handled by Chairman Wang or carried on under his guidance. . . . We will be guided by the Central Executive Committee and we must therefore show nothing but explicit obedience."[32]

Wang, according to his own biographer, "felt very uncomfortable" about Chiang's telegram. He did not approve the methods which Chiang Kai-shek proposed to use in eliminating Communist influence from the ranks of the Kuomintang. He, too, "visualized the necessity of separating from the Communist Party," only he was "against any precipitate break [and] wanted to settle all the disputes outstanding in a regular, peaceful way." Wang tried to persuade Chiang Kai-shek that they could attain the desired end without resort to violence or "illegality." According to one account, Wang promised that Borodin would be dismissed, that the decisions of the Third Plenary Session of the Kuomintang Executive Committee in March, which deposed Chiang from the party chairmanship and the supreme military command, would be revised, that the disarmament of the Shanghai pickets would be approved and Chiang's civil appointments in the Shanghai district sanctioned. Wang tried later to deny that he had come to any such agreement with Chiang. But his own biographer records that he left Shanghai for Wuhan to persuade his colleagues there "to come down to Nanking to hold the plenary session with Chiang and the rest, so as to maintain the unity of the party," adding that Wang "believed that he could get the support of the great majority of the pure Kuomintang members of the C.E.C. to effect a revision of the decisions taken by the Third Plenary Session."[33]

But Chiang Kai-shek and his friends were intent now not upon party compromises but upon direct action. The apparent agreement with Wang Ching-wei helped to increase the mounting confusion in the opposing camp as the decisive moment approached. To increase it further, they reached out through Wang to the Communists, with results that must have far exceeded their expectations. Chiang Kai-shek, the returned prodigal, was moving toward power, aiming a decisive blow against a foe who had already, in effect, surrendered to him.

Chapter 10

THE CONSPIRACY OF SILENCE

To THE workers of Shanghai, the hour of the arrival of the Nationalist troops had been represented by their Communist leaders as the
hour of liberation for all the oppressed. The central slogan of the
victorious insurrection of March 21 had been: "Hail the National
Revolutionary Army! Welcome to Chiang Kai-shek!" Quite unaware that the troops had been halted at Lunghua in the hope that the
workers would be broken in the battle against the Shantung soldiers,
the workers greeted the arrival of the first Nationalist detachment
on the evening of March 22 with delirious joy. Two days later, when
foreign newsmen flocked to Lunghua to interview General Pai
Ch'ung-hsi, they witnessed an unusual sight: "A striking example of
the impression the Cantonese arrival has made on the minds of the
laboring classes of Shanghai was furnished during the interview.
. . . A procession of 1,800 factory workers, 300 of them women,
entered the yamen bearing a multitude of gifts which they piled outside the door of the inner building as a mark of their pleasure, kettles,
teapots, boxes, baskets, cloth. . . ." The day after Chiang Kai-shek's
arrival a welcome demonstration was staged for him at West Gate
where a throng of 50,000 workers gathered to hear Communist
speakers who were "superlatively laudatory . . . toward Chiang
Kai-shek."[1]

The Shanghai workers and Chinese Communists were not alone
in saluting Chiang and his army as the saviors of the people. All the
parties in the Communist International reacted in the same manner,
for everywhere it was understood that Chiang bore with him to the
gates of Shanghai nothing less than the standard of the world revolution. No one had ever been advised differently. Two days after
the Shanghai insurrection, *Rote Fahne*, central organ of the German
Communist party, featured a photo of Chiang Kai-shek, describing
him as the heroic leader of the "revolutionary war council of the
Kuomintang." A similar photo appeared in *L'Humanité*, French

Communist daily, on the same day, with a report of a mass meeting in Paris at which Chiang's entry into Shanghai was greeted as the inauguration of "the Chinese Commune," opening a "new stage in the world revolution." An editorial spoke of the Cantonese victory as the "liberation of Shanghai" which meant "the beginning of liberation for the workers of the world."[2]

As late as April 10, *Pravda*, the guiding organ of the Comintern, was proclaiming the need, above all else, of maintaining in China "the bloc of four classes" and insisting upon the unassailable unity of all classes under the leadership of the Kuomintang. At the same time, from the end of 1926 and into the early months of 1927, the Comintern press was also, in accordance with the "line" of the Seventh Plenum, issuing broad, generalized warnings about the forthcoming defection of the national bourgeoisie. These articles[3] invariably deprecated the strength of the Right Wing of the Kuomintang, invariably exaggerated the strength of the "Left" Wing, and in no case mentioned Chiang Kai-shek as the actual spearhead of the gathering forces of reaction. Whenever they did mention Chiang, it was to give renewed assurance that he was leading the revolutionary forces to victory and that all would be well. To support this assurance, the Comintern press had to deny all the rumors and reports, growing in number and plausibility, that Chiang Kai-shek was heading in Shanghai toward an open break. The result was a veritable conspiracy of silence around an impending catastrophe.

It seems impossible that the Comintern leaders, at least, were unaware of the actual course of events. In a few weeks, their whole press would furiously belch forth denunciations of Chiang Kai-shek, with all the information suppressed for a year pouring out in a hot stream. The letter of the three Comintern delegates in Shanghai, from which we have so extensively quoted, showed that Chiang's plans were no secret to the men on the spot. But there is even more striking evidence of deliberate concealment. A Comintern delegation, consisting of Earl Browder of the United States, Jacques Doriot of France, who was later to find his way from Stalin's top staff to French Fascism, Tom Mann of Great Britain, and a Russian, Sydor Stoler, arrived in Canton in February 1927. The delegation traveled up through Kiangsi at the heels of Chiang Kai-shek during March. It came into direct contact with the terror which had already been laid across the province like a black whip. The members of the delegation were themselves treated with formal courtesy, Chiang having left instructions that they be wined and dined and sent on their way. Thus wherever they went, as Browder himself naïvely admitted later, they "had the experience of actual street fighting being suspended during our visit while leaders of both sides talked to us." As their subsequent reports showed, the delegates made copious notes of names, dates, places, and incidents. They passed through town after town where the unions had already been driven underground and in Kanchow they received detailed information on the murder of Ch'ên Tsan-hsien, the local trade-union leader killed by Chiang's orders only a few weeks previously.

They did not miss the significance of what they saw. Doriot wrote, later, that "the Kanchow incidents taught us a precious lesson. We knew from that moment on—well before the split—that the conflict between the bourgeoisie and the Chinese working class would take on the bloody forms it has since assumed." Browder wrote, also later, that he saw in the Kanchow affair "one whole phase of the deepgoing split that was tearing the Kuomintang into two separate warring bodies throughout China." Finally, when they met General Chang Chun, one of Chiang's close aides, at Nanchang on March 26, he made the matter quite explicit. Doriot quoted him as saying: "The marshal [Chiang] cannot speak now. . . . He is not free enough. He has not enough territory. He has left for Nanking and Shanghai. There he will speak. There he will have his word!"[4]

The Comintern delegation arrived at Kiukiang only a few days after Chiang arrived in Shanghai. They landed upriver at Hankow on March 31. It was a critical time of decision. Chiang's strength in Shanghai was uncertain, the workers' strength was great. They were being assured that there was no split, that there was no possibility of a clash, that Chiang Kai-shek would not act against them, that the thing above all was not to provoke him. If it were a simple matter of ignorance of the facts, Browder and Doriot and the other members of the Comintern delegation were now clearly in possession of the facts. They had seen the pattern set by Chiang Kai-shek's course through Kiangsi. They had been told he would have "his word" at Shanghai. They were in a position to warn the workers of Shanghai that Chiang was not their savior but their mortal enemy, that they had at all costs to keep their arms, strengthen themselves, and prepare to repel the attack that was clearly coming. It is of course impossible to know what would have happened if three responsible Comintern leaders had spoken up at that moment. The fact is that they did not.

Browder's first statement on arrival in Hankow was anything but a denunciation of Chiang Kai-shek. His interview with the *People's Tribune* on April 1 ran as follows: "Everywhere . . . the contact between army, union, and peasant groups was one of the most pleasing aspects of his visit, Mr. Browder stated. . . . Everywhere they went . . . they found that the people, without exception, were solidly in support of the party (the Kuomintang). . . . The peasants were in complete co-operation with all other groups in the Nationalist revolution." He cautiously remarked that in Kiangsi "the movement has been working under difficulties" but hastened to add that "the workers were not at all discouraged." Except for a single statement which he later claimed[5] to have given to a Chinese newspaper, Browder did not mention Chiang Kai-shek by name as the author of the "difficulties" in Kiangsi. In a formal report of their trip published eight days later, Browder-Doriot-Mann again described the fine co-operation between the "revolutionary army" and the mass organizations in Kiangsi. They ventured to say that they saw "a definite differentiation going on" and mentioned that at Kanchow they found the workers mourning for a leader murdered by "agents of reaction." The identity of these agents remained unrevealed.[6]

Less than two weeks later, Chiang Kai-shek relieved the Comintern representatives of the need for concealment. When he had, in his own time, successfully struck his blow at Shanghai, it became time for the Delegation to reveal in the *People's Tribune* of April 22, that the "agents of reaction" were soldiers "acting in the name of Marshal Chiang Kai-shek," that in Kiangsi "the trade unions must hold their meetings secretly, all premises being occupied by troops." These were, evidently, the army-union contacts which Browder found so "pleasing" in his first version. Only now it appeared that in Kiangsi "the Kuomintang represents only the mandarins and the capitalists, as the workers and peasants have no voice whatever."[7]

The same kind of deliberate concealment and misrepresentation, coupled with staggering misjudgment of the realities of the political situation in China, filled the columns of the international Communist press right up to the eve of Chiang Kai-shek's coup d'état. A few examples will suffice. In *La Correspondance Internationale* on March 23:

Now that we are on the eve of the taking of Nanking and Shanghai, the imperialists are issuing reports about the so-called splitting tendencies within the Kuomintang. The results of the executive session of the Kuomintang . . . showed exactly the contrary. The united front inside the party is today as solid as before. . . . Far from dividing, as the imperialists say, the Kuomintang has only tightened its ranks.

Again, a week later, under the title, "The Victory of the Shanghai Workers":

A split in the Kuomintang and hostilities between the Shanghai proletariat and the revolutionary soldiers are absolutely excluded right now. . . . Chiang Kai-shek has himself declared he will submit to the decisions of the party. A revolutionist like Chiang Kai-shek will not ally himself, as the imperialists would like one to believe, with the counter-revolutionary Chang Tso-lin to struggle against the emancipation movement. There were, indeed, negotiations last November between Chang Tso-lin and the Cantonese armies, but only for tactical reasons. . . . The Kuomintang has promised the workers to satisfy all their demands. The only danger for the Shanghai proletariat is an imperialist provocation.[8]

That same week *L'Humanité* reported a meeting in Paris where the workers cheered wildly when they were assured of the "indefectible unity of the Kuomintang."[9]

In Moscow, the same reassurance was given in reply to Trotsky and the Russian Opposition, who were warning of a blow and were demanding the unconditional independence of the Chinese Communists. Stalin's drive against the Opposition had already begun to take on the proportions of a pogrom. Oppositionists were shouted down at party meetings and denied space in the press to air their views. The issue in the internal party struggle already embraced the entire internal and external orientation of the Soviet State. The events in China, obviously moving toward a crisis, became a major issue in this struggle. Stalin was gambling the whole international position of Russia on the successful emergence in China of a strong Chinese nationalist ally against Britain. Trotsky, with astonishing clarity considering the paucity of information at his disposal, saw that Stalin was actually leading the whole Chinese revolution toward incalculable disaster. Although hardly a speech or an article by any Stalinist spokesman in this period failed to belabor Trotsky for his demand that the Chinese Communists be allowed to free themselves from their Kuomintang strait jacket, Trotsky was never allowed to express his views publicly. On April 3, 1927, Trotsky submitted for publication an article entitled "Class Relations in the Chinese Revolution." It was not printed. It was a warning against the rise of a "Chinese Pilsudski."* Trotsky wrote:

> If the Polish Pilsudski required three decades for his evolution, the Chinese Pilsudski will require a much shorter period for the transition from national revolution to national fascism. . . . The policy of a shackled Communist Party serving as a recruiting agent to bring the workers into the Kuomintang is preparation for the successful establishment of a Fascist dictatorship in China at that not very distant moment when the proletariat, despite everything, will be compelled to jump back from the Kuomintang. . . . To drive the workers and peasants into the political camp of the bourgeoisie and to keep the Communist Party a hostage within the Kuomintang is to carry on a policy equivalent objectively to betrayal. . . . The Kuomintang in its present form is the embodiment of an "unequal treaty" between the bourgeoisie and the proletariat. If the Chinese revolution as a whole demands the abolition of the unequal treaties with the imperialist Powers, then the Chinese proletariat must liquidate the unequal treaty with its own bourgeoisie.[10]

Despite suppression, Trotsky's views became known and were made the object of a violent campaign in the whole press. Its object was to reassure the Russians that all was well in China, that the revolution was marching with great strides toward the ultimate victory, that far from threatening to develop into a Chinese Pilsudski, Chiang Kai-shek was submitting to the revolutionary mass movement and could not do otherwise.

On March 16, *Pravda* published an article entitled "The Chinese Revolution and the Kuomintang" which declared that "now particularly, the military question is the main political question of the Chinese revolution." It spoke of Right-Wing elements who "with varying degrees of vacillation" were aiming for a deal with the imperialists but added reassuringly: "We have a strong Left wing in the Kuomintang which reflects the interests of the masses. . . . For quite understandable reasons, the imperialist press is employing all means to exaggerate the strength of the Right Kuomintang, who are alleged to have already turned the revolution on to 'moderate' lines and con-

* Pilsudski was the military dictator who crushed the revolution in Poland.

centrated power in their hands. The imperialist press has predicted the complete degeneration of the Kuomintang, a split, and paralysis of the Chinese revolution. . . ." It then proceeded to attack the Trotskyist Opposition for demanding immediate withdrawal of the Communists from the Kuomintang: "They see the Right fraction of the Kuomintang but they do not see its kernel and they do not see the masses. . . . Even the Right circles in the Kuomintang, government, and the army are forced to yield to the pressure of the revolutionary masses. In this regard the declaration of Chiang Kai-shek . . . is a very important document. [This refers to his pledge of discipline.] Chiang Kai-shek is compelled . . . to swear his devotion . . . to submit to the leadership. . . . The plan which the extreme Right Wing of the Kuomintang had hoped to carry out and which the imperialist bourgeoisie regarded as its trump card . . . has failed. Now even the American capitalist press has been compelled to recognize the failure of the Right-wing plot."[11]

Blandest statement of all was made by Stalin himself, who rose on April 5 before a meeting of three thousand functionaries in the Hall of Columns in Moscow to answer Trotsky's criticisms:

Chiang Kai-shek is submitting to discipline. The Kuomintang is a bloc, a sort of revolutionary parliament, with the Right, the Left, and the Communists. Why make a coup d'état? Why drive away the Right when we have the majority and when the Right listens to us? The peasant needs a worn-out jade as long as she is necessary. He does not drive her away. So it is with us. When the Right is of no more use to us, we will drive it away. At present, we need the Right. It has capable people, who still direct the army and lead it against the imperialists. Chiang Kai-shek has perhaps no sympathy for the revolution but he is leading the army and cannot do otherwise than lead it against the imperialists. Besides this, the people of the Right have relations with the generals of Chang Tso-lin and understand very well how to demoralize them and to induce them to pass over to the side of the revolution, bag and baggage, without striking a blow. Also, they have connections with the rich merchants and can raise money from them. So they have to be utilized to the end, squeezed out like a lemon, and then flung away.[12]

A few days earlier, Stalin had told a meeting of young Communists:

It must be said that until now they [the imperialists] have secured one result: the deepening of the hatred of the Chinese for imperialism, the cohesion of the forces of the Kuomintang, and a new swing to the left of the revolutionary movement in China. No one can doubt right now the

imperialists have achieved the exact opposite of what they wanted. . . .
It is said, not without truth, that the gods strike blind those whom they
would annihilate.[13]

Blindness and annihilation were, indeed, on the order of the day,
but not in the manner that Stalin calculated. The blow was about to
fall on the Shanghai workers and they were deprived not only of
advance knowledge but of the means to defend themselves. According to T. Mandalyan, one of the Comintern representatives in Shanghai, the precise instructions given in this fatal week to the Chinese
Communists were the following:

On March 31, when the preparations of the bourgeoisie for the overturn became apparent, the E.C.C.I. gave the following directive: Arouse
the masses against this overturn now being prepared and conduct a campaign against the Right. Open struggle is not to be launched at this time
(in view of the very unfavorable change in the relationship of forces).
Arms must not be given up but in any extremity, they must be hidden.

Ch'ên Tu-hsiu's account of these events says: "The International
telegraphed us to hide or bury all the weapons of the workers to avoid
military conflict between the workers and Chiang Kai-shek."

The fact itself was confirmed a few weeks after the events by the
second highest possible authority, Bukharin, who in a defense of his
policies wrote: "Was it not better to hide the arms, not to accept
battle, and thus not permit oneself to be disarmed?"[14]

These instructions amounted to an invitation to the Chinese Communists in Shanghai to put their heads docilely on the executioner's
block. If they were not to mobilize for "open," i.e., armed, struggle
against Chiang Kai-shek, obviously they had to do everything in their
power to propitiate him. The "campaign against the Right" obviously
could not mean a campaign against Chiang himself, whose fidelity
was being proclaimed by the highest spokesmen of the Comintern.
It could only subside into angry whimpers against the politicians and
generals and bankers in Chiang's entourage. The order not to give
battle, to hide or bury all arms, meant that if Chiang did not choose
to be propitiated he was free to act and that the workers of Shanghai
were completely at his mercy. "The Kuomintang," said the leading
periodical of the Comintern in March, "is suffering from a lack of
revolutionary worker and peasant blood. The Communist Party must
infuse such blood and thereby radically change the situation."[15] This
was, in Trotsky's phrase, "an ominous play of words," for the trans-

fusion was now at hand. Only it was to come in a manner least expected by the strategists in the Kremlin.

It has been necessary to go at this length into the Comintern estimate of the situation in Shanghai in March–April 1927, because after a few halfhearted attempts to defend the policies actually pursued, the legend was before long to be created and to persevere in all the literature of the Communist International that responsibility for the Shanghai debacle rested wholly upon the Chinese Communist leaders, notably Ch'ên Tu-hsiu, who were to be accused of stubbornly rejecting instructions they received from Moscow. The record plainly shows, however, that the instructions received made the debacle absolutely inevitable and that the Chinese Communists, by scrupulously carrying out the instructions, hopelessly disarmed the Shanghai workers in the face of the impending blow.

All rumors of a threatening coup were met in Shanghai, as abroad, with indignant denials. "How can the Shanghai workers clash with the army, the same army which they have only to welcome and respect?" asked the General Labor Union in a public statement. "Rumors are being disseminated to the effect that there is a possibility of a breach between the Nationalist army and the laboring classes. . . . Needless to say, these rumors are groundless and the public is requested not to believe them."[16] Open predictions in the daily press that an attack on the workers was forthcoming were denounced as "machinations of the enemy to sow discord." The Communist organizations appealed to Chiang Kai-shek to suppress the guilty newspapers for publishing news "prejudicial to the united front." In accord with the Moscow instructions to "conduct a campaign against the Right," flaming denunciations of "reactionaries" were issued almost daily. On April 4, the General Labor Union even publicly threatened a general strike if any action was taken by the "reactionaries" against the armed pickets and the workers. But Chiang's name was never mentioned in connection with these threats and often the term "reactionaries" was specified to mean only the Western Hills group and Kuomintang Right-Wing politicians like Wu Chih-hui and Chang Ching-chiang. The fact that Chiang Kai-shek had openly associated himself with these men was ignored, or concealed, or worried over in the privacy of Communist headquarters.

Every effort was made to propitiate Chiang. After his arrival, the Communists even prepared a reception and banquet in his honor, but neither Chiang nor his staff showed up. The Communists accepted the insult meekly. They joyfully greeted every gesture that could be interpreted as being conciliatory. Chiang's telegram of April 3 endorsing the leadership of Wang Ching-wei brought forth a flood of congratulatory messages from all the Communist organizations. They hailed it as a virtual settlement of all disputed issues and expressed pious hopes that henceforth all would be well. Since Chiang had apparently agreed and "submitted" to Wang Ching-wei's leadership, the Communists hastened to do the same. Discussions between Wang and Ch'ên Tu-hsiu, the Communist leader, produced a joint statement issued on April 4. Its salient passages:

The Chinese Communist Party resolutely recognizes that the Kuomintang and its principles are necessary to the Chinese revolution. Only those who are unwilling to see the Chinese revolution advance could advocate the overthrow of the Kuomintang. No matter how misguided it is, the Chinese Communist Party could never advocate the overthrow of its ally, the Kuomintang, to please our imperialist and militarist enemies. . . .

Now the national revolution has reached the stronghold of the imperialists, Shanghai. This has aroused all the counter-revolutionaries, here and abroad, who are fabricating all sorts of rumors designed to create tension and sow discord between our two parties. Some say the Communists will organize a workers' government, will rush into the foreign concessions in order to embarrass the Northern Expeditionary Army, will overthrow the Kuomintang power. Others say the Kuomintang leaders will expel the Communist Party, will suppress the labor unions and the pickets. It is not clear whence come such rumors. The resolutions of the recent plenary session of the Central Executive Committee of the Kuomintang demonstrated to the whole world that such things as the expulsion of the Communist Party and the labor unions can never take place. The Shanghai military authorities have announced that they will obey the central government. Although there are dissensions and misunderstandings, none of them is insoluble. The Communist Party is not the last in loving peace and order. It agrees with the policy of the Nationalist government against taking back the Shanghai settlements by force. The Shanghai General Labor Union has also issued a manifesto against any independent action in rushing into the concessions. The Communist Party also agrees with the policy of collaboration of all classes in the municipal government. These are hard facts and leave no room for fabricated rumors. . . . We must stand on the common ground of the revolution, give up mutual suspicions, reject rumor-mongering, and respect each other. . . . Then all will be well with both parties and with the Chinese revolution.[17]

This policy of total subservience of the Communist leadership was guaranteeing the victory of the gathering counterrevolution. But it stood in such apparent contradiction to the immense and growing power of the mass organizations that right up to the last moment that victory seemed hardly assured. The insurrection had enormously heightened the authority of the Communists. The workers were streaming into the unions. "At the rate agitators are enrolling new members," said the *North China Herald* on April 9, "upwards of half a million laborers will be subject to the strike demands of the General Labor Union in the course of the next few weeks."[18] It was not out of mere hysteria that the foreign and Chinese capitalists of Shanghai anticipated imminent expropriation at the hands of the workers. Warships and troops might protect the foreigners' settlements but they could not make the wheels go around. They also knew that Chiang Kai-shek's forces were limited, that he could be isolated from his own army, that with a twist of pressure the whole counterrevolutionary plot could be smothered. They did not misjudge the actual situation. It justified their fears and even their hysteria. What they did misjudge was the caliber of the Communist leadership and its real intentions. Nothing was further from its mind than an attempt to assert its authority or to compete for power. "The keys to Shanghai were handed over by the victorious workers to the Canton army," exclaimed *Pravda* on March 22. "In this fact is expressed the great heroic act of the Shanghai proletariat."[19] This "heroic act" was one of unwitting surrender.

In the Provisional Municipal Government inaugurated under Communist auspices on March 29, a majority was voluntarily assigned to representatives of the Shanghai bourgeoisie. Only five of the nineteen government members were nominated by the trade-unions. Chiang Kai-shek, who was putting his own men into key administrative posts and quickly setting up the framework of his own civil authority, refused to recognize the Provisional Government, declaring through his spokesman, Wu Chih-hui, that it was "contrary to the party system of government." As soon as Chiang's attitude became known, the bourgeois representatives one after another declined the proffered posts. Yü Ya-ch'ing, banker and compradore, ignored the appointment. K. P. Ch'ên, general manager of the Shanghai Commercial and Savings Bank, formally declined. Wang Hsiao-lai, of the General Chamber of Commerce, who had been named chairman after he had publicly indicated his willingness to serve, now said that since he was a silk merchant and spring was his busy season, he would prefer to cede his position to a wiser man. Wang Han-liang, another prominent merchant, announced that with the occupation of Shanghai all his past efforts were amply rewarded and he desired no further honors. Soumei Chêng, a woman lawyer and judge closely connected with the upper and under worlds of Shanghai, said she was "too busily engaged in her official duties." Francis Zia, managing editor of the *China Courier*, pleaded illness. All the other nominees made similar excuses.

Thus boycotted, the union delegates to the municipal government pleaded helplessness. The *Sin Wen Pao* on April 4 reported:

At the fifth delegates' conference on April 3, the chief secretary of the Municipal Government [Lin Chün, a Communist] said that . . . petitions from the masses calling upon them to take over local institutions, or reporting local acts in taking over institutions, or urging the government to take measures against the gentry, or to settle school disputes, had been pouring into the government offices like snowflakes. But the members of the government, owing to the fact that they have received a letter from Commander-in-chief Chiang asking them to postpone doing anything, did not actively conduct their work.

It did not occur to the participating members of the government to go ahead on their own initiative in response to the many popular demands made upon it. Instead they addressed a letter to Chiang Kai-shek in the style of a *ch'êng wên,* the form used in the old mandarinate for petitions from lower to higher orders, respectfully asking him to hand over the municipal institutions in which he had already placed his own appointees and asking his benevolent support for the municipal administration elected by the mass organizations. While waiting for his reply, the government attempted no measures in behalf of the people. It did issue a manifesto with a program of demands that it promised to satisfy, but no steps were taken to implement them. The Provisional Government's only other activity in its brief existence was the passage of resolutions welcoming Chiang Kai-shek and the Nationalist army, welcoming Wang Ching-wei when he returned, congratulating Chiang for his promise to obey party discipline, and greeting with particular joy the Ch'ên-Wang manifesto. Supported by hundreds of thousands of trade-unionists, the government provided no concrete social program behind which they could rally. With the Kuomintang soldiery in Shanghai wavering and unclear on what was happening, it made no attempt to approach them or to encourage fraternization between workers and soldiers. Such acts might have saved the day for them in Shanghai. But it would have jeopardized the "national united front." In a few localities, as in Pootung, the workers asserted themselves more aggressively, taking over local organs of power, setting up their own courts, and empowering the pickets to perform police functions. These acts were never supported by the Provisional Government but were on the contrary deplored and criticized.

The General Labor Union, which directly controlled the swelling mass organizations, was likewise doing its best to avoid "open" struggle. It tried to limit the strike movement and to keep the worker-pickets within strict bounds. On April 4, it issued a set of new strike regulations forbidding any spontaneous walkouts. According to the new procedure laid down, demands "were not to be too exacting" and were first to be negotiated directly by the workers themselves. If these initial parleys failed, the matter was to be referred to the next higher union body, the district committee, and finally to the union center, which would negotiate with the employers. As these new orders took effect, the employers were already hitting back at the labor movement by ordering lockouts. The General Labor Union's response was to adopt a resolution meekly asking the Provisional Municipal Government to ask employers "not to close their factories without good grounds or on simple pretexts."[20]

Strict orders were issued forbidding pickets from making arrests. Their duties were to be confined to "the maintenance of order in co-operation with the army and the police." Heavy penalties were imposed for infractions. The union leaders displayed an attitude of servility toward the military commanders. One evening, for example, some members of the family of General Liu Chih, one of the more notorious Right-Wingers in Chiang's entourage, were arrested on suspicion by a picket patrol. Next morning the G.L.U. overflowingly apologized. General Liu was asked to "pardon" the four pickets whose "actions were so reckless and thoughtless as to encroach upon other comrades and to disturb the division commander's family. We have disarmed them, expelled them from membership in the picket corps, and will punish them severely."[21]

The same meekness was shown in relation to the foreign interests in Shanghai, barricaded behind their bristling Settlement barriers and at times employing force directly against Chinese workers and students. American participation in the bombardment of Nanking on

March 24 had come as a shock to many Chinese who still believed that the official United States attitude toward Chinese nationalism was benevolent. Again, on April 7, in Shanghai, an American military patrol broke up a demonstration outside the Oriental Spinning and Weaving Company. On the night of April 8, a detachment of two hundred British soldiers raided the Great China University, wounded eight students, searched the dormitories, seized students' property, and made a number of arrests. Japanese marines were repeatedly using bayonets on workers in the Japanese mills in the Settlement. The Communists at this juncture, however, did not intensify their anti-imperialist propaganda or concentrate on severing every nerve that linked the Settlement to the rest of the country. They confined themselves to making reassuring promises that there would be no repetition in Shanghai of the Hankow and Kiukiang events. In an advertisement inserted in all Shanghai newspapers on April 2, it was stated that "in the question of the rendition of the concessions, the General Labor Union, jointly with the army and the merchants, will back the foreign policy of the National government. It will not undertake to rush into the concessions. In the question of law and order, it will co-operate with the army and the merchants to preserve it."[22] In a declaration on March 30, it had already promised it would "await patiently the outcome and a peaceful settlement of forthcoming negotiations in which the National government and the foreign Powers will enter." It deplored the fact that "residents of the International Settlement are considerably agitated" by rumors of an attack. "While it is our desire to expand our propaganda movement, we desire to remove all unnecessary alarm. The Shanghai General Labor Union strongly supports the movement for the rendition of the Settlement but the responsibility for this is vested in the proper authorities of the National government. . . . Our action with regard to diplomatic affairs will be similar to and will be guided by those who are higher than we, namely the National government."[23]

In this way, step by step, the Communist party in Shanghai abdicated its opportunities. Government power in the city could be exercised only in co-operation with the bourgeois leaders or not at all. "Law and order" were surrendered to "the army and the merchants." The fight against imperialism was to be guided only "by those who are higher than we" and any settlement made was unquestioningly accepted in advance. Finally, if anyone suggested that preparations were under way to smash the Communist party and the unions, he was guilty of circulating counterrevolutionary rumors designed to disturb the "national united front." Writing more than a year later, P. Mif, the Comintern specialist on China, said: "The Shanghai comrades still lived hypnotized by the old line and could not imagine a revolutionary government without the participation of the bourgeoisie. . . . The bourgeoisie, again according to the old tradition, was given the leading role."[24] Unfortunately, the "old line" and the "old tradition" were at the time in Shanghai the only line and the only tradition. The Chinese Communists were simply carrying out, to the best of their ability, the instructions they had received from Moscow. Stalin had said he was squeezing lemons, that the lemons gave him connections with Chang Tso-lin and the rich merchants which had not yet been fully utilized. Chiang Kai-shek did have these connections but was employing them not in behalf of the revolution but to stage a counterrevolution. Stalin had said that Chiang and the other "capable people" in command of the army could not "do otherwise than lead it against the imperialists" and that to avoid any "open" struggle it was necessary for the Shanghai workers to hide or bury their arms. This was the "old tradition" that was guiding the Shanghai Communists when almost at the zero hour they were presented with an opportunity to assume full command of the whole First Division, which was Chiang Kai-shek's own garrison force in the city.

The First Division included some of the most seasoned and most politically minded troops in the Kuomintang army. These were the men who had chafed at Pai Ch'ung-hsi's restraining orders on March 21 and had finally marched into the city the next day in defiance of his orders. One of Chiang Kai-shek's first objects after his own arrival was to remove these forces from the scene and during his first week in Shanghai he issued orders for them to leave. General Hsüeh Yüeh, the division commander, was a man who was either at the time infected with the revolutionary spirit or with personal ambitions of his own, or both. He felt acutely the pressure of his own ranks and he also saw the chance to play a role that would completely transform the situation in Shanghai and in the revolution generally. With Chiang's orders in his hands, he went to the headquarters of the Central Committee of the Communist party.

The record of this story exists in obscure bits and pieces scattered through contemporary documents and subsequent reports. In its essentials, it is confirmed by a variety of sources.[25] They all agree substantially on the following details. Hsüeh Yüeh said to the Central Committee: "I have been ordered by Chiang Kai-shek to leave Shanghai. What shall I do?" He offered to arrest and imprison Chiang on charges of plotting counterrevolution. Ch'ên Tu-hsiu, the other members of the Committee, the Comintern representative Voitinsky, and a whole assorted group of Comintern advisers were all apparently present or else soon apprised of this startling offer. They hesitated, then decided to temporize. According to an account published later in Moscow: "To this proposition for a decisive attack on Chiang Kai-shek no clear answer was given. They advised Hsüeh Yüeh to sabotage, to pretend illness." But Chiang Kai-shek accepted no delay. "The moment arrived when it was impossible to put it off. Hsüeh Yüeh received an ultimatum and when he addressed himself again to the party, there was no other way out: either take up arms against Chiang (he proposed) with the support and under the leadership of the Communist Party, or obey, i.e., take out of Shanghai a large, and from the revolutionary point of view, precious force."

The Communists and the Comintern representatives in the end did not dare accept this bold offer. Instead they addressed respectful petitions to Chiang Kai-shek and his chief of staff, Pai Ch'ung-hsi, humbly requesting them to keep the First Division in the city. To the workers they repeated their assurances that all was well. (There were men, if André Malraux is to be believed, who desperately wanted to keep these troops and to organize resistance. His central character, the Communist Kyo, wanted to fight, "but the official speeches of the Chinese Communist Party, the whole propaganda of union with the Kuomintang, were paralyzing him."[26]) The decisive moment passed. Hsüeh Yüeh's troops were moved, first out of Chapei, the working-class district, then up the railroad out of Shanghai altogether. The soldiers, uncomprehending but still confident in the Communist leadership, moved out without protest.* They were replaced by the troops of Pai Ch'ung-hsi, Liu Chih, and Chou Fêng-ch'i, the recent renegade from the Northern militarist ranks, who saw to it that the new garrison in working-class Chapei was made up of men impervious to popular contacts and revolutionary appeals.

* Hsüeh Yüeh later became one of Chiang's most faithful lieutenants and led troops in the bitter campaigns against the Communist armies in Central China in 1930–34 and later against the Japanese. He was Chiang's last governor in Kwangtung in 1949.

At the same time—it was the first week in April—piecemeal attacks began to take place on local Communist centers. Scores were arrested and several picket patrols were disarmed. The city Kuomintang headquarters, staffed by Communists, was closed down. Protesting these acts, the staff of the Political Department of the army met on April 5 and adopted a resolution asking Chiang to prove his fidelity to the Kuomintang by releasing the arrested men. In reply the next day a company of Chiang's soldiers descended on the office of the Political Department and arrested nineteen men. An official communiqué took pains to announce that these arrests did not signify any ill will toward the Communists. "The people in control of the Political Department," it said, "are secretly fostering reactionary forces and are hindering the development of the Northern Expedition."[27]

That same day soldiers of the Northern war lord Chang Tso-lin, acting with the permission of the Diplomatic Corps, raided the Russian Embassy in Peking, arresting twenty Chinese found there, among them Li Ta-chao, a founder of the Communist party.* Chiang hastened to wire the Soviet Embassy expressing his "indignation" and "regret." He called the raid an "unprecedented outrage" and begged to extend to the Soviet chargé d'affaires his "sincerest condolences."[28] In Moscow Chiang's telegram was promptly cited as further evidence that he could not possibly be planning a coup against the workers.[29] But when in Shanghai the foreign authorities followed the example of the Peking raid by throwing a cordon around the Russian Consulate General and searching all who came and went, Chiang remained discreetly silent. "It is suspected in foreign circles," reported an American correspondent, "that Chiang Kai-shek's faction may not be averse to the curtailment of the Soviet consulate's liberties."[30]

At one of the ceremonies arranged for Chiang by the Communists just after his arrival, Chiang had actually presented a banner to the pickets inscribed "Common Action." The kind of common action he had in mind was disclosed on April 6, however, when orders were issued in Lunghua: "All armed pickets of the labor unions are to be under the command of the headquarters of the commander-in-chief, otherwise they will be regarded as conspiratorial organizations and will not be permitted to exist."[31]

---

* Li Ta-chao and the nineteen others arrested were later executed by strangulation.

The time for gestures and concealment was coming to an end. While congratulatory telegrams greeting the Ch'ên-Wang manifesto were still coming in from Communist and Left-Wing organizations, Wu Chih-hui, Chiang's spokesman, addressed a meeting of the Right-Wing group in Shanghai where he said: "The Ch'ên-Wang manifesto was simply diplomatic friendly talk between leaders of the two parties. It has no bearing on the policies of the party at all."[32] To replace the Provisional government, by now almost extinct, Chiang appointed a Provisional Committee, headed by Wu Chih-hui, to take over all organs of civil administration. Almost everything else was in readiness. The week before he had sent a force of his own most trusted troops up the line to Nanking to clear that city of units hostile to him. He made a quick trip there himself to inspect the results. That operation was completed by April 9. It was done painlessly, with most of the offending troops submitting to disarmament without resistance. They had no idea of what was going on.[33] Now in Shanghai the three weeks of talk, of maneuvers and gestures, of negotiations and cunning compromises and pronouncements were drawing to a close.

The approach of zero hour could almost be plotted graphically in the half-page advertisements run daily in the Chinese press by the political department of Pai Ch'ung-hsi's headquarters. In huge black characters during the first few days of the Nationalist occupation, these advertisements repeated the familiar slogans: "Down with imperialism! Exterminate the feudal forces!" But beginning April 7 their tone changed, first subtly, soon with brutal directness.

April 7: "Down with the reactionaries who are wrecking the National revolution!"

April 8: "Whosoever opposes the Three People's Principles is opposing the revolution!"

April 9: "Down with the disruptive elements in the rear!"

April 10: "For the new Shanghai Provisional Committee!"

April 11: "We the soldiers are fighting at the front at heavy cost. Honest workers in the rear will not strike on any pretext whatever or cause any disorder."

On April 12 the advertisement read: "Consolidate the great national united front of peasants, workers, students, merchants, and soldiers, to strive for the realization of the San Min Principles!" On that morning, just before dawn, the blow fell. The sound of machine-gun and rifle fire crackled over the awakening city. The workers rose to discover the unthinkable, the impossible, coming to pass. Where they could, they sprang to the arms they still had to defend themselves. But they could well have asked, hurrying along with Malraux's Kyo some hours before that dawn: "How would they fight, one against ten, in disagreement with the instructions of the Chinese Communist party, against an army that would oppose them with its corps of bourgeois volunteers armed with European weapons and having the advantage of attack?"[34]

Chapter 11

THE COUP OF APRIL 12, 1927

AT FOUR O'CLOCK on the morning of April 12 a bugle blast sounded from Chiang Kai-shek's headquarters at the Foreign Ministry Bureau on Route Ghisi. A Chinese gunboat at anchor off Nantao sounded a blast on its siren. "Simultaneously," reported the *China Press*, "the machine guns broke loose in a steady roll."[1] The attack was launched at the fixed hour in Chapei, Nantao, the Western District, in Woosung, Pootung, and Jessfield. It came as no surprise to anyone except the workers, for as the local British newspaper revealed: "All the authorities concerned, Chinese and foreign, after midnight were made secretly cognizant of the events which were to take place in the morning."[2]

Members of Shanghai's underworld gangs "had feverishly worked through the night organizing secret parties to appear at dawn as though from nowhere." They wore white armbands bearing the Chinese character *kung* (labor). The *North China Daily News* called them "armed Kuomintang laborers." The Shanghai Municipal Police Report referred to "merchants' volunteers." The *China Press* contented itself with "Nationalist troops." More bluntly, George Sokolsky reported: "Arrangements were made with the Green and Red Societies, so that one morning they, as 'white' laborers, fell upon and shot down the Communists."[3] They did not appear from "nowhere," but at the given signal, as the *Shun Pao* and other newspapers frankly stated, they "rushed out of the concessions" and in the adjoining Chinese areas made contact with picked detachments of Pai Ch'ung-hsi's troops. Together or separately, according to detailed, prearranged plans, they attacked the headquarters of working-class organizations scattered throughout the city. In most cases, as at the Foochow Guild in Nantao and the police station in Pootung, the objectives were won after sharp but brief battles. Their quarters once occupied, the pickets and their supporters were given short, brutal shrift. Their arms were seized and "even their clothes and shoes ripped from them."[4] Every man who resisted was shot down where he

175

stood. The remainder were lashed together and marched out to be executed either in the streets or at Lunghua.

In a few places the attackers tried guile. A band of some sixty gangsters began firing on the Huchow Guild in Chapei at about 4:30 A.M. This building housed the headquarters of the General Labor Union and was defended by several scores of pickets. The surprised guards shouted out to ask the attackers what union they belonged to; "To the Northern Expeditionary Army," was the reply, and the attack continued and the pickets returned the fire. Twenty minutes later, a company of soldiers, headed by an officer named Hsin Ting-yu, appeared on the street. Hsin shouted orders to cease firing. "Do not fire at us!" he cried out to the pickets. "We've come to help you disarm these men." The shooting stopped. He proposed from the street that both sides hand over their arms. Ostentatiously he proceeded to disarm some of the gangsters and, under the suspicious eyes of the pickets, even bound some of them in ropes. At that, the gates were opened. Hsin and his men were invited in. The Communist who tells this story, a participant in the scene, adds that tea and cigarettes were brought out for the guests. The officer told Ku Chên-chung, commander of the pickets, that he had been appointed to conduct "armed mediation" under the new martial law regulations. He asked Ku to accompany him to headquarters. The picket leader complied and with six of his men left the premises with Hsin. A few steps down the street Hsin turned to Ku: "We've disarmed those guerrillas. We've got to disarm your squads too," he said. Ku stopped short. "You can't," he said. "Those men are gangsters. Our pickets are revolutionary workers. Why disarm us?" Hsin did not answer. Instead his men closed in on the group. Ku and the six men were disarmed and brought back to the G.L.U. headquarters. A few minutes later a force of some three hundred gangsters who had been waiting near by rushed into the building and while the soldiers stood by, they savagely attacked the astounded pickets. In the melee, Ku and his vice-commander, a young man named Chou Ên-lai, escaped.* The

---

* Ku remained with the Communist party until 1931 when he deserted it for the Kuomintang. He became one of the most rabid killers, and eventually the chief, of Chiang Kai-shek's anti-Communist terror organization. Chou Ên-lai emerged as one of the leaders of the later Communist movement in the peasant hinterland. Ku and Chou were reunited in Chiang's camp during the second "united front" period early in the war against Japan. Chou Ên-lai negotiated the rescue of Chiang Kai-shek when he was "kidnaped" in Sian in 1936. Chou later conducted most of the futile negotiations that preceded the renewal of civil war in 1945. He became premier and foreign minister of the Communist government established at Peking in 1949.

Huchow Guild had meanwhile fallen. Similar methods achieved similar results at most of the other workers' centers in the city.[5]

By midmorning the last workers' stronghold was the big building of the Commercial Press, where some four hundred pickets continued to hold out against overwhelmingly superior forces. When the gangsters attacked and the soldiers came on the scene with their demand for a cessation of hostilities, the defenders inside the building answered with a renewed fusillade. The soldiers thereupon simply joined in the attack and all further attempts at deception were discarded. Siege was laid to the building from all sides. Paoshan Road dinned with gunfire for several hours. The defenders fought on until most of them were dead and the rest without ammunition. It was nearly noon before the attackers gingerly stepped inside the bullet-riddled building.

"What action the soldiers took beyond disarming the Communists is naturally not known. It is not going to be advertised by the Chinese authorities," complacently reported the *North China Daily News*. Early foreign reports minimized the casualties of that first day, but the British-controlled Shanghai Municipal Police later came nearer the actual toll when it reported that nearly four hundred workers were killed in the day's operations. Other reports put the death toll at close to seven hundred.[6] Among the missing was Wang Shao-hua, chairman of the General Labor Union. It was not discovered until some time later that he had been kidnaped by gangsters the previous afternoon and carried off to military headquarters at Lunghua, where he was executed. At four o'clock, the military authorities announced they had the situation "in hand."

Ch'ên Ch'ün, secretary and aide to the gang leader Chang Hsiaolin and newly appointed Political Director of Pai Ch'ung-hsi's army* announced plans for the immediate "reorganization" of the General Labor Union along the lines already made familiar in Kiangsi and Chekiang in March. "The policy of the government is to have labor working in harmony with the revolutionary army and the government," he said. "But when labor becomes a disturbing element, when it arrogates to itself tasks which are detrimental to the movement and disturbing to law and order, labor must be disciplined." His newly

---

* Ch'ên Ch'ün and Yang Hu personally commanded Chiang Kai-shek's execution squads. They later made trips to Ningpo and other cities to complete the "reorganization" of the labor movement by executing hundreds of people. A saying became current: "In Shanghai wolves and tigers [hu] stalk abroad in packs [ch'ün]."

created "Workers Trade Alliance" at once took over the occupied union quarters and introduced itself as follows:

The Shanghai General Labor Union was manipulated by a few Communist scoundrels. They bullied and deceived the workers and made them sacrifice themselves. Workers who have lost their jobs owing to strikes are daily increasing in number. The General Labor Union wanted to starve and ruin the workers to create opportunities for committing crimes against society and the state. The aim of the Workers' Trade Alliance is to realize the Three People's Principles of the Kuomintang, to secure for the workers their most concrete interests, to aid in China's reconstruction so as to win freedom and equality in the family of nations. . . . Now the pickets of the G.L.U. have all been disarmed. They can no longer oppress our workers. Now our workers are completely free. It is hoped that the workers will send delegations to get in touch with us and wait patiently for a settlement.[7]

The General Labor Union and other Communist organizations were still in existence. They were still addressing appeals and petitions to Chiang Kai-shek. The Shanghai *tangpu*, the local Kuomintang branch, long since driven from its headquarters, issued an exhortation: "Our working masses must not shrink from reorganizing their ranks. . . . The military authorities should also more properly protect the workers' organizations and return their arms to them." The defunct Provisional Government still existed in name and it addressed a letter to General Pai: "The workers' pickets made heavy sacrifices to aid the Northern Expeditionary Army and to expel the Chihli-Shantung bandit troops. . . . After the capture of Shanghai, they cooperated with the army and the police to maintain order and they have rendered no little service to the city. Therefore even Commander-in-chief Chiang highly approved of them and presented them with a banner inscribed 'Common Action'. . . ." The letter concluded with a respectful request for the return of the arms taken from the pickets.[8] That night Communist speakers addressed crowds in the streets of Chapei. They complained that the workers "had consistently assisted the Nationalist government for years and had only recently captured Shanghai for them. . . . They had always maintained discipline . . . and had not only observed the law but assisted in upholding it." Resolutions were adopted at these street meetings urging "that the authorities be again requested to give back the arms taken."[9]

It was at this moment, with the battle lost and the moment for

action irretrievably buried in the blunders of the past, that the General
Labor Union called, on April 13, for a general strike of protest. "We
shall fight to the death . . . with the national revolution as our banner. It is glorious to die in such a way." The workers had obediently
followed the Communists to the slaughter but were now asked "to
be prepared to sacrifice all, to renew the war against the forces of
the Right Wing."[10] They might well have asked: what war against
the Right Wing? They had been told all would be well, that they
should retreat, bury their arms, and avert "open" struggle. Now the
open struggle had been carried to them by the enemy and they were
helplessly caught unprepared. Nevertheless, the strike call of the General Labor Union produced striking evidence of the strength and
discipline of these workers. Some 100,000 of them quit work.[11] The
waterfront was tied up. The tramway workers went out. Most of
the textile workers in the Western District and about half the workers
in the Yangtzepoo mills answered the call.

At noon on April 13, a great crowd of workers gathered in a mass
meeting on Chinyuen Road in Chapei. Resolutions were passed demanding the return of the seized arms, punishment of the union-
wreckers, and protection for the General Labor Union. A petition
was drafted and a parade formed to march to Second Division headquarters to present it to General Chou Fêng-ch'i. Women and children
were in the parade. None of the men had arms. They swung into
Paoshan Road under a pouring rain. As they came abreast of San
Tê Terrace, a short distance from the military headquarters, machine
gunners waiting for them there opened fire without warning. Lead
spouted into the thick crowd from both sides of the street. Men,
women, and children dropped screaming into the mud. The crowd
broke up into mad flight. The soldiers kept firing into the backs of
the fleeing demonstrators. From adjacent alleyways the attackers
fell upon the crowd, swinging bayonets, rifle butts, and broadswords.
They pursued the fleeing marchers right into the houses in Yi Ping
Terrace, Paotung and Tientungan Roads—streets thickly clustered
with working-class tenements. Men and women were dragged out.
"Those who resisted were either killed on the spot or wounded. . . .
Many of the wounded were left to die where they dropped. It was
an hour before the street was cleared," reported one eyewitness. Another a little later saw bodies being carted off in vans. He counted
eight truckloads filled with corpses. More than three hundred were

killed and a much larger number wounded.* Many of the wounded were "carried away and buried with the dead."[12]

Foreign forces co-operated directly in the reign of terror now instituted throughout the city. The contribution of the French authorities was especially notable, since the head of the French Concession detective force was Pockmarked Huang Ching-yung himself, leading member of the triumvirate ruling the underworld gangs of the city. In the International Settlement, foreign municipal police and detachments of the British and Japanese defense forces carried out a series of raids beginning on the night of April 11, several of them in Chinese territory adjacent to the so-called extraconcessional North Szechuen Road. These measures were taken "with permission from the Nationalist military authorities at Lunghua."[13] On the night of April 14 British armored cars joined squads of Japanese marines in minor raids in the extraconcessional area during which machine guns were several times brought into play. Everywhere house-to-house searches were carried out and wholesale arrests made.[14] Prisoners were handed over in batches to the military headquarters at Lunghua. There they faced military courts set up under martial law regulations issued by General Chiang Kai-shek. Run by officers expressly empowered to "use their own discretion" in the event of any "emergency," these courts became the chief instrument for a system of official terrorism which in the following months claimed the lives of thousands.

This reign of terror, directed above all at the workers and the Communists, likewise for a time crossed the bounds of property which it was instituted to keep inviolate. The Chinese bankers and merchants had found it necessary to call in Chiang Kai-shek and the gangsters against the workers. Now they were forced to submit themselves to the predatory raids of their own rescuers. Like the French bourgeoisie, which in 1852 "brought the slum proletariat into

* The workers of Shanghai were shot down as "reactionaries." A manifesto issued by Chiang Kai-shek accused them of "conspiring with the Northern militarists to ruin the cause of the revolution." There is nothing ever new, it would seem, in the methods of counterrevolution. The Jacobins were guillotined as "agents of Pitt." Lenin and Trotsky in 1917 were "agents of the Kaiser." In Stalin's Russia, dissenters became successively "agents of England," "agents of Hitler," "agents of the Mikado," or "agents of Wall Street," according to the shifting requirements of Soviet foreign policy. In Spain in 1936–39, Stalin's party shot down anti-Stalinist revolutionists as "agents of Franco." The "agents of Chang Tso-lin" slaughtered by Chiang Kai-shek's executioners and the Mauser-wielding squads of the Green Gang in Shanghai were members of a great historic company.

power, the loafers and tatterdermalions headed by the chief of the Society of December the Tenth,"[15] the Chinese bourgeoisie in 1927 elevated over itself the scum and riffraff of the cities headed by the chiefs of the Green Gang and the man who was sometimes called the Ningpo Napoleon, Chiang Kai-shek. Like its French prototype, the Chinese bourgeoisie had now to pay heavily for professional services. It had, again in the peculiarly applicable words of Karl Marx, "glorified the sword; now it is to be ruled by the sword. . . . It subjected public meetings to police supervision; now its own drawing rooms are under police supervision. . . . It had transported the workers without trial; now the bourgeois are transported without trial . . . [and their] money bags are rifled. . . . The words of the bourgeoisie to the revolution were unceasingly those of St. Arsenius to the Christians: *Fuge, tace, quiesce*! The words of Bonaparte to the bourgeoisie are the same." Like Louis Napoleon, Chiang Kai-shek ordered the moneyed men of Shanghai to flee, be silent, and submit. More explicitly, he added: "Pay!"

The bankers, industrialists, compradores, and merchants had rallied to Chiang's banner on condition that he would free them of the Communists, of the rebellious workers, of strikes and insurrections. With a ruthlessness that should have satisfied the most exacting and worried capitalist, he acquitted himself of this task. He carried out, in the words of a British account, "such a cleanup of Communists as no northern general would have dared to do even in his own territory." But here came the hitch. This same account continued: "The anti-Communist campaign should have ended there and the people [*sic*] would have been happy. But every form of persecution was resorted to on the pretext of hunting Communists. Men were kidnapped and forced to make heavy contributions to military funds. . . . No reason or justice was evident . . . no courts of law were utilized. . . . Men possessing millions were held as Communists. . . . No one is safe, even at this moment, from the inquisition which has been established."[16]

"The plight of the Chinese merchant in and about Shanghai is pitiable," reported the correspondent of the *New York Times* on May 4. "At the mercy of General Chiang Kai-shek's dictatorship, the merchants do not know what the next day will bring, confiscations, compulsory loans, exile, or possible execution. . . . The military authorities have ordered the reorganization of the Chinese Chamber of

Commerce and other institutions with new directors, presumably satisfactory to Chiang Kai-shek and Pai Ch'ung-hsi, as they ordered the reorganization of the labor unions. . . . Outlawry against the better class of Chinese is rampant." When the raising of the $30,000,000 loan for the new Nanking government lagged, the merchants received "military advice to subscribe, with intimations that arrests may follow failure to do so. . . ."[17] Even Yung Chung-chin, well-known leading industrialist, was not exempt. Chiang asked him for a half-million dollars. When Yung tried to bargain, Chiang had him arrested forthwith. Yung reportedly bought himself out of prison with $250,000. Others had to pay more.[18]

It has been aptly said that Fascist or military dictators are like ferocious bodyguards who sit at the table of frightened employers and help themselves almost at will to the feast that is spread there. Chiang Kai-shek, like other militarists before him, appeared to be a brigand garbed in the authority of state power, but he remained, nevertheless, a hireling. His price was high but it was small compared to what he saved his employers by smashing the mass movement. The bankers and merchants rallied quickly enough to the government that Chiang now set up at Nanking. Within a few days after the Shanghai coup, similar blows were struck at Ningpo, Foochow, Amoy, Swatow, and Canton. In all these cities the turnover took place in circumstances that almost exactly reproduced those at Shanghai.

A delegation of Russian trade-unionists en route to Hankow arrived in Canton on April 14. They came in time to be witnesses of the raids on the trade-unions, mass arrests, and executions carried out at the orders of General Li Chi-shên, following the lead of Chiang Kai-shek. Li too, only a short time before, had been one of those listed in Stalin's directory of "revolutionary generals."* Trade-unionists fleeing from Canton brought to Hankow the belated message: "We regret to say that the cradle of the national revolution has become a stronghold of reaction."[19]

In Hankow the Left Kuomintang and the Communists were, up to the last hours and beyond, still engaged in the business of propi-

* In later years Li Chi-shên was alternately an ally and an opponent of Chiang Kai-shek. During the last years of the war against Japan he tried and failed to set up an opposition group of generals and politicians in Southwest China. Through the Democratic League he subsequently joined the Communist camp and when the Communist government was set up at Peking in 1949 he occupied a nominally high post as one of the "democratic" appendages of the Communist regime.

tiating Chiang Kai-shek. Wang Ching-wei had arrived there to tell his colleagues about the agreement with Chiang to hold a joint plenary session of the Kuomintang Central Executive Committee for the "peaceful" settlement of all disputes. News now came to Wuhan that Chiang was about to convene his own separate plenary session in Nanking. On April 13, the day after the Shanghai coup, the delegation of the Communist International in Hankow, now led by the Indian Communist, M. N. Roy, sent Chiang Kai-shek the following telegram:

The delegation of the Third International is now in China and has always been eager to visit you; but it could not be done because we have been visiting separately distant parts of the country. . . . Now comes news that you have decided to convene several members of the Central Committee and the Central Control Committee at Nanking. This act obviously violates your agreement with Wang Ching-wei that all questions of conflict inside the party would be placed before a plenary session of the Central Committee, which should be called at Wuhan and in which you would participate. Your convening a meeting of a few members of the Central Committee at this critical moment will naturally be interpreted by the enemies of the revolution as a rupture in the ranks of the Kuomintang. At this moment when international imperialism unites in an insolent attack upon the Chinese nationalist revolution, the unity of the revolutionary forces is a supreme necessity. . . . In view of the dangerous situation, we advise you to abandon the projected Nanking conference which will practically split the party. And the grave responsibility for breaking the nationalist front at this critical moment will rest on you. We advise you to stand on the agreement to place all contentions on inner party questions before a plenary session of the Central Committee. If you take this advice, we shall be glad to visit Nanking in order to discuss with you personally all outstanding questions. The Third International will lend all its services to help the formation of a united nationalist front of all revolutionary forces. Signed, for the delegation of the Third International, M. N. Roy, April 13, 1927.[20]

This remarkable communication was dispatched more than twenty-four hours after the beginning of Chiang's coup in Shanghai. This would seem to exclude the possibility that the news of what was happening in Shanghai had not yet reached Hankow. In any case, the Comintern representatives there were fully aware of the events in Kiangsi, the progressive attacks on the unions and other organizations from city to city along the Yangtze and, just before the Shanghai outbreak, in Hangchow. The telegram of April 13 makes it plain that the Comintern agents, Roy, Earl Browder, Jacques Doriot, and

Tom Mann, together with Borodin and the other master strategists, were ready to overlook these developments if Chiang would, even now, only accept their "advice." From Peking some days later, the well-informed Walter Duranty, who knew his Kremlin, wired to the *New York Times* his conviction that "the Moscow leaders will do their utmost to restore Kuomintang unity, even at the sacrifice of the more extreme Communists."[21] The plea of the Hankow Comintern agents, dispatched to the executioner even while the heads were rolling in Shanghai's streets, showed how far the Comintern was ready to go in sacrificing the interests of the Chinese revolution to the Kremlin's conviction that the only ally it could have in China was the Chinese ruling class. It showed how hopelessly the Kremlin had misunderstood and miscalculated the play of forces in China.

In Moscow first there was silence. Information passed around the Soviet capital and in the headquarters of the Comintern only in the form of rumors. News of the Shanghai events came like the blow of some utterly shattering catastrophe. It was, on the face of it, incredible. A full day passed before any statement was made. There is a total blank in the available record as to what went on in the Kremlin in those hours. Finally a brief announcement was made. "After persistently denying reports of serious discord between Chiang Kai-shek and the extremists of the Kuomintang," foreign correspondents were at last able to wire, "the Soviet authorities at Moscow this evening announced it was unfortunately true and deplored the fact that fighting occurred at Shanghai between detachments of the Nationalist Army and 'armed labor fraternities' and that the Nationalist Army is busy disarming labor fraternities in other southern towns."[22] In the Comintern, the surprise was complete and the consternation unbounded. Articles written by Comintern "experts" right up to the day of the coup d'état firmly denying any and all possibility of a coup were still being published in the central organ of the International for days after the coup occurred. The April 16 issue of *La Correspondance Internationale*, for example, featured an article by Ernst Thaelmann, the future leader of the German Communist party who was destined to figure six years later in the capitulation to Hitler. He wrote: "The bourgeois Right wing in the Kuomintang and its leadership had been defeated" back in 1926. Chiang, he said, "must submit." He closed deriding the "illusions" of the imperialists about the chances of Chiang's defection.[23] On April 20 the same publication

contained an article by one Victor Stern of Prague which announced
that "the hopes of a split . . . and a compromise of the Right wing
with the militarists . . . are lies and have no chance of succeeding."
The same day, bearing the same date, a special issue was released
under the heading: "The Treason of Chiang Kai-shek!"[24]

Chiang's coup, bad enough in itself for the Kremlin's cause, was
particularly embarrassing because it so crushingly confirmed the
warnings and predictions of Trotsky and the Opposition in the Russian Communist party. This was in many ways, from Stalin's point
of view, Chiang Kai-shek's most unforgivable crime. Events might
prove Trotsky right, but the struggle against Trotskyism had to go
on. It had been felt all the way to Shanghai where, in Malraux's
words, the Chinese Communist leaders, "knowing that the Trotskyist
theses were attacking the union with the Kuomintang were terrified
by any attitude which might, rightly or wrongly, seem to be linked
to that of the Russian Opposition." Accordingly, in the name of
unity with the Kuomintang, they had led the workers to the slaughter.
Even now it was impossible for Moscow to admit that events had
overtaken a thousand lies and specious arguments. A spokesman for
the Comintern unblinkingly declared: "The treason of Chiang Kai-
shek was not unexpected."[25] Stalin himself, on April 21, announced
that events had "fully and entirely proved the correctness" of the
Comintern "line."[26]

But papal bulls of infallibility could not displace the facts. In
Shanghai the workers had died on the cross of Kuomintang "unity."
Under it, the militarists and the bankers now gambled and bargained
for the spoils.

Chapter 12

MOSCOW: "THE REVOLUTIONARY CENTER"

CHIANG KAI-SHEK's Shanghai coup d'état dealt a crushing blow to the revolution but it need not have been mortal. In Hunan and Hupeh the revolutionary tide was just sweeping in. The peasants were rising to seize the land; and the workers, in degree of organization and potential power, were already quite capable of becoming the leaders and the guardians of the agrarian revolt. Together they represented a force strong enough to defeat the reaction which ruled in the east with Shanghai as its center and Chiang Kai-shek as its master. By his coup, Chiang had grasped power where he sat, but he still did not by any means hold it firmly in his hands.

Chiang had struck his blow in the interests of a deal with the foreign Powers, but by the same act he had weakened his bargaining position. He had cut the arteries of the national revolutionary movement, but for the sake of maintaining his own position he could not entirely divest himself of its claims and purposes. He had still to claim for himself and for the Kuomintang the leadership of the "anti-imperialist struggle." He had still to denounce the "unequal treaties" and demand, at least in form, their abrogation. But the foreign interests concentrated at Shanghai were content for the moment that Chiang had removed the immediate threat of the mass movement. Now they sat back to wait for further proofs of his right to their benevolent guardianship.

We would not for a moment underrate what General Chiang has done [said the *North China Daily News*]. With conditions as they were in this district a fortnight ago the only thing to do was to act ruthlessly and to shoot down the Communists without mercy. And, situated as General Chiang then was, it needed a good deal of moral courage to take this step and to act with the determination that he evinced. Furthermore, we fully recognize the truth of the old saying that "Rome was not built in a day." At the same time much more must be done both by General Chiang Kai-shek and the Kuomintang before their assurances can be accepted at face value.[1]

From the Kiangsu-Chekiang capitalists, as we have seen, Chiang exacted a heavy price for his services, in extortion, terror, and taxation. Compared to his impositions, the burdens of the old militarists must have seemed to some of them an easy load to carry. After April 12 there was no love feast between Chiang and his wealthy mentors. He had to lash them savagely to him and they, without any other choice, had to suffer themselves to be lashed—for nothing was secure. Chiang's plight was desperate, his military position precarious. Under the counterattack of the Fengtien army, Hsuchow fell. The Northerners mockingly dropped shells into his capital at Nanking from their entrenchments across the river at Pukow. Chiang himself acknowledged that his army was in a state of disunity and demoralization.[2] He too had to pay a price for turning on the mass movement, for without the popular support that made it real, the legend of Nationalist invincibility waned. Military victories came far less easily and the chances of defeat in the field loomed large before him instead. If he was weak in relation to the Northern militarist forces, he was even more vulnerable to counterattack by the revolutionary movement itself. Isolated at the mouth of the Yangtze, Chiang could have been engulfed in an avenging wave sweeping down the river from the aroused provinces.

But this depended on what the Communists did in the weeks now to come. It was a matter of how they would understand the disaster that had befallen them on the road from Canton to Shanghai. They had subordinated themselves to the leadership of Chiang Kai-shek and the Kuomintang and thereby yielded themselves to catastrophe. Now at Wuhan sat the government of the so-called Left Kuomintang, consisting of Wang Ching-wei and his little coterie of politicians on the one hand and a group of ambitious Central China militarists on the other. In the cities and in the country, literally millions of workers and peasants were in motion, seeking a leadership that would express their interests. What was Wuhan, and what was the "Left" Kuomintang, and how should the Communists orient themselves in relation to this government and to the masses? That was the question. What answer the Chinese Communists would have made if left to themselves is difficult to say. Any impulses toward self-assertion within the party leadership had long since been stifled. Now doubts and protests were stilled; the party leadership made no choices. The decisions were made in Moscow.

The swift course of events had given the Chinese revolution first place on the long list of issues and fundamental differences that now openly divided the ruling group in Russia, led by Stalin, and the Opposition, led by Trotsky. Once again, the reader of this history has to remember that in 1927 the Stalin regime in Russia was only just consolidating its power. It had not yet eliminated its internal opposition. It had begun to substitute police terror for political methods inside the ruling party itself, but the process was not as yet very far advanced. It was already a regime motivated by the purely national interests of the state as conceived by the ruling bureaucracy, but it still had to justify itself in the terminology of revolutionary internationalism. Stalin's real talent lay in the removal of obstacles by force, but he had not yet grown strong enough to express himself fully in this manner either at home or abroad. Stalin still had to defend his political infallibility by argument and prescription. He had even now to prepare a thesis on the Chinese revolution to present to the Eighth Plenary Session of the Executive Committee of the Communist International, scheduled to meet in Moscow later in May. He was already preparing to trim away these superfluous quasi-parliamentary trappings, but at this time he still had to engage in a certain amount of debate and to justify himself by the traditional modes of Marxist and Bolshevik party politics.

To this role, Stalin brought mediocre talents and all the limitations of the bureaucratic mentality. In the realm of ideas he tended to flounder amid abstract categories with which he could never identify living social forces. He was a specialist in the mechanism of power, and above all of power in Russia. His knowledge and grasp of social movements and politics abroad was extremely limited. Where and when he had to function at the ideological level, however, Stalin did display a certain consistent pattern. He had never accepted the idea that the proletariat could really wield power, and even less the idea that such power could be wielded in a democratic manner. This is why he was almost left behind by the events in Russia in 1917. Afterward, he readily enough seized upon the power that had been won in order to fashion it into an oligarchy after his own design. On the world scene he again and again showed that his fundamental idea was either the imposition of totalitarian power by brute force, or, failing that, the manipulation of working-class or other popular movements as pressure upon a bourgeois power that he could understand and deal with, as one self-interested oligarchy to another. This was essentially his approach to the problem of China in April 1927. He had calculated that Chiang Kai-shek would lead the Chinese people to victory in the national revolution and create in China a strong ally for Russia against the common enemy, England. Events proved that he had been monumentally wrong. Having already embraced the doctrine of infallibility that goes with monolithic rule, he could not acknowledge his error. He could only insist upon the correctness of his course and look about in China for another potential source of power at whose disposal he could now place the Communist-led mass movement. He thought he found it in the so-called Left Kuomintang at Wuhan.

Against Stalin, Trotsky—and in general the Opposition faction which he led—represented the surviving socialist and internationalist current in Bolshevism. Trotsky and his followers were bound by the dictatorial political system and the one-party regime which had also emerged from Bolshevism. But they were still the revolutionists who never dreamed that the power emerging from the revolution could assume the form that Stalin gave it. They still believed that the future of Russia, as a socialist state, depended wholly on the successful broadening of the international proletarian revolutionary current. Unlike Stalin, Trotsky had a superb and almost intuitive grasp of the dynamics of the revolutionary struggle almost everywhere. Although the information available to him was scanty, Trotsky's analyses and warnings about the course of events in China proved to be strikingly accurate. He believed that the revolution in China, like that in Russia, could succeed only if the working class assumed the leadership of the peasant mass. Because the tasks of the revolution in China were "bourgeois," he argued, it did not follow that, at this late date in history, especially in a semicolonial country, the bourgeoisie or any part of it could successfully carry out those tasks. They would be accomplished only under working-class leadership by a telescoping of the bourgeois and socialist revolutions and, beyond that, only as part of the revolutionary transformation of the decisive areas of the world. The subordination of the workers and peasants and the Communists in China to the bourgeois Kuomintang could only lead to defeat, he had warned, and that is precisely what had happened at Shanghai.

That was precisely what would happen again, he now warned once more, if the mass movement was subjected to the government of petty bourgeois radicals and militarists at Wuhan.

Stalin's thesis, "The Questions of the Chinese Revolution," was published in *Pravda* on April 21.[3] Trotsky's counterthesis, "The Chinese Revolution and the Thesis of Comrade Stalin,"[4] was submitted on May 7 for publication in the press according to the regular procedure. It was, however, barred from print. Stalin was still subject to debate but was already using his power to keep the debate as one-sided as possible. Both the documents were prepared for the Comintern session due to take place several weeks later, but it is important to counterpose them at this point because within those weeks, before the session actually convened, events in China had already passed comment upon them.

Stalin began by saying that events in China

proved that the line laid down was the correct line. . . . This was the line of the close cooperation of the Left Wingers and the Communists within the Kuomintang, of consolidation of the unity of the Kuomintang . . . of making use of the Right, of their connections and their experience so far as they submitted to the discipline of the Kuomintang. . . . The events which followed have fully and entirely proved the correction of this line.

Trotsky replied:

We know very well how the bourgeoisie submitted to "discipline" and how the proletariat utilized the Rights, that is the big and middle bourgeoisie, their "connections" (with the imperialists) and their "experience" (in strangling and shooting the workers). The story of this "utilization" is written in the book of the Chinese revolution with letters of blood. But this does not prevent the theses from saying: "The subsequent events fully confirmed the correctness of this line." Further than this no one can go!

The events, said Trotsky, had in reality revealed the ruinous nature of the official policy. That the class struggle could not be "exorcised by the idea of the national united front is far too eloquently proved by the bloody April events," he wrote, "a direct consequence of the policy of the bloc of four classes." To refuse to understand this was "to prepare a repetition of the April tragedy at a new stage of the Chinese revolution."

Only a new course, he urged, guaranteeing the organizational and political independence of the Chinese Communist party and the formation of Soviets as organs of dual power to lead and protect the agrarian revolution in the provinces offered any security against new and still greater disasters. The formation of Soviets meant the creation in town and countryside of authentic organs of the mass movement itself. Workers, peasants, and soldiers would democratically elect their own delegates, unite them in common assemblies sitting side by side with the organs of the regular government to guarantee the prosecution of the struggle for the land, the struggle against the militarists and the imperialists. This unity at the base would provide a constant check and a constant threat to the petty bourgeois radicals who occupied the seats of power in Wuhan. It would render the masses independent of vacillation and compromises at the top. It would create, in a word, the dual power as a transition to a further stage in the revolution.

According to Stalin, however, complete reliance was still to be placed in the Kuomintang, in its "Left" section, in the Wuhan government. It now had become the center of the revolution. The workers and peasants were to rely on it to carry on the fight against militarism and imperialism and to stand sponsor for the agrarian revolt.

Chiang Kai-shek's coup [he wrote] means that from now on there will be in South China two camps, two governments, two armies, two centers, the center of the revolution in Wuhan and the center of the counter-revolution in Nanking. . . .

This means that the revolutionary Kuomintang in Wuhan, by a determined fight against militarism and imperialism will in fact be converted into an organ of the revolutionary democratic dictatorship of the proletariat and the peasantry. . . . [We must adopt] the policy of concentrating the whole power in the country in the hands of the revolutionary Kuomintang. . . . It further follows that the policy of close cooperation between the Lefts and the Communists within the Kuomintang acquires special force and special significance . . . and that *without such cooperation the victory of the revolution is impossible.*

The slogan of Soviets, therefore, was inadmissible, because it would mean

issuing the slogan of a fight against the existing power in this territory . . . of the fight against the power of the revolutionary Kuomintang, for in this territory there is at present no power other than the power of the revolutionary Kuomintang. This means confusing the task of creating and consolidating mass organizations of the workers and peasants in the form of strike committees, peasants' leagues and peasant committees, trade councils, factory committees, etc., upon which the revolutionary Kuomintang is already based, with the task of setting up a Soviet system as a new type of power in place of the revolutionary Kuomintang.

Trotsky replied:

These words fairly reek with the apparatus-like, bureaucratic conception of revolutionary authority. . . . The government is not regarded as the expression and consolidation of the developing struggle of the classes, but as the self-sufficient expression of the will of the Kuomintang. The classes come and go but the continuity of the Kuomintang goes on forever. But it is not enough to call Wuhan the revolutionary center for it really to be that. The provincial Kuomintang of Chiang Kai-shek has an old, reactionary, mercenary bureaucracy at its disposal. What has the Left Kuomintang? For the time being nothing, or almost nothing. The slogan of Soviets is a call for the creation of real organs of the new state power right through the transitional regime of a dual government.

For Stalin, in the coming period,

the main source of the power of the revolutionary Kuomintang is the further development of the revolutionary movement of the workers and peasants and the strengthening of their mass organizations, the revolutionary peasant committees, the workers' trade unions, and the other revolutionary mass organizations as the elements which are to form the Soviets in the future.

"What should be the course of these organizations?" asked Trotsky—

We do not find a single word on this in the thesis. The phrase that these are "preparatory" elements for the Soviets of the future is only a phrase and nothing more. What will these organizations do *now*? They will have to conduct strikes, boycotts, break the backbone of the bureaucratic apparatus, annihilate the counter-revolutionary military bands, drive out the large landowners, disarm the detachments of the usurers and the rich peasants, arm the workers and peasants, in a word, solve all the problems of the democratic and agrarian revolution . . . and in this way raise themselves to the position of local organs of power. But then they will be Soviets, only a kind that are badly suited to their tasks. . . . During all the preceding mass movements, the trade unions were compelled to fulfill functions closely approaching the functions of Soviets (Hongkong, Shanghai, and elsewhere). But these were precisely the functions for which the trade unions were entirely insufficient. They do not at all embrace the petty bourgeois masses in the city that incline toward the proletariat. But such tasks as the carrying through of strikes with the least possible losses to the poorer population of the city, the distribution of provisions, participation in tax policy, participation in the formation of armed forces, to say nothing of carrying through the agrarian revolution in the provinces, can be accomplished with the necessary sweep only when the directing organization embraces not only all sections of the proletariat but connects them intimately in the course of its activities with the poor population in the city and country.

One would at least think that the military coup d'état of Chiang Kai-shek had finally hammered into the mind of every revolutionist the fact that trade unions separated from the army are one thing and united workers' and soldiers' Soviets on the other hand are quite another thing. Revolutionary trade unions and peasant committees can arouse the hatred of the enemy no less than Soviets. But they are far less capable than Soviets of warding off its blows.

If we are to speak seriously of the alliance of the proletariat with the oppressed masses in the city and country—not of an "alliance" between the leaders, a semiadulterated alliance through dubious representatives— then such an alliance can have no other organizational form than that of Soviets. This can be denied only by those who rely more upon compromising leaders than upon the revolutionary masses below.

While he rejected the slogan of Soviets, Stalin declared that the "most important counter-measure [antidote] against the counter-revolution is the arming of the workers and peasants."

The arming of the workers and peasants is an excellent thing [answered Trotsky], but one must be logical. In southern China there are already armed peasants; they are the so-called National armies. Yet, far from being an "antidote to the counter-revolution" they have been its tool. Why? Because the political leadership, instead of embracing the masses of the army through soldiers' Soviets has contented itself with a purely external copy of our political departments and commissars, which, without an independent revolutionary party and without soldiers' Soviets, have been transformed into an empty camouflage for bourgeois militarism.

The theses of Stalin reject the slogan of Soviets with the argument that it would be "a slogan of struggle against the government of the revolutionary Kuomintang." But in that case what is the meaning of the words: "The principal antidote to the counter-revolution is the arming of the workers and peasants"? Against whom will the workers and peasants arm themselves? Will it not be against the governmental authority of the revolutionary Kuomintang? The slogan of arming the workers and peasants, if it is not a phrase, a subterfuge, a masquerade, but a call to action, is not less sharp in character than the slogan of workers' and peasants' Soviets. Is it likely that the armed masses will tolerate at their side or over them the governmental authority of a bureaucracy alien and hostile to them? The real arming of the workers and peasants under present circumstances inevitably involves the formation of Soviets. . . . To declare that the time for Soviets has not yet arrived and at the same time to launch the slogan for arming the workers and peasants is to sow confusion. Only the Soviets, at a further development of the revolution, can become the organs capable of really conducting the arming of the workers and of directing these armed masses. . . .

. . . It is said: The Hankow government is nevertheless a fact. Fêng Yü-hsiang is a fact. T'ang Shêng-chih is a fact, and they have armed forces at their disposal; neither the Wuhan government nor Fêng Yü-hsiang nor T'ang Shêng-chih wants Soviets. To create Soviets would mean to break with these allies. Although this argument is not openly formulated in the theses, it is nevertheless decisive for many comrades. We have already heard from Stalin on the Hankow government, the "revolutionary center," the "only governmental authority." At the same time an advertising campaign is launched for Fêng Yü-hsiang in our party meetings, "a former worker," "a faithful revolutionist," "a reliable man," etc. All this is a repetition of the past mistakes under circumstances in which these mistakes can become even more disastrous. The Hankow government and the army command can be against Soviets only because they will have nothing to do with a radical agrarian program, with a real break with the large landowners and the bourgeoisie, because they secretly cherish the thought of a compromise with the Right. But then it becomes all the more important to form Soviets. This is the only way to push the revolutionary elements of Hankow to the left and force the counterrevolutionists to retire.

In sum, Stalin favored a continued bloc with the bourgeois radicals of the Kuomintang and opposed any independent organization of the masses into their own councils which might prejudice the bloc at the top. This was the course that the Chinese Communist party actually pursued. Trotsky demanded the independence of the Communist party, the formation of Soviets or councils in the towns and villages, and a program "to set the connection with the petty bourgeois masses higher than a connection with their party leaders, to rely upon ourselves, upon our own organizations, arms, and power."

The Chinese Communists, however, were never able to compare notes between the views of the Opposition and their own experience. They understood that "Trotskyism" was some pernicious doctrine that was adequately answered not with argument but with epithets. Only the most bowdlerized versions of its views were published, while the broadest possible publicity was given to a series of articles expounding the official "line" laid down by Stalin.[5] These articles all reproduced the remarkable argument that the slaughter at Shanghai was entirely in accord with the prognoses of the Comintern and could not, in any case, have been prevented. The actions of the Communist party leadership at Shanghai, later to be bitterly attacked for its alleged violation of Comintern directives, were now strongly defended. In his own document, Stalin wrote:

The Opposition is dissatisfied because the workers of Shanghai have not undertaken a decisive fight against the imperialists and their lackeys. They do not understand, however, that the revolution in China cannot develop at such a rapid tempo. . . . They do not understand that one cannot undertake a decisive struggle under unfavorable conditions . . . that not to avoid a decisive fight under unfavorable conditions (when it is possible to avoid it) means rendering easier the work of the enemies of the revolution.

"It was necessary," wrote another defender of the Comintern's strategy, "not to permit oneself to be provoked and to await the propitious moment for action. The coup d'état of Chiang Kai-shek, carried out under the pressure and under the protection of armed foreign imperialism, *could not have been prevented*."[6]

In a chapter hastily added to a report made to the Moscow party organization in April, Bukharin defended the policy of "hiding arms and not accepting battle" and insisted that "the authority of the Communist Party will necessarily increase, since long before the armed coup, the Communist Party had conducted a vigorous campaign against the bourgeois dictator." A little later, when he had already begun to attack the Chinese Communists for carrying out the policies which he had himself drafted, Bukharin still said: "It is necessary to affirm that even had they done all that could have been done, we could not, in the present period, have triumphed over Chiang Kai-shek in direct conflict. . . . The imperialists could have shattered in blood the workers of Shanghai in a single day's armed conflict."[7]

One entire article in the central organ of the Comintern was devoted especially to proving that the Communist party of China had unflinchingly followed the directives of the Comintern. After a lengthy review, it concluded: "All this proves that the young Communist Party of China has in recent times kept aloof from any vacillations and hesitations and has grasped the fact that the tactics of stimulating the mass movement are the only right tactics for the vanguard of the Chinese proletariat."[8]

Bukharin, who performed the role of chief ideological aide and drafter of briefs and resolutions for Stalin but who was destined despite this to pay with his life for Stalin's drive to power, made it plain that there would be no abandonment of the Kuomintang policy.

"It would be a great mistake," he declared, "to hand over the Kuomintang banner to the clique of Chiang Kai-shek."⁹ On the contrary, it was explained, the Communist object would be to bring the masses into the Kuomintang to support the government of Wuhan which "is fighting . . . the imperialists and the Chinese militarists" and "has put the agrarian revolution on the order of the day."¹⁰ It was a matter of reposing all confidence, all support, and all faith in the Left Kuomintang.

All of this, wrote Trotsky, meant

to bring one's head voluntarily to the slaughter. The bloody lesson of Shanghai passed without leaving a trace. The Communists, as before, were being transformed into cattle herders for the party of the bourgeois executioners.¹¹

Again, on May 18, Trotsky warned:

The leaders of the Left Kuomintang of the type of Wang Ching-wei and Co. will inevitably betray you if you follow the Wuhan heads instead of forming your own independent Soviets. The agrarian revolution is a serious thing. Politicians of the Wang Ching-wei type, under difficult conditions, will unite ten times with Chiang Kai-shek against the workers and peasants.¹²

It was to take less than six weeks for this prophecy to be fulfilled.

The "revolutionary center" discerned by Stalin at Wuhan had a most ephemeral existence. The petty bourgeois leaders, whom Stalin confused with the great masses of poor in city and country and without whose co-operation he said the victory of the revolution would be impossible, turned out to be political middlemen in the repression of the mass movement. Stalin thought that with them he was forming a new "bloc of the workers, peasants, and petty bourgeoisie." But these petty bourgeois leaders were infinitely closer to the so-called "big" bourgeoisie than they were to the masses of the poor. They were glib with radical promises for tomorrow but were invariably shocked and frightened by the "excesses" of today whenever workers or peasants reached out to satisfy their own demands. They had submitted fearfully to Chiang Kai-shek and he had scorned them. Now in Wuhan they fawned on the local militarists, upon whom, especially after Chiang's defection, they felt more dependent than ever.

Chief among the military men in Hankow was the Hunan war lord, T'ang Shêng-chih. T'ang was himself a big landholder in Hunan and upon him the Hankow Chamber of Commerce and related gentry relied for protection. Borodin himself was the author of an apt figure of speech that described the mutual relations between the Wuhan politicians and General T'ang. Anna Louise Strong, the Kremlin publicist, was in Hankow at the time. She asked Borodin about the civilian and military power in Wuhan. She thought that "if the civil power stood firm, the military would have to yield."

He laughed. "Did you ever see a rabbit before an anaconda," he said, "trembling, knowing it is going to be devoured, yet fascinated? That's the civic power before the military in Wuhan, staring at the military and trembling."

"So he had few illusions," commented Miss Strong, "regarding the courage of the Chinese intellectuals with whom he was working and who made up the Wuhan government. But he was their chief source of steadfastness and revolutionary purpose to the end."[13]

The Wuhan radicals, who were seen in Moscow as revolutionary paragons and viewed in Hankow even by Borodin as anemic rabbits, were a small and ineffectual band, undistinguished except by their total incapacity for power and leadership. Chief of them was Wang Ching-wei, whom we have seen bend and fold under Chiang Kai-shek's pressure in Canton and Shanghai. He was indecisive in all things except his readiness to retreat before stronger personalities. One of the most vocal was one Hsü Ch'ien, onetime Confucian scholar, who was fond of making radical speeches that singed even his Communist colleagues. He would be the first to flee from gathering difficulties. Ku Mêng-yü, editor of the central organ of the Kuomintang in Hankow, had in 1926 characterized the peasant upsurge as "a movement of vandals, scoundrels, and idle peasants." Sun Fo, son of the late Leader, Sun Yat-sen, was a squirmy politician who changed his views and allegiances so often that even his own colleagues, hardly noted for their steadfastness, contemptuously called him "Sun Wu-k'ung," after the mythical monkey who covered 10,000 miles in a single leap. Best-known to the foreigners, possibly, was the brilliantine Eugene Ch'ên, artisan of the well-turned purple phrase and master of diplomatic invective, barred by his ignorance of the Chinese language (he was born in Trinidad) from playing any role but that of spokesman to the Powers. Soong Ching-ling, youthful and earnest widow of Sun Yat-sen, was only nominally among the leaders. Of the whole group only Têng Yen-ta, who had succeeded Liao Chung-k'ai as political director of the army in Canton, had the kind of courage of his convictions that lifted him a long notch above his fellows.

These were the main props of the "revolutionary center" upon whom everything, according to Stalin, now depended. Their strength, wrote Doriot, "resides essentially in the support of the working masses. . . . The General Federation of Labor with its 3,000,000 members. . . . The peasant unions, with their 15,000,000 adherents . . . are grouping themselves around the Kuomintang banner."[14] Unfortunately, the rallying of the masses to the Wuhan government was one thing. The rallying of the Wuhan government to the masses was quite another. Six months later, addressing a party conference in Moscow, Chitarov, one of the Russians in Hankow at the time, said: "One thing was left out of sight in connection with this: that while the bourgeoisie was retreating from the revolution, the Wuhan government did not even think of leaving the bourgeoisie. Unfortunately among the majority of our comrades, this was not understood. . . ."[15] Again, Borodin, also long after the event, told Fischer: "The world thought Hankow Communist but the Left Kuomintang ruled and the Left Kuomintang was neither Bolshevik nor Socialist and the generals who shared their condominium in Hankow certainly opposed everything Communist."[16]

This was the real Wuhan which in a few weeks would make a macabre joke out of Stalin's theory of the "revolutionary center." According to this theory there was supposed to be a clear-cut and diametric opposition between the forces of the revolution (Wuhan) and the forces of the counterrevolution (Nanking). As Mif put it: "For the initial moment it was characteristic that there was a full contradiction between these two centers."[17] Or, as the Chinese Communist leaders put it: "The secession of the big bourgeoisie relieved the national revolutionary movement of the causes of internal conflict and disharmony and caused the movement as a whole to be directed to one simple goal."[18]

But only a few weeks later, startled readers of *Izvestia* would learn that the Left Kuomintang leaders proved to be "playthings in the hands of the generals."[19] Readers of the foreign Communist press would be told "there is very little, if anything, to distinguish the generals and generalissimos of the counterrevolutionary camp from the generals and generalissimos of the Nationalist government."[20] Mif had to record that "in the end . . . the Wuhan leaders knelt before Nanking."[21]

The "full contradiction" quickly and completely dissolved, and for a long time the only explanation was that handy device, the "dialectics of the class struggle." But a somewhat more honest, and more dialectic explanation appeared under the imprint of the Chinese Communist party in 1931:

> The rupture between Nanking and Wuhan did not bring about the immediate and distinct appearance in Wuhan of the bloc of workers, peasants, and petty bourgeoisie. To the contrary, not only the power of the bourgeoisie, but also that of the landlords and the gentry still existed there. The latter especially held great power. The internal conflict in Wuhan possessed the same social features as that in Nanking, that is, the democratic revolution of the workers and peasants was struggling against the gentry and the landlord class. The internal decomposition of Wuhan had begun even before the Wuhan government was completely organized.[22]

To advance this view years after the event was apparently good dialectics. To breathe it in 1927, while it was happening, was apparently counterrevolutionary Trotskyism. Trotsky had warned that Wuhan would go with the generals against the agrarian revolution. Stalin insisted that Wuhan would go with the agrarian revolution against the generals. It needed only, he said, the unqualified and unreserved support of the Chinese Communists and the mass movement. Stalin, of course, prevailed, and the Chinese revolution plunged on toward new defeats.

Chapter 13

WUHAN: "THE REVOLUTIONARY CENTER"

THE COMMUNIST INTERNATIONAL had declared that Chiang Kai-shek's Shanghai coup d'état was entirely in accord with its own predictions. It went further and declared that the slaughter of the Shanghai workers "could not have been prevented." In Wuhan the Left Kuomintang could not quite approximate this blandness. "A long time ago we knew of this intrigue," said the Kuomintang Central Executive Committee in a manifesto anathematizing Chiang, "and now we regret that we failed to act until it is too late. For this we offer sincere apology." In another statement it said: "It is to be regretted that the wrong choice of a military commander has led to such difficulties. The comrades of the party, prompted by the spirit of leniency, have again and again, for the sake of saving the party, overlooked, though reluctantly, many irregularities."[1] In Hankow all the leaders were explaining how they had "overlooked" Chiang's waywardness and had "hoped" he would not carry it too far. The Comintern delegation, which only three weeks before had enthusiastically hailed the idyllic relations between the army and the people in Kiangsi, was now giving names, dates, places, and details of the ruthless terror inflicted on that province by Chiang Kai-shek beginning in February. Even now, it seemed, his worst crime was the establishment of a rival government at Nanking. This act, said the delegation in a formal statement,

is more unpardonable than his previous numerous acts of violation, namely the coup d'état of March 20, attacks upon the revolutionary wing of the Kuomintang, suppression of the workers' and peasants' movement in Kiangsi and Chekiang, and finally the murder of the Shanghai workers. We watched all these violent actions of Chiang Kai-shek and his agents with great anxiety, but hoped that he would hesitate to turn a barefaced traitor to the nationalist movement. At this critical period of the nationalist revolution preservation of the united front is so imperative that all crimes of those who fight against imperialism can be temporarily overlooked. But . . . Chiang Kai-shek's crimes did not stop at the massacre of the Kiangsi and Shanghai workers. They culminated in a revolt against the people's party and the people's government.[2]

The statement went on to recall how the delegation had telegraphed Chiang on April 13 urging him to call off his separatist moves and offering, if he accepted their advice, to visit him to talk things over. "He did not answer our telegram and proceeded with his plan to disrupt the party." In other words, even now, had Chiang been willing not to set up a separate regime, all his other crimes could be "temporarily overlooked." It was not the bloody slaughter that made him a "barefaced traitor." It was his act in setting up a rival "Nationalist government" at Nanking. The Comintern had hoped he would heed its advice. He had not done so. The workers of Shanghai paid with their heads for this error in judgment.

Wang Ching-wei was also among those whose ill-founded hopes had proved so costly to the Shanghai workers. Discussing his meeting and agreement with Chiang in Shanghai two weeks earlier, Wang now said: "I still hoped for the awakening. I still hoped that he would sever his connections with reaction. . . . I promised him to propose to the Central Kuomintang the calling of a conference to settle all outstanding disputes. . . . When I arrived here, I was still hoping against hope for a change. I made no attack against Chiang in my report."[3] Wang had believed that he had persuaded Chiang to wait for the "peaceful and legal" liquidation of his grievances. He had agreed with Chiang on the essential objectives: a ban on the Communists and recognition of the paramountcy of the military. But events had shown that Wang had simply been used to cover preparations for the coup. The worst of it, from Wang's point of view, was the fact that under his "agreement" with Chiang he would have preserved the titles of office that smelled so sweetly in his nostrils, for he looked upon himself as the heir and successor of Sun Yat-sen and the chief standard bearer of the revolution. Chiang's act in setting up a rival government at Nanking mortally affronted these pretensions. Wang was dismayed to discover that the ruling class preferred Chiang's services and Chiang's methods to his own. The Comintern to the contrary, Wang was not concerned with leading the agrarian revolution. He wanted to find out, as Ch'ü Ch'iu-po of the Communist Central Committee later acknowledged, how "to compete with Chiang for the sympathy of the southeastern (Chekiang-Kiangsu) bourgeoisie."[4] Wang, the petty bourgeois radical on whom the Comintern pinned its faith, hoped to prove to the bankers and big merchants that Chiang "oppressed" them and that he, Wang, would save them both from the menace of the mass movement and the impositions of the militarists.

Under Wang's leadership, the Kuomintang Central Executive Committee issued its mandate of April 17, excommunicating Chiang and all his associates, cataloguing their crimes, expelling them from the party, and depriving them of all government posts. But this was as far as it would go. The only possible means of making this mandate effective was to move on Chiang with military force. He was vulnerable enough. But Wuhan was too conscious of its affinity with Nanking. When asked if they would attack Chiang, Wuhan leaders blandly asserted that they would leave that task to the workers and peasants in Chiang's own territory. "The people would soon rise against Chiang and his friends," promised the Kuomintang leader T'an Yen-k'ai, "so the Nationalist government does not consider their revolt of serious importance, because they are bound to fail."[5] Borodin dutifully echoed this pious hope. Asked by a Japanese correspondent if the Nanking revolt would be put down with arms, he replied: "This will hardly be necessary. The process of disintegration has already set in in Nanking. Allow them a little time to run their course and they will be finished from within."[6] Chiang Kai-shek, for his part, made no military gestures hostile to Wuhan. Precarious as was his own position, he doubtless had his own ideas about who would be "finished from within."

"All hostility and personal accounts notwithstanding and despite the actual break, some ties with Chiang Kai-shek remained intact. . . ." said the *post factum* analysis of Fischer-Borodin. "Much divided Hankow from Nanking. But something drew them together." Thus instead of the irreducible antagonism between the "revolutionary center" and the "counterrevolutionary center" there was "something" that linked them in fundamental affinity. This "something" was the fundamental common political interest that both served. Wang Ching-wei and his military ally, T'ang Shêng-chih, figured that if they could extend Wuhan's domain, if they could first wrest Honan province from the Northern armies, again in the words of Fischer-Borodin, "they could come to terms with Chiang Kai-shek."[7] A military victory culminating in the occupation of Peking would assuredly send their stock up and Chiang's stock down on the bourgeois exchanges of the country. If they could swing it (and the success of the plan depended entirely, as we shall see, on the military co-operation of Fêng Yü-hsiang) they would become the rulers of the country and Chiang Kai-shek would have to settle with them.

Such were the real calculations of the "revolutionary" leadership of the Kuomintang at Hankow. That they jibed perfectly with the private Napoleonic aspirations of General T'ang Shêng-chih was, moreover, no accident. The Hunan general, now daily protesting his revolutionary loyalty, dreamed of the day when he too would have completely in his hands a movement powerful enough to betray in his own interest. So, simultaneously with its expulsion of Chiang Kai-shek, the Wuhan government issued orders for the advance into Ho-nan and its armies were set immediately in motion. But Peking could not be taken in a day and in the interim the Wuhan leaders had to face the multitude of difficulties created for them by Chiang's coup. More difficult still, they had to cope with the mass movement.

The Shanghai events had occurred just as the mass movement was reaching its peak in the central provinces. In Hunan and Hupeh the peasants were in their own plebeian way beginning to translate words in action and to strike out for themselves. The landlords and local gentry, who had been retreating precipitously, were greatly emboldened by Chiang's coup. They began to organize themselves and to strike back. The Wuhan leaders tried to insert themselves between these contending forces. While the issue was being decided in the fields and in the towns, the radicals in Wuhan continued to feed on the illusion that with their committees, their decrees and pronouncements, they were settling the fate of the nation. Actually the gap between their professions and their practices was being closed by forces over which they exercised no real control. The Wang Ching-weis were not Chiang Kai-sheks. Between the closing clamps they would not strike out boldly. They would squirm and wriggle, check and demoralize, vacillate and temporize, until more aggressive agents than they seized the reins from their hands, but until the end, they would do their utmost to prove, to the imperialists, the factory owners, the landlords and gentry, that not Chiang alone spoke in their name.

The Shanghai events had put an entirely different complexion on things so far as the imperialist Powers were concerned. They understood clearly that the balance of forces had shifted in their favor. Until now they had been giving way, step by step, before the advance of a mass movement they knew they could not smash themselves. They had been probing gingerly for the point at which they could come to terms with the Chinese bourgeoisie. The bombardment of Nanking in March had hastened the bargain. On April 12 it was sealed. Now their tone stiffened. The flow of foreign armed forces to strategic ports increased. On April 21, the 9,750-ton cruiser *Vindictive*, largest British warship in Chinese waters, joined a line of thirty-five foreign warships stretching for a mile and a half along the Hankow Bund. Within a week additional vessels arriving from Shanghai increased the total to forty-two, drawn from the navies of Britain, Japan, the United States, France, and Italy.

In Tokyo the newly installed premier, Baron Tanaka, "clearly indicated that the period of leaning back in China affairs was at an end." Correspondents in Tokyo reported that "Chiang Kai-shek's successful stroke against the Reds brings that change in the Chinese situation which Japanese observers have been hoping for." In London it was joyfully announced that "the diplomatic situation as regards China . . . has completely changed. [The Wuhan government] is no longer in the saddle and in a few weeks may have faded from the picture altogether."[8] In the United States an abrupt easing of the official pulse was reflected in the disappearance of China news from the front pages of the metropolitan press.

The attitude of cool defiance toward the foreign Powers, nourished by the diplomatic successes which had followed the seizure of the British Concession by the Hankow workers in January, disappeared. The Wuhan leaders abruptly resumed the posture of respectful supplication. Anti-imperialist posters were torn off Hankow's walls. Foreign missions and church buildings, occupied by workers, peasants, and soldiers, and used as headquarters for mass organizations, were restored to their owners. "The foreign office, instead of being merely courteous and sympathetic had now become energetic and even decisive in foreigners' difficulties," wrote a delighted Hankow resident.[9] "The topic everywhere," wired the correspondent of the *New York Times* on April 25, "is the metamorphosis which has occurred in the last two or three days."

New edicts were issued by the government and in duplicate by the Hupeh General Labor Union restraining the police powers of the pickets and forbidding any actions which might irritate foreigners or prejudice foreign property and trade. Detailed penalties were prescribed for workers guilty of disobeying these orders.[10] Foreign Minister Eugene Ch'ên cited these decrees in a personal appeal to the United States Consul General and a delegation of businessmen whom he saw on April 23. "The Minister outlined the measures which are being taken to assist the restoration of conditions for the conduct of foreign business and trade and he emphasized the fact that Labor had resolved to impose on itself revolutionary discipline in order to carry out these measures of the government."[11]

The government sharply called to task workers in Changsha who had begun a general strike against American enterprises because of the United States Navy's role in the bombardment at Nanking. The workers were ordered to evacuate the Y.M.C.A. they had occupied and to suspend their strike against American coal and oil firms in the Hunan capital on the grounds that "any free and unrestrained action, no matter whether in itself good or bad, must seriously interfere with the unification policy of the party and at the same time inflict a heavy blow upon the anti-imperialist movement. . . . Any undue action . . . must now be rectified and its recurrence in the future must be prevented."[12]

While the Wuhan press began explaining at length the need for "adapting" the government's foreign policy, the Wuhan leaders crudely attempted to apply the traditional Chinese policy of playing off one barbarian against the other. The hopes aroused in Nationalist breasts by the seemingly contradictory zigzags of American policy had been dashed by the events at Nanking, where American guns had spoken louder than all the rest. But Japan's guns had kept silent, and a Japanese subaltern had even sought refuge in hara-kiri from the shame of his government's forbearance. The Wuhan anti-imperialists now turned disingenuously to Japan with special appeals.

"Whereas the Chinese revolution is affecting the very roots of British imperialism," wrote the official organ of the Kuomintang Central Executive Committee, "it assists a friendly Japan in stabilizing her position as a world power and can offer her all possibilities for unprecedented development of her trade and prosperity. . . ." The British and American imperialists, they went on, were trying everywhere to block Japan's expansion. "The best course for Japan's politicians would be to take sides with the Chinese nation against her enemies, to prove that Japan does not approve or assist either the militarists or the imperialist policy of intervention . . . Japan and

China must combine to oppose British imperialism."[13] Within a few weeks Japan replied in her own way to Wuhan's attempt at a flirtation. Japanese troops moved into Shantung, occupying Tsinan and taking over the railway to the sea.

Great Britain, on its part, was thoroughly content. On May 9 in the House of Commons, Sir Austen Chamberlain, the Foreign Secretary, gave official voice to the delight of the Powers with Chiang's coup and the subsequent turn of events. Eugene Ch'ên's note sent in reply to the Powers' protests concerning the Nanking affair was rejected as "unsatisfactory in substance and detail." When the Powers' notes were presented, said Sir Austen,

China south of the Yangtse was apparently united under the Nationalist Government, whose seat was in . . . Hankow. . . . Within four days after the date of Mr. Ch'ên's reply that united government in South China no longer existed. . . . Not two months ago it seemed as if the southern party and the Nationalist armies would sweep China from the south to north. Nanking has already checked this victorious career, if it has not wrecked it altogether. [The Communists] have been punished by the Chinese Nationalists themselves with a severity and effectiveness of which no foreign Power was capable. In Shanghai, Canton, and other towns the extremist organizations have been broken up and their leaders executed. The Nationalist Government at Hankow has lost its dominating position and is at present little more than the shadow of a name.[14]

To the outraged dismay of the British community in China, which wanted swift and direct and terrible military reprisals, Chamberlain made it plain that Britain was content for the moment to let Chiang Kai-shek serve as its deputy. A week later the British diplomatic representative at Hankow was withdrawn.*

The diplomatic consequences of the events in China reverberated in Europe. Stalin had counted on the victory of Chiang Kai-shek in China to give Russia a strong bastion in China and inflict a serious defeat on Britain, the premier Power in China and leader of the anti-Soviet capitalist world. He had built his hopes of support in England itself on the so-called Anglo-Russian Trade Union Unity Committee. Chiang's coup blasted all these hopes and calculations. The British recognized at once that it meant the defeat of Russian purposes in China. At home, in London, on May 12 British police descended on

---

* As if to emphasize the nature of this withdrawal, the British government chose the same day, May 17, to announce the award of decorations to the crew of the British gunboat that wantonly bombarded Wanhsien, on the upper Yangtze, eight months earlier.

the offices of Arcos, Ltd., the Soviet trading organization. Charges of espionage were brought. The trade-union committee blew up. On May 26, Britain severed diplomatic relations with the Soviet Union. Russia's whole international position was palpably worsened. It was more than ever isolated. In Moscow the British moves touched off a panicky war scare.

In London it had been understood immediately that Wuhan offered no serious threat, that it was but the "shadow of a name," and the British government had acted accordingly in its own interest. In Moscow, however, the fiction of Wuhan as a strong revolutionary center still governed and was the resort of last, desperate hopes that the situation in China, and with it the whole international picture, could yet be revised in Russia's favor.

But even the Comintern's own representatives in Hankow felt the difference, even if they did not understand or acknowledge it. The whole atmosphere in relation to the Powers had changed. The foreign warships in the Yangtze, which had hitherto seemed such a puny threat when set against the mass movement rolling across the hinterland, now became grim sea dragons laden with menace. Wuhan's Left Kuomintang leaders acutely felt the new pressure of that long gray line of vessels in the river. Roy, the delegate of the Comintern, felt it no less.

Not only Shanghai [he wrote] but the entire Yangtze River is packed with war vessels. The Yangtze River, the main artery of trade in China, is under the direct control of imperialist guns. This is a "holdup" on a grand scale. The imperialist bandit is saying "Hands Up!" to revolutionary China. The seat of the Nationalist government, Hankow, is practically a beleaguered city. A formidable array of cruisers, destroyers, and gunboats arrogantly challenges the right of the Chinese people to govern this country in their own way. English, American, French marines crowd the streets of the Nationalist capital. The Nationalist government smarts under this indignity for on the slightest provocation the bandit will blow out his brains.[15]

Wuhan had indeed lost its "dominating position," politically, militarily, and psychologically. Thanks to Chiang's coup and the pusillanimity of the Left Kuomintang, Britain, which had come to Wuhan in January with hat in hand, left it in May with a contemptuous shrug. The "youthful optimism, superb confidence, and bold aggressiveness" that a British observer had seen there had utterly collapsed. Only fearful uncertainty remained. "Before three months are ended," blustered Eugene Ch'ên, "we shall conquer our way across Honan to Peking where in the name of Nationalist China and the Kuomintang I will speak a language which cannot be ignored by Sir Austen Chamberlain. . . . The revolutionary armies under Fêng Yü-hsiang and T'ang Shêng-chih together with the forces under Yen Hsi-shan, are now closing in on the bandit soldiery of Chang Tso-lin. . . ."[16] But Fêng failed him. T'ang failed him. Yen failed him. Eugene Ch'ên never again had a chance to be ignored by Chamberlain.*

For employers of labor in Wuhan, Chiang Kai-shek's drive against the labor unions was a heartening promise of things to come. Feeling the new support that came from Nanking, they resisted with fresh vigor the demands and the strikes of the workers. They closed down factories and shops. They deliberately organized runs on local banks. They shipped all the silver they could down river to Shanghai. They deliberately set out to sabotage and paralyze the economic life of Wuhan and the whole area economically dominated by it.[17] Merchants and usurers in the surrounding provinces hoarded their money or smuggled it down to Shanghai. Peasants were refused loans on any terms. There was no other ready cash available anywhere and in many places peasants were unable to buy seed and other supplies to carry them over the spring months. Speculators deliberately drove the price of rice up to unreachable levels. Foreigners co-operated in this program of sabotage by closing down their enterprises, curtailing river steamer schedules, and instituting a virtual blockade of Wuhan. In May there were nearly 100,000 workers locked out of factories and shops and within four weeks this figure nearly doubled. The owners of capital preferred to risk ruin rather than meet the demands of the workers.

A "revolutionary" regime, such as the Comintern believed existed in Hankow, might have taken bold countermeasures. Closed factories might have been seized and operated. Rice hoards might have been confiscated. Peasant co-operatives might have been set up and supplied with capital secured from public confiscations of hoarded money and goods. Support of the peasant drive to seize the land was

* In 1933, while he was Foreign Minister of the short-lived Fukien government, set up at Foochow in revolt against Chiang Kai-shek, Eugene Ch'ên ruminated over the past: "*Then, then,* I could speak with authority because I had the masses with me!" he told the writer. He never understood that he had lost that authority because he had failed to be with the masses. Driven from Foochow, as he was from Wuhan, by Chiang Kai-shek, Eugene Ch'ên faded into well-deserved obscurity. He died in 1944.

the first marker on the road toward reorganization of village life. The Communist International "advised" the Left Kuomintang to take over the banks, factories, and shops. But the Left Kuomintang was interested in protecting, not violating, bourgeois property. It went hat in hand to the Hankow Chamber of Commerce and pleaded with it to let trade resume its normal course, promising to rein in the mass movement. Blame for the economic difficulties was laid by the Wuhan leaders not on the sabotage of the capitalists but on the "excesses" of the workers. The demands of factory and shop employees, they complained querulously, were ruining trade and industry.

These demands bear examination. Between January and April of 1927, the strikes of the wharf workers in Hankow had brought their wages up from three to seven Chinese dollars a month. In the textile mills women and children who formerly earned twelve cents a day fought for and won increases to twenty cents a day—that is, a raise from a monthly rate of $3.60 to $6.00.* In the match factories, strikers won increases of seventeen to forty coppers for a twelve-hour day. In the silk filatures, employing mostly women, a twelve-hour day was won by a series of bitter strikes. Formerly they had worked seventeen hours. In some dyeing plants, not all, wage increases from eighteen to fifty coppers a day were won. The highest wage paid to industrial workers was still $20 a month. The average had been raised from about $10 a month to $14. Yet a wage and living cost survey conducted in Wuhan by a government bureau fixed $27.46 as the minimum subsistence budget for a family of four. In the matter of hours little improvement had been made. Children of seven and eight were still working as long as adults for ten cents a day. The demand for an eight-hour day for child labor remained on paper. A survey by the labor department of the Kuomintang at the end of June revealed that the majority of shop employees in the city were still working twelve to fourteen hours a day. Some were fighting for a reduction from seventeen hours to fifteen, or sixteen to fourteen. The demands of the apprentices, still held under conditions much worse than bond slavery, were scarcely heard at all.[18]

An interviewer for the *People's Tribune* saw some union leaders in March when the cry of "unreasonable" demands was already on Kuomintang lips. "At the mention of the word 'unreasonable,' the

* One Chinese dollar was at that time worth fifty American cents. The rate of coppers to the Chinese dollar ranged, between 1925 and 1928, from 240 to 285.

union leaders smiled. They were mill workers themselves. All their lives they had been wondering about 'reasonableness.' They asked me about it. All their lives, they said, they had been looking for some 'reason' for their existence. So far, unless to starve that others might be clothed and fed, they had found none. Where, they asked, was the reason in this?"[19]

None of the gains made by the Wuhan workers enabled them as yet to come within "reasonable" reach of the minimum subsistence standard of living—and the Western reader has to bear in mind that "subsistence" in China meant then, as now, a standard that anywhere else would be regarded as starvation. It was an "excess," therefore, when the workers dragged before their own tribunals merchants who were speculating in grain and food. It was an "excess" when the workers of Hanyang decided to open the factories and run them and when the workers in Puchih and other Hupeh towns took over shops that had been deliberately closed down. It was an "excess" when local peasant committees in Hunan and Hupeh placed local embargoes on shipments of rice in order to resist the hoarders and speculators who were trying to starve them into submission. It was above all an "excess" when the peasants seized the rice hoards of the landlords to feed their families. These and similar acts were excesses, said the leaders of the Left Kuomintang, and were ruining trade and disrupting economic life. They had to stop forthwith. One of Wang Ching-wei's first official acts upon his return to Wuhan was to break up the workers' co-operative that was operating fifteen factories in Hanyang, force the surrender of the plants, and order the dissolution of the Hanyang Kuomintang branch which supported the workers.[20]

At the end of April regulations were issued abolishing the judicial and police functions assumed by the trade-unions, which were henceforth permitted to act only against their own members. These regulations were issued by the government and the Hupeh General Labor Union in duplicate. Arbitration courts were set up and "unjust demands" for higher wages were prohibited.[21] Hsiang Chung-fa, Communist secretary of the General Labor Union, issued a proclamation, posted on all the walls of the city, asking the workers to make a "supreme effort" and ordering that "new struggles against the capitalists should temporarily be suspended."[22]

On May 20, the Kuomintang Central Executive Committee published a manifesto on the "all-class nature of the revolution." It expressed most clearly the particular class nature of the Wuhan Left Kuomintang:

Whether or not the revolution will be a success will depend on the measure of support given to it by the manufacturers and merchants. Whether or not they can effectively support the revolution will depend upon the willingness of the peasants and laborers to treat them as their allies. . . .

Since the Northern Expedition was launched . . . it is regrettable that the peasant and labor organizations in the Yangtze Valley, by reason of their rapid development, have been unaware of their blunders. . . . They have not considered the future of the revolution as a whole and have belittled their allies, the manufacturers and the merchants. Excessive demands, for instance, have been made to the employers by the peasant and labor bodies through their own ignorance of the economic aspect of the situation. Factories and shops have been closed by armed pickets and exorbitant demands, impossible to carry out, have been forced upon the employers or owners. Consequently the manufacturers and merchants have felt that they have been denied protection by the government and that they cannot enjoy freedom in respect to both person and property. They have also felt that not only has the revolution failed to benefit them in any way, but that it has endangered and jeopardized their welfare and safety. Therefore they have stayed away from the battle line of the revolution and bitterly hate the peasants and laborers who should be their revolutionary allies. As a result the peasants and laborers may find themselves in a state of isolation and committing suicide and the very foundation of the revolution may be shaken.

The party . . . cannot ignore the isolated condition of the peasants and laborers lacking guidance; and especially cannot neglect the interests of the revolutionary allies, the manufacturers and the merchants, and deny them adequate protection. It is our policy to unite them all on the same battle front, never to be torn asunder, and enable them all to benefit equally from the revolution. In order to carry out this policy, the National Government is ordered to put into effect the following:

1. The Labor Ministry and the provincial authorities shall adopt arbitration rules and organize arbitration boards for the settlement of disputes between laborers and factory owners;

2. Enact a Labor Law, regulate workers' hours . . . fix the scale of wages in accordance with living conditions . . . and provide for the protection of the laborers;

3. Prohibit laborers and employees from making excessive demands and interfering with the administration of factories and shops; all demands made to be examined by a special joint committee to be organized by the labor union and the merchants' union, which committee shall impose suitable limitation on the demands;

4. No labor union or picket corps is permitted to threaten, impose fines

upon, or adopt any mode of oppression against shopkeepers or factory owners. . . ."[23]

Dutifully, in its turn, the Communist General Labor Union "cooperated" with the "revolutionary government."* A few days later it proclaimed "revolutionary discipline" for the workers, urged them "not to forget the interests of their allies, the manufacturers and the merchants," and issued the following regulations: (1) Workers who violated revolutionary discipline were to be punished; (2) serious offenders were to be handed over to the government for trial and punishment; (3) unions were prohibited from arresting, fining, "or in any way oppressing persons other than laborers."[24]

Rising prices were blotting out the meager gains of a hundred strikes. The workers instinctively moved toward more revolutionary solutions of their problems but were held in check by the Communists to wait for action by the Wuhan government, action that never came. The Communist Central Committee "ordered the labor unions not to struggle for the workers' demands but to submit to labor discipline . . . not to occupy factories even when the factory owners deliberately closed them as an act of sabotage, not to close shops even when the shopkeepers deliberately raised prices."[25] Earl Browder addressed a meeting of unionists in Hankow on April 29 and said the government would have to regulate prices and that any failure to do so would mean "disaster to the revolutionary forces."[26] The government did fail. The Communists submitted to this failure. The result was disaster.

The same yardstick of property interest measured the position taken by the Left Kuomintang on the cardinal question of the land.

* Anna Louise Strong described how Hanyang arsenal workers crowded eagerly around a visiting delegation of Russian trade-unionists. "During your revolution," they asked, "what attitude did you take toward sabotage in government industries? During your revolution when did the metal workers begin to get any benefit? Did they benefit as soon as the exploiters were overthrown or did they have to suffer long and make many sacrifices before the revolution was finally established?" Miss Strong omitted to mention what reply, if any, was made by the Russians, but went on: "Many were the sacrifices they were already making for their revolutionary government. They gave up their demand for an eight-hour day to work thirteen to seventeen hours in the arsenal 'because our revolutionary government is menaced.' They postponed the demand for a child labor law. I myself saw children of seven and eight working ten hours in Wuchang cotton mills and was told by union organizers, Wuhan is blockaded; we must not attack production, especially foreign-owned production.' They had reason to sacrifice for Wuhan, for elsewhere their situation was far more serious. In Shanghai, Canton, and Hunan, workers were being executed. In Wuhan they still had the chance to raise their heads and argue a little. They were pathetically grateful for this meager privilege." *China's Millions*, p. 41–42.

Stalin had promised that the Left Kuomintang would display the utmost determination in solving the agrarian problem. What developed instead were evasions of the land issue, growing into complaints against the "excesses" of the peasants, and passing over to forcible repression as soon as the peasants began on their own initiative to deal with their problems in their own way.

The leaders of Wuhan were by no means insensible to the motive power of the peasant masses. So long as warmly spoken phrases placed that power at their disposal, they were used abundantly. For example: "The realization of the aims of the national revolution depends upon the awakening of the peasants of all China. Our party will always defend and struggle for the interests of the peasants in order that all privileged classes oppressing them be deprived of support . . . in order that the oppressed peasants be really emancipated." Again, as late as March 19, a government manifesto affirmed that "the revolution must work great changes in the village . . . in order to suppress finally the activities of the local parasites, lawless gentry, landlords, and counterrevolutionaries, under the power of the peasants. . . . This is the only road. . . . If the peasants are not given the possibility of possessing their own land they will not be able to support the revolution to the victorious end."[27]

In words no less radical than those used in the resolutions of the Communist International, the Kuomintang had even proposed the arming of the peasants. In its March "Declaration to the Peasants," the Kuomintang Central Executive Committee had said:

"In order to ensure . . . victory . . . the peasants will need arms for their protection. The armed forces employed by the feudal landlords . . . should be disarmed and their munitions should be handed over to the peasants. In addition the party should devise measures to enable the peasants to buy arms at cheap prices. In short, it should enable the peasants to have ample arms for self-protection. This is to ensure the permanence of the victory of the rural revolution and to ensure that democratic influences overthrow the old feudal influences."[28]

These were strong words, but words alone could not give the peasant his land. Because they were words and nothing but words, the difficulties began for those who uttered them as soon as the peasants of Hunan and Hupeh began to show in action that they took them seriously. The Kuomintang "Platform for Workers and Peasants" adopted in October 1926 actually promised the peasants nothing more than a 25 percent reduction in land rent and the "prohibition" of usury, with the proviso that interest on loans should not exceed 20 percent per annum. The rent-reduction plank remained wholly ineffective. The peasants by themselves, moreover, came quickly to the conclusion that the issue was not one of limited reforms but of the land itself. The Kuomintang Plenary Session in March 1927 admitted that "the cardinal question in the problem of poor farmers is the land question," but the only practical solution it offered was a proposal to set up farmers' banks to make loans at 5 percent per annum in order to meet the lack of capital among the poor peasants.[29] This Plenary Session created a Land Commission which was supposed to bring together statistical and other information for the purpose of concretizing the Kuomintang's land policy. This Commission began its sessions on April 27. It was composed of the principal Kuomintang leaders, with T'an P'ing-shan representing the Communist party. As culled from various sources,[30] the deliberations of this Commission went as follows:

Everyone agreed in principle at the outset that the peasant had to be made master of the land. But then the question arose: What peasants should be masters of what land? "Land to the tillers!" had a nice radical ring to it. But whose land? Certainly not the land of the small landlords, said Wang Ching-wei. The party's duty was to protect the small landlords, for were they not part of the petty bourgeoisie? Certainly not the land belonging to the officers of the army, said T'ang Shêng-chih. The peasants in Hunan, he complained, were already seizing the estates of army officers or of their relatives. Why, in Chienchih, they had even taken a regimental commander who also happened to be the owner of a large local estate, bound him, put a dunce cap on his head, and paraded him through the streets! And the sister-in-law of Ch'ên Ch'êng, a Kuomintang general, had actually been forced to bob her hair to show her solidarity with the new order of things! This would never do. Maybe the rank and file soldiers, landless peasants all of them, would approve, but the officers would never stand for it. The army, mind you, would be split on the question of the land, and, after all, we cannot afford a split in the army, can we?

No, by no means, quickly agreed the commissioners.

Well, then, the land of the big landlords? Yes, the land of the big landlords! But then again, how are we to know which landlords are big and which small? Moreover, if, as T'ang Shêng-chih demanded, "we have to think out concrete means for guaranteeing intact the land belonging to the officers of the national revolutionary army," then we also have to distinguish between those "big" landlords related to the officers and those who are so unfortunate as not to have a son or brother in an officer's uniform.

"We must establish the criterion of confiscation," echoed Wang Ching-wei and Sun Fo.

Hsü Ch'ien had a solution all his own. He discovered somewhere that only 15 percent of the land in all China was under cultivation. "Then there is no purpose," said he, "in taking the land from the landlords when we can give the peasants the land which nobody cultivates." But Hsü Ch'ien was unable to verify his figure, and, anyway, most of the uncultivated land was in Tibet and Turkestan and in the Northwest. The wholesale transportation of the peasants of Hunan and Hupeh did not sound like a particularly practicable proposition. So later Hsü Ch'ien agreed with T'an Yen-k'ai that it might be possible to confiscate only the land of the "especially malicious or evil landlords and the evil business men." Now then, which landlords were evil or (one shudders to think of such people) especially malicious?

Hm, said everybody.

When the idea of buying the land from the small landlords was discussed, T'an Yen-k'ai rubbed his chin. "That will not satisfy the small landlords," he said, "because they still have very little faith in the National government. If we give them our bonds, they cannot live by eating the paper. The land will have to be left in their hands."

On behalf of the Communists, T'an P'ing-shan timidly suggested that only the land of the "counterrevolutionary landlords" be confiscated. Wang Ching-wei leaped into the breach. "Political confiscation!" he snorted. "That is an extremely general phrase which says nothing. If the peasants in any given district are strong enough, they consider every landowner to be counterrevolutionary in order to expropriate his land. Under political confiscation there is no criterion. Where the peasants are strong, they go straight ahead to economic confiscation. Where they are weaker . . . they fall first on the small landlords who thus suffer before anyone else, and we want to keep the small landlords on our side." Completely confounded, the Communists withdrew their proposal.

After three weeks it was finally decided, amid general sighs of relief, that the revolution was still in its military period and that, according to Sun Yat-sen, the solution of such problems as the land would have to await the final military victory and unification of the country, which would usher in the period of "political tutelage." A resolution was accordingly adopted recognizing in principle the desirability of confiscating big landed properties—fixed at the astronomical figure of 500 mow—but recommending that for the time being land rents should not exceed 40 percent of the harvest. This decision was a partial retreat even from the standard plank for a 25 percent rent reduction, since land rents, amounting to 70 percent of the crop in some places, were more commonly set at 50 to 60 percent. Nevertheless, the Communists acquiesced. When the Commission further decided not to publish any record of its deliberations "for fear of creating confusion," the Communists again concurred. The army was saved. The landlord was saved. The Kuomintang was saved. The issue was settled to the satisfaction of everyone but the peasants. They had to be patient. If they would only keep on supporting the National government while they waited, all would be well.

Unfortunately, the initiative was already being seized by other hands. Inspired by the success of Chiang Kai-shek and directly instigated by him, militarist rebellions against Wuhan's authority rose on all sides. In northern Hupeh, a general named Yü Hsüeh-chung defied the government. In the west another militarist, Yang Shên, started moving his troops against the Nationalist capital. Hsia Touyin, the Nationalist commander who held the western front against Yang, abruptly mutinied on his own and with a handful of troops careered through the country south and west of Wuhan, burning, looting, and coming to the aid of the landlords and gentry against the peasants. Ch'ü Ch'iu-po, of the Communist Central Committee, records that the peasants in the area were already so confused and disoriented by the failure of the Wuhan government to support its own promised reforms that efforts to organize the peasants for resistance to Hsia brought little or no response.[31] Yeh T'ing, a Communist officer, managed by heroic efforts to stave off Hsia's threat to Wuchang, on the south bank of the Yangtze opposite Hankow. But the Nationalist capital remained beset on all sides, militarist revolts threatening from without and economic stagnation within.

On May 18, in the midst of panic, the editor of the *People's Tribune* watched frightened people "with laden carts, bearing household goods, going by our windows" and "heard whisperings of woe in the air. . . . Disaster is impending, say panic-stricken people in the city. . . . Foreigners have been half-frenzied, half-elated. They have seen the end of the hated rule of Nationalist Hankow. . . . Tomorrow morning they expect to see the dawn of a new regime in Wuhan."[32] The editor scoffed both at the panic of the Chinese and the hopes of the foreigners and prophesied an early victory for the Nationalist cause on all fronts, but his optimism was forced. The clamps were closing in. The Left Kuomintang did not even consider taking the bold steps that might have given it a chance to defeat its rising array of enemies. The great masses of peasants and workers had risen in their own behalf but had been left leaderless. There was no organization of local power in the villages, no program of action offered to them to enable them to move forward. There was nothing but an immense milling about, confusion, disarray, and uncertainty.

The Communists, for their part, were tied hand and foot to the Left Kuomintang leadership. The Comintern had "advised" bold measures in city and country but the leaders of the Left Kuomintang did not accept this advice. The Comintern had also said that without the co-operation of the Left Kuomintang victory was impossible. From this the Communists concluded that they had no choice but to concede. This was eminently satisfactory to Wang Ching-wei, who appeared as guest of honor at the opening of the Fifth Congress of the Chinese Communist party in Hankow on April 27. Here he said that he and his colleagues "gladly accepted the perspectives of the Communist International" and "completely agreed" with the report of the chief Comintern delegate, the Indian Communist M. N. Roy. Mif, present at the Congress, wrote that Roy gave the Chinese Communists "for the first time, a really Leninist prognosis" of the events taking place, "a thoroughly thought-out perspective of the movement" and "directives on a series of cardinal questions."[33] Before long, the Fifth Congress and Roy himself, much to Mif's embarrassment, would come under attack in Moscow for ignoring the Comintern "line" but at the time the central organ of the Comintern published Roy's report with full responsibility and without adverse comment. With all due modesty, Roy wrote: "The Fifth Congress had a great many complex and difficult questions to solve. . . . A clear perspective for the future development of the revolution had to be traced and firm leadership given to it. It was the historic role of the Fifth Congress to give this perspective, to trace the line of conduct for the proletariat, and to help create clear-thinking, devoted, and energetic leaders indispensable to the victorious march of the revolution. The Congress fulfilled this task."[34]

Roy later claimed that he had fought hard to get the Chinese Communist party to pursue a bolder revolutionary course even if it meant a break with the Left Kuomintang. His own reports published at the time fail, however, to back him up in this claim. Here is how he estimated the situation in the report he made to the Comintern on the Fifth Congress itself:

The differentiation of the classes within the Kuomintang has strengthened the bonds between its Left Wing and the Communist Party. The departure of the big bourgeoisie has permitted the transformation of the Kuomintang into a revolutionary bloc composed of the industrial proletariat, the peasants, and the petty bourgeoisie (in addition to several strata of the bourgeoisie). . . . The Chinese revolution continues to develop on the basis of a class coalition and cannot yet be submitted to the exclusive leadership of the proletariat. . . . The leading members of the Kuomintang participated in the opening meeting of the Congress and declared that they were ready to fortify the bloc with the Communist Party.[35]

This was plainly a simple repetition of the formulas laid down in Moscow. Writing one year after the rude jolt of events had smashed both the revolution and Roy's untouchability, Ch'ü Ch'iu-po said:

Roy's political view was that the Lefts and the petty bourgeoisie had no other way out but by following us. He did not point out the possibility of new betrayals and the concrete, complicated tasks the Communist Party should have undertaken against the possibility of such new betrayals. Therefore the atmosphere of the Fifth Congress was governed by the slogan: "Long live the cooperation of Communism with the Three People's Principles to the end!"[36]

In his report to the Congress as general secretary of the party, Ch'ên Tu-hsiu acknowledged that although the peasants were moving on their own initiative to seize the land, "we have carried out too pacific a policy." He agreed that large estates should be seized but added: "At present the alliance with the small landholders is still necessary. We must not fall into extreme leftism but must follow a centrist line. We must also wait for the development of the military movement before seizing the large and middle landholdings. The only correct solution at the present moment is that the extension of the revolution must take place before it is deepened."[37]*

The deliberations of the Congress on the land question followed the pattern of the discussions at the meetings of the Kuomintang Land Commission. In the end, the Communist Congress approved in principle the confiscation of large landholdings. But, it added, "land belonging to the small landowners and land belonging to the officers of the revolutionary army is not subject to confiscation."[38] This meant evading the issue of the land altogether, for there was scarcely a subaltern in the armies of Wuhan, to say nothing of the generals, who was not kin to landowners in Hunan, Hupeh, or other provinces. Ch'ên Tu-hsiu himself had pointed out in his report that "the officers are young men from the landlord class." To concede to them was to abandon the peasantry.

The tendencies of the Fifth Congress were described by Ch'ü Ch'iu-po as follows: "Borodin's line was to retreat and slacken the agrarian revolution . . . concessions to the petty bourgeoisie . . . concessions to the so-called industrialists and merchants; concessions to the landlords and gentry; ally with Fêng Yü-hsiang to overthrow Chiang Kai-shek; and with such a policy to lead the Left leaders against the Right reactionary forces of Wuhan and Nanking. Roy was for relative concessions to the business men . . . against conceding anything to the landlords and gentry [but] for small concessions to the small landlords and revolutionary generals." The Central Committee of the party was for "complete concessions to the business men, complete concessions to the landlords and gentry, considering that the agrarian revolution could not be realized immediately but required an adequate period of propaganda . . . considering it best to let the Left [Kuomintang] lead and for us to go off the path a bit so that the revolution should not be prematurely advanced."[39]

These were shadings, but they all added up to one view: to retreat.

---

* When this statement was published, without comment, by *Pravda*, in Moscow, Trotsky added a footnote to his reply to Stalin's thesis on China: "This road is the surest, most positive, the shortest road to ruin. The peasant has already risen to seize the property of the large landowners. Our party, in monstrous contradiction to its program, its name, pursues a pacific-liberal agrarian policy. . . . The agrarian policy of Comrade Ch'ên Tu-hsiu, who is bound hand and foot by the false leadership of the representatives of the Comintern, is objectively nothing more than the formula of severance of the Chinese Communist Party from the real agrarian movement." Trotsky, *Problems of the Chinese Revolution* (New York, 1931), pp. 77–78.

The important task, the Congress proclaimed finally, was to "unite all democratic elements under the banner of the Kuomintang."[40] To accomplish this it was necessary not merely to evade the radical demands of the peasants but to curb them. It was necessary to sacrifice every popular demand to the requirements of the bloc with the little band of top leaders of the Wuhan Kuomintang. The Comintern would soon be denouncing this course and charging the Chinese Communists with exclusive responsibility for the debacle that followed. But the record shows that the Chinese Communist party was with literal fidelity carrying out the directives it had received from Moscow. In Hankow, in any case, were Borodin, Roy, Mif, the Russian trade-union leader Lozofsky, Browder, Doriot, and a whole staff of "Bolshevik" advisers hanging on to the end of wires from the Kremlin. Not one of them spoke up for any different course. Every one of them helped chart and endorsed the path that was followed.

Moscow had imposed a formula which canceled itself out: victory was impossible without the agrarian revolution; victory was also impossible without the co-operation of the Left Kuomintang. But, as we have seen, under the leadership of the Left Kuomintang, it was impossible to have the agrarian revolution. Hence, on Moscow's terms, victory was impossible.

Chapter 14

THE STRUGGLE FOR THE LAND

THE RISING of the peasants in Central China in the spring of 1927 was the greatest since the days of the long-haired Taipings. It was another one of those moments in Chinese history when the peasant saw the chance to hope for more from life than the right to toil and to die. He saw himself as a man and the will rose in him to live like one. It drove him, in his millions, to struggle against everything that had made him the little-heeded hewer, drawer, and bearer of burdens in a civilization thousands of years old.

Ignorant leaders had tried to draw moral distinctions for him among those who held him down. There were "bad" gentry to be overthrown and "good" gentry who were his friends. There were big landlords whose land, at some future time, he would be permitted to recover, and there were smaller landlords who were his "allies." His enemies in the village were the *t'uhao*, the local bullies, officials, and hirelings of the landlord; but all the relatives of Nationalist officers, although they were landlords and usurers and petty officials, were his friends and liberators and were not to be offended by threats to their property. But as the pressure grew and the "revolutionary" government showed no sign of implementing even its mildest promises, the peasant began to see that the slogan: "Down with the *t'uhao* and bad gentry!" corresponded not to his interests but to the interest of those who wanted his services without paying for them. There was an awakening in the villages. The slogan underwent a plebeian face-lifting and soon ran: "All who have *t'u* (land) are *hao* (oppressive) and there are no gentry who are not bad!"[1]

The Kuomintang said, "Down with the unequal treaties!" But the only unequal treaties the Hunan peasants knew were the tenancy agreements which compelled them to surrender to the landlords up to 70 percent of their crops, to make noninterest-bearing cash deposits in advance on their rent, to make gifts to the landlords at festival times, to serve without wages when a betrothal, a marriage, or a funeral in the landlord's family required preparation for ceremonies or the conveying and serving of guests. To the Hunan peasant the "abolition of the unequal treaties" meant abolition of thralldom on the land. The Kuomintang promised only a 25 percent reduction in rent and a "restriction" of interest rates to 20 percent per annum. It spoke of "equalization of tenants' rights" without ever explaining what it meant. The tenants soon gave it a meaning that made sense to them. When the Left Kuomintang proved unwilling or unable to carry out its own program, the peasants moved with swift and direct logic to take over for themselves the land they tilled. In their thinking and in their deeds, they moved with that draconic simplicity which suspends all subtleties and challenges all encrusted traditions. It was a fearful thing for those who stood to lose by it and they fled. By the end of April across widening areas of Hunan and Hupeh, confiscation of land and property was the order of the day. In Central China the struggle for the land brought nearly ten million peasants into the orbit of new mass organizations in a few short months.

The accumulated oppression of centuries had laid charges deep in the soil, and when the Nationalist revolution touched them off, everything in the old society was shaken, everything that was old, corrupt, degenerate, and decadent. Bandages were torn from the bound feet of children. Young girls, with bobbed hair and an air of defiant energy, streamed into the countryside to awaken their sex and free it of chains that bore the mold of generations.* Confucius, the high priest of privilege and submission, was torn from the shrouds of a reactionary morality and paraded in effigy through the village streets. Buddhist temples were taken over and turned into schools and meeting-places. Foreign missionaries, who had never been able to make much of an impression on Chinese who knew better than to believe in a single truth, packed and fled from something they called anarchy because it was beyond their understanding. Superstitions and old habits suffered. "The clay and wood gods have already lost their dignity," said a report from the country. "The people no longer need

* "I have lived eighty years," said an old woman to a girl propagandist in the field, "without seeing such a short-haired, big-footed, uniformed female creature like you." In a letter to a Hankow friend, the girl told how, sitting in a meadow at Chiayu, in southern Hupeh, she spoke to a group of peasants about the evils of foot-binding. A well-to-do, middle-aged woman with three-inch "golden lilies" hobbled up to her and said: "Your feet are so big. Won't your husband get into your shoes some time by mistake?" All the soldiers and peasants who stood around laughed. The girl blushed, and then began to laugh herself. From "A Letter from the Field," *People's Tribune* (Hankow), June 22, 1927.

the Five Classics and the Four Books. What they want is political reports. They want to know the conditions in the country and in the world. The *mên shên* [door gods] which used to be pasted on the gates have now been covered with slogans. Inside the houses even the *chao-mu kao-piao* [ancestral tablets] have been crowded out by placarded slogans."[2]

Evils which had been deeply rooted in the old society were swept away in the flood. One of them was opium smoking. "Ever since the last days of the Manchus," said a report from Hunan, "the government has repeatedly prohibited opium. But in fact the opium prohibition bureau has always been the bureau for selling opium. Only petty smokers were fined. The greedy officials and gentry, even though they smoked right out in the open, were never touched. . . . But the ban that was a ban in vain for twenty years became a ban in fact after the peasants rose. The village peasant associations decreed that anyone found smoking would be fined and paraded. After many prominent gentry had been paraded in dunce caps, nobody in the villages of Hunan dared again to smoke. The peasants smashed the pipes of the gentry. To eradicate gambling, the Pioneers (boys of twelve to fifteen) made house-to-house searches. Mah jongg and other gambling paraphernalia were burned on the spot. Footbinding was abolished. Dams and roads were built, waste lands put under cultivation. . . . Establishment of schools and smashing of superstitions became the most enthusiastic work in the villages. . . . The peasants created a peaceful village. No matter how you describe the tumult of the Hunan villages, they have been in fact more peaceful than when the landlords ruled. . . ."[3]

The peasant went about his task with a grim thoroughness and often not without the humor that is one of his universal traits. In Hwangkang, Hupeh, the dunce caps used for the gentry who were paraded through the town in disgrace were the three-*do* three-*sen* measuring containers which the landlords used when they divided the grain at rent-collection time. Peasant justice was swift and simple in the villages. It was astonishingly lenient. Few executions were ordered or carried out. In most cases heavy fines or prison sentences were imposed on the landlords and their followers who had committed crimes against the peasants. Justice was administered by the local peasant committee sitting before a mass meeting of the peasants. Disputes and claims had previously been settled by the local magistrate or by the local big landlord who enjoyed the privileges of a feudal baron before the law. He would sit in his own courtyard and dispense justice as it pleased him. This was now all changed. The local peasant committees took up the long list of unsettled grievances and swiftly settled all outstanding cases. Their decisions reflected the fact that they wanted to have done forever with landlords and usurers.

The peasant organizations faced the economic problems of the village with the same incorrigible simplicity of purpose. They could solve nothing in the absence of a radically new economic policy in the urban centers. But they tried. With confiscated hoards and stocks of food and commodities, they set up co-operatives in many places and took steps to regulate the movement of grain and to prevent speculation. Some of these co-operatives even issued notes which were readily accepted by the peasants of the locality. When it came to the matter of land rent due to the landlords, they simply declared it abolished. Loans outstanding at usurious rates were simply declared canceled. They tried in their own way, too, to get at the root of one of the worst miseries of peasant life: the sale of women and children into prostitution and slavery. Traffic in human lives had long been a trade which thrived on human misery. Each year tens of thousands of women and children were sold into brothels or into the homes of the wealthy as chattel slaves. In Yanghsin, the delegates of the hsien, or district, peasant association voted to appropriate part of the funds confiscated from the gentry to feed the hungry "so that they would not need to sell their wives and children in order that they might live." But every partial, crude effort they made to cope with their economic difficulties brought the peasants in the end to the basic problem of the land itself. No hunger was greater than the land hunger and in district after district the peasants reached out to satisfy their craving. They began to declare the land confiscated and to divide it among themselves.

In many places this was accomplished in the beginning with surprising ease. Out of fear for their lives or with the characteristic hope that they would be left at least a share in the division, many landlords voluntarily surrendered their land to the peasant associations. They felt that this movement was far too strong for them. The government at Wuhan, the armies sweeping across the land, all seemingly devoted to the idea of a revolutionary transformation, were more than they could prudently oppose. If they did not have the means to flee, many landlords prepared to make the best of the new dispensation, to adapt themselves to the new power that spoke, they thought, for the peasant. But this soon changed, as the landlords and village gentry began to realize that in Wuhan no such power existed, that in Wuhan there was only irresolution, vacillation, and a fear of the peasants that was, if anything, greater than their own. Their self-confidence returned. They began to group themselves, by village and by dis-, trict, for resistance to peasant demands. They rallied their bands of plug-uglies, village scoundrels, and formed them into *min t'uan,* or militia. Paid off with money and spurred by promises of prefer-ment later on, these bands began to prey on the village organizations and were soon marauding through the countryside with growing boldness.

A detailed report of the situation in the Hunan countryside made by the local peasant association described the situation in the follow-ing passages:

The Hunan peasants at the present time cannot be said to have overthrown the *haoshên.** We can only say that they are rebelling against them. Those who do not know the real conditions say that in Hunan the conditions are terrible, that too many *haoshên* were killed. But the facts are otherwise. . . . The *haoshên* killed numbered only tens but the number of peasants killed by the *haoshên* is astounding. . . . Many people know that the peasants are conducting a revolution in Hunan but few know the cruelty and cunning of the *haoshên.* . . . It has been very common in all hsien for the *min t'uan* to lynch peasants. . . . Torture was freely used. . . . After being arrested peasants would be killed outright or mutilated first, muscles of the feet extracted, genitals cut away and so on. . . . The *min t'uan* in Tsalien burned alive in kerosene a student who had come to the district to work in the peasant movement. . . . After being driven from the villages by the peasants, the *haoshên* and the dregs of the *min t'uan* often sought alliance with the bandits to fight the peasant associations. Nine reports out of ten coming to the provincial peasant association tell about the gath-ering of the *t'uhao* with the bandits to drink wine and cock's blood† for the overthrow of the peasant association, for the extermination of the party commissioner. . . .

They also formed reactionary organizations. In Siangsiang, they called it the Association for the Maintenance of Town and Village. In Hengyang, it was the White Party. In Liling and Liuyang, the San-Ai Party. In Liling, there was also the Association for Beating Dogs, the

* *Haoshên,* a term embracing the landlords and the gentry and their local tools and hirelings, the latter being known as *t'uhao,* or oppressors on the land.

† A ceremonial oath of alliance.

dogs meaning the peasants. In many parts of Hunan, there was the Party for the Preservation of Property. These organizations planned and carried out the massacres of peasants and raids on peasant associations. . . . Sometimes these plots were uncovered by the peasants but the organizations were never dissolved. . . . Another method used by the *t'uhao* was to mingle in the peasant associations . . . to disrupt them. Or else they organized their own peasant associations. They also agreed wholeheartedly in words with the peasant movement. . . . They would organize on a clan basis in order to set one hsien against another, one name against another.* They would entice clansmen into the association with promises of cheap grain. They also deceived the higher organs and got themselves recognized as special village or district peasant associations.[4]

The families of the gentry, who fled to Changsha, Hankow, and all the way to Shanghai, spread the wildest tales they could devise. Among them was that hoary old reliable that has cropped up in every revolution, East or West, since 1789. They spread reports, among soldiers particularly, that within six months all their wives and sisters in Hunan would be "communalized." This accusation came from members of the gentry who normally kept as many concubines as they could afford, from landlords whose exactions forced peasants to sell their womenfolk into slavery and prostitution, and who were often the owners or at least the chief patrons of the fanciest brothels in their cities and towns. They also tried to outrage the filial sensibilities of the ordinary Chinese by alleging that in Hunan the Red peasants were massacring all foes over fifty years old.

Reports of the Hupeh peasant organizations closely paralleled those from Hunan. The principal difference was that in Hupeh, where the movement had been slower in getting under way, the gentry had often been more successful in capturing control of the peasant associations at the outset. "In many villages in the peasant associations there are no peasants at all," said a Hupeh report, "only the long-gowned and broad-sleeved gentlemen going out and coming in." Where the peasants did succeed in retaining control of their own organizations, the gentry concentrated their attention on the local Kuomintang branches. Once in control there, they would set up rival peasant associations under their own auspices and would maintain a clear line of demarcation between the peasants and the party. "In Chi-hsui hsien there were even such things as refusals to let peasants join the party." In Hupeh, also, there sprang up under various names

---

* In many hsien, most of the inhabitants bear a single surname and belong, in varying degrees of relationship, to the same clan.

reactionary bands like the *Ta Tao Hui* (Big Sword Society), the *Ch'üan T'ou Hui* (Fist Society), and others, financed and led by the landlords. Contact between the gentry and the rebelling militarists was quickly established. When Hsia Tou-yin rebelled in May, a reporter in the area described how his troops marched

from Chiangling to Chienli, Hsienti, Tungyang, everywhere opening the prisons to release the *haoshên*, who then acted as guides to hunt down the commissioners of the peasant associations and the executive committee members and to slaughter them. They killed right and left almost all the way to Wuchang. In the hsien adjacent to Honan, the gentry united with the Red Spears to massacre the peasants. In western and northern Hupeh they joined with Chang Lien-shen and Yü Hsüeh-chung. . . . In Yanghsin they poured kerosene over the peasants and burned them alive. In Hwangkang they used red hot irons to sear the flesh and to kill. In Lotien they bound their victims to trees and put them to death with one thousand cuts into which they rubbed sand and salt. They cut open the breasts of the women comrades, pierced their bodies perpendicularly with iron wires, and paraded them naked through the streets. In Tsungchang, every comrade was pierced twenty times.[5]

The Hupeh Provincial Peasant Association estimated that 4,700 peasants, including 500 women, were slain in this manner in the province between February and June. It listed the means of execution: "Beheading, burying alive, shooting, strangling, burning . . . cutting into pieces."[6] Whatever the crude and unlettered country folk lacked in refinement, they learned in these harsh days from those who defended their masters' culture, so aged, so delicate, so beloved of so many sentimental foreign Sinologues. The peasants never succeeded in perpetrating even a fraction of the horrors inflicted upon them by their betters when the struggle was reduced to raw violence.

For the peasants of Hunan and Hupeh were virtually defenseless. They had nothing but their numbers and their newly awakened will to change the conditions of their lives. In this they were alone. They had not been allowed to create any effective organs of local power. Beyond them, in Wuhan, no central power supported them. The government never got around, as report after report testified, to enforcing its own promises of rent reductions. What it did do was to block at every turn the efforts the peasants made to carry out their own program for themselves. Petitions from peasant associations repeatedly urged the government to define its policies clearly, to set up standards for the solution of the land problem. To these demands the government spokesmen replied only with lectures about the "excesses" of the peasants.[7]

In Hunan, the traveling delegation of the Communist International was again discovering facts that failed uncomfortably to accord with the analyses made in Moscow. According to an account by Sydor Stoler, the Russian member of the group, they found that the Kuomintang program of rent and interest reductions could not be realized "because of the resistance of the landlords." A Kuomintang representative told them: "There is a general and loud demand by the peasants of the province for *land*. They want the division of the land. They say they will be obedient to the Nationalist government but they at the same time demand that the government do something. They want the land!"[8]

In Moscow, Stalin was rejecting the idea of soviets, or local people's councils, because, it will be recalled, this would mean a struggle against the "revolutionary center" of Wuhan, the "only governmental authority." Trotsky was retorting that the "revolutionary center" was a fiction, that the machinery of revolutionary power had to be created on a popular basis in the towns and villages themselves. These sharply counterposed views are strikingly measured by the reports of those in the field who had never seen either Stalin's or Trotsky's theses on the subject. The Hankow representative of the Hupeh Provincial Peasant Association said in May that the most urgent need was "immediately to establish organs for the maintenance of the political system. The political organs now existing are not really a power at all."[9] Stoler, Browder, and Doriot were discovering in Hunan that the peasants were trying, in their own way, to create precisely the kind of local organs of power of which Trotsky spoke, and that Stalin's "only governmental authority" really did not exist at all.

"While the militarists have been defeated and driven out," they reported, ". . . the magistrates and gentry, like the landlords, remained. We saw them everywhere. . . . They still exercise their feudal dictatorship over the population. . . . A revolution without the destruction of the old system of local government is unthinkable. . . . This is keenly felt and understood by the masses everywhere. . . . In Hunan the process of supplanting the old system has also proceeded further than in any of the other provinces we passed through. . . . Special commissions were being set up in various districts of the province to take over the administration of local affairs. These commissions are composed of representatives of the Kuomintang, the trade unions, and the peasant unions. . . . While the old magistrates are still officiating in the villages, they are gradually being pushed out and supplanted by so-called citizens' councils, which are directly elected by the population. . . . But it is appropriate to remark here that all this work of sweeping out the old rotten system . . . still lacks in system and planfulness. The absence of a definite program of action for the reorganization of local government is keenly felt. Of course it can be explained by the preoccupation of revolutionary China with the war against the militarists and the struggle against imperialism." Everywhere the Comintern visitors heard the cry: "Arms to the peasants! We have no guns or ammunition. The peasants must be armed!" They found peasants organizing defense groups with picks and plows and they listened to plans being hopefully made in almost every district for obtaining arms and ammunition. "Cases were cited where the peasants had captured thousands of rifles from the Northern troops, but invariably these arms were handed over to the National government or the army."[10]

The peasants wanted land and arms and were trying to organize "citizens' councils" to rule and defend themselves against the counterattacks rising on all sides. The secretary of the Comintern group wrote that it would be a "fatal error for the National government to neglect to tackle the agrarian problem in the most decisive revolutionary manner," but the National government was making this "fatal error" and the Communists were deprived of any power to rectify it. In Wuhan when it was a matter of carrying out any kind of an agrarian program, there was evasion, confusion, and lack of policy; but when it came to efforts to rein in the peasants and keep them from acting in their own behalf, there was never any lack of decisive action. When the peasant associations began exercising political power in the villages, the Wuhan regime ordered them to desist. Unable or unwilling itself to deal with the bands of *min t'uan* marauding through the countryside, the Wuhan government prohibited the holding of trials by the peasant associations and a little later even ordered them not to make any arrests of any kind.[11]

"Unscrupulous landlords and gentry are denounced by the Party for the reason that they have persistently fleeced the peasants by oppressive means," said the Central Executive Committee of the Kuomintang. ". . . It must be pointed out, however, that it is only after clear and conclusive evidence is established concerning such fleecing and oppressive conduct that landlords and gentry should be dealt with by legal organs. Those innocent and well-to-do families in the villages and districts who are not opposed to the national revolution are under the protection of the Nationalist government. Our party comrades should definitely instruct the masses against reckless attack on others' liberty of person, property, profession, or religious faith. Anyone who is bent upon disturbing the local public order . . . is opposed to the revolutionary interests and his conduct is tantamount to anti-revolutionary offenses. The party headquarters in the various localities should take heed to check such actions. . . ."[12]

"The peasants are glad to give the government this task of judging," said the secretary of the Hupeh Provincial Peasant Association, "but the government has no legal officers in all these districts. Our greatest demand is that the Wuhan government should quickly establish local governments. . . . Such a government we peasants will still defend with our lives if the government will grant us arms."[13]

But the government did not want a revolutionary power in the villages. Instead it ordered the dissolution of peasant associations which attempted to wield such power. Each peasant association was permitted, in theory, to have only fifty armed militiamen, and there was a decree that said that these fifty might use their arms only against bandits, not against the landlords. In all Hupeh, where by June there were no fewer than three million peasants organized, the peasant associations possessed seven hundred revolvers, and these were scattered all over the province.[14]

"Many hsien have sent people to the capital to request the purchase of rifles," reported the Hupeh Provincial Peasant Association delegate to the Kuomintang. "They have brought sufficient funds, asking only aid in buying them. This is not only the demand of the village peasant associations, but the universal demand of the peasants." These delegates were turned back empty-handed and all other appeals went unanswered. "The peasants . . . were without arms and were continually subject to attack by counterrevolutionaries. Unfortunately it was generally impossible to meet the requests for military aid sent in from the country," said an official report of the Kuomintang.[15]

"In the Huang An district, for instance," said a Hupeh peasant association secretary, "reactionaries killed twenty-one of the most responsible peasant leaders. The union has begged the government to send troops to protect them. But the government says the troops are busy at the front. The union then asks for the right to use its own arms; but this also the government forbids, allowing it only against recognized bandits who attack villages, but not for civil conflict within the village. What can we do? The reactionaries recognize no law; they kill as they wish. But we must recognize law, for we are a responsible union. Yet the law cannot help us and only forbids us to help ourselves. . . . We won the confidence of the peasants by promising relief from bad conditions. . . . This is not carried out. . . . The ordinary peasant only cried: 'Liars! You did nothing for us. Now we won't listen to your empty words.' We are trying to break down feudalism. But feudalism is based on the present economic structure of the village. The gentry have all the money. The poor must borrow every spring for seeds, fertilizer, even for their own food. Now the gentry refuse to lend any more because they hate the peasants' union. Two-thirds of the peasants can get no money for seeds. They begin to blame the union. We promised to organize cooperatives but for this also we have no money. . . . The law forbids us to take land from the gentry till the new land policy is settled and the courts decide. . . ."

"Against this terrific list of difficulties," Miss Strong added, ". . . he told me that the peasants' union made only two simple demands, immediate establishment of local governments with enough militia to support them against bandits and lawless reactionaries; and immediate establishment of cooperative stores and government credits to the peasants. . . . Such elementary and necessary demands," she concluded, "but under the military, financial, and political situation of Wuhan—such utopian dreams!"[16]

This was the revolutionary center, not in the fictional Moscow version but as it actually existed in Central China. As their most elementary demands became "utopian dreams," the peasants soon regarded as "liars" not only the Wuhan spokesmen but their own organizations as well. "The peasant unions," reported a speaker at a Hupeh conference on June 25, "have gradually lost the confidence and support of the peasant because what the peasants get from their struggle is often nothing but trouble or massacre."[17] When Hsia Tou-yin rebelled in May, it never occurred to him to haul down the flag of Wuhan. "Because he still put up the Kuomintang banner and did not clearly express his attitude," said a field report, "the peasants were attacked off their guard. The onslaught was sudden, arrests were made, many fled, so that the peasants lost their leaders and the organizations collapsed. Therefore they did not help in the fighting nor in transport."[18]

In the government at Wuhan there now sat two Communist ministers, holding, appropriately, the portfolios of Labor and Agriculture. The Communists had been originally ordered into the National government by the Comintern plenum at the end of 1926. The Kuomintang plenary session in March named T'an P'ing-shan Minister of Agriculture, and Hsü Ch'ao-jên, the Canton trade-union leader, Minister of Labor. Earl Browder wrote on April 10 that "the appointment of Communists to head these two posts signifies a deepening of the social phase" of the revolution. He said it meant a "turn to the left" that would "undoubtedly come as a surprise and shock to American and British imperialism."[19] Arthur Ransome, a British journalist, understood somewhat better than Browder what the position of the new Communist Minister of Labor would actually be:* "He will not be a tool of the trade unions," he wrote, "but a mediator between the government and labor."[20] In fact, the entry of the Communists into the Wuhan government preceded a sharp turn to the right that held surprises and shocks only for the workers and peasants.

As ministers, the Communists carried on in the role of hostages and compliant agents of Kuomintang policies. In its guiding directive for Communist leaders sitting with the Kuomintang leaders in the so-called Joint Conference, the Communist Central Committee reminded its representatives that any concrete proposals "should keep in mind . . . the solidarity with the Kuomintang Left Wing." They concurred without question when Wang Ching-wei announced that

---

* Arthur Ransome astutely summarized the Comintern's contribution to the Chinese revolution when he wrote in February 1927 that Russia taught the Kuomintang "how to turn Dr. Sun's pious program of a raised standard of living for the workers into a stout weapon of offense and defense. Borodin may be said to have taught Dr. Sun to rely on classes rather than on individuals after having taught him to rely on a party instead of on himself. Borodin could show how the revolution of 1905 was brought about by the workmen . . . for the benefit of the Russian bourgeoisie. He could show how agrarian revolution in France . . . crushed the feudal lords for the benefit of the bourgeoisie. . . . These are dangerous weapons, but no other could have brought about the result achieved. In bringing these weapons into active operation the obvious agents to use were the Chinese Communists, and on them will fall the heaviest blows if and when the Chinese revolution finds it necessary to blunt them." *The Chinese Puzzle*, London, 1927.

only the Kuomintang Central Committee had the right to publish the proceedings and decisions of the Joint Conference. The Communist committee also ordered its members working on newspapers* "to work in the spirit of the Kuomintang resolutions."[21]

At the formal induction of T'an P'ing-shan as Minister of Agriculture on May 20, Wang Ching-wei said: "The peasant movement has grown rapidly. . . . What we need now is a man who can lead and direct the peasants. . . . Comrade T'an is such a leader. He is unusually equipped to cope with the peasant problems." In his reply, T'an said: "I feel it is my solemn duty to work hard to carry out the government's agricultural policy . . . the agricultural program of the Kuomintang and the late Tsungli [Sun Yat-sen]."[22] This inaugural address, it was pointed out long after the event, "cannot be called other than shameful. He was silent on the agrarian revolution, on the confiscation of land, on the elimination of the power of the *t'uhao* and the gentry in the villages. He spoke at length about the liberal reform of peasant conditions and inveighed against 'excesses.' After assuming his post, T'an P'ing-shan immediately issued instructions to the peasants forbidding 'rash acts' against the *t'uhao* and gentry, threatening 'severe punishment.' "[23]

"At present there is a crisis in the peasant emancipation movement," said T'an in one of his first manifestoes as Minister of Agriculture. "[It is] a transitional period . . . a period of much struggle and chaos, of acts that are premature and of deeds that confuse the main issue. Some of this is attributable to excessive demands on the part of the peasants. While excessive demands must be attributed to, and are logical results of, the long suppression of the peasants . . . it remains a matter of necessity that they be checked and controlled. . . . The government therefore announces its policy that all irresponsible acts and illegal deeds of the peasants be nipped in the bud in the interests of the majority of the peasants and the larger phase

* The Communists never published any daily newspaper of their own, out of respect for the conditions of their bloc with the Kuomintang, nor were they ever instructed by the Comintern to do so. Of this party Stalin said in April: "While fighting in the ranks of the revolutionary Kuomintang, the Communist Party must preserve its independence more than ever before." "Preserve?" echoed Trotsky, "but to this day the Communist Party has had no such independence. Precisely its lack of independence is the source of all the evils and all the mistakes. Instead of making an end once and for all to the practices of yesterday, [Stalin] proposes to retain it 'more than ever before.' But this means that they want to retain the ideological and organizational dependence of the proletarian party upon a petty bourgeois party, which is inevitably converted into an instrument of the big bourgeoisie."

of the peasant movement. . . . All elements in the village sympathetic to the cause of the revolution must be gathered and organized
under its banner and to that end peace must reign in the villages. It
must not be annihilated by the peasants' excessive demands. As to
the local tyrannical landlords and gentry, these must be left to be dealt
with by the government. Free action by the peasants resulting in their
[the landlords'] arrest or their execution is punishable by law."[24]

Jên Hsü, general secretary of the All-China Peasant Association,
complained that "the peasant movement in Hupeh developed too
rapidly" and announced that the association had decided to "moderate" the peasant upsurge in order to ensure protection of the land of
the "revolutionary officers." The Hupeh Provincial Peasant Association obediently followed suit, "In compliance with the instructions of
the Central Kuomintang and the Nationalist government," it ordered
all branch associations "to prevent immature actions in the peasant
movement. . . . Efforts must be made to consolidate the front and to
seek for closer cooperation between the propertyless peasants, the
small landlords, the merchants, and the manufacturers. . . . Confiscation of the property of military men of the revolution or the property of those who are not local rowdies and bad gentry is banned."[25]
Wang Ching-wei, according to his biographer, complained to Borodin
that the peasants were not heeding these instructions and were seizing
the land wherever they could. "Borodin denied that he was responsible for the movement. . . . Wang then asked Borodin what he proposed to do about it. Borodin could only answer to the effect that the
only way was to modify the movement."[26]

But while the Wuhan politicians and the Communists were trying to "modify" what the Communist Central Committee on May 15
called "the infantile acts of the poor peasants,"[27] their time was already running out. They hoped for "restoration of order" and believed that they could accomplish this by official decrees and directives,
by complaints, pleas, and orders. In Hunan, these were now all
brushed aside. The "revolutionary" army now moved in to do the
job of restoring order in its own way.

On the night of May 21 in Changsha, capital of Hunan, the business of really "modifying" the peasant movement got under way.
General Hsü K'ê-hsiang, commander of the local garrison and a
subordinate of General T'ang Shêng-chih, ordered his men, the 33rd

Battalion of the 35th Army, to tie white bands around their arms. At their head he marched to the headquarters of the Hunan Provincial General Labor Union. Four pickets, two women, and a fifth man were shot down at the gate and the soldiers swarmed into the building. In quick succession similar raiding squads moved in on the provincial Kuomintang headquarters, the party school, and the quarters of all the many workers', peasants', and students' organizations. The offices were wrecked and their occupants either arrested or shot. The shooting continued almost until dawn. The next morning the city was plastered with bills: "Down with the extremists!" "Support Chiang Kai-shek!" Hsü K'ê-hsiang announced that he had been "forced" to take action because the pickets and peasant guards were planning to disarm his own men. Hsü likewise announced that the Hunan provincial Kuomintang and government would be "reorganized," and a committee, appointed by the military, was set up for that purpose.

News of the events in Changsha on May 21–22 trickled slowly into print in Wuhan. Not until four weeks later did the press carry full accounts[28] and that was when a delegation arrived from Hunan to petition the government for protection from marauding troops who had established a reign of terror throughout the province. By then, indecision and betrayal had finished what the militarists had begun.

The raids on May 21 proved to be the opening phase of the bloodiest chapter in the history of a bloody year. To the open space outside the west gate of Changsha at nightfall and at dawn, arrested men and women and boys and girls were marched and killed in batches. The solders amused themselves with the women victims, dispatching them with bullets fired upward into the body through the vagina. The men were subjected to nameless tortures. Many who were not decapitated were sliced through the body at the hips. After the first wave of killings, Changsha settled down to a routine of at least ten, and often as many as thirty, executions daily. Once begun at the provincial capital, the terror spread through the province. Within a few days, more than 100 were killed at Hengyang. On May 24 at Changteh, 600 active members of the local peasant association were slaughtered in a mass execution by machine guns. When the shootings began at the village of Liuyang, many peasants fled toward Changsha. There, near the city wall, Hsü K'ê-hsiang's soldiers met them and left 130 men and women dead and dying in front of the city gate. During the course of the next few months an estimated total of 20,000 people fell before this onslaught. For the scores killed by the revolution, the reaction took the lives of thousands.

Immediately after May 21 an attempt was made to mobilize the scattered peasant guards for a counterattack. Local leaders ordered the concentration of armed detachments in the hills outside of Changsha. Groups made their way with their rifles to the appointed place. Within a few days a peasant army said to number several thousand, men bitter with the loss of wives and sisters, fathers and brothers, stood ready to march on Changsha, which Hsü K'ê-hsiang then held with a force of 1,700 men. They counted on bottling up the Changsha garrison while they gathered forces on a province-wide scale. They counted, above all, on quick aid from Wuhan.

They were already on the march to begin the attack on Changsha when word came from the Central Committee of the Communist party in Wuhan to cancel plans for the attack on Changsha and "to await action of the National government for a settlement of the question."[29] The All-China Trade Union Federation and the All-China Peasant Association sent a joint wire on May 27: "To the Provincial Peasant Union and the Provincial Labor Union, care of the Siangtan and Siangsiang unions: The Central Government has appointed a committee of five which left here this morning for the settlement of the Changsha incident. Please notify all peasant and labor comrades of the province to be patient and wait for the government officials in order to avoid further friction."[30] The representative of the Communist Central Committee in Hunan immediately issued orders for the retreat of all the peasant units. They reached all but two detachments of men from Liuyuanghsien, who marched up to the gates of the city at the appointed time and were there wiped out by Hsü K'ê-hsiang's machine guns. The delay enabled General Ho Chien, who was due to hold the province in fief from Chiang Kai-shek, to send two regiments down from Yochow to reinforce the Changsha garrison. In a few days the opportunity to strike back and mobilize the whole province was lost.[31]

The "committee of five" sent down from Wuhan was headed by T'an P'ing-shan. Ch'ü Ch'iu-po records that Borodin also accompanied the party that left Hankow on May 26 "to carry out the task of restoring order." But they got no farther than the Hunan border. At Yochow they were turned back by the troops of General Ho Chien.

The task of restoring "order" had already been taken in hand by abler instruments of the counterrevolution.[82]

The "reorganized" provincial government ordered the immediate restoration of the *lien pao* system (collective family and village responsibility for the offenses of individuals). Decrees were issued offering protection to those who would denounce Communists and active leaders of the mass organizations. In the process of "reorganizing" the various public bodies, all the former leaders, wherever caught, were shot without ceremony. All land seized from the landlords or from the temples was ordered restored to the "rightful" owners. The plan to hold a provincial delegates' assembly was canceled and the hundred-odd delegates already in Changsha awaiting the first session, scheduled for June 1, were executed en masse. Schools were closed down. Girl students, especially those marked by the telltale bobbed hair, were subjected to gross indignities. The old newspapers which had been suppressed resumed publication. *Haoshên émigrés* who had fled the province returned in droves and filled the posts in the newly reorganized party and government. With them they brought the money with which they filled the private coffers of the militarists, Hsü K'ê-hsiang and Ho Chien.

Chapter 15

ᘓᘓᘓ

MOSCOW: THE "SUFFICIENT AUTHORITY" OF STALIN

WHILE IN CHANGSHA and a hundred other Hunan towns workers and peasants were being led out for execution by the soldiers of the Kuomintang, delegates from all over the world were meeting in Moscow at the eighth plenary session of the Executive Committee of the Communist International. Although Hsü K'ê-hsiang's military coup in Changsha took place three days after the plenum opened, only a handful of those present in Moscow knew that the ensuing days, until the plenum ended on May 30, were the bloodiest days of the terror in Hunan. The plenum itself, however, met in an atmosphere of terror all its own.

Theoretically, the Executive Committee of the Comintern was, after the world congress, the highest policy-making body in the International. Actually, policy was made by the Russian delegation and the Russian delegation was dominated by Stalin. Stalin's drive against Trotsky and the Opposition was entering its final phase. The real issue for Stalin was power, and his goal, now not far off, was the physical liquidation of dissenters and an end to the annoying need to answer for the consequences of his policies. But here he still had to account for his course and to defend himself against opposition to his leadership at home and abroad. The agenda was filled with urgent and critical questions of which the most urgent and the most critical was the fate of the Chinese revolution.*

---

* The Opposition was not a homogeneous body. It was composed of the original Left Opposition, led by Trotsky, and the so-called Leningrad Opposition, led by Zinoviev and Kamenev. The latter had in 1923 joined Stalin in a triumvirate directed against Trotsky and had passed into opposition only in 1926. There were differences between the two groups, and between Trotsky and Karl Radek, especially on the problems of the Chinese revolution. In formulating their joint platform, the Trotsky group, over Trotsky's protest, made several concessions to Zinoviev in the China question for the sake of their general agreement on other important issues. These differences involved not only such questions as "worker-peasant parties" and the "democratic dictatorship of the proletariat and the peasantry" but also involved, on Zinoviev's part, differing estimates of the Wuhan government and the Kuomintang. Trotsky in the debate continued to present his own views, which had been consistent

The plenum met at a time when Stalin's failures had become too patent to conceal. His internal policies had already begun to corrode the foundations of the regime.[1] More obvious, especially to the foreign delegates, was the dead end of Stalinist policies in Britain and China. The two pillars of his fight against British imperialism—the bloc with the British trade-unionists, Purcell, Hicks, and Citrine,[2] and the bloc with Chiang Kai-shek in China—had collapsed. The diplomatic break with Britain occurred while the plenum was in session. The same week the Anglo-Russian Trade Union Unity Committee, devised by Stalin as his prime weapon against the anti-Soviet moves of Downing Street, dissolved into thin air. While the plenum sat, too, the new articles of faith in Wang Ching-wei, T'ang Shêng-chih & Company in Wuhan were being blotted out by the blood of Hunan peasants.

In these circumstances, Stalin was not inclined to provide the Opposition with a public forum for its criticism. The plenums of the Executive Committee of the Comintern had previously taken place in Andreyev Hall, the former throne room of the Czars, inside the Kremlin. Hundreds of Russian and foreign Communists would always fill the large hall to listen to the reports and speeches. These were always reproduced verbatim in day-to-day accounts published in the Russian press and in the English, German, and French organs of the Comintern. This procedure was still being followed as recently as the two plenums held in the preceding year. The reports of the Sixth Plenum in February-March 1926 filled nine numbers of *International Press Correspondence*, taking up 202 closely printed pages. Reports of the Seventh Plenum, in November, were even bulkier, taking up

since 1923. The Stalin-Bukharin majority was able to make much of baiting the Opposition for its internal contradictions on this question. There were real and important differences, but the essential logic of the Opposition standpoint as a whole led directly to the demand for withdrawal of the Chinese Communist party from the Kuomintang and this was recognized by the majority as the Opposition's major demand. On the key question of Soviets, there was no difference within the Opposition. References in the text to the Russian Opposition refer primarily to the consistent Left Opposition led by Trotsky. Zinoviev, Kamenev, and Radek capitulated to Stalin the next year but this did not save the two former from execution and the latter from imprisonment in the purge trials eight years later. The differences within the Opposition on China would form part of a study of the whole course of the Opposition to Stalin, a history which remains to be written. Those relating to China are touched on briefly in a letter from Trotsky to Max Shachtman in 1930, published by the latter in his introduction to Trotsky's *Problems of the Chinese Revolution*, pp. 18–20. Zinoviev's views will be found in his "Theses on the Chinese Revolution," printed in the appendixes to the same volume.

sixteen whole issues of the same publication. This system was now abruptly scrapped. The Eighth Plenum met under semiconspiratorial conditions. Only a brief eight-line communiqué announced, somewhat belatedly, that it had convened.[3] The French Communist, Albert Treint, then a member of the presidium of the Executive Committee of the Comintern and also a member of the subcommittee of the Plenum on China (and a confirmed opponent of "Trotskyism") described the session as follows:

The last plenum of the Executive was held in the small room usually used for meetings of the Presidium—and this on the pretext that in Moscow, capital of the world revolution and the proletarian state, there was no other room available for the Executive Committee of the Comintern. In reality, it was a question of preventing the Russian comrades, usually invited to our international sittings, from attending the discussions, where they could have learned some of the things hidden from them. Political documents, bearing no secret character whatever, were delivered to the delegates only on the eve of the opening session of the Executive. Then the sessions of the plenum and its committees went on in unbroken succession, giving the delegates time to read these documents only most superficially if at all.

Delegates were forbidden to take copies of the stenograms of their own speeches or to communicate them to anyone. As soon as the plenum ended, all documents had to be returned immediately, on pain of not receiving permits to leave. They tried to forbid members of the Executive from making declarations when voting, but in the end, following several protests, this decision was applied only to members of the Opposition. For the first time in the history of the International, no record of the discussions was published either in the press of the U.S.S.R. or in the international Communist press. Only the resolutions adopted and a few statements made during the discussion were published, but these lost their real meaning when detached in this way from the discussion from which they emerged.[4]

Besides the resolutions, a brief editorial by *Pravda* on May 31, and a communiqué by the secretariat of the E.C.C.I., the press a month later published Stalin's speech and a report made by Bukharin about the plenum to a Moscow party meeting. It was not until a year later, after oppositionists abroad had begun to publish the speeches made by Trotsky, that the Comintern issued a slim pamphlet in German containing a few of the speeches on the Chinese question at the plenum.[5] The full report of the proceedings was never published.

Yet it was here that the differences in China were brought forward in boldest relief, especially when considered in conjunction with the events that were in precisely those days taking place on the territory of the Wuhan government.

In his speech, delivered on May 24—that is, three days after the Changsha overturn—Stalin reiterated his opposition to the creation of Soviets on the grounds that the Hankow government and the Kuomintang were the organs of the agrarian revolution in China.

The agrarian revolution [he said] constitutes the foundation and content of the bourgeois democratic revolution in China. The Kuomintang in Hankow and the Hankow government are the center of the bourgeois democratic revolutionary movement.

. . . Does the Opposition understand that the creation of Soviets of workers' and peasants' deputies now is tantamount to the creation of a dual government, shared by the Soviets and the Hankow government, and necessarily and inevitably leads to the slogan calling for the overthrow of the Hankow Government? . . . It would be quite another matter were there no popular, revolutionary democratic organization such as the Left Kuomintang in China. But since there is such a specific revolutionary organization, adapted to the peculiarities of Chinese conditions and demonstrating its value for the further development of the bourgeois democratic revolution in China—it would be stupid and unwise to destroy this organization, which it has taken so many years to build, at a moment when the bourgeois democratic revolution has just begun, has not yet conquered, and cannot be victorious for some time.

. . . Since China is experiencing an agrarian revolution, . . . since Hankow is the center of the revolutionary movement in China, it is necessary to support the Kuomintang in Wuhan. It is necessary that the Communists form a part of that Kuomintang and its revolutionary government, on condition that the hegemony of the proletariat and its party be secured both within and without the ranks of the Kuomintang. Is the present Hankow government an organ of the revolutionary dictatorship of the proletariat and the peasantry? No. So far it is not, nor will it be so very soon, but it has all the chances of developing into such an organ in the further development of the revolution. . . .[6]

Stalin wanted the "hegemony of the proletariat" in the Kuomintang and the Hankow government, which he expected to carry through the agrarian revolution. Trotsky argued in reply that the Wuhan leaders would break on the issue of the agrarian revolution and that the "hegemony of the proletariat" was realizable only if the masses were mobilized into soviets, or people's councils, really capable of leading the peasants in the crucial struggle for the land. "The bloc of Hankow leaders is not yet a revolutionary government," he warned. "To create and spread any illusions on this score means to condemn the revolution to death. Only the . . . Soviets can serve as the basis for the revolutionary government."[7]

Stalin [said Trotsky] has again declared himself here against the workers' and peasants' Soviets with the argument that the Kuomintang and the Wuhan government are sufficient means and instruments for the agrarian revolution. Thereby Stalin assumes and wants the International to assume the responsibility for the policy of the Kuomintang and the Wuhan government, as he repeatedly assumed the responsibility for the policy of the former "national government" of Chiang Kai-shek. . . . We have nothing in common with this policy. We do not want to assume even a shadow of responsibility for the policy of the Wuhan government and the leadership of the Kuomintang, and we urgently advise the Comintern to reject this responsibility. We say directly to the Chinese peasants: The leaders of the Left Kuomintang of the type of Wang Ching-wei and Company will inevitably betray you if you follow the Wuhan heads instead of forming your own independent Soviets. . . . Politicians of the Wang Ching-wei type, under difficult conditions, will unite ten times with Chiang Kai-shek against the workers and peasants. Under such conditions two Communists in a bourgeois government become impotent hostages, if not a direct mask for the preparation of a new blow against the working masses.[8]

This new blow, as we have seen, had already been struck in Hunan, where disorganized workers and peasants were being shot down in wholesale batches. If there was to be violence—and he assumed it was unavoidable—Trotsky wanted it the other way around. He called upon the Chinese workers and peasants to organize themselves into powerful councils that could win the soldiers' allegiance away from the generals. "Shoot the generals who do not recognize the Soviets," he said in the same speech. "Shoot the bureaucrats and bourgeois liberals who will organize uprisings against the Soviets. Only through the peasants' and soldiers' soviets will you win over the majority of Chiang Kai-shek's soldiers to your side."

The resolution adopted, however, of course followed the line prescribed by Stalin. Its key passages:

The Executive Committee of the Communist International deems erroneous the point of view of those who underestimate the Hankow government or deny its reality, its great revolutionary role. . . .

The Executive Committee of the Communist International particularly calls the attention of the Chinese party to the fact that now, more than ever, contact between the revolutionary government and the masses is necessary. It is only by this contact, realized primarily with the aid of the Kuomintang, only through determined orientation toward the masses, that it will be possible to strengthen the authority of the revolutionary government and its role as the organizing center of the revolution. The task of the Communist Party is to assure such an orientation on the part of the Hankow government. Without the realization of this task, without the unfolding of a mass movement, without the agrarian revolution, without a decisive improvement in the situation of the working class, without the transformation of the Kuomintang into a large and real organization of the toiling masses, without the future strengthening of the unions and the growth of the Communist Party, without the closest connection between the Hankow government and the masses, it is impossible to lead the revolution to its crowning victory.

In the present conditions in China, the Communist Party is for the war waged by Hankow. It is responsible for the policy of the Wuhan government, into which it enters directly. It is for facilitating the tasks of this government by every means. That is why the Communist Party can have nothing, "in principle," against the tactic of proceeding cautiously. Responsible for the policy of the government, the Communist Party would commit an utter folly if, whatever the circumstances, it rejected the tactic of compromise, that is, undertook to fight on all fronts at the same time. That is why the E.C.C.I. considers that this question must be settled concretely in conformity with the concrete conditions, which cannot be foreseen in advance. . . . The admissibility of a tactic of tacking must be reflected in the economic policy of the government. . . .[9]

This resolution ordered the Chinese Communists to "deepen" the agrarian revolution, to arm and mobilize the masses. But they were not to do this themselves. Nor was it to be done by letting the masses organize themselves. It was to be done through the "organizing center of the revolution," the Hankow government without whom, again, it would be "impossible" to lead the revolution to victory. In the matter of going along with the masses, it was the duty of the Communists "to assure such an orientation on the part of the Hankow government." But the question was: suppose the Hankow government proved unwilling to be oriented? What if it not only proved unwilling to go along with the agrarian revolution but openly opposed it? This question was neither raised nor answered in the formal resolution adopted by the plenum. In the private sessions of the subcommittee on China, however, according to the testimony of Albert Treint, it came up with perfect clarity. Stalin and Bukharin spoke publicly of the "great revolutionary role" of Hankow but they acknowledged privately it would not go very far with the peasants. On the other hand, the cooperation of the Hankow politicians and generals was indispensable, they believed. Hence it was necessary to keep the agrarian revolt within limits that would not frighten these allies away.

This was the point of view expressed by Bukharin to the sub-committee, which was composed of himself, Ercoli of Italy,* and Treint of France. Treint, who neither then nor afterward belonged to the Trotskyist opposition, balked at this, declaring it would lead to the armed suppression of the peasants. Called into the meeting by Bukharin, Stalin said that failure to check the peasants "would turn the Left bourgeoisie against us." He displayed telegrams from Borodin, Treint says, which showed that "the leadership of the Kuomintang was determined to fight against the agrarian revolution even if it meant a break with the Comintern." Against this danger, Stalin said, it was necessary to "maneuver."

"To fight now means certain defeat," argued Stalin. "To maneuver is to gain, with time, the possibility of growing stronger and of fighting later in conditions where victory will be possible. It is possible to maneuver without compromising anything. The agrarian revolution frightens the Kuomintang only to the extent that it directly strikes at its own members and the officers of the armies. I propose to send instructions to Borodin to oppose the confiscation and division of land belonging to members of the Kuomintang or officers of the Nationalist army."

When Treint thereupon demanded to know whether the Communists would be expected to support Hankow in the armed suppression of the peasants, Bukharin, he says, replied in the affirmative. At this point Stalin interjected: "Bukharin is drawing extreme logical conclusions, but things will not happen that way. We have sufficient authority over the Chinese masses to make them accept our decisions."†

But even as it was going on, this discussion was already academic. Long before the resolution of the Eighth Plenum and Stalin's tele-

---

* More recently better known as Togliatti.

† Treint adds that he insisted on having the instructions specifically order opposition to any attempt at use of force by the Hankow regime against the peasants. "We are agreed in principle," Stalin replied, according to his account, "but it is useless to send instructions relating to problems that are not before us. I repeat that we have enough authority over the masses in China to have no need of using force." Treint's record of this discussion was included, in its essence, in a public statement he made on July 22, 1927. (See "Déclaration de Camarade Treint," p. 64.) He expanded it from his notes at the request of the author in Paris in August 1935. His memorandum was subsequently published with the title "Compte Rendu Analytique de la Petite Commission Chinoise, Mai, 1927." It was reprinted in English in the *New Militant*, New York, February 8, 1936. Treint made no strong stand for his views at the Eighth Plenum but he was nevertheless expelled before the end of 1927 by the French Communist party.

gram of instructions arrived in Hankow on June 1, the Kuomintang generals were already exercising their own sufficient authority over the peasants. The documents from Moscow did not prove very helpful to the Chinese Communists. They were supposed to get the Left Kuomintang leaders to sponsor the agrarian revolution but they could not break from these leaders if they refused to accept Communist advice. They could not call upon the peasants to organize their own organs of power because that would have meant struggling against the Kuomintang. Publicly, the Comintern demanded the advancement of the agrarian revolution. Privately, Stalin's telegram required that it be kept within the limits needed to preserve the Kuomintang alliance. These directives canceled each other and left the Chinese Communists in hopeless confusion. They could do nothing but fall back on what the E.C.C.I. resolution called "the tactic of proceeding cautiously."

Stalin's June 1 telegram, as given by Ch'ên Tu-hsiu who received it,[10] contained the following points:

1. *"Confiscate the land . . . but do not touch the land of the military officers."*

This repeated, in essence, the formula adopted in principle both by the Kuomintang Land Commission and the Fifth Congress of the Communist party. Wang Ching-wei had bitterly opposed any form of land confiscation precisely because, according to his biographer, he realized that "from the gentry of Hunan and Hupeh the majority of the subaltern officers of the Second, Sixth, and Eighth armies were drawn."[11] As Ch'ên Tu-hsiu later put it: "Not a single one of the bourgeoisie, landlords, war lords, and gentry of Hunan and Hupeh provinces but was the kinsman, relative or old friend of the officers of that time. All the landowners were directly or indirectly protected by the officers."[12] Trotsky said six weeks later, when the text of Stalin's telegram became known, that these instructions converted the armies "into mutual insurance societies for the landlords, large and small."[13]

2. *"Check the peasants' overzealous action with the power of party headquarters."*

"We did execute this shameful policy," Ch'ên Tu-hsiu later acknowledged. But the overzealousness of the peasants was already being more effectively "checked" not by the Communist party but by the militarists of the Kuomintang.

3. *"Destroy the present unreliable generals, arm 20,000 Com-*

munists and select 50,000 worker and peasant elements in Hunan and Hupeh to create a new army."

In Hankow, the Communists gaped at this passage. They were supposed not to come into conflict with the generals or the Kuomintang but they were supposed to get rid of the generals and create a new army. "I suppose," said Ch'ên Tu-hsiu in the same subsequent document, "that we should still have pitifully begged the Central Executive Committee of the Kuomintang to discharge them."

4. *"Put new workers and peasant elements in the Central Executive Committee of the Kuomintang to take the place of the old members."*

Writing of this a year later, Ch'ü Ch'iu-po did not dare to quote directly from Stalin's telegram but ventured to quote a parallel passage from No. 71 of the *Communist International* which said : "On the one hand we must consolidate the national revolutionary army and the Kuomintang. . . . On the other hand . . . we must seek means whereby, not shaking the united front, we shall change the class groupings within the Kuomintang, in the National government, and in the armies." This, commented Ch'ü cautiously, "was extremely difficult because to change the class groupings in the army meant the capture of the army by the Communist Party. . . . [It meant] a certain social policy had to be put in force boldly to solve the livelihood problems of the soldiers, the peasants, and the broad masses."[14]

5. *"Organize a revolutionary court with a well-known member of the Kuomintang as its chairman to try the reactionary officers."*

This was, presumably, the suggested means of "destroying" the reactionary generals. On this basis the Communists approved the appointment of General T'ang Shêng-chih to judge the actions of his subordinate, Hsü K'ê-hsiang. Subsequently it meant the attempt to get Wang Ching-wei to judge T'ang Shêng-chih, a proposal actually made a few days later by M. N. Roy.

In general, the members of the Communist Central Committee, already confused and overwhelmed by the accumulated effects of their own previous policies, were dumbfounded and perplexed by these instructions. Ch'ên Tu-hsiu somewhat inelegantly expressed their feelings when he said it was like "trying to take a bath in a urinal." Even Borodin, Stalin's deputy, he relates, "saw no possibility of carrying them out." After considering the communication from Stalin for some time, the Central Committee finally voted to wire its thanks to Moscow with the accompanying plea that the goals designated "could not be realized immediately."[15] Roy, however, thought he had the solution. He promptly showed Stalin's telegram to Wang Ching-wei and asked him to endorse it. "I am quite sure," he is quoted as saying to Wang, "that you would approve of it."[16] But Wang did not approve at all. He did not want to destroy the unreliable generals. He wanted to ally himself with them. Roy discovered, to his dismay, that the Left Kuomintang did not have to follow Communist advice. It could go the other way. This was the one small flaw in Stalin's whole program: it required the approval of Wang Ching-wei and this it did not get.

On May 28 in Moscow, all unaware of these developments, Trotsky had written in a letter to the plenum: "The whole revolution cannot be made dependent upon whether or not the pusillanimous bourgeois leadership of the Kuomintang accepts our well-meaning advice. It cannot accept it. The agrarian revolution cannot be accomplished with the consent of Wang Ching-wei but despite Wang Ching-wei and in struggle against him. . . . But for this we need a really independent Communist Party, which does not implore the leaders but resolutely leads the masses. There is no other road and there can be none."[17] But no one was listening to Trotsky at the plenum. A special resolution was passed condemning him for advocating the creation of soviets, or councils, in China. A brief communiqué announced that "the plenum approved the transformation of the Wuhan government and the Kuomintang into a democratic dictatorship of the workers and peasants" and *Pravda* solemnly proclaimed that "the decisions of the Communist International on the Chinese question give the only correct answer to the most important questions of the Chinese revolution."[18]

In Hankow on June 1, the day Stalin's telegram arrived, a group of Communist-led organizations, headed by the Hupeh General Labor Union and the provincial Peasant Association, issued a joint appeal for patience pending the government's "settlement" of the Changsha militarist uprising. "Unfortunately," the appeal said, "a misunderstanding has arisen among the workers, peasants, and soldiers in Hunan province. But this will not interfere with our sacred task of revolution. The government has despatched a special commission for conciliation. A satisfactory settlement may be expected in a few days. . . . We have decided unanimously to carry out all the policies and orders adopted and promulgated by the government. We shall do our best to strengthen the united front of workers, peasants, and merchants to support the peasant policy of the party. We thoroughly understand that the only way to save the present difficult situation is practical cooperation between the government and the masses of the people. . . . As regards the incident in Hunan, we hope that the government will settle the case . . . and will guarantee that hereafter similar incidents shall not occur."[19]

Wang Ching-wei, however, declared that those responsible for the Changsha events were really the peasants who had dared to seize the land for themselves. "He opposed the proposal of Borodin and the Communists that the Central Executive Committee [of the Kuomintang] should order the attack on the revolting army and the punishment of the guilty officers, as he realized that they had been acting under grave provocation. Instead T'ang Shêng-chih was sent to Changsha to investigate into the affair and restore peace."[20] To this decision the Communists bowed. They announced their policy to be one "waiting patiently for a settlement." Actually, they had no other choice. They had no effective links whatever to the rank and file of the Nationalist army, no channels through which they could appeal to the soldiers—who were, after all, mostly landless peasants—on grounds of revolutionary solidarity.* Having tried in vain to "pacify" the peasants, the Communists now hoped to "pacify" T'ang Shêng-chih, assuring themselves and trying to convince others that he was a loyal believer in the Three People's Principles and would see that justice was done. When T'ang arrived from the Honan front on

---

* *Die Kommunistische Internationale*, Berlin, February 25, 1927: "The Chinese Communist Party and the conscious Chinese workers must not in any circumstance pursue a tactic which would disorganize the revolutionary armies, just because the influence of the bourgeoisie is to a certain degree strong there."

Trotsky's *Theses*, May 7, 1927: "The political leadership, instead of embracing the masses of the army through soldiers' Soviets, has contented itself with a purely external copy of our political departments and commissars which, without an independent party and without soldiers' Soviets, have been transformed into an empty camouflage for bourgeois militarism." *Problems of the Chinese Revolution* (New York, 1932), p. 49.

Ch'ü Ch'iu-po, a year after the events: "We did not pay any attention to the soldiers. . . . We paid attention only to the connections with the army divisional commanders or to the decorative work of the political departments. These political departments beautified the ugly counterrevolutionary faces of the division and army commanders. If the masses were disgusted with the military, they often expressed it in a disgust for the soldiers. The soldier masses were thereby very easily deceived by the militarists and persuaded that the workers, peasants, and Communists were against the armies, seeking only to destroy provisions and cause troubles in the rear." *The Chinese Revolution and the Communist Party* (Shanghai [?], 1928), chap. ii.

June 14 on his way to Changsha, the Communists issued a leaflet which insisted that the "Hunan coup was a revolt against T'ang Shêng-chih because T'ang . . . has expressed goodwill toward the oppressed peasants."[21]

In an attempt to develop a campaign in favor of a punitive expedition against Hsü K'ê-hsiang, several mass meetings were held and manifestoes issued by various Communist-led mass organizations. A group of refugees from Hunan called at Central Kuomintang headquarters. "Although the Hunan delegates have been in Wuhan for more than twenty days," their petition said, "still terror reigns in many districts of Hunan. The Central Kuomintang must send a punitive expedition against Hsü K'ê-hsiang." A large group of delegates from Hunan organizations called on General T'ang to ask for action against the Hunan militarists. "Laborers and peasants never will be suppressed," he promised them, "although some immature actions of the labor and peasant movements should be corrected . . . Long live the revolutionary masses in Hunan!"[22] The Communist party's supreme effort to carry out the instructions it had received from Moscow took the form of a letter sent on June 16 to the Central Executive Committee of the Kuomintang:

The moment for carrying out the agrarian policy is the present. This is the historic task of the Kuomintang. The future of the revolution depends upon whether or not the Kuomintang takes decisive steps in this question. . . . The Central Committee of the Chinese Communist Party proposes the following measures for the suppression of the counterrevolution: The Nationalist government must issue a decree declaring the committee of the insurrectionaries in Changsha to be counterrevolutionary and calling upon all soldiers to overthrow it. This committee must be dissolved and the rightful government of the province re-established. A punitive expedition must be sent immediately to suppress the insurrection. T'ang Shêng-chih must be authorized to send troops to overthrow the counterrevolution. The usurping local committee of the Kuomintang must be dissolved. . . The workers' and peasants' organizations and the Communist Party must continue to exist unmolested in the province of Hunan. The Nationalist government must order all arms to be returned to the workers' and peasants' guards. The peasantry must be armed to create a guarantee against further reactionary outbreaks. The Kuomintang must now take closer feeling with the masses of the people and lead them unanimously against the counterrevolution. Unless the Kuomintang and the Nationalist government do this, the revolution will be endangered."[23]

It all availed nothing. There was no punitive expedition nor even any thought of one. T'ang Shêng-chih made a quick trip of "investigation." His report was brief: "I have found," he wired from Changsha on June 26, "that the workers' and peasants' movement, under the misguidance of their leaders, has broken loose from control and precipitated a reign of terror against the people. In defiance of the explicit orders of the Central government for the protection of the revolutionary soldiers' families, they have everywhere extorted taxes and fines, abused people, and even murdered people. . . . Seeing this state of affairs . . . the soldiers who were stationed in Hunan rose for their self-defense. . . . Although Hsü K'ê-hsiang's actions were animated by a passion for justice, he has overstepped the limits of law and discipline. He should receive a light punishment in the form of a demerit but should be retained in the army service." T'ang concluded with a demand that the provincial regime be "reorganized" and asked for power to deal with "a few party members who are . . . planning to defy the government."[24] Three days later the government obediently responded by naming T'ang Shêng-chih chairman of the Hunan provincial government and distributing all the important provincial posts to his underlings.

On the same day that the text of T'ang Shêng-chih's telegram was published in Hankow, the central organ of the Communist International boasted reassuringly: "The panic-mongers of the Opposition have made much noise about the Changsha coup. They have spoken of a new defeat for the Chinese revolution. Their cries will convince no one. Our party is closely following the events in China . . . confident in the strength of the Chinese revolution. The uprising of the officers at Changsha, which met with the decided resistance of the workers and peasants, has already been suppressed."[25]

But what had already been suppressed was the revolution in Hunan. The mass executions were now sanctified by the authority of General T'ang Shêng-chih and the Wuhan government itself. A few days later, the new dispensation was established in neighboring Kiangsi province. There another militarist, General Chu P'ei-tê, who held Kiangsi nominally in the name of the Wuhan government, expelled all Communists, trade-union and peasant leaders, political commissioners, and party workers. The Communists in Hankow decided not even to raise this new issue publicly because, as they later explained, "they feared to drive General Chu away from the revolution" and hoped to "neutralize" him by keeping quiet.[26] The circle narrowed around Wuhan itself. In near-by Hupeh districts, "in

Chienmen, Yitsang, and other hsien, the massacre goes on," ran the somber report of a peasant union official on June 13. "Even ten *li* [three miles] from Hanyang, the *t'uhao* are surrounding and killing the peasants. There used to be fifty-four hsien with peasant associations. But last week there were only twenty-three. According to our estimate, the day before yesterday of these twenty-three hsien there were only four in which the peasants were holding their own. Today not one hsien is left."[27]

In the midst of this carnage, the Communists persisted in their delusions and their pleas. On June 23 the central organ of the Comintern told its readers that "the mass of the poor peasants is the reliable basis of the revolutionary Wuhan government." Tu Ch'êng-tsu, chairman of the General Miners Union of Hunan, said: "The workers have faith in the Kuomintang leadership. They feel that the central party will never sanction the suppression of labor and it is on this basis that they give the party their support."[28] The Communist leaders were still desperately trying to act in the spirit of the Moscow instructions, to ensure the "orientation of the Hankow government toward the masses." But the Wuhan leaders shrugged. "The Communists propose to us to go together with the masses," declared Wang Ching-wei at a meeting of the military council. "But where are the masses? Where are the highly praised forces of the Shanghai workers or the Kwangtung or Hunan peasants? There are no such forces. You see, Chiang Kai-shek maintains himself quite strongly without the masses. To go with the masses means to go against the army. No, we had better go without the masses but together with the army."[29]

Wang Ching-wei would not go with the masses, but that did not prevent the Comintern and the Communist party from going along with Wang Ching-wei to the bitter end. Borodin said later that it would have been premature in the spring of 1927 to take an independent revolutionary road because "the possibilities of collaboration with the Left Kuomintang had not yet been completely exhausted."[30] One after another, these possibilities had been probed; first Chiang Kai-shek, now Wang Ching-wei. It was not yet time to leave off imploring leaders, because not all the "possibilities" had even yet been exhausted. There still remained Fêng Yü-hsiang.

Chapter 16

WUHAN: THE DEBACLE

FÊNG YÜ-HSIANG, obese and unscrupulous, was a militarist who had risen to power in the Northwest by a series of shrewd and timely betrayals of his superior officers and allies. Originally nurtured on the bosoms of foreign missionaries, he first appeared in the world's headlines as the "Christian General" who taught his hymn-singing soldiers the homely virtues of rustic simplicity. In 1924, he discovered that Moscow made up in generosity what it lacked in spiritual piety. He shed his Christian skin and joined the ranks of that peculiar species, raised exclusively on Chinese soil by Stalin and Bukharin, the "Bolshevized" militarists. The Holy Grail proved no match for Russian arms, Russian money, Russian advisers. Fêng was quickly converted to the idea that a Russian gun in hand was worth a dozen halos in the hereafter, especially when military reverses at the end of 1925 cut his "People's Army" off from all other sources of supply.

He left for Russia early in 1926. "Fêng Yü-hsiang is coming to Moscow," said a dispatch to the New York *Daily Worker*, "to work as an ordinary workingman in a factory and thus amid labor surroundings to acquire a firsthand education and experience of all phases of economic and political life in the Soviet Republic. He is entering into this self-imposed exile in order to equip himself the most thoroughly to carry out the principles of the Kuomintang."[1] What Fêng wanted was to "equip himself most thoroughly" with the goods to be found in Soviet arsenals, and on his arrival at the Soviet capital he found that the open sesame to these riches was a simpler formula than the Lord's Prayer. He had himself and his henchman, Yü Yu-jên, photographed in the center of admiring Russian comrades. He predicted "new battles and new victories awaiting the future of the Chinese nation." Before very long he learned to call "special attention" to the "labor and peasant movement taking place throughout China" and to declare his conviction that "in the future the proletariat will ultimately gain a victory in China." On August 19, 1926, in an interview with *Pravda*, Fêng promised that his army would fight "for the emancipation of the nation" and "the consummation of the national revolution."

Although he had renamed his army the "Kuominchün" or "People's Army," the wily Fêng had for years evaded friends who importuned him to throw in his lot with the Kuomintang. "But when he visited Moscow," marveled a Japanese journalist, "the Christian General allowed himself to be a disciple of Lenin before anyone was aware of it." It was immensely easy, pleasant—and profitable. Delighted with his conquest, Stalin plied Fêng with arms and funds and shipped him back to his army, which had already started on a long trek southward from Nankow Pass through Shensi province toward the Honan border. Back among his soldiers, Fêng proclaimed on September 17, 1926: "I am the son of a laborer," and announced that it would henceforth be the object of his armies "to awake the masses . . . sweep away the traitorous military clans, break down imperialism, and secure the freedom and independence of China."[2] Fêng was now a full-fledged recruit in the ranks of Stalin's reliable allies and stepped boldly along the path already trod by Hu Han-min, Chiang Kai-shek, Li Chi-shên, T'ang Shêng-chih, and Wang Ching-wei. Secure behind the mountains in his great northwestern territory, he acquired huge stocks of Russian arms and ammunition, entrenched himself at Tungkwan Pass, overlooking the Honan plain, listened politely to his Russian advisers, and waited for his opportunity.

It was not long in coming. While he waited, the Northern Expedition swept to the Yangtze. Chiang Kai-shek, who had earlier learned how easy it was to unlock the doors to Russian arsenals, entered Shanghai and there broke, not his faith with Stalin, but Stalin's faith in him. T'ang Shêng-chih and Wang Ching-wei were by now also in the process of breaking away, although this was not yet officially admitted in Moscow. In any case, for Moscow there was still Fêng. He, surely, would come out of his western stronghold and save the day for the "revolutionary Kuomintang"! He was a solid man, closer to the soil, more deeply rooted in it than the thin reeds Moscow had until now leaned upon. He was, even now, reiterating by wire his undying fealty to Wuhan. News dispatches reaching Moscow indicating that Fêng was in touch with Chiang Kai-shek's emissaries, that Fêng would force Wuhan to come to terms with Chiang, were kept out of the Russian press and elsewhere hotly denied.

"Recently the imperialists have again been circulating rumors that Chiang Kai-shek would be reconciled with Wuhan or that he would collaborate with Fêng Yü-hsiang. This is false," said *La Correspondance Internationale* on June 8, 1927. "None of the leaders has any connection with Chiang Kai-shek. Fêng Yü-hsiang and his army have no confidence in this traitor either. . . ." Fêng was Moscow's last trump. To suggest that he would fall down on the job was the rankest Trotskyist heresy, for only Trotsky was warning, once more, that to put faith in Fêng meant to court a repetition of the experiment with Chiang Kai-shek.[3]

Wuhan, too, counted, almost piteously, on Fêng Yü-hsiang. Wuhan, it will be recalled, had decided to move northward against the Fengtien troops rather than against Chiang Kai-shek, in the hope that a military victory and the occupation of Peking would bring Chiang to heel. The success of this plan rested decisively with Fêng Yü-hsiang, sitting tight with his fresh forces back of Tungkwan Pass. In the first part of May the best divisions of the Kuomintang army had accordingly been moved up the railroad into Honan. Led by the famous "Ironsides," it fought its way northward in a series of battles which reached their climax at the end of June on the fields north of Chumiatien. Behind the lines in Hankow, workers toiled at the arsenal for thirteen, fifteen, and seventeen hours a day. Over their heads fluttered banners: "You are the rear guard of the revolution. . . . Unless you give your all, there can be no army, no revolution, no struggle to free China from its oppressors. . . . Our revolutionary soldiers do not fight in eight-hour shifts. Do you want to work only eight hours?" At the front the soldiers, too, thought they were fighting "to free China from oppressors." With unexampled heroism they hurled themselves at the better-fed, better-equipped armies of the Northerners, commanded by Chang Hsüeh-liang, the young son of Chang Tso-lin. The Fengtien forces were defeated but the Nationalists paid for this victory with the destruction of their best forces. They lost fourteen thousand killed and wounded.[4] The men fought as men had rarely ever fought before in China because they were animated by the hope that in fighting and dying they were helping to put an end to the hated poverty and degradation of their own people. But their sacrifice was futile. They had been sent into battle not for these ends but to feed the Napoleonic ambitions of T'ang Shêng-chih and the hopes of the Wuhan leaders that they could force Chiang Kai-shek to come to terms. These, too, were frustrated. Wuhan had put up the stakes, the flower of its army. It was Fêng Yü-hsiang who raked in the winnings.

Fêng had remained carefully aloof during the fighting. He now moved down from Tungkwan Pass along the Lunghai railway. Scarcely losing a man, he occupied Loyang and by June 1 was ensconced in new headquarters at Kaifeng. The rout of Fengtien and the decimation of Hankow's armies made him military arbiter of Central China. The march on to Peking depended entirely upon him. As if to underline that fact, he sent telegrams announcing his "victory" with fine impartiality both to Nanking and to Wuhan. He then summoned the Wuhan leaders to Chengchow for a conference on June 12. Here they came in a body to learn their fate.

Fêng waited until the Wuhan party had arrived at Chengchow before coming down the line to meet them. Anna Louise Strong watched Fêng alight, "with ostentatious simplicity," from a freight car, which he used because his "brother soldiers also travel in freight cars." She related that "a long time afterward" she heard that Fêng had entered the freight car at the last station before Chengchow, having traveled thus far in a comfortable private car on the same train. The Kremlin and its agents might have pondered the fact that only a year before Fêng had arrived in Moscow in a political freight car decorated with the name of the Chinese proletariat. Now, "a long time afterward," they were about to learn that he had only temporarily left his own, more comfortable private car labeled: "Reserved for the Chinese bourgeoisie."

When Fêng gathered together with the group of Wuhan leaders, he found himself in agreement with them on one thing only: the workers, peasants, and Communists had to be crushed. "Even the Wuhan Government had decided this," added Miss Strong. Beyond this, Fêng wanted no more truck with Wuhan. He wanted strong allies from whom he could filch advantages, not weaklings from whom he had nothing further to gain. After the formalities of feasting were over and Wuhan had endowed Fêng and his principal henchmen with titles to grace his military grip on Honan (from which Wuhan had already voluntarily withdrawn all its political workers),

Fêng brought the conference to an abrupt close and sent his "allies" packing back to Hankow.[5]

"All the forces under Fêng Yü-hsiang are pledged to obey the resolutions and orders of the Central Executive Committee at Wuhan and of the Nationalist Government," hopefully reported the *People's Tribune* on June 13. But just one week later, accompanied by Ku Mêng-yü and Hsü Ch'ien, two Wuhan luminaries, Fêng Yü-hsiang traveled down to the eastern terminus of the Lunghai railway, Hsu-chow, and there met Chiang Kai-shek, with whom he struck an immediate bargain. On June 22 at the Hsuchow station, Fêng told eager newspapermen of his "sincere desire to cooperate with the Nationalists and to extirpate militarism and Communism,"[6] and handed them a copy of a telegram he had sent to the leaders of the Wuhan government.

When I met you gentlemen in Chengchow [the telegram read], we talked of the oppression of the merchants and other members of the gentry, of labor oppressing factory owners, and farmers oppressing landowners. The people wish to suppress this form of despotism. We also talked of the remedies for this situation. The only solution which we discussed is, as I see it, as follows: Borodin, who has already resigned, should return to his own country immediately. Secondly, those members of the Central Executive Committee of the Hankow regime who wish to go abroad for rest should be allowed to do so. Others may join the Nationalist Government at Nanking if they desire. . . . Both Nanking and Hankow, I believe, understand their mutual problems. I do not need to remind you gentlemen that our country is now facing a severe crisis. But in view of this I feel constrained to insist that the present is a good time to unite the Nationalist faction in a fight against our common enemies. It is my desire that you accept the above solution and reach a conclusion immediately.[7]

This ultimatum wiped out the last lingering hopes of the Wuhan politicians that Fêng Yü-hsiang might still ally himself with them against Chiang, or at least help them to extract a better bargain from Chiang. Fêng, characteristically, had made his deal with the stronger force. He now demanded the total capitulation of Wuhan to Nanking on the basis of a common drive for the extirpation of the mass movement. He may even have figured, at least for a while, that as the arbiter who brought about the "unity" of the two factions, he would be in a position to dominate the reunited government. But whatever Fêng's calculations, he struck the final blow that toppled the tottering structure at Wuhan. Instead of proving to be the "reliable ally" advertised in the Comintern press, instead of rallying the revolutionary forces against the reactionary Chiang Kai-shek, he had joined hands with Chiang against the revolutionary forces. He was the last of Moscow's "possibilities" of co-operation.*

Returning from the meeting in Chengchow, General Galen (Vassily Blücher), chief Russian military adviser to the Kuomintang, had noticed from the train window some barely distinguishable shapes hugging the ground beneath the trees and in the gullies. These were "the bodies of Cantonese who had died advancing by this pass and railway . . . boys of Kwangtung and Hunan who had marched forth for a hope that most of them were only beginning to understand." They had died, wrote Anna Louise Strong, so that "their allies who survived might establish a military dictatorship based upon the joint suppression of the workers and peasants." To come to terms with this dictatorship as swiftly as they could was now the sole remaining purpose of the Wuhan politicians.

Wang Ching-wei's biographer relates how he "at once got to work, preparing for the expulsion of the Communists." T'ang Shêng-chih made his hurried trip to Hunan, and there, as we have already noted, he "confirmed the existence of the Communist conspiracy against the Kuomintang." In the press and from public platforms, the Kuomintang leaders opened a campaign against the Communists to pave the way for the split.[8]

This campaign had some ironic twists. The Chinese Communist party was desperately trying to carry out Moscow's instructions to curb the independence of the mass movement. In a few weeks, Moscow was going to turn savagely on these Communists and charge them with having ignored orders by failing to develop such independence. But now, in Hankow at the end of June, Wang Ching-wei and the other Kuomintang leaders approvingly quoted Stalin and the Com-

---

* In subsequent years Fêng Yü-hsiang alternately fought and "co-operated" with Chiang Kai-shek. Defeated by Chiang in a civil war in 1930, Fêng went into retirement, re-embraced Buddhism, and although he held high nominal titles in Chiang Kai-shek's government, he spent most of the years of the war against Japan writing poetry and perfecting his calligraphy. In 1947 Fêng came to the United States where, for the first time in many years, he publicly attacked Chiang Kai-shek. He refused an order to return to Nanking but left for China announcing his intention of making a political comeback in some new anti-Chiang combination. Obviously hoping to form part of some new coalition with the Communists, Fêng sailed from New York on a Russian vessel, intending to visit Moscow before going back to China. But a mysterious fire reportedly broke out on the ship while it was crossing the Black Sea. On September 5, 1948, the Russians announced that Fêng had died in the fire.

intern against the workers and peasants and individual Communists who were committing the "excess" of independence in the country-side. In a speech at the Hupeh Kuomintang delegates' conference, held at Wuchang on June 26, Wang cited the resolutions of the Seventh Plenum of the E.C.C.I., "which clearly stated that the Chinese revolution must take its stand on the alliance of the workers and peasants and small capitalists. In view of this fact, members of the Chinese Communist Party itself viewed with disapproval the inconsiderate acts recently perpetrated, for example, in Hunan province."[9] To stress the differences between China and Russia in respect to the problems of social revolution, Wang quoted what he called "Stalin's admirable comparison" between the China of 1927 and the Russia of 1905 and 1917, a comparison Stalin had made to refute and deride Trotsky's arguments that soviets, or popular councils of power, were needed to carry the Chinese agrarian revolution through to its conclusion.* It was a striking fact that Wang Ching-wei, Sun Fo, and other Left Kuomintang leaders managed in the whole discussion to sound exactly like Stalin, quoting him and reproducing his ideas and using his terminology, while the workers of Wuhan and the peasants of Hunan and the nameless leaders of the mass movement were credited with ideas and statements that sounded strangely like echoes of Trotsky.

"I have heard frequently from those who are conducting the mass movement," wrote Wang Ching-wei, "the saying: 'Don't place your confidence in the strength of the Kuomintang or the Nationalist government. Place confidence in yourself.' . . . As a result, the people have refused to accept orders or follow the instructions of the government or party [Kuomintang]. It has not only alienated the

---

* "Can it be stated that the situation in Russia in March–June 1917 was analogous to the present situation?" asked Stalin at the plenum in May. "No it cannot . . . not only because Russia was then on the threshold of a proletarian revolution, while China is now facing the bourgeois democratic revolution, but also because the Provisional Government of Russia was then a counterrevolutionary government whilst the present Hankow government is a revolutionary government in the bourgeois democratic meaning of that word. . . . The history of the workers' Soviets tells us that such Soviets can exist and develop only in the event of favorable conditions for the direct transition from the bourgeois democratic to the proletarian revolution. Was it not because of this that the workers' Soviets in Leningrad and Moscow in 1905 came to grief, just like the workers' Soviets in Germany in 1918, because conditions were not favorable? It is possible that in 1905 there would have been no Soviets in Russia had there existed at that time in Russia broad organization similar to the present-day Left Kuomintang in China. . . . It follows that the Left Kuomintang in China is playing approximately the same role in the present Chinese bourgeois democratic revolution as the Soviets played in 1905." J. Stalin, "The Revolution in China and the Tasks of the C.I.," *Communist International*, June 30, 1927.

people from the party, but has also placed the people in the precarious position of conducting an independent war with the counterrevolutionaries without the direction of the party. . . . As a consequence the masses have been surrounded by counterrevolutionaries and the Party has found it impossible to rescue them."[10]

In an article entitled "Revolution and the Masses," Sun Fo protested that the masses had ignored Wuhan's ban on the assumption of local civil power by the mass organizations. Unions and peasant associations in many places were still performing police functions, he complained; peasants were seizing the land, and workers were taking over factories and shops "in open disregard of the government's decisions." Thereby they "are actually committing counterrevolutionary actions."

"If the people regard their actions as proper, then they have openly refused," he went on, "to take the Nationalist government as the only governing organ of the revolutionary movement and the government of the national revolution. They are under the impression that the Nationalist government can no longer enforce its authority and so they must form independent administrative organs. . . . In opposing openly the revolutionary government, their actions can be taken as being of a counterrevolutionary character. . . . They refuse to admit that all mass movements in China should be directed and unified under the Kuomintang. They believe that the Communist Party should take part in leading movements. They have not yet been convinced that the Nationalist government is the only representative organ of the revolutionary movement."[11]

Sun Fo may have seen Stalin's theses of April. It is less likely that he had seen Stalin's plenum speeches in May. It is certain he never saw Trotsky's replies. But this was, in any case, conscious or unconscious plagiarism from Stalin. The Chinese workers and peasants, like Trotsky, rejected the dictum that the Wuhan government was "the only governmental authority" (Stalin) or "the only governing organ of the revolutionary movement" (Sun Fo). The masses were convinced that Wuhan could "no longer enforce its authority" just as Trotsky in Moscow had said that Wuhan's power "was nothing or nearly nothing." The masses, according to Sun Fo, were demanding and creating "independent administrative organs" even as Trotsky in Moscow was calling for the creation of soviets, or independent councils of the workers, peasants, and soldiers. Stalin de-

nounced Trotsky as "counterrevolutionary" and Sun Fo called the
workers and peasants "counterrevolutionary." These resemblances
were hardly accidental.

In these final days of dissolution, the Chinese Communist leaders
were caught helplessly in the midst of conflicts they could not resolve.
Moscow had ordered them to cling to the Left Kuomintang. As late
as June 29, when the Left Kuomintang had already indicated its intention to squeeze out of the Communist embrace, the Comintern was
still listing all its arguments against any independent policy for the
Communists in China. Wrote one of its specialists on that day:

"Who will realize the agrarian revolution? By its historic past, its
social composition and the perspectives of its development, the Kuomintang can and must be transformed into an organ of the democratic dictatorship. . . . The Kuomintang is a sort of cross between a party and a
national parliament. . . . Soviets will be necessary at the moment when
the revolution will be nearing the achievement of its bourgeois democratic
tasks . . . This moment cannot be foreseen with precision. Nevertheless
it is clear that it is not close enough for it to be necessary to advance immediately among the masses the slogan of Soviets. The Communist International and the Communist Party of China are now responsible for the
fate of the Kuomintang, and of the Wuhan government, in other words,
for the fate of the Chinese revolution. They cannot therefore permit themselves to issue loose slogans and formulas."[12]

But while Moscow continued to deal in these abstract and paralyzing formulas, in the Chinese countryside the peasants were desperately
trying to forge for themselves the instruments of power that would
help them accomplish their own purposes. A glimpse of this emerges
from the report of a special Kuomintang commission that had been
sent to investigate conditions in Kiangsi. Its report, published at the
beginning of July, included this passage: "The government cannot
even participate in or supervise the activities of the public organizations. . . . Very often we see the districts neglecting the direction of
the provincial Kuomintang, or the peasant and labor unions opposing
the resolutions of the provincial Kuomintang. . . . The party
branches have made arrests and punished people freely. Public organizations did the same thing. Thus everywhere there have been the
phenomena of multiple governments. This is just as dangerous as
anarchy. . . . The greatest fault of the peasant and labor movement
leaders is their misunderstanding of the slogan: 'Support the interests of the peasants and laborers.' "[13] It seems that the masses thought

the slogan, "Support the interests of the peasants and laborers" meant support for the interests of the peasants and laborers. This was, according to the Kuomintang, their greatest fault. But they stubbornly persisted in it. Isolated and scattered in the towns and villages, the local unions of workers and peasants and other mass organizations found themselves colliding with the Kuomintang and with the "organizing center" of Wuhan. These "multiple governments" completely lacked any connection with one another. Their impulse was to broaden themselves into representative councils, to link up village to village, town to town, to bring common forces together and to pursue a common policy in "the interests of the peasants and laborers." But these would have been soviets which Moscow had banned. The result was that the mass movement, in Trotsky's phrase, was "splattered into froth."

Moscow was hammering at the Communist leaders to preserve the alliance with the Wuhan politicians. The Wuhan politicians were blaming the Communists for the excesses of the mass movement. The mass movement was plunging away from all the organized parties, leaderless, blinded, and easy prey for the local militarists. The Communist leadership, trying to obey Moscow and trying to refute the Left Kuomintang charges of conspiracy, simply abandoned the turmoil in the countryside and tried desperately to find any remaining avenues of retreat that would preserve the "united front" with the Left Kuomintang.

For a short time it tried to maneuver with the idea of diverting Wuhan in the direction of a punitive expedition against Chiang Kai-shek. On the same day that Fêng Yü-hsiang had issued his ultimatum demanding the destruction of the trade-union movement, the refugee delegates of the Shanghai General Labor Union in Hankow wired an appeal to Fêng: "We hope that you, who are the true believer in Kuomintang principles and the real supporter of the . . . policies of the Tsungli [Sun Yat-sen], will lead . . . the revolutionary armies for a punitive expedition against Chiang Kai-shek."[14] After Fêng's defection became obvious, attention centered for a while on General Chang Fa-k'uei, the commander of the "Ironsides," who was personally most bitter against Chiang Kai-shek. Ch'ü Ch'iu-po wrote later that the Central Committee thought it might "fool the 'revolutionary generals' into attacking Chiang first and the Communists later."[15] Meetings were staged. Manifestoes were issued. Roy went to Wang

Ching-wei and tried to persuade him to carry out the proposal in Stalin's telegram to form a new Communist army and proposed that Chang Fa-k'uei be given the command. Wang showed no enthusiasm for the plan. He and Chang Fa-k'uei had actually toyed with the idea of trying to mount an attack against Nanking. Some troop movements in this direction were actually begun, but the other Wuhan generals would not play. "We will not fight Chiang Kai-shek for the Communists," said Ho Chien and the other generals. The campaign fizzled into nothing.

Everyone now clearly understood that the expulsion of the Communists impended. All the propaganda for the so-called "Eastern Expedition" against Nanking was coupled with the most fervent pleas for continued co-operation between the two parties.[16] The panic-stricken Communist Central Committee decided to issue a manifesto declaring that if the Kuomintang "really" wanted to carry out the policies of Sun Yat-sen it "had" to fight Chiang Kai-shek and "had" to remain allied to the Communists. But when the members of the Communist Political Bureau met, every member present offered a different draft and no agreement was reached on the terms of the proposed declaration. Finally on June 20 an enlarged meeting of the Central Committee adopted a statement embodying eleven points, of which the most important were:

4. The Kuomintang, since it is the bloc of the workers, peasants, and petty bourgeoisie opposed to imperialism, is naturally in the leading position of the national revolution.

5. Communist members of the Kuomintang, although participating in government work, both central and local, are participating as members of the Kuomintang and not as members of the Communist Party. . . . The Communist members now in the government may ask leave in order to reduce the difficulties of the political situation.

6. The workers' and peasants' mass organizations should accept the leadership and control of the Kuomintang. The demands of the workers' and peasants' mass movement should be in accordance with the resolutions of the Kuomintang congresses, the decisions of the Central Executive Committee, and the decrees and laws of the Government. But the Kuomintang should also protect the organizations of the workers and peasants and their interests, also in accordance with the party resolutions and government decrees.

7. According to Kuomintang principles, the masses must be armed. But the armed groups of the workers and peasants should submit to the regulation and training of the government. In order to avoid political

troubles, the present armed pickets at Wuhan can be reduced or incorporated into the army.

8. The labor unions and workers' pickets may not assume judicial or administrative functions, arrest people, try them or patrol the streets without the permission of the *tangpu* [local Kuomintang branch] or government.

9. Shop employees' unions should be organized jointly by the *tangpu* and the men sent by the General Labor Union. The economic demands of the shop employees shall not exceed the economic capacities of the shopkeepers. The unions shall not interfere with the shopkeeper's right to hire and fire. They shall not insult the shopkeepers with arrests, fines, putting on dunce caps, etc.[17]

There was a suppressed mood of rebellion against this wholesale retreat when four hundred delegates gathered the same week in Hankow for the Fourth All-China Trade Union Conference. They claimed to represent three million organized workers in eight provinces, although almost everywhere by now the unions had been destroyed or driven underground. The conference dutifully cheered Wang Ching-wei when he appeared before it on June 23, but the feeling of the delegates was so strong that even Lozofsky, present as a fraternal delegate of the Russian trade-unions, had to make an unusually radical speech threatening the reactionaries. The manifesto of the conference was somber: "Counterrevolution is gaining strength every day. In the territory of the Nationalist government, the labor movement can only be conducted openly at Wuhan. Counterrevolutionaries are in power in Hunan, Kiangsi, and Honan. . . . Laborers are suffering under a new kind of tyrannical rule. Under these circumstances it is possible for the reactionaries to dominate Wuhan some day. We must struggle hard to maintain the existence of the labor unions. We are now in a reign of white terror."[18]

"Here labor is in a free atmosphere," the *People's Tribune* had said on June 22 as the conference opened. "The heavy hand of unsympathetic or actively antagonistic militarists is absent here. Organized labor in Nationalist China is loyal to the Wuhan government because it is only under this government that it can confidently count upon holding on to labor's first and most vital right: to work in the open . . . unafraid and fearless." But on the morning of June 30, the final session had barely ended with the shouting of the slogan "Long live the Nationalist government!" when the "heavy hand of antagonistic militarists" descended sharply and directly on the trade-union headquarters in Wuhan. Soldiers marched in and began to loot and destroy the property and records of the All-China Labor Federation. Panting protests were made. The soldiers were ordered withdrawn. They had apparently acted a little ahead of schedule. Anna Louise Strong caught Hsü Ch'ao-jên, the Communist Minister of Labor, as he raced past her in the street. She asked him if the soldiers would be punished. "He smiled wearily. He was glad enough to get the building. 'We have it to work in today. . . . Who knows what will happen tomorrow?' he replied."[19] The federation never did get its building back.

The Communist party went ahead with its pledges of retreat. It had offered to disarm and dissolve the small force of pickets in Hankow and this was now done. In Shanghai the order had been given to "hide or bury" arms in hopes of averting the impending blow. In Hankow, the Central Committee decided to give up demonstratively the small stock of arms they still possessed. On June 29, a delegation of the Hupeh General Labor Union, headed by Hsiang Chung-fa, went to the headquarters of the Kuomintang Military Council. There, according to the *People's Tribune*, "it stated that in view of the complaints that union pickets were a factor in the reluctance on the part of businessmen to restore normal economic conditions, they wish to offer either to deliver their arms or be incorporated in the army."[20] The military authorities accepted the delivery of the arms.

Next day the Hupeh General Labor Union issued a further explanatory statement: "For the purpose of consolidating the united front of the troops and laborers and in order not to give grounds to support the charges made by reactionaries and counterrevolutionaries, the union ordered the dissolution of the armed pickets on the 28th inst. Arms and ammunition were handed to the Hankow office of the Wuhan garrison for custody. . . . We have petitioned the government for protection in order to show our sincere intention to support it. . . . As to the reactionaries, we hope the government will mete out strong measures for their punishment."[21]

The Communist Central Committee had also authorized the Communists in the government "to ask leave in order to reduce the difficulties of the political situation." Accordingly, on June 30 T'an P'ing-shan, the Communist Minister of Agriculture, petitioned the government for "leave of absence," apologizing for his failure "to put the peasant movement on the right track."

"Ever since I assumed office as Minister of Agriculture," he wrote, "I have tried my best to perform the important duty of improving peasant conditions. I have consistently done my best to set the peasant movement right. Recent developments have made the political situation so serious that to put the peasant movement on the right track has been too heavy a responsibility for me. Since I am physically unfit to go on with my work, I request leave of absence."[22] Hsü Ch'ao-jên, Communist Minister of Labor, had long since ceased attending to his office. His letter of resignation, stating that "owing to recent developments, I can no longer remain in office," was made public a few days later. Hsiang Chung-fa and other Communists who held posts in the Hupeh provincial government had already withdrawn. Panic and demoralization were complete. The Central Committee itself fled across the river to Wuchang. It had done all it could to preserve the alliance with the Left Kuomintang, to "strengthen the authority of the organizing center of the revolution." But it had all been to no avail. For it was now known that the Kuomintang leaders had already decided to expel the Communists and that this decision remained only to be formally adopted at a session of the Kuomintang Political Council called for July 15.

In these hours of desperation, Ch'ên Tu-hsiu had finally arrived at the conclusion that the only course left open was the withdrawal of the Communist party from the Kuomintang. He consulted with Borodin. "I quite agree with your idea," said the High Adviser, "but I know that Moscow will never permit it."[23] According to Wang Ching-wei's amanuensis, Borodin had been regarded ever since the Changsha events at the end of May as merely "an honored guest" and no longer "a trusted adviser." He was apparently still probing in these final hours for any "possibilities" of co-operation that he might have overlooked. According to Ch'ü Ch'iu-po, Borodin toyed with the idea of leading Mrs. Sun Yat-sen, Têng Yen-ta, and Eugene Ch'ên out of the government as a demonstrative act against Wang Ching-wei. But events had already rolled over Borodin's head. The Communist leadership was falling apart. The rank and file of the party were scattered and demoralized. Ho Chien's troops were in the saddle in Wuhan and were riding their own way. One by one the headquarters of unions and other organizations were occupied. Arrests were made and executions began to take place. The tide of the terror was engulfing Stalin's "revolutionary center." The *Izvestia* correspondent wired that yesterday's reliable allies had today become "playthings in the hands of the generals."[24] The ship of Wuhan was sinking and the rats began to act in the traditional manner.

In Moscow on July 6, Bukharin suddenly issued new and rather startling advice for the Chinese workers and peasants: "Trust in your own forces alone! Do not trust the generals and officers! Organize your armed troops! . . . Fêng Yü-hsiang has gone over to the camp of the opponents of the people's revolution. We must declare merciless war upon him!"[25] Announcing the Wuhan plan to expel the Communists from the Kuomintang, Bukharin said that "the friends of Chiang Kai-shek are ready to accept this plan," and then, in parenthesis added his last stubborn hope: "Wang Ching-wei is not among them. He is firmer than the others." But within less than a week it became clear, even to Bukharin, that Wang was firmer than the others only in his desire to be quit of the Communist alliance. Bukharin thereupon proclaimed[26] that "an abrupt turn in the Chinese revolution" had taken place. He solemnly declared: "The revolutionary role of Wuhan is at an end." This Kremlin reversal was set forth on July 14 in a new resolution of the Executive Committee of the Communist International, a remarkable document in which the Comintern abandoned the entire course it had been following, declared that it had been entirely correct in everything it had done and advised, and charged the consequences of its acts to the "opportunist deviations" of the Chinese Communist leaders. Its main passages:

The revolutionary role of the Wuhan government is played out; it is becoming a counterrevolutionary force. This is the new and peculiar feature which the leaders of the Chinese Communist Party and all the Chinese comrades must fully and clearly take into account.

The support given to the Northern Expedition was perfectly correct so long as it aroused a revolutionary mass movement. And the support given to Wuhan was equally correct so long as it acted as the opponent of Chiang Kai-shek's Nanking government. But this same tactic of blocs becomes fundamentally wrong in the moment at which the Wuhan government capitulates to the enemies of the revolution. What was correct during the previous stage of the revolution is now absolutely unsuitable.

All this involves certain difficulties for the leadership of the party, especially in the case of so young and inexperienced a party as the Communist Party of China. . . . The acute tension of the revolutionary situation requires a rapid grasp of the features peculiar to each moment. It requires skillful and timely maneuvers, rapid adaptation to slogans . . . and the decided rupture of blocs which have ceased to be factors of the revolutionary struggle and have become obstacles in its way. If at a certain stage of the development of the revolution, the support of the Wuhan government by the Communist Party was necessary, such support at present would be disastrous to the Communist Party of China and would plunge it into the bog of opportunism.

In spite of the advice given by the Comintern, the heads of the Kuomintang have not only failed to support the agrarian revolution but have unfettered the hands of its enemies. They have sanctioned the disarmament of the workers, the punitive expeditions against the peasants, and the reprisals of T'ang Shêng-chih & Co. They have postponed and sabotaged the campaign against Nanking under various pretexts.

The Communists should remain in the Kuomintang, in spite of the campaign carried on by its leaders for the expulsion of the Communists. They should seek closer contact with the mass of the members of the Kuomintang, who should be induced to accept resolutions decidedly protesting against the actions of the C. E. C. of the Kuomintang, demanding the removal of the present leaders of the Kuomintang, and to make preparations on these lines for the Party Conference of the Kuomintang.

[The Communists should now] intensify the work among the proletarian masses . . . build up labor organizations . . . strengthen the trade unions . . . prepare the working masses for decisive action . . . develop the agrarian revolution . . . arm the workers and peasants . . . organize a competent fighting illegal party apparatus.

. . . The E.C.C.I. considers it its revolutionary duty to call upon the members of the Communist Party of China openly to fight against the opportunism of the Central Committee. . . . Take measures to make good the opportunist errors of the Central Committee of the Communist Party of China in order to render the leadership of the party politically sound . . . fight decisively against the opportunist deviations of the party leaders . . . change the character of the leadership . . . disavow those leaders who have violated the international discipline of the Communist International.[27]

To the Chinese Communists this came as a truly stupefying final blow. What was fundamentally right yesterday became fundamentally wrong today. The "new and peculiar fact" of Wuhan's opposition to the agrarian revolution and the mass movement had been evident for months to the simplest Wuhan worker or Hunan peasant and even to the Communist leadership. In Canton, Shanghai, Changsha, and now in Wuhan, the standard bearers of the "revolutionary Kuomintang" had changed from sterling allies of the revolution into cruel butchers of the revolution. At each new catastrophe, the Comintern announced it had foreseen everything and had been correct in its policies before, during, and after the events that took place. The bloc with the Kuomintang politicians which only six weeks earlier had been an absolute condition for the victory of the revolution now, on July 14, became an obstacle in its path. But during those six weeks, and for a long time before, the Communists had been rigidly prevented from doing anything to protect themselves against the coming blow. The bloc became "absolutely unsuitable" only at the precise moment when the ex-ally-turned-enemy struck. It had been "correct" to support Chiang Kai-shek up to the moment he loosed the slaughter in Shanghai, the Hunan militarists up to and beyond the day when they turned their executioners loose on the peasants, and the Wuhan politicians up to this moment, on July 14, when the "organizing center" of the revolution suddenly, by Moscow fiat, turned into a "counterrevolutionary force." Even now—and this was perhaps the clearest evidence of the blind panic that had gripped the Kremlin strategists—it was still necessary to wave the Kuomintang banner in the face of disaster and to talk of carrying the revolution from new crest to new crest as though nothing, or almost nothing, had happened.

To this the hapless Chinese Communist might well have replied: But how? How are we to act now, when our great organizations have been smashed, our comrades tortured, killed, and scattered? How are we to "prepare for decisive action" the masses whom we have led to the execution ground? How are we to "develop the agrarian revolution" when only in the last few weeks we let it beat itself out against the armed opposition of the militarists? These were, possibly, the "difficulties" to which the resolution referred. But these misfortunes were not in any respect the responsibility of the Comintern. They were due to the Communist party leadership which had, in Bukharin's words, "in recent times obstinately sabotaged the decisions of the Comintern" and therefore had to be deposed and replaced. The Chinese Communist leaders were the selected scapegoats and it became henceforth the "revolutionary duty" of all Comintern scribblers to echo the charge that the Chinese Communist leaders, hapless victims of their own gullibility and ignorance and subservient faith in the leadership of Moscow, were alone responsible for the catastrophe that overtook them.

While the Kremlin took refuge behind palpably dishonest resolutions, in Wuhan events took their final course. In accordance with the latest instructions, the Communists demonstratively "withdrew" from the government they had already left, announcing at the same time that they "had no reason to leave the Kuomintang or to refuse to co-operate with it" and that they would not permit "the generals who have betrayed the revolution and the vacillating politicians to misuse the name of the Kuomintang and hide themselves under the banner of Sun Yat-sen."[28]

Unimpressed, the generals and the politicians proceeded to "misuse" the name of the Kuomintang. On July 15 the Kuomintang Political Council ordered all Communist members of the Kuomintang to renounce their Communist party membership on pain of immediate extreme penalties. Four days later the Military Council ordered a similar purge throughout the army. "Punishment without leniency" was ordered for all recalcitrants.[29] Within a few days, execution squads were carrying out the "expulsion" order. Communists who were not caught up in the net fled. Ch'ên Tu-hsiu, overcome by the utter hopelessness of his position, resigned from the Central Committee.* "The International," he wrote, "wishes us to carry out our own policy on the one hand and does not allow us to withdraw from the Kuomintang on the other. There is really no way out and I cannot continue with my work."[30] The remaining Communist leaders, Ch'ü Ch'iu-po, Chang Kuo-t'ao, Li Li-san, Mao Tsê-tung, and others, fled. On July 27, with executions going on in the streets of Hankow, the leaders of the Left Kuomintang gathered at the railway station to bid farewell to their "honored guest," Borodin. He left nominally

---

* Ch'ên Tu-hsiu was formally deposed from the leadership at the Party Conference of August 7, 1927. He withdrew into retirement while the whole Comintern press echoed and re-echoed the Moscow charge that he had been responsible for the disaster that had befallen the revolution. Ch'ên opposed the policy of futile adventurism on which the Communist party subsequently embarked. In August 1929, he addressed a letter to the Central Committee formally declaring himself opposed to the policies of the party and demanding a general discussion. In reply he and eighty others who had signed his declaration were expelled forthwith from the party. In February 1930, the Comintern invited him to Moscow "to talk things over" but Ch'ên refused to go. He became one of the leading figures in the Trotskyist Opposition in China with which he remained until arrested by the Kuomintang in 1932. (A list of his principal letters and articles pertaining to the events of the revolution and the subsequent internal party struggles will be found in the Bibliography at the end of this book.) Because of his immense personal prestige, Ch'ên Tu-hsiu had to be given a semipublic trial; he took full advantage of it to make a stirring defense of his political views and a strong attack on the Kuomintang dictatorship of Chiang Kai-shek. He was sentenced to thirteen years' imprisonment but was released five years later, in 1937, during the confusion of the early Chinese defeats in the Sino-Japanese war. Ill and physically broken, he lived in forced and guarded retirement in West China until May 1942, when he died at the age of sixty-three.

"to confer with Fêng Yü-hsiang," but everybody understood that he was starting on the long trek across the northwestern provinces to the distant Soviet frontier, Moscow's retreat from Hankow.

The military authorities proceeded with the systematic destruction of the trade-unions. The Hankow Garrison Headquarters issued a ban on strikes. Between July 14 and 19, detachments of soldiers were "billeted" on the premises of twenty-five unions, whose archives and effects were confiscated. Simultaneously throughout Honan province Fêng Yü-hsiang was carrying out similar measures. "In the last few weeks the Chinese labor movement in the territory of the Wuhan Government has lived through a period of the most brazen reaction. . . ." reported the Pan-Pacific Trade Union Secretariat in one of the last issues of the *People's Tribune*. "The military . . . have carried out such enormous work of destruction directed against the mass organizations . . . that it will require a very long period and gigantic energy to make good the losses and to enable the trade unions to resume their normal functions. Many of the trade union leaders and organizers in the different provinces and districts . . . have been driven out, arrested, or killed. The other leaders of the Chinese trade unions, among them the most prominent leaders of the All-China Trade Union Federation, were compelled to flee."

On July 30, two thousand Hankow ricksha men stormed a police station to force the release of an arrested comrade. Two of them were killed and six wounded. Police sent a letter to the Ricksha Pullers' Union to send representatives to a parley. But no one was there. The union leaders had fled. There were only the pullers in the streets on strike. Martial law was proclaimed and the death penalty formally instituted. The strike ended. It was the last open manifestation of the Hankow labor movement for a long time to come.

A few days later, Nanking and Wuhan were exchanging congratulatory telegrams. Nanking wired compliments to Wuhan on its decisive action and invited the leaders to Nanking: "If all feelings of aversion are resolutely given up . . ." replied Wuhan on August 10, "your former measures devised to meet emergencies will be wholeheartedly excused by us all."[31] The "former measures"—the massacre of thousands—were wholeheartedly excused. Thus ended the "complete contradiction" between the "revolutionary center" at Wuhan and counterrevolutionary Nanking.

Of the important Wuhan leaders, only Têng Yen-ta and the widow of Sun Yat-sen, Soong Ching-ling, dissociated themselves publicly from the new course. "From Yang Yü-t'ing [Chang Tso-lin's deputy] to Chiang Kai-shek . . . all are either Kuomintang members or are going to become members. Kuomintang banners are hoisted everywhere. But is this not the same situation we faced in the 1911 revolution?" wrote Têng on July 6. "Is not all economic, political, and military power still in the hands of the militarists? . . . We wanted to utilize the military but we were being utilized by them."[32] A few days later Têng resigned as head of the Political Department of the Military Council. Having no fetish of infallibility to preserve, Têng spoke plainly: "Those who formerly advocated the full protection of the laborers and peasants have started to massacre them. . . . The revolutionary significance of the Kuomintang will be lost. . . . The natural result will be that the Party itself will become counterrevolutionary. . . . The revolution will be a failure, as it was in 1911."[33] Following Têng, Soong Ching-ling declared that the Kuomintang had become "a tool in the hands of this or that militarist. It will have ceased to be a living force working for the future welfare of the Chinese people, but will have become a machine, the agent of oppression, a parasite battening on the present enslaving system."[34] Têng Yen-ta and Soong Ching-ling, accompanied by Eugene Ch'ên, fled into European exile. Thus ended the myth of the "Left Kuomintang."*

The revolution which had swept China for three years ebbed away. For its failures, tens of thousands of Chinese working people and a whole generation of China's best youth were now paying a terrible price. Over the prisons and execution grounds flew the banner of the Kuomintang that had been sanctified for them by the Kremlin. Under it the people had risen. Under it, uncomprehending, they had been struck down.

---

*Wang Ching-wei, after vainly trying during the next five years to form a successful anti-Chiang combination, finally became, in January 1932, the civilian fig leaf on Chiang's military dictatorship. When the Japanese invasion passed over, in 1937, to an attempt to conquer all of China, Wang ended an ignoble career ignobly, as a puppet of the Japanese and while playing that role died in Nanking in November 1944. Sun Fo gravitated in and out of office during the years of Chiang's rule, at times enjoying a wholly undeserved reputation as a "liberal" member of Chiang's entourage. Têng Yen-ta returned to China from exile in 1930 and organized the "Third Party" in opposition to both the Kuomintang and the Communists. He was soon arrested by the French authorities in Shanghai, handed over to Chiang Kai-shek, and was executed in Nanking by order of Chiang Kai-shek. Mrs. Sun Yat-sen returned from European exile in 1931. She was the only survivor of the "Left Kuomintang" who kept faith, although often unhappily, with the Communists. She concerned herself mainly with welfare work and when the Communists won power in 1949 was appointed to a nominally high post in the Communist regime in Peking.

Chapter 17

AUTUMN HARVEST AND THE CANTON COMMUNE

COLLAPSE of the Wuhan government completed the victory of the counterrevolution. From Canton to Nanking, from the sea to the hills of Hunan, the generals were in power. Already at war among themselves, they waged in common a ruthless campaign of extermination against the mass movement, its organizations, and its leaders.

"Here are the facts of the suppression," reported the *China Weekly Review* on August 20, 1927. "For four months a systematized massacre has been going on in the territory controlled by Chiang Kai-shek. It has resulted in the smashing of the people's organizations in Kiangsu, Chekiang, Fukien, and Kwangtung, so that in these provinces one finds Kuomintang headquarters, and labor, peasant, and women's unions transformed from forceful, determined organs into docile, spineless organizations, so effectively 'reorganized' that they will carry out the will of their reactionary masters.

"In the past three months, the reaction has spread from the lower Yangtze until today it is dominant in all the territory under so-called Nationalist control. T'ang Shêng-chih has proven himself an even more effective commander of execution squads than of armies in battle. In Hunan his subordinate generals have carried out a clean-up of 'Communists' that Chiang Kai-shek can scarcely parallel. The usual methods of shooting and beheading have been abetted by methods of torture and mutilation which reek of the horrors of the dark ages and the Inquisition. The results have been impressive. The peasant and labor unions of Hunan, probably the most effectively organized in the whole country, are completely smashed. Those leaders who have escaped the burning in oil, the burying alive, the torture by slow strangulation by wire, and other forms of death too lurid to report, have fled the country or are in such careful hiding that they cannot easily be found. . . ."[1]

"The toll of executed trade union leaders and organizers is growing from day to day," reported the Pan-Pacific Trade Union Secretariat on September 15. "Not a day passes without the execution of several workers and trade unionists. . . . The mass movement is crushed for the moment. All the labor organizations and the peasant unions are being 'reorganized,' which means that they are first disorganized and broken up, and then what remains of them is put under the whip of some appointee of the militarists. . . . In Kiukiang, as in Wuhan, all the trade union organizations have been dissolved and many trade union leaders executed. . . . Soldiers have occupied most of the trade union buildings and have worked havoc with the property and the documents and valuable archives of these organizations. . . . What is happening in Wuhan is an exact repetition of what took place some time ago in Canton, when General Li Chi-shên destroyed and then 'reorganized' the trade unions and peasant organizations, and also of the Chiang Kai-shek regime in Shanghai."[2]

The defeat of the mass movement could not be measured merely by the extent of its physical annihilation. The workers and peasants had not merely fallen before a stronger enemy. They had been decapitated by their own leaders, by the men and organizations they had been taught to regard as the standard-bearers of their own revolution. The moral and psychological demoralization that resulted from this fact incalculably deepened the effects of the counterrevolution. The masses of people fell away from the political arena. The brutal and, for them, entirely unexpected assault of the counterrevolution drove them into passivity. They left their shattered organizations. A spokesman for the Communist trade-union apparatus had early acknowledged that it would take "a very long time and gigantic energy" to restore the unions.[3] The peasant associations that had counted nearly ten millions in their ranks disappeared almost entirely. Only scattered rebel bands that took to the hills remained to harass the columns of soldiery that went through the countryside like a scourge. In the cities the workers left the ranks of the Communist party by the thousands. In April 1927, it had been an organization of nearly sixty thousand members, 53.8 percent of them workers.[4] Within a year that percentage fell by four-fifths and an official report admitted that the party "did not have a single healthy party nucleus among the industrial workers."[5] Thus in their own way the workers passed their verdict on the party that had led them to disaster. They never did return to its ranks. The essentially nonurban character of the Chinese Communist party, originating in these circumstances, was preserved right up until its conquest of power two decades later.

For its part, the leadership in Moscow had once again "foreseen" everything and "acted correctly" in every respect. The debacle confirmed its wisdom, sufficient for itself at least, if not for the thousands in China now paying with their lives for the lessons learned. Lenin and Trotsky had won leadership by their superior grasp of the internal laws of the social process. For this, Stalin had substituted a pragmatic and eclectic empiricism which reduced social forces to mechanical robots and history to a pedantic and docile succession of stages. Stalin had "foreseen" that the bourgeoisie would abandon the revolution and regarded this as a necessary and unavoidable "stage" in the revolutionary process. A corollary to this was the idea that the revolutionary party had to wait until the bourgeoisie had "discredited" itself in the eyes of the people by openly taking the road of counterrevolution. Only then could the party proceed with a bolder revolutionary course which the masses could thereafter comprehend, having lost all their previous illusions. This notion was organic with Stalin. In the critical days of March 1917, before Lenin had returned to Russia, Stalin had said: "We must bide our time until the Provisional Government exhausts itself, until the time when in the process of fulfilling the revolutionary program it discredits itself . . . until the moment when the events reveal the hollowness of the Provisional Government." Now, like an echo ten years old, Stalin wrote on the morrow of the collapse of Wuhan:

Should the Chinese Communists have set up the slogan six months ago: "Down with the leadership of the Kuomintang"? No, for that would have been a very dangerous and precipitate step and it would have rendered the approach to the masses more difficult for the Communists, for the masses at that time still believed in the leadership of the Kuomintang and this would have isolated the Communist Party from the peasantry. This would have been false, for at that time the leadership of the Kuomintang in Wuhan had not yet achieved its highest point as a bourgeois revolutionary government and had not yet discredited itself in the eyes of the masses through its fight against the agrarian revolution and by its defection to the counterrevolution. We always said that no attempt should be made to discredit and overthrow the leadership of the Kuomintang in Wuhan so long as it had not exhausted all its possibilities as a bourgeois revolutionary government. . . . Should the Chinese Communists now set up the slogan, "Down with the leadership of the Kuomintang in Wuhan"?

Yes, of course they must. Now that the leadership of the Kuomintang has already discredited itself by its struggle against the revolution and has created hostile relations between itself and the masses. . . . Such a slogan will meet with a tremendous response. Now every worker and peasant will see that the Communists are acting correctly.[6]

Stalin overlooked only one thing. In the process of "discrediting itself" and reaching its "highest point" while the Communists passively waited, the Kuomintang counterrevolution successfully crushed the organizations of the mass movement. The workers and peasants, defending themselves as best they could against the blows of the terror, were no longer in a position to see that the Communists were now "acting correctly." Stalin's academic calculations had little in common with the grisly reality on the ground in China.*

Now, one after another, the "leaders" of the revolution solemnly summed up the "lessons" of the catastrophe. Borodin, who had stood by to the end, pumping steadfastness into Stalin's Kuomintang allies until all their "possibilities" were exhausted, was now on his way back across the wastes of Northwest China. En route he was politely entertained by Fêng Yü-hsiang and other lesser generals. Anna Louise Strong, who accompanied Borodin on this long retreat from Hankow, has written on this another of her unintentionally valuable vignettes:[7]

"Borodin seemed weary and bored by all these generals. He saw too clearly behind their nationalist slogans the desire for military assistance. He remarked: 'When the next Chinese general comes to Moscow and shouts: "Hail to the World Revolution!" better send at once for the G.P.U. . . . all that any of them wants is rifles.' "

Miss Strong protested that their host for the night "seemed a friendly soul and fond of Russia." But "Borodin answered wearily: 'He's young. They are all good when they are young.' " A few nights later, sitting on a campstool beneath a rising Chinese moon, Borodin delivered himself of what Miss Strong called "the most complete and leisurely exposition of the forces involved in China's revolution that I had yet heard him give. There had been no time for such discussion in Hankow. Now, removed by many days and miles from the scene of action, it was as if he summed it up for his own soul also." Said

---

* At the back of the same issue of the periodical containing this article by Stalin, was a reprint of a fragment from Lenin, dating from 1917, in which the following sentence occurred: "It is precisely the first steps which we must learn to recognize, if we are not to fall into the ridiculous role of a dull-witted philistine who cries out at the second step, although he helped to take the first."

Borodin: "The big bourgeoisie can never unify China because they are not really against the imperialists; they are allied with them and profit by them. The small bourgeoisie cannot unify China because they vacillate between the workers and peasants on the one hand and the big bourgeoisie on the other and, in the end, go over to the latter. The workers and peasants did not unify China because they trusted too much to the small bourgeoisie."*

Stalin's other acolyte in China was the Indian Communist, M. N. Roy, who had devoted himself to the strenuous task of "advising" Chiang Kai-shek, then Wang Ching-wei, not to "discredit" themselves. Spurned, he fled from the wreckage to write:

Rather than sacrifice the sectional interests of the reactionary landlords and capitalists, the bourgeois nationalist leaders betrayed the revolution. Class solidarity cut across national solidarity. . . . Development of the revolution menaced the interests of the capitalist and landowning classes. Further fight against imperialism would inevitably have caused revolution in the internal social-economic relations. The land should have been given to the peasantry. The peasantry should have been secured against unlimited capitalist exploitation. In short, imperialism could not be overthrown unless its native allies were destroyed. Complete national liberation could be realized . . . only by seriously encroaching upon the privileged position of the classes whose representatives led the Nationalist movement. . . . The petty bourgeois radicalism of the Wuhan government went bankrupt. It capitulated . . . to the counterrevolutionary feudal bourgeois militarist bloc which had already sold the country to imperialism. The nation was sacrificed on the altar of class interests. The democratic (non-class) ideals of the Kuomintang were lost in the fierce clash of class interests. The lessons of these revolutionary and counterrevolutionary events in China are that the nationalist bourgeoisie in the colonial and semicolonial countries are essentially counterrevolutionary; that the national revolution to be successful must be an agrarian revolution; that not only the big bourgeoisie but even the petty bourgeoisie, in spite of their radical phrases, cannot and will not lead the agrarian revolution; that the petty bourgeoisie, when placed in power by the support of the workers and peasants, do not share and defend this power with the working class, but hand it over to the counterrevolutionary bourgeoisie; and that the working class operating through its independent political party (Communist Party) is the only guarantee for the success of the national revolution.[8]

* This, so far as we know, is the only place where Borodin passed verdict upon himself and his deeds. Back in Moscow he lapsed into obscurity. Reverting to journalistic hackwork as editor of the English-language *Moscow Daily News*, Borodin managed miraculously to survive the purges of subsequent years and, at least as recently as 1945, was still in Moscow where, occasionally bibulous and indiscreet, he would tell foreign journalists about Stalin's tragic blunders in China.

In the book he published a few years later Roy conservatively estimated[9] that 25,000 Communists lost their lives in the first months of the terror in 1927 after the "nonclass ideals" of the Kuomintang changed overnight into the "fierce clash of class interests." Only yesterday Stalin, echoed by Roy, was "foreseeing" that the bourgeoisie (not Chiang Kai-shek, not Wang Ching-wei) would "abandon" the revolution. At the same time he was teaching these 25,000 to believe that Chiang Kai-shek and Wang Ching-wei were the "reliable allies" of the revolution, that Chiang's Canton and later Wang's Hankow were the authentic "organizing centers" of the agrarian revolution, that "no attempt should be made to discredit and overthrow" them until they had "discredited" themselves, that is, until they had snuffed out the lives of the uncomprehending 25,000 and after them the lives of thousands more, and the life of the revolution itself. This price evidently had to be paid to confirm the prognoses of Moscow and to enable Stalin, Bukharin, Borodin, Roy, and all their friends to arrive at the "correct" conclusion that the Chinese bourgeoisie could not lead the agrarian revolution and that "imperialism could not be overthrown unless its native allies were destroyed." To have foreseen any of this prior to the events was counterrevolutionary Trotskyism. After the event, it became part of the holy writ of Stalin's infallibility. Following a detailed report by Bukharin, Stalin's Central Committee on August 9, 1927, issued the following summary:

The experience of the past development shows plainly that the bourgeoisie is not capable of solving the problems of national emancipation from the yoke of imperialism since it is conducting a fight against the workers and peasants, that it is not capable of conducting a consistent fight against imperialism and is becoming more and more inclined to a compromise . . . which in fact leaves the domination of imperialism almost completely undisturbed. The national bourgeoisie is equally incapable of solving the inner problems of the revolution, for the reason that it not only fails to support the peasantry, but actively combats them. . . . It is almost impossible for the bourgeoisie to enter into any compromise with the peasantry, since in China even the scantiest land reform would involve expropriation of the gentry and small landowners, an action of which the bourgeoisie is absolutely incapable. . . . The Communist Party must declare that the victory over imperialism, the revolutionary unification of China, and its emancipation from the yoke of imperialism are only possible on the basis of the class struggle of the workers and peasants against the feudal lords and capitalists.[10]

When Trotsky in the period of the greatest upswing of the mass movement had urged a bold and independent course, his proposals had been derisively rejected. Then events had extracted their remorseless toll. Veering rudderlessly and driven from one pole to the other by the impact of events they could not control, the Kremlin leaders *now* proclaimed that the time for aggressive action had come. Since, in accordance with the Kremlin's forecast, the bourgeoisie had "abandoned" the revolution and "discredited" itself, it was obvious that now, in the words of Stalin's Central Committee, the revolution "was striding forward to the highest phase of its development, to the phase of the direct struggle for the dictatorship of the working class and the peasantry." Trotsky had been accused of skipping over the bourgeois democratic stage of the revolution. Stalin now sought to skip over the disastrous consequences of his own policies. He ordered the Chinese Communist party to take the path of open insurrection.

The Chinese party, which in Ch'ên Tu-hsiu's bitter words had "learned in the past only how to capitulate," now suddenly, in the face of terror, decimation, and dispersal, had to attack. It was compelled to affirm that the policies of the Comintern had been completely correct, that the failure at Wuhan was due to the "sabotage" of the Chinese Communist leadership, that the defeat had raised the revolution to a "new and higher stage." Yesterday, with huge masses in forward motion, the Communists had been taught only how to check and demoralize the movement by subjecting it to hostile class forces. Today that movement had been splattered into froth and the remaining Communists were driven pitilessly from the one extreme of compromise to the opposite pole of adventurism in the hope that by belated military action they could retrieve positions that had now been irretrievably lost.

Most of the Communist party leaders made the turn obediently. Ch'ên Tu-hsiu, who had been selected as the chief scapegoat for the defeats of the past, was deposed, but most of the other members of the Political Bureau remained. The new group included Ch'ü Ch'iu-po, Chang Kuo-t'ao, Li Li-san, Chang T'ai-lei, Chou Ên-lai, and Li Wei-han, all of whom shared with Ch'ên Tu-hsiu the responsibility for what had gone before. It was Chou Ên-lai who had helped lead the Shanghai workers into the hands of Chiang Kai-shek's executioners. It was Li Wei-han (later better known as Lo Mai) who, as chairman of the Hunan Provincial Committee of the Communist party, had ordered the retreat of the peasant detachment from Changsha the week after the militarist coup of May 21. All of them now purchased the continued patronage of Moscow by putting the entire blame on Ch'ên Tu-hsiu and a few others whose only major crime had been their effort to carry out faithfully the orders they had received from Moscow. The new leaders, schooled only in retreat when it had been time to attack, were now ordered to attack when it was time to retreat.

They made the mechanical turn on orders from above, heedless of what was going on in the country and without at first even changing the basic policies of the party in its attitudes toward the Kuomintang or toward the agrarian revolution. At a conference of the new leadership, hastily convened on August 7 "by the telegraphic instructions of the Communist International and its new representative, Lominadze," the Communist party was called upon "to organize uprisings of the workers and peasants under the banner of the revolutionary Lefts of the Kuomintang."[11] Disaster had also legalized the slogan of "Soviets"—only yesterday Trotskyist contraband—*Pravda* declaring on July 25 that "the crisis of the Kuomintang places the question of Soviets on the order of the day. The slogan of Soviets is correct now. . . . The former partisans of the immediate formation of Soviets . . . wanted to force the masses to jump over stages through which the movement had not yet passed."[12] Now they were going to be forced to jump over the ruins of the revolutionary movement. The August 7 conference issued a lengthy letter to all the remaining members of the party, detailing the "mistakes" of the deposed leadership and declaring that Ch'ên Tu-hsiu had stubbornly refused throughout to carry out the impeccably correct instructions of the Comintern. Every drop of ambiguity was squeezed out of the cunning and self-insuring qualifications inserted by Bukharin in his resolutions in order to prove that the Comintern had been infallibly right before, during, and after all that had occurred. The conference declared that the new regime would "guarantee that henceforth there will be correct, revolutionary, Bolshevik leadership."[13] Hua Kang's official history said the conference "saved the party from impending dissolution and put it on the Bolshevik path." In Moscow, it was officially announced that "the right deviation in the leadership of the Chinese brother party has now been liquidated and the policy of the leadership corrected."[14]

Voices were raised, by Ch'ên Tu-hsiu and by others in the party, against the new policy of uprisings. But their objections were smothered. Moscow had said the time had come for "direct struggle." Putschist moods, born of desperation, were strong. If the necessary conditions for successful attacks did not exist, then they had to be created. The Communists plunged on into a series of adventures in the fall of 1927 known as the "Autumn Harvest Uprisings." The first of them occurred at Nanchang, capital of Kiangsi province, on August 1. Two Communist officers, Yeh T'ing and Ho Lung, commanding about three thousand men, raised the banner of revolt. Among the members of their "Revolutionary Committee" they listed not only the names of the Left Kuomintang leaders, Mrs. Sun Yat-sen, Têng Yen-ta, and Eugene Ch'ên, then en route to European exile, but also Generals Chang Fa-k'uei and Huang Ch'i-hsiang, of the "Ironsides" Army. The Comintern press trumpeted: "A new revolutionary center is being formed."[15] But the new center lasted only a few days. Chang Fa-k'uei moved his troops toward the city to attack the rebels and Yeh T'ing and Ho Lung were forced to flee. Waving their Kuomintang banners in the face of an apathetic population, they marched southward and were defeated and dispersed in battles before the towns of Chaochow and Swatow in northeastern Kwangtung. Remnants of the Yeh-Ho army fled into the East River districts, where the peasant movement had been cradled and where now, in its ebb, there were still bands of stubborn insurgents. That was the end of the Yeh-Ho adventure.[16]

Similar outbreaks, although on an even smaller scale, took place elsewhere in Central China and even in some districts in the north. They all had one feature in common: the masses, instead of making the "tremendous response" Stalin had predicted, simply refused to co-operate. In most cases, the Communists met the passive reluctance of the masses by ignoring them altogether and seeking salvation in alliances with little local military satraps. A small force of troops in Hupeh led by another Communist officer named Chang Fao-cheng tried to unite with one local militarist against another but was wiped out in its first battle. A similar defeat was met in northern Kiangsu. In some districts of Hunan and Hupeh there were sporadic uprisings of small bands of peasants, armed with pikes and spears. They were uniformly crushed. In Shanghai, the Kiangsu Provincial Committee, encouraged by brief peasant outbursts in two country districts early in November, decided that "the time for an insurrection has now really arrived." The difficulty was that the workers were uninterested. According to the party's own report, it tried to overcome this lack of interest by sending bands of "armed Red terrorists to intimidate workers into striking, factory by factory, thinking that if a general strike could be manufactured in this way, the uprising would surely be successful."[17] In Wuhan, the Yangtze Bureau of the Communist party had received, and at first rejected, orders to stage an insurrection after the first series of Autumn Harvest uprisings in the countryside had failed. It was immediately barraged with charges of "opportunism" and "cowardice." It backed down and, according to Ch'ü Ch'iu-po, issued orders for a general strike and insurrection. When the day came, however, the remaining party members in the city panicked and fled. The Northern Bureau of the party adopted a "General Plan for Uprising" that was so elaborately preposterous that even Hua Kang, the official party historian, was compelled, later, to call it "material for a historical joke."

While these abortive adventures were in progress, the Political Bureau of the Communist party finally decided to furl the blue banner of the Kuomintang. On September 19, 1927, the bureau declared that "the uprisings can under no circumstances take place under the Kuomintang banner."[18] For the blue banner of the Kuomintang flown in the period of the great revolutionary upswing, the Communist party now substituted the red banner of the Soviets in the period of the revolution's ebb. On September 30, in Moscow, Stalin's *Pravda* proclaimed: "The propaganda slogan of Soviets must now become a slogan of action!"[19] In November, a plenary session of the Communist Central Committee dutifully proclaimed the new course: "All power to the delegates councils of the workers, peasants, soldiers, and city poor—the Soviets!" From the collapse of the Yeh-Ho adventure, from the defeats of the Autumn Harvest, the Communist leadership drew the now-familiar conclusion: "After the Yeh-Ho defeat, the Chinese revolution not only did not ebb, but rose to a new, higher, stage." The course toward insurrection still held. "The enormous experience of the last three months," the plenum concluded, "is eloquent testimony that the tactic of the Chinese Communist Party was, on the whole, perfectly correct."[20] From Canton to Shanghai to Wuhan, they had moved from defeat to disaster to debacle. The cycle had now to be completed. In Canton, once more, they lurched toward a new catastrophe.

In Kwangtung province, General Li Chi-shên ruled with a heavy hand. The repressions of 1926 were followed by bloodier purges in April 1927, after Chiang's Shanghai coup. The peasant unions had all been wiped out and the great workers' organizations in Canton had all but disappeared. The Communists had taken to the desperate expedient of terrorism, making several unsuccessful attempts to assassinate Li Chi-shên. When the Wuhan collapse came and the Communist party was driven by Comintern orders along the road of insurrection, they gathered their remaining cadres in Canton for a final, desperate effort. In September, when the Yeh-Ho army was careering southward through Kiangsi, plans were hastily made for an uprising in the expectation that Yeh-Ho would actually be able to storm Canton itself. When the Yeh-Ho force was scattered, the plans were not abandoned but merely postponed.

A few weeks later a conflict developed in Canton that seemed to the Communists to offer a fresh opportunity for action. Chang Fa-k'uei and Wang Ching-wei were plotting there to oust Li Chi-shên and as their plans became known, the Communist Central Committee ordered the Kwangtung organization "to utilize the opportunity of the civil war resulting from the coup d'état in order resolutely to expand the uprisings in the cities and villages." The coup against Li Chi-shên took place on November 17 and the forces of the opposing generals squared off for battle along lines that began some forty miles from the city of Canton itself. On November 26, the Communist party in Canton decided to organize an insurrection and a few days later the date was set for December 13.*

In the events that followed in Canton, myopia, delusions, and insane adventurism culminated in gross tragedy. Heinz Neumann, the

* By a peculiar "coincidence," the Canton insurrection was fixed for the date of the meeting of the 15th congress of the Russian Communist party, at which Stalin expelled the Trotskyist Opposition. Trotsky has charged that the uprising in Canton was timed to give the Stalinist majority a "victory" in China "to cover up the physical extermination of the Russian Opposition." *Problems of the Chinese Revolution,* pp. 291–92. Cf. Victor Serge, *De Lenine à Staline* (Paris, 1937,)p. 31 ; Serge, *Russia Twenty Years After* (New York, 1937), p. 160; Boris Souvarine, *Staline* (Paris, 1935), p. 434. A member of the group of Left Kuomintang *émigrés* in Moscow at the time has told the present writer that the whole group understood that the Canton events had been forced for the purposes of the C.P.S.U.'s 15th Congress.

German Communist adventurer, had come down to take personal charge. Neumann, himself executed by Stalin a decade later, left behind a book in which he gave his own detailed version of the Canton events. A group of Comintern representatives and leading Chinese Communist participants a year later contributed chapters to an even more detailed history published by the Communist party. From these accounts, the following narrative is largely drawn.[21]

The insurrectionists felt sure that the impending battle between the militarists would favor their enterprise. A year later, Lozofsky wrote that they "should have known that as soon as the banner of revolt was raised, the quarrels in the camp of the counterrevolution would immediately come to an end." They also believed that the sporadic outbursts of peasant anger in the East River districts portended another rising surge of the peasant movement. P'êng Pai had returned to Haifeng and Lufeng, 150 miles from Canton, where he had started his career five years before.* With small bands of survivors of the Yeh-Ho army, he had set up peasant "Soviets." These, together with similar tiny centers in a few other remote districts, were but flickering sparks. The plotters saw them magnified and felt sure that the whole country would burst into flame when they rose in Canton. "Obviously," confessed the Comintern agent Lominadze a year later, "we far too greatly exaggerated the extent of the development of the peasant uprisings at that time."

In Canton itself the conspirators counted up their resources. Assembling the reports of the Communist military commander Yeh T'ing, of "Comrade A" (presumably Neumann), and of the Canton Revolutionary Committee, Ch'ên Shao-yü† estimated the armaments of the revolutionists at their highest figures as follows: "Revolvers and automatics, at most 30; grenades, at most 200; rifles in the hands of workers, at most 50; rifles in the hands of soldiers, at most 1,600." Neumann's own report said that the proposed insurrectionary force, recruited mainly from remnants of the Canton-Hongkong pickets, had only 29 Mausers and about 200 grenades. The single military detachment at their disposal was a regiment of former Whampoa cadets among whom were 200 members of the Communist party. The actual number of participants in the uprising was given by Yeh T'ing as 4,200. "Comrade A" gave the total as 3,200.

* P'êng Pai was captured by the Kuomintang and executed in August 1929.
† Later better known as Wang Ming, for some years during the 1930's secretary-general of the Communist party.

According to Yeh T'ing's account, the Canton military authorities had 5,000 well-armed soldiers in the city, in addition to 1,000 policemen and 1,000 armed gangsters of the Mechanics' Union (a famous name in the history of the Canton labor movement, now used to cloak a Kuomintang-controlled strong-arm squad). These forces had more than 5,000 rifles, a good number of machine guns, and 35 small trench mortars and cannon. In addition, several Chinese and foreign gunboats were anchored in the river. On the outskirts of the city there were nearly four full regiments and only two or three days' travel away there were the combined armies of Chang Fa-k'uei and Li Chi-shên, totaling about 50,000 men. Among these forces, there was no trace, by Neumann's own admission, of any Communist influence. On the other hand, he argued defensively, these troops "were surrounded on all sides by revolutionary ferment" and if one takes this factor into consideration, "one can say that the military forces in Canton were equal."

The "revolutionary ferment" was so great that the Communist party did not dare issue a call for a strike. When Neumann and the Communist committee pondered the strategy to be followed, they thought for a moment of calling a general strike. They abandoned the idea almost at once, Neumann reported, "because it seemed to the revolutionary committee that if they did not succeed in taking the enemy unawares by a sudden night attack, the chances of victory would singularly diminish." The last attempt to call out the Canton workers had ended in failure on October 23, when Chang Fa-k'uei, already sharing power in the city, had broken up most of the remaining trade-union centers and arrested many of the underground leaders in the factories. Wang Ching-wei, the liberal leader lately the "reliable ally" in Wuhan, had also carried out the task from which even the militarists had shrunk: he had seen to the forcible eviction of the surviving Canton-Hongkong pickets from the dormitories they had still occupied on the outskirts of the city. The pickets had dispersed and only about five hundred of them remained at the disposal of the Communist party. After these events, the Communists ceased trying to regain the confidence of the workers in the factories. The result was, according to Lozofsky, that when the insurrection occurred it came "suddenly and like an accident" to the masses of Cantonese workers. The same "sudden" and "accidental" character was given to the "Soviet" which was to emerge from the uprising. Four days before the insurrection, fifteen men were selected, nominally representing the workers, peasants, and the cadet regiment. These fifteen constituted nothing less than the "Canton Council of Workers' Peasants' and Soldiers' Deputies."[22] After the insurrection, it was supposed to be enlarged to a membership of three hundred.

To make matters worse, the military authorities learned of the Communist plans several days ahead of time. According to Huang P'ing, a member of the Revolutionary Committee, the word came from Wang Ching-wei, who had gone to Shanghai for a conference with Chiang Kai-shek. There he learned what was being plotted and wired an urgent warning to Chang Fa-k'uei. Chang immediately ordered his chief aide, Huang Ch'i-hsiang, one of the dashing revolutionary heroes of the old "Ironsides" Army, to detach sufficient troops and return to Canton to reinforce the Canton garrison. Huang arrived in the city on the morning of December 10 with his troops only a few hours' march behind him. In the face of these developments, the Revolutionary Committee simply moved the date for the uprising from the 13th to the 11th.

At seven o'clock on the evening of the 10th the insurrectionists began to gather at their appointed stations. The new orders were sent to the cadet regiments' barracks, and within a few hours' time the die was irretrievably cast. The authorities, however, had been alerted, and through the evening hours, heavy police patrols and armored cars were thick in the streets. Pedestrians were searched in all the main thoroughfares. One of the concentration points was actually uncovered and ninety "Red Guards" were arrested and a cache of sixty grenades seized. There was brief wavering among the Communist leaders but it was too late to change their plans now. By midnight, in any case, the authorities seemed reassured, for most of the police patrols were gone from the streets. At 3:30 A.M. firing began in the northern end of the city. The cadet regiment had risen. The regimental commander and several officers were shot. Climbing into motor busses, the cadets split into parties of one and two companies and moved off to the selected points of attack. Simultaneously the waiting squads of armed pickets moved into action.

The first raids were almost all successful. At several points in the city small detachments of hostile troops were disarmed or scattered after brief skirmishes and some additional rifles were added to the slim store of weapons held by the insurrectionists. In the center of town a combined worker-cadet force stormed and quickly occupied the central police headquarters and the headquarters of the military gendarmerie just across the same street. At Chang Fa-k'uei's staff headquarters, and at the fortresslike mansion of Li Chi-shên, the attackers were repulsed by machine-gun fire which proved impassable. By dawn, when most of the city was in the hands of the insurrection, these points still held out and fighting continued there well into the next day.

At six o'clock on the morning of December 11 the Canton "Soviet of Workers', Peasants', and Soldiers' Deputies" formally established itself in the police headquarters and began to function as the *de facto* government of Canton. There were only thirteen men present to launch the "Soviet." Two of the selected peasant delegates did not arrive in time to participate. One of the government's first acts was to release more than one thousand political prisoners, most of whom immediately joined the forces of the insurrection. Arms seized from the enemy were doled out as fast as they were secured. Firing was still plainly audible in the city when the first decrees of the "Soviet Government" began to be issued.

The manifesto of the revolutionary government had been printed a few days before but the printing plant where the copies still were held was in the line of fire and could not be reached. Hurriedly new handbills were run off in shops located within the captured area. Motor cars were commandeered. Youthful propagandists made off in them to spread the freshly printed sheets among the workers of Canton to let them know that the revolution had at long last taken place, that the blue banner of the Kuomintang had at last been replaced by the red flag of the Soviets. The manifesto called for the confiscation of the property of the big bourgeoisie, the banks, and the money exchange shops. The houses of the wealthy were to be turned into dormitories for the workers. The pawnshops were to be taken over and all the articles in them returned freely to their owners. "All our martyrs have struggled and given their lives for such things. We must continue their struggle."

The program of the Canton Commune called for an eight-hour day; wage increases; state aid to the unemployed according to the regular wage scale: nationalization of all big industries, communications, and banks; recognition of the All-China Labor Federation as the national organization of the Chinese proletariat. It called for the nationalization of land; the extermination of all landlords and *haoshên*; destruction of land deeds, leases, debt bonds, and land boundaries; and the establishment of the Soviet power in the villages. The city poor were to be relieved by the distribution of property confiscated from the wealthy. All debts to pawnshops and usurers were ordered canceled and all miscellaneous taxes and contributions imposed upon the toilers abolished. The arming of the workers, the immediate release of all political prisoners, freedom of speech, press, and assembly, and the right to organize and strike were proclaimed for the working population.

This program, launched in an hour of hopeless desperation, was its own comment on the whole previous course. In the days of sweeping mass power, the Communists had confined themselves to the limited and timid reforms approved by the Kuomintang and had in the end suffered disastrously from their lack of boldness. Now, when they were a handful venturing in the presence of an inert mass to attack well-armed and well-entrenched reaction, they were ready to speak in bold terms that went unheard amid the din of bloody repression. Only a few Canton workers joined them. Some drivers, some printers, some ricksha coolies quit work to grasp rifles. But the railroad workers and river sailors remained at their jobs, largely ignorant of what was happening. They transported the troops being brought in to crush the uprising. They helped Kuomintang officials to flee the districts held by the insurrectionists. "The masses took no part in the uprising," wrote Yeh T'ing, who had arrived only six hours before the outbreak to take command of the military forces. "All the shops were closed and the employees showed no desire to support us. . . . Most of the soldiers we disarmed dispersed in the city. . . . The reactionaries could still use the Canton-Hankow line. . . . The workers of the power plant cut off the lights and we had to work in the dark. The workers of Canton and Hongkong, as well as the sailors, under the pressure of the British imperialists, did not dare join the combatants. . . . The river sailors placed themselves shamefully at the service of the Whites whom they helped to cross the river while we were not even able to learn about some of the points of embarkation. The railway workers of the Hongkong and Canton-Hankow lines transmitted the telegrams of the enemy and transported their soldiers. The peasants did not help us by destroying the tracks and did not try to prevent the enemy from attacking Canton. The workers of Hongkong did not display the least sympathy for the insurrection."

"It is true," wrote Deng Cheng-tsah, another leading participant, "that not all the workers of Canton participated. . . . But some people say only 5,000 men were involved. This is . . . a slander. Surely more than 20,000 took part." Even so, Deng stopped to consider: "Still, we must say that its social basis was not broad. There were, for example, before the betrayal of the Kuomintang about 200,000 workers under the Communist Workers' Delegates Council." Heinz Neumann's report, which did its best to maximize the degree of popular support, also acknowledged that the workers had remained passive and that "there was no important revolutionary movement among the peasants in the districts adjacent to Canton."

Only two years earlier, with their own forces and their own strength, the workers and peasants of Canton and Kwangtung had demoralized the armies of the old militarists, paralyzed mighty Britain's Hongkong, and made possible the political unification of the province and the establishment of the Kuomintang's national government. At that time the Communists had taught them to expect nothing in return. Now, with their forces reduced, to take Deng's figure, to a tenth their former size in the city, with the revolution everywhere shattered and the reaction everywhere triumphant, the Communists were staging an uprising under the banner of the Soviet power. But the masses were no longer there to follow them. Two years earlier the Communists had seen their forces through the broad end of binoculars—minuscule and impotent—when in reality they were formidably strong. Today they were looking at them through the narrow end, magnified and distorted. They never did see their forces as they really were and were now paying with their lives for their failures.

By midmorning of December 11, the Kuomintang troops had already begun to strike back. At half a dozen crude street barriers, the defenders of the Canton Commune were already desperately trying to repel the counterattack which grew stronger every hour. Feverishly the few squads of youthful propagandists tried to arouse the people, spreading word by mouth and by handbills, that a monster mass meeting would take place at noon that day. At the appointed hour, a bare three hundred people were present. That evening it was decided to try again for another mass meeting at noon the next day outside the

Taiping Theater. Concerning this meeting Huang P'ing, who had been made "Foreign Affairs Commissar" of the Commune, is silent. Deng Cheng-tsah, another participant, wrote flatly that it failed to materialize. Ch'ên Shao-yü, who had the advantage of not having been in Canton but in Moscow at the time, wrote that ten thousand workers gathered to ratify the decrees of the Commune. According to the agenda of the meeting, the fifteen-man Soviet was supposed to have been confirmed in its functions, its program endorsed, and its membership increased to three hundred. Whether these measures were ever taken was not recorded and it no longer mattered, for by the afternoon of December 12, troops were attacking the city in force and a battle was going on in which workers and cadets, sparsely armed, were stubbornly holding out against the greatly superior artillery and machine-gun fire of the attackers.

During the fighting several fires began in the central district of the city. These were subsequently charged to the incendiarism of the Communards. In fact, the principal fires, which partially destroyed the Central Bank and neighboring buildings, had resulted from the bombardment of the city from the river, where Chinese, British, and Japanese gunboats had joined in the battle of repression. They went into action to cover the defenders of Chang Fa-k'uei's headquarters and also laid down a barrage to cover the crossing of troops now arriving in large numbers to retake the city. According to the eyewitness account of the correspondent of the *Peking Morning Post*, the shelling ignited a powder magazine, starting fires which quickly spread through the vicinity. The *Ta Kung Pao* reporter also described the actions of the Kuomintang's own gangsters, who "took the opportunity to commit arson and to loot." The Peking *Yi Shih Pao's* firsthand report said that the gunboat shelling caused at least ten fires.[28]

Enemy troops moved on the rebels from three different directions. Chang Fa-k'uei, Huang Ch'i-hsiang, and Li Fu-lin directed operations from a gunboat anchored in the river. Among the commanders marching to the suppression of the Commune was Hsüeh Yüeh, who only nine months earlier had offered his division to the Communists to oppose Chiang's Shanghai coup. From the West River front, from Kungyi in the north and from Whampoa and Honan in the east, some 45,000 troops were being moved toward the city. There, about one thousand well-armed gangsters were already attacking the forces of the Commune. The main Communist body was entrenched behind sandbags on the river bank and was under fire from across the river, from the gunboats, and from the gangsters in the rear. The Communists were already so isolated that several enemy detachments landed and came within 150 yards of the Revolutionary Committee's headquarters before being spotted. Despite this, the headquarters held out until ten o'clock on the morning of the 13th, when they finally fell back from the sandbag barricade, fighting from street to street. Some leaders gathered part of the cadet regiment and a few Red Guards—Neumann says they totaled 1,500 men—and escaped the cordon of enemy troops, leaving the city to march toward Hailufeng. At noon the remaining Communists were making their last stand at the Bureau of Public Safety, where the "Soviet" had briefly held sway. Here, surrounded on four sides, they resisted extermination in a two-hour battle. They threw back five attempts to rush their lines. Shortly after noon the red flag was finally pulled down from police headquarters. For a few hours longer small groups held out here and there, until their ammunition was exhausted or until they were trampled down by the attackers. By the afternoon of December 13, the last of them had been wiped out.

Most Kuomintang and foreign accounts refer to the Canton events of December 11–13 as the "three days of terror." During its brief existence, the Commune, according to the Communists, had killed 210 and imprisoned 71. A report by a Chinese correspondent to the *China Weekly Review* estimated that the Communists had killed 600, including those Kuomintang troops killed during the fighting.[24] Not until the Kuomintang's avenging executioners set to work on the night of December 13 did the real reign of terror begin. Li Chi-shên, Chang Fa-k'uei, and Huang Ch'i-hsiang turned their soldiers loose on the city. Long after the fighting ended, the streets echoed the gunfire of executioners and were strewn with the blood and the bodies of the dead. A correspondent of the *Ta Kung Pao* saw women Communists "wrapped in cotton padded blankets, soaked in gasoline and burned alive." Soldiers seized any women they found with bobbed hair, which was regarded as infallible evidence of radicalism. Hundreds of girls were shot or otherwise killed after being subjected to indescribable indignities. "Canton is like hell itself," wired a reporter on the scene. "Uncleared corpses are piled up along the roads."[25]

A correspondent of the Peking *Shuntien Pao* ventured out into the streets:

The first thing I saw as I turned out of the small lane was the body of a worker lying face up. It was covered with dirt. On its head was a red kerchief. The forehead and right cheek had been shot away. Flies swarmed on the dead flesh. . . . Behind the fallen brick walls, propped up against trees and lying at the street curbs, floating on the surface of the river, wherever you looked, dead men. . . . In every street everywhere were the corpses of massacred men and women. . . . Blood seemed to be running in rivers. . . . There were thick reddish-black clots staining the ground, strewn with brains and bowels and entrails. Stones, bamboo swords, and wooden spears still lay about the streets. . . . The corpses lying stiff in their blood stank horribly. . . . At the square of the park, I saw three trucks piled high with corpses. In the shrubs to the right were ten bodies, seemingly newly-shot. . . . There were mournful shrieks and in the distance there still seemed to be shooting going on.

Under the photo of corpses in Canton's streets, a Shanghai editor captioned: "The bodies of the dead were collected as so much cordwood and carted away for burial in a common grave."[26]

Among them were the bodies of Chang T'ai-lei, head of the Revolutionary Committee, killed in battle on December 12, and of five Russians, shot by Li Fu-lin's soldiers when they raided the Soviet Consulate on the 15th. Most of the leaders had escaped. Heinz Neumann, according to Yeh T'ing, had been one of the first to flee. Behind them, grotesquely sprawled on the streets of Canton, they left the remains of the revolutionary organizations of the city. The final toll of the counted dead was 5,700.

For months afterward, Communist resolutions twisted themselves around the harsh facts of the Canton uprising. Some voices were raised in criticism of the Kwangtung Provincial Committee, but they had to be quickly silenced. The chain of responsibility for the insurrectionist course ran too plainly and too directly from the Kwangtung Committee to the Central Committee, from the Central Committee to the Comintern, and from the Comintern to Stalin. The crime of Canton had to be justified in order, once more, to preserve the myth of an infallible leadership.

It had been "correct" and "necessary," the resolutions said; the analysis of the situation on which it had been based was "completely in accord with the facts." So much so that the Political Bureau of the Chinese Communist party, on January 3, 1928, and the Ninth Plenum of the Executive Committee of the Comintern a month later both declared that there had only been "mistakes of the leadership" committed on the spot and that the Communist party, overcoming such

292 THE TRAGEDY OF THE CHINESE REVOLUTION

"mistakes" had to go on to the organization of new and bigger and more successful uprisings on the crest of the "new revolutionary upsurge" of which Canton had been the harbinger.[27] Not until the Sixth Congress of the Communist International and the Sixth Congress of the Chinese Communist party met simultaneously in Moscow in July 1928 had the time come to acknowledge that the Canton uprising, while beyond doubt "correct" and "necessary" had been a "rearguard battle."[28]

Actually, it had been a bloody sacrifice, imposed from above and from the outside, on a small band of disoriented survivors of a shattered revolution.

Chapter 18

THE IMPRINT OF THE CHINESE
REVOLUTION OF 1925–27

TWENTY-TWO YEARS after the defeat of the revolution in 1927, the Communists conquered power in China. In mid-October 1949, Chinese Communist troops entered the city of Canton. Shanghai and Nanking had already fallen to them. Two weeks earlier, on October 1, the Communist People's Republic, headed by Mao Tsê-tung, had been proclaimed at Peking. Chiang Kai-shek and those generals and Kuomintang politicians who had remained with him were fugitives on the island of Formosa. The wheel had turned full, from Canton to Canton within less than a generation, well within the lifetime of some of the principal participants in both sets of events.

As it flickered out, the defeated revolution of 1927 had left behind it a trail of sparks that inevitably re-ignited the combustibles in Chinese society. The crisis in Chinese life remained, sharpened by the revolution and the counterrevolution. It arose, more insistently than ever, out of all the unsurmounted obstacles and all the unresolved dilemmas and out of the hastened pace of the country's decay. The Communists, decimated and dispersed in 1927, had regathered tiny forces in the remote countryside. Resuming political life at the head of small peasant and guerrilla bands, they went on through years of wars and failures and persistent survival, rising again to new strength out of the conditions created by the Kuomintang's misrule, Japan's invasions, and the onset of the second World War. When that war ended, the struggle for power in China was renewed as the Communists moved in to replace a Kuomintang regime no longer capable of maintaining its authority. This conflict, unfolding against the backdrop of the new Russian-American struggle for world power, quickly revealed that the Kuomintang had exhausted its capacities, even for misrule. During 1948–49, Chiang Kai-shek's regime fell apart. For the Kuomintang the civil war was mostly a matter of disintegration, abdication, and flight. For the Communists it was mostly a matter of

293

taking over the power that fell into their hands. Under its new masters in Peking, and beyond them in Moscow, China moved into a new phase of its effort to overcome its backwardness. Internally this involved the beginnings of the creation of a new totalitarian dictatorship. Externally, it meant that China's new relationship with the Western world would be defined by China's new place within the Russian power orbit. For the rest of Asia and the world, this began a transformation of incalculable dimensions. For the Chinese people it was the opening of a new act in the unending tragedy of their years.

Looking back and down from their present heights of power in China, the Communists view their defeat of two decades ago as an episode, a momentary setback on their road to ultimate victory.* But this view flattens the jagged course of history into an uninformative curve that hides from us too much of the meaning of both past and present. In fact, the imprint of the Communist defeat of 1927 lies heavily marked not only upon the Communist victory of 1949 but upon all the catastrophic history of the intervening time.

The defeated revolution of 1925–27 in China was one of the major episodes in human affairs in the years between the first two world wars of this century. It has to be grouped in this sense with the abortive German revolution of 1923, the world economic depression that began in 1929, the Japanese invasion of Manchuria in 1931, the rise of Hitler in 1933, the French general strike of 1936, and the Spanish civil war of 1936–39. The events in China in 1927 contributed in culminating degree to the shaping of Russia into a nationalist-totalitarian state. Within China itself, the defeat of the revolution exposed the country within a few years to Japan's attempted conquest. This in turn aggravated all the tensions and circumstances that finally exploded into the Pacific war of 1941–45. The psychological and political imprint of the 1927 events was deeply imbedded in the thinking and behavior of both sides in the renewed civil war after Japan's defeat. It remains also, despite all the attrition and changes of the years, a basic element in the new Chinese-Russian relations inaugurated by the Chinese Communist conquest of power.

There is an immediate as well as a historical importance, there-

* In a major document written on the eve of victory ("The Dictatorship of the People's Democracy," written for the twenty-eighth anniversary of the Chinese Communist party, July 1, 1949), Mao Tsê-tung was able to compress the entire history of 1925–27 into a single sentence: "Sun Yat-sen died and the power passed to Chiang Kai-shek." (*Soviet Press Translations*, September 1, 1949.)

fore, in the effort to see the imprint of the Chinese revolution of 1925–27 on all this crowded history. This is, to be sure, history through which we are still living. It is certainly no easier for the student than it is for the statesman, politician, journalist, or plain citizen, to bring it into focus. In all their variety and magnitude, events have outrun the record. Yet there is an urgency in our need to understand it that the future historian will never feel. Hence, with whatever inadequacy, we can here at least attempt to trace the imprint and the consequences of 1927 in the rise and fall of the Kuomintang, the fall and rise of the Communist party, the evolution of Russia, and the prospects of totalitarianism in Asia. We can hope thereby to see how the initial phases of the revolution that began in China just over two decades ago helped shape the dilemmas that face us in the present day.

I. THE RISE AND FALL OF THE KUOMINTANG

The defeat of the revolution ushered in for China a period of terror, renewed militarist wars, deepening economic disintegration, and foreign invasion. Unable to give effect to the most elementary social and economic reforms, the Kuomintang could establish itself only in the form of a brutal military dictatorship. This was not a monolithic, self-sufficient dictatorship. Chiang Kai-shek and his associates in Nanking shared power with groups of rival military satraps and remained largely dependent upon the military, political, and financial support of the Western Powers. The regime grew into a monstrous parasite on the stricken body of the nation. Its generals and bankers, its landlords and bureaucrats, its jailers and executioners, inextricably interlaced, mercilessly drained the country. The land, the people, even the most limited kind of economic enterprise, became sources not merely of profit but of plunder. All the existing means of exploitation that had been vainly challenged by the revolution were not merely preserved but sharpened to an unprecedented degree.

The Kuomintang ruled largely by naked force. Unable to win popular support, it compelled submission. Incapable of developing— much less utilizing—democratic institutions, it simply imprisoned or destroyed its opponents and its critics. There was a certain amount of play for contending elements within the Kuomintang regime itself, but it was basically a product of the paternalistically authoritarian ideology of Sun Yat-sen operating through an organization that was created by copying the Russian Bolshevik party. Hence it was, throughout its twenty-two-year tenure, a single-party regime, complete with its thought-control apparatus, its secret police, and its unremittingly merciless treatment of all dissenters. Its first years were its bloodiest. No one has ever been able to estimate accurately the number of those who died under the scourge of Kuomintang terror. No one has ever known exactly how many political prisoners choked stinking jails from one end of the country to the other in the years of its rule, nor how many of them died of disease or torture.

For the record there are fragmentary statistics culled from official announcements and the press in which, at least until 1932, the regime quite proudly announced the daily or weekly toll of killings. One study, for example, indicated that between April and December 1927, there were 37,985 persons formally condemned to death and 32,316 imprisoned. These figures obviously did not include the uncounted victims of the wanton slaughters that occurred during the suppression of the mass organizations and the establishment of the Kuomintang government. Among these there was, for example, the massacre of 20,000 persons in Hunan province alone. Between January and August 1928, there were 27,699 acknowledged executions. In 1930 one rough estimate held that at least 140,000 people had been killed by the regime up to that time. In 1931 a collection of reports from only six provinces produced a total of 39,778 executions that year.[1] Some of these figures come from Communist sources, but it is doubtful if they are seriously exaggerated. The terror was too publicly waged and its toll too openly acknowledged even in the Kuomintang and foreign press of the time. After 1931, the publicity waned but the terror did not. For, in this period, 1932 to 1937, the most common crime was opposition to Chiang Kai-shek's rigorously imposed policy of nonresistance to Japanese encroachments. Suppression of the anti-Japanese movement kept the prisons full and the execution grounds busy. Throughout the period of Kuomintang rule, secret police governed the press and terrorized the faculties and student bodies of China's schools. Forced conscription for the army and labor corps added to the ravage of the villages. None of this includes any measure of the cost, in human life and suffering, of the repeated large-scale punitive military campaigns waged against the Communist-led insurgent peasant armies in Central China through most of the years of this dark and bloody decade.

When he came to power, Chiang Kai-shek substituted a new militarism for the old. He decked it in nationalist trappings and invoked the name and doctrines of Sun Yat-sen as formal sanction for the one-party dictatorship through which he ruled. Sun's provision for a period of "political tutelage" governed the entire period of Kuomintang rule. None of the promulgated constitutions or hand-picked assemblies ever seriously mitigated the absolutism of the Kuomintang regime. In behalf of the landlords, the Kuomintang preserved the backward and unproductive system of land tenure and cultivation which drove great masses of peasants either into open rebellion, or else into wandering pauperism, into the swollen armies of the militarists, and into banditry, or left them prey to death through uncontrolled flood or unrelieved famine. In behalf of the bankers, it floated huge loans from which enormous profits were made by a few favored families and individuals, and subjected all business enterprise to the drain of unchecked speculation, peculation, and corruption. In behalf of the generals, it spent all but a tiny fraction of the national revenues and carried out or permitted wholesale requisitions which stripped towns and villages of their meager resources year after year. In behalf of the bureaucrats and politicians, it sucked up what remained of the national loot through ruinous taxes and through the unofficial but immensely lucrative opium monopoly.

The "unification" of China under the Kuomintang remained a myth. Chiang eliminated some of his militarist rivals by civil wars; some he absorbed by purchase; others he neutralized by mutually profitable alliances. Kuomintang "reconstruction" produced a mountain of paper plans, laws, decrees, special commissions, and promises. The results were some showcase industrial projects, a few miles of highway, a few miles of railway, some pretentious government buildings in Nanking, and an imposing monument to Sun Yat-sen, a façade for the wholesale plundering of the country's waning wealth. Natural and man-made disasters progressively destroyed more and more of China's capacity to sustain itself. China, a huge agricultural country, had to apply a steadily increasing proportion of its normal exports to pay for imports of food. The onset of the world economic crisis, especially after 1931, simply hastened and deepened the process of economic disintegration of which the Kuomintang regime was the prime agency.

It was upon this prostrate China that Japan, in September 1931, resumed its imperialist offensive. Choosing its moment shrewdly, it moved into the vacuum created in world politics by the intense Western preoccupation with the economic crisis on the one hand and with the strategy of creating a *cordon sanitaire* around Russia. It moved into Manchuria, meeting only scattered local resistance unsupported by Chiang Kai-shek's government. It then moved across the Great Wall into China proper, alternating military attacks and political pressure aimed to bring the entire country and ultimately the whole continent of Asia under its control. For nearly six years, in the face of recurring Japanese blows, Chiang Kai-shek retreated, temporized, and yielded, seeking a basis for satisfying Japan's demands while preserving his own power. This attitude reproduced, on Chiang's own level, the attitude of Japan's Western rivals, who did not oppose Japan's advances in the hope they would not go too far. Wherever in China resistance was offered to the Japanese, it was despite Chiang Kai-shek and in defiance of his orders. This happened at Shanghai in 1932 when the Nineteenth Route Army, by the decision of its own commanders, stood off a combined Japanese land, naval, and air attack for thirty-four days while Chiang withheld his support. In the end his representatives stepped in and negotiated the "truce" which demilitarized the Shanghai area. The Tangku truce of 1933 yielded up the region immediately contiguous to the Great Wall and gave Japan a firm foothold in North China. In 1934, Chiang's representatives gave *de facto* recognition to Japan's Manchurian conquests by agreeing to resume postal and rail connections between "Manchukuo" and North China. In 1935 two further agreements accepted Japan's claim to eastern Chahar and cleared Hopeh province of all Chinese government forces.

Kuomintang apologists have always insisted that in this period Chiang was buying time with space, preparing for the ultimate defense of the country. But far from acting like a leader who was gathering his country's forces for resisting foreign invasion, Chiang Kai-shek matched his surrenders to the Japanese with ruthless suppression of popular resistance to his "nonresistance" policy. Anti-Japanese movements were put down with blood and iron. Students and others who openly protested were shot, cut down, or jammed into crowded prisons. Chiang's prime preoccupation was, in fact, the maintenance of his own position. He hoped with each successive capitulation to the Japanese that they would leave him untouched in his own bailiwick, the Yangtze Valley. In that area, while claiming military impotence in the face of the Japanese, he expended the bulk of his armies and his weapons in campaigns against the insurgent armies led by the Communists.[2]

It was not until 1937, when the Japanese took off from the spring-boards Chiang had yielded to them and embarked upon a campaign obviously designed to conquer all of China, that Chiang was finally compelled to resist. Even then, he proved capable only of throwing huge, poorly led, poorly trained forces into futile, sacrificial battles, and of withdrawing westward as the Japanese bore down upon him. He shied from acceding to demands for even limited reforms that might have mobilized the people, whom he still feared more than he feared the invaders. When Japan's war against China finally became a war among the major Powers, Chiang Kai-shek simply hung on tenaciously in his western refuge, waiting to be rescued by American armed might. In the process, however, his regime lost its grip on power. The struggle against the Japanese in the large occupied areas of the country created its own forms and its own leadership and before long passed under the influence and control of the Communists. The Communist armies, previously bottled up in the northwest, filtered eastward, provided an organized outlet for the people anxious to resist the hated invader, won great popular prestige and following, and established the basis for their later swift expansion. When American power finally reduced Japan, when Russian armies moved into Manchuria, and when the undefeated Japanese armies in China abruptly laid down their arms, the Communists had acquired the forces and the positions that enabled them to challenge the Kuomintang in a contest for the mastery of all China.

II. THE FALL AND RISE OF THE CHINESE COMMUNIST PARTY

The re-emergence of the Chinese Communists in such spectacular strength in 1945 and their march to power by the end of 1949 have obscured the history through which they passed in the two decades after their defeat in 1927. Yet it is to that history that one must go for clues to an understanding of what this Communist movement became.

The defeat of 1927 was nearly one of annihilation. The Communist party had been founded only seven years before and had been led to disaster mainly—as we have seen—because it was so totally dependent upon Russian guidance and subject to Russian control.

After the defeat, the Chinese Communists did not cease to be subject to Russian pressure and dictation, but they were not and did not become merely an alien graft. In the remote hinterlands of Central China they found their own means of survival and new paths to power. The Kuomintang victory brought no solution to China's persistent social crisis but served only to deepen it. Over the next twenty years, through defeat and isolation and through hardy and bitter adventures, the Chinese Communist movement regained strength and acquired a new character by blending itself into the kind of partisan warfare that has a tradition in China almost as old as the history of the country itself.

Recurring peasant wars through China's many centuries had often toppled dynasties and erected new ones without significantly transforming the social relations among the different classes of the population. Through long historical periods during the rise and decline of successive ruling houses, partisan bands of rural dissidents continued here and there to challenge the established authority, creating a continuous tradition of dissent and violence while, for most of the time, the society itself remained statically unchanged. This was the vicious historical circle within which China stagnated while the Western world transformed itself. Less than a century before the mass uprising of 1925–27, South and Central China were swept by the great Taiping rebellion, which some historians believe might have germinated radical changes in Chinese society. But it was crushed by the intervention of the European powers acting in support of the Manchu Court at Peking, and became another abortive dynastic revolt. The revolution that rose in the same corner of the country shortly after the first World War also drew on the long tradition of peasant disaffection, but it introduced a new ingredient. This was the possibility of an urban workers' revolution capable of uniting the new class of city industrial workers with the great masses of the scattered peasantry, creating a new relationship between town and country and placing China's productive forces on a new footing. If this possibility did exist, it was extinguished by the events of 1925–27. Even the chance of an urban workers' revolution would not, as events proved, come again.

For, on the one hand, the successful counterrevolution shattered, physically and psychologically, the organizations of the city workers. On the other hand, the urban proletariat, so newly grouped in its factories in the years during and immediately after the first World War, suffered from 1927 onward an uninterrupted series of blows which reduced its numbers and weakened its powers of recovery. The decade after the revolution was marked by the onset of the world economic depression, foreign invasion accompanied by wholesale destruction of factories, and, afterward, ruinous inflation and economic paralysis. The accumulation of these circumstances prevented the Chinese working class from regaining the position it had held in 1925–27 as a distinct and politically significant class in Chinese society. The Communist road to power, therefore, never again led through the cities and the factories. The Chinese workers never won their own revolutionary victories; they were ultimately "liberated" by military forces which moved in on the city, in the classic Chinese manner, from the countryside.

The fact is that while the Communist party had helped create the huge working-class organizations of 1925–27, it never did in all its history pursue a policy that was fundamentally proletarian in its conduct or its objectives. The resulting defeat in 1927 drove the Communist movement physically from the cities and, in a political sense as well, further than ever from the working class. What the Kuomintang terror did not fully accomplish the Communists themselves achieved in the years of their wild adventures from the end of 1927 to the end of 1930. In mad little uprisings, they decimated their remaining urban membership and widened still further the gap between themselves and the workers in the factories. The party retained its claim to being the "party of the proletariat" but with that purely ritualistic label it actually set out upon a wholly new path.

The counterrevolution was securely triumphant in the cities. In the country the agrarian revolt had likewise been dispersed, its organizations destroyed, thousands of its leaders lost in the scourge of the terror. But it was impossible to extinguish all the impulses and all the people that had been stirred to action. Survivors and stubborn dissenters had a broad and remote and mountainous hinterland in which to seek refuge. They had, too, a tradition in which they could take shelter and find moral and psychological support for their persistence. Defeat and frustration were, after all, far more common than success in the long history of peasant struggle. From time almost immemorial those who would not accept such defeats had lived on in the mountains, in shadowy secret societies, in small bands, half-outlaw, half-insurgent. The Communist survivors of the defeated revolution in 1927 made themselves part of this tradition in Chinese life.

In twos and threes and in scattered bands, these survivors made their way to the mountainous border regions of Kiangsi, where they formed into small guerrilla bands which slowly enlarged into armies. Gradually they established a measure of control over scattered rural districts in the regions bordering on Hunan and Fukien and in several neighboring provinces. In the tiny Kiangsi village of Juichin on November 7, 1931, they proclaimed the "Chinese Soviet Republic." Its largest single piece of territory was the "central Soviet district," an area covering some seventeen counties astride the Kiangsi-Fukien border with a total population of about three million. The Communist armies and partisan forces of this period learned to become, in the old Chinese phrase, like "flowing water and moving clouds," constantly changing in size and location. For nearly five years, they successfully outwitted Chiang Kai-shek and his best generals and foreign advisers, evading or successfully parrying the repeated attacks of incomparably larger and better-armed Kuomintang forces. They developed a superb mastery of guerrilla tactics based upon the assistance and friendly support of the local population—an experience which prepared them for their future, more spectacular achievements.

But within their tiny areas and in the face of almost constant attack, the Communists were unable to carry out any consistent program of agrarian reform or to establish any kind of stable regime. The geographic remoteness and the absence of roads and rails, which stood them in such good stead in a military sense, proved the undoing of their political and economic objectives. Cut off from the cities and towns, they were unable to make the local economy function except on the basis of the crudest kind of village self-sufficiency, and even this had to be bolstered by "illicit" trade with the neighboring Kuomintang areas. Their attempts at land division cut the production of precious rice and had to be abandoned. In the end, they were all but overwhelmed by accumulated internal obstacles and external pressures. In 1934, the fifth Kuomintang offensive, planned and carried out under the direction of a corps of German advisers headed by General Hans von Seeckt, finally recovered the districts of the "Soviet Republic" of Kiangsi. But the Kuomintang offensive failed in its object, which was the destruction of the Communist armies. With great skill and ingenuity, the Red forces eluded capture, broke through the carefully planned cordon, and started on their famous long march across the provinces of Hunan, Kweichow, and Szechwan, ending up, after great feats of endurance, valor, and cunning, in the sparse lands of Shensi in the Chinese Northwest.*

This retreat to an even remoter hinterland widened still further the gap between the Communist movement and the urban working population in the cities of the central provinces and the east. In the years of the Kiangsi Soviet experiment, the Communist nuclei in these cities had narrowed down to shrinking groups of intellectuals, students, and a tiny handful of workers. They performed the function of a "rear" for the peasant forces in the countryside, carrying on agitation about their accomplishments and even recruiting workers and intellectuals to leave the cities for the distant Red districts. The other main focus of their activity was anti-Japanese propaganda designed to force the Kuomintang to cease its war against the Reds and abandon its policy of nonresistance to the Japanese. When the Kiangsi "republic" was finally snuffed out in 1934, the Communist apparatus in the eastern cities was demoralized and for a time almost completely disappeared. There were wholesale desertions to the Kuomintang, including some by prominent Communist leaders like Huang P'ing, "foreign minister" of the short-lived Canton Commune of 1927. There were numerous betrayals. Many a Communist bought his immunity by going to work for the Kuomintang secret police. Party members feared to walk the streets lest they be spotted by ex-friends now working for Chiang Kai-shek. Many fled, or lapsed into despairing passivity, or else tried to find places in the anti-Japanese movement which had also been driven underground by Kuomintang repression. Meanwhile the surviving Communist armies doggedly sustained themselves in far-off Shensi. They were in an impasse from which a number of distant pressures now combined to liberate them. New orientations were imposed both upon them and on Chiang Kai-shek and opened a fresh phase in their complementary history.

* The original chapter of this work dealing in documented detail with the Kiangsi Soviet period, 1928 to 1934, appears as an appendix to this edition, beginning on page 323. However, the titles referred to in the notes to the Appendix do not appear in the Bibliography. These titles will be found in the "Draft Survey of Materials Relating to Communism in China, 1927–1934," collected by Harold R. Isaacs (Hoover Institute and Library on War, Revolution, and Peace, Stanford, Calif., August 16, 1948, mimeographed, 57 pp.).

The Chinese Communist party's links to the Communist Inter national had thinned but had never been broken. Throughout thi period, Comintern representatives—Russians, Germans, and even few Americans—had guided the party apparatus from havens dee in the Shanghai underground. From time to time they had impose arbitrary changes upon the party leadership and its policies. But the played little or no role in the hinterland movement, which governe itself. In 1935, however, the Comintern itself made a broad tac whose consequences reached all the way to China's inland provinces The victory of Hitler in 1933 had been facilitated to a decisive degre by the myopic actions of the German Communist party, which unde Russian guidance insisted that the German Social Democrats, not th Nazis, were the main enemy of the German workers. After Hitle triumphed, the Kremlin boasted that Nazi rule would finally cleanse the German workers of their social-democratic illusions and pave the way for a Communist conquest of power. During the next five years, however, the Kremlin maneuvered to turn away from itself the shar edge of this new German power. On the one hand, it began the ob- scure maneuvers which ultimately resulted in the Hitler-Stalin Pact of 1939. On the other hand, it began to seek allies against Hitler, turning to Western Europe with offers of pacts. The Communist parties were ordered to parallel the pacts between states by new pacts between classes, the so-called People's Fronts, whose prime purpose and policy was the support of alliances between their respective coun- tries and the Soviet Union.

This turn, signalized by the Seventh, and last, Congress of the Comintern in 1935, was translated in China into renewed offers of a united front with Chiang Kai-shek against Japan, the Far Eastern end of the anti-Comintern Axis. Chiang Kai-shek, for his part, was finding it increasingly awkward to carry out his policy of propitiating the Japanese while simultaneously attacking his internal enemies. The issue was brought to a head late in 1936 when Manchurian troops in Shensi refused to carry out an ordered attack against the Commu- nists and demanded the chance to turn their guns against the Japanese. When Chiang flew to Sian that December to make his commands effective, he was ignominiously kidnaped and anti-Japanese demands were served upon him. His life was saved only when Communist emissaries, headed by Chou Ên-lai, stepped in to offer him their co- operation if he would oppose Japan. Chiang reluctantly agreed and was released. The terms of a new "united front" were negotiated on the basis of a complete abandonment by the Communists of their radical land policies and their claims to political independence and a promise by Chiang to mobilize his forces to resist the Japanese. When even months later, in July 1937, the Japanese finally launched their final effort to bring all of China under their control, they were opposed by a tenuous alliance of the Kuomintang and Communist armies.

The "united front," however, proved to be of only brief duration. Chiang continued to fear the Communists more than he feared the Japanese. He feared social reforms more than he feared military defeats. His own position steadily worsened. The Kuomintang leadership split wide open under Japan's attack. One whole wing, led by the onetime "liberal" Wang Ching-wei, stayed behind in Nanking to become puppets of the Japanese. Chiang Kai-shek retreated, first to Hankow and then to Chungking, behind the craggy Yangtze Gorges. His chief preoccupation, even while Chungking quivered under Japanese air attacks, remained the careful husbanding of his own forces and the blockade of the Communists in the northwest. At the beginning of 1941, the Communist New Fourth Army, which had formed in the Yangtze Valley, attempted to cross to the north bank of the river. It was suddenly attacked by Chiang's troops. Heavy casualties were inflicted upon its columns, crowded with women and children accompanying the force on what had been intended as a nonfighting maneuver. The army's commander, Yeh T'ing, was arrested and held prisoner until the end of the war.* The "New Fourth Army incident" to all intents and purposes terminated the Kuomintang-Communist alliance.

What followed was a poorly kept truce. The Communists, making maximum use of their limited resources and their experience as political guerrillas, concentrated on extending their zone of influence. With the Kuomintang backed up against the western mountains and its forces largely inactive, the Communists spread their partisan activity eastward—around, across, and beyond the narrow communication lines and cities held by the Japanese. The Kuomintang simply

* Yeh T'ing had reappeared as a Communist military commander after a period of prolonged retirement. He was released from prison in March 1946, in one of the brief honeymoon periods of Kuomintang-Communist negotiations under the sponsorship of General George Marshall. On April 12, 1946, a United States Army plane taking Yeh and a group of other Communist leaders from Chungking to Yenan crashed in the hills, killing all aboard.

tightened the screws of extortion on the people in the western provinces it still controlled. It soon dissipated whatever shreds of popular
support its anti-Japanese stand had won for it. Its armies, as the
Americans before long discovered to their dismay, were sodden with
corruption, starvation, and untended disease. By contrast, the Communists carried out limited but effective administrative reforms wherever they went, threw out corrupt officials, regularized tax collections,
encouraged an ingenious system of local production, helped organize
local militia, gave concrete form and an outlet to the intense feeling
aroused by Japanese brutalities, and won immense popular prestige
and support. From 1941 onward, the war against Japan in China
resolved itself into a stalemate, marked by sporadic Kuomintang-
Communist clashes, widespread pinpricking guerrilla activity by the
Communists against the Japanese, and rarer battles between Kuomintang forces and the Japanese. With the involvement of the United
States at the end of 1941, Chiang Kai-shek dug in more stubbornly
than ever, counting on American power to pull the Japanese off his
back and assure his postwar return to power.

The American-Chinese war alliance during the next three years
was marked chiefly by angry cross-purposes: the American military
command under General Joseph Stilwell wanted to reorganize, re-
train, and re-equip Chiang's forces for action against the Japanese,
whereas Chiang wanted to husband strength and accumulate supplies
to maintain his balance of power vis-à-vis the Communists. In the
end neither purpose was accomplished successfully. The Americans
discovered, through difficult and often grim experience, that Chiang's
armies mirrored Chiang's regime and could be transformed only if
the regime were renovated at the same time. Stilwell's attempt to
meet this dilemma head-on cost him his command, but in the end
China was written off as a decisive theater of war. Instead, Japan was
reduced to defeat in the western Pacific and the Japanese home islands
themselves.[3]

At the war's end, the Kuomintang and the Communists moved
to seize the strategic advantage in the eastern provinces where the
occupying Japanese forces laid down their arms. The Communists
moved in force into Manchuria, where, with the help of the Russian
army (which had moved in during the last few days before Japan's
surrender), they fell heir to large quantities of Japanese weapons and
stores. The American air force, on the other hand, transported whole

armies of the Kuomintang by air to the main centers in the east to enable Chiang Kai-shek to re-establish his prewar positions. The balance was a precarious one, with the advantage obviously on the Communist side. Negotiations were begun, under American auspices, to bring about a coalition that would avert full-scale civil war. General George Marshall was sent out at the beginning of 1946 to see if, through successful negotiations, the power of the Communists could be neutralized and the advance of Russia's influence in China thereby halted. The truce he arranged was short-lived, for no real basis for it existed. Chiang Kai-shek still blindly believed in his power to maintain himself, and the Communist leadership, by no means blindly, was intent upon winning power for itself. The civil war burgeoned into a full-fledged struggle for mastery of the country. It developed into a spectacle of Kuomintang disintegration and swift Communist victory. By the end of 1948, the Communists were in complete control of Manchuria and all of North China. Radical land reforms were stepped up in these areas, providing both rapid political consolidation and an impetus to further advance. There was little enough to prevent this advance, for the Kuomintang was already in the final stages of self-destruction.

During its brief tenure of restored power in the eastern cities and provinces, Kuomintang officialdom had outdone itself in sheer rapacity. Its lean days in hinterland exile had lasted a long time. Popular jubilation over Japan's defeat quickly gave way to dismay, anger, and disgust over what followed. The looting by officials and official favorites was widespread and indiscriminate. One of the more spectacular performances in this period was the diversion to private profit of the bulk of the international relief supplies and funds, largely supplied by the United States through UNRRA, the international postwar relief agency. The revulsion was universal. People refused to accept this as the shape of the long-sought liberation from the Japanese. A profound desire for a change spread over the entire country and among all sections of the population. The Communists rode it, like a tide, to power. In Chinese terms, Heaven's mandate to the Kuomintang had exhausted itself. In large areas its authority was never successfully re-established. In the face of Communist military advances, whole Kuomintang armies surrendered or fell apart while the population waited passively, even hopefully, sometimes enthusiastically, for the Communist arrival; in city after city the victors were

welcomed as liberators. By the autumn of 1949, the Communists ha
taken Nanking, Shanghai, and Canton, and all but completed thei
conquest of power over the whole country.

The party which thus assumed control over China had come
long way from the nascent Communist movement of the years 1925-
27. The Russian Communist party under Stalin had taken many year
to divest itself of its proletarian roots and ideology and to become
power machine rooted in the new ruling bureaucratic caste. The Chi
nese Communist party came to power already equipped to play thi
role, already fashioned into a power mechanism with an almost uniqu
capacity to balance itself among and above the classes of the popu
lation.

In all the years of its physical and political separation from th
urban workers, the Communist party had continued to call itself "th
party of the proletariat." This formal fiction persisted throughout th
years of the Kiangsi experiment and later in the northwest. It wa
dropped only briefly during the period of the second alliance with th
Kuomintang. It was restored thereafter and, with the assumption o
power, the party claimed to exemplify, in itself, the "hegemony o
the proletariat" in the new order of things. Like so much else in th
semantic labyrinth of "Marxism-Leninism-Stalinism," this reflecte
not any social or political reality but rather the rationalizing mystiqu
of the Communist movement. The first party representatives wh
went to take over government-owned enterprises were, says one earl
Communist account, "unfamiliar with the running of industry, sinc
they had long engaged in rural and army work," and they found tha
the "masses of industrial workers did not at once realize that th
revolution had made them the real masters of the state-owned enter
prises. They were not prepared to assume their great new responsi
bilities."[4] Between March and August 1949, hundreds of thousand
of workers were marshaled into new trade-unions, created by orde
of the Communist party, to facilitate the re-education of the new "mas
ters" of the country. Actual mastery, of course, remained with th
party itself. The real nature of this ruling power bore little resemblanc
to its descriptions of itself; it was actually a unique kind of instrument
even among Communist parties.

During the two decades following 1927, the Communist party
became a party of de-urbanized intellectuals and peasant leaders whos
main strength lay in the military force which they created and witl

which they ultimately won power. Apart from its broadly agrarian character and preoccupations, this party and this military force had no stable or consistent class base through the years. In accordance with changes of line, purpose, and circumstances, it shifted from one section of the peasantry to another, now seeking the support of the lower strata, now of the upper strata, at times adapting itself without undue difficulty even to the landlords. It appeased, when it needed to, the merchants and local shop-owners and capitalists. It developed support by *dispensing* reforms and benefits designed to win the gratitude and support of the beneficiaries. It came as a force from the outside, bringing its program with it. This program varied, in different periods, from the most radical kind of land confiscation and division to the mildest kind of amelioration of abuses. It created and encouraged village organization, carefully nursing it from birth, shaping it, fixing its limits, and adapting itself to local prejudices and economic and social relations.

The literature of the Chinese Communist movement is full of evidence of its essentially paternalistic character, mildly authoritative when occasion suited, but vested with harsh and unlimited power which it used whenever circumstances required. The party liked to boast, for example, that by its own magnanimous decision, local and district committees were to include one-third Communists in their total membership. This was partly a means of creating a "democratic" atmosphere, partly a means of encouraging participation of all village classes. But in any case, the programs followed were invariably laid down by the party or were subject to its approval. Defections or serious dissent were dealt with, as a rule, in the manner in which Communists have become so expert. Thus with the sanction of force always in the background, the Communists would come as bringers of good things which they persuaded the peasants to share and which the peasants, once convinced that the other side would not come back, readily embraced. Whole manuals were written to explain to party officials how to win the peasants' confidence, how to get them to participate in the new affairs of the village. During periods of more stable occupation of different areas during the long war years, they initiated ingenious and successful schemes for expanding local handicraft production and for increasing agricultural output. In this sphere, in its hinterland years, the Communist leadership performed impressive feats of improvisation. But their focus was always the development of a stronger material base for the army and the creation of a friendly population in the area of its operations.

In its eastward expansion after the end of the Japanese war, this army came upon towns and cities in the traditional role of a conquering force, coming out of the countryside to "liberate" the people. It brought with it initial relief from intolerable abuses to win the ready acquiescence of great masses of people ripe for a change. The new conquests, however, brought new and major problems signalized in the shift from the countryside to the cities, a change in center of gravity formally proclaimed by the party's Central Committee in March 1949. The well-being of the peasant could no longer be the sole or even the major preoccupation of the regime. In fact, in South and Central China especially, owing to the unexpected speed of the conquest, it was found necessary to yoke the peasant rather harshly to the new regime's requirements without the prefatory period of prolonged persuasion and demonstration and winning of allegiance that had been possible earlier in the hinterland and in the northern and northeastern provinces. The dragooning of the population by force under the new dictatorship began south of the Yangtze immediately after the conquest of power.

This shift in dealing with the peasantry was not so difficult for the party to carry out as might have been supposed. The whole hinterland history had been, as has been pointed out, one of constant shifts in relation to different sections of the peasantry. Moreover, by this time the Communist army consisted of much more than the early cadres of trained and indoctrinated peasant soldiers who might have been expected to hold on more stubbornly to their village outlook. In the course of the civil war, the Communist forces were swelled by enormous additions, by whole armies of Kuomintang troops which switched allegiance in the field, ex-puppet forces originally created to police the country under Japanese control, and semi-independent partisan armies which had operated previously at great distances from effective Communist control. The Communist armies became an agglomeration of plebeian soldiery with roots in the land and in the peasantry but with no fixed social or economic orientation. They had nothing to lose and everything to gain from the success of their new allegiance. They were, by and large, declassed masses of men, held together by submission to the authority of the party and of the army and by acceptance of the party program and promises and orders as the quintessence of the higher wisdom. The party leadership itself consisted of a hard core of skilled and able men, practiced in balancing themselves above and between different class groupings, with a well-established system of monolithic party authority and of suppression of any significant dissent. It was able to draw, as its victory became inevitable, on the student youth, with all its passionate and uncritical devotion, as well as upon the inevitable horde of latecoming adherents, band-wagon jumpers, deserters from the old regime, and middle-roaders leaping into the new orthodoxy. These were, in general, elements which could be counted on to be even more zealously uncritical, and far less high-minded, than the older party cadres. Thus the party and the army both had been converted into instruments quite capable of carrying out, without undue wrenching, any tasks of organization and reorientation that the situation required.

Hence the Chinese Communist party, coming to power for the first time over the whole of China, was well equipped by nature, character, organization, and experience to function as an authoritarian, bureaucratic, paternalistic leadership. It would, through whatever intermediate phases, tend to shape itself into a party bureaucratic dictatorship, holding itself above the dispersed and disoriented classes of a disintegrating society, whipping it into new shapes by main force. Much has been made, both by his admirers and by his critics, of Mao Tsê-tung as the ideologist of the "New Democracy," Chinese-style. But an examination of Mao's theoretical and historical writing discloses that ideological analysis has become just so much baggage, secondary to the central issue of power itself. With that issue settled, the rest is a matter of what the leadership deems expedient.

The regime created by the Communists upon their conquest of power was represented to be a resurrection of the same "bloc of classes" that had featured the initial Communist-Kuomintang alliance, with the difference that it was now "under the leadership of the working class," which in turn was "exemplified" by the position of the Communist party itself in the commanding role. It was, therefore, a "people's democracy" in which the power to define the "people" remained with the Communist leadership. It was, in a word, a dictatorship of the party itself. The most candid of Mao Tsê-tung's own definitions of this regime appears in a programmatic statement written in July 1949:

We are told: you are establishing a dictatorship. Yes, my dear sirs, you are right. We are actually establishing a dictatorship. . . . This means that the reactionaries must be deprived of the right to express their opinion and that only the people can have the right to vote, the right to express its opinion. Who are the "people"? At this stage, the people in China comprise the working class, the peasant class, the petty bourgeoisie, and the national bourgeoisie. Under the leadership of the working class and the Communist Party, these classes have united in order to form their own state and to elect their own government for the establishment of a dictatorship over the lackeys of imperialism—the land-owning class and bureaucratic capital—so as to suppress them and to permit them to function only within permissible limits. . . . If in their speech or actions they attempt to exceed these limits, they will be restrained and immediately punished. . . . These two aspects, the democracy of the people and the dictatorship over the reactionaries, constitute the dictatorship of the people's democracy.

The formula, "dictatorship of the people's democracy," is itself a fair example of the semantic cloud that has been thrown over political thought by the modern Communist totalitarians. But Mao's context makes its meaning quite clear. Any virtue or benevolence or limited democratic procedures within this regime will be a matter of the will of the Communist leadership and, on the local plane, of its subordinate bureaucracy. Institutionally, the machinery established is a machinery of absolutism, governed by the tight and small oligarchy at the top. The terms "dictatorship of the people's democracy" and "dictatorship of the proletariat" may reflect certain differences in the tactical approach to class relations, but both, in their essence, are identical with a dictatorship of the Communist party, which is in turn ruled absolutely by its top leadership.

Given the pressure of circumstances—and this pressure was immediately forthcoming—the logic of dictatorship had to assert itself. During the first year of its existence, the regime imposed its own absolute uniformity on the press and the schools of the country. It began employing force to exact peasant compliance, to carry out its financial policies and, before the year was out, its military policies. The pressing needs of internal reconstruction were subordinated to a costly external military adventure in Korea, as part of a tactical operation in the world power struggle initiated by Russia. To deal with the resulting stringency, the regime turned to the inevitable expedient of terror to deal with rising dissent. On February 20, 1951, the Communist government in Peking proclaimed the death penalty for a series of vaguely defined "counterrevolutionary offenses." In all the major cities of the country the executions had already begun. In ensuing months the number of executions officially announced by the regime ran into the thousands. The first—and surely not the last—great Communist purge was under way in the same places the Kuomintang had drenched in blood in the same manner when it came to power twenty-four years earlier.

But the Communist power that came into being in China did not stand by itself or in a vacuum. It became part of the Russian national power orbit in the midst of an acute world power struggle. Its fate, like that of the rest of the world, was linked in large measure to the ultimate resolution of that struggle. Indeed, the new role of Russia in this context was perhaps the greatest of the transformations that had taken place in world affairs in the two decades between the defeat of the Communists in China in 1927 and their victory in 1949.

In 1927, the forces confronting each other beyond the rising masses and contending classes in China were British imperialism, still paramount in the world, and the new Soviet Russian state, a weak, beleaguered regime whose greatest asset was still the revolutionary idea from which it originally sprang. In the intervening two decades the balances of power affecting China were violently transformed. Japan rose in its immense conquering effort and fell. Great Britain was driven from its premier position. The United States emerged as the major power of the Pacific basin. Russia, in the full panoply of a national superstate based upon formidable military force, emerged at the same time to contest with the United States the opportunity to dictate the new shape of things in Asia.[5]

III. THE RE-EMERGENCE OF RUSSIAN POWER IN ASIA

When it reappeared as a major factor in the affairs of Asia at the end of the war with Japan in 1945, Russia had long since outgrown the weaknesses, uncertainties, and contradictions of its totalitarian adolescence. It had become a hardened, powerful, supernationalist police state, ruling through maximum centralized police power at home and through the cynical use of political and military force in establishing its national domination or influence abroad. Of the many elements and circumstances that shared in this transformation, the defeat of the Chinese revolution in 1927 was not the least.

As we have already suggested, Soviet Russia had, at the time of its first impact upon the political life of China, only just shifted from the socialist-internationalist premises of the 1917 revolution to the bureaucratic-nationalist premises of Stalinism. Out of its isolation and its backwardness, out of its traditions of autocracy, and out of the one-party system of dictatorship fostered by Bolshevism, and out of the conditions of prolonged civil war, the new oligarchy headed by Stalin had already taken shape. By the time the ferment in China after 1919 had opened a whole new field of revolutionary possibilities, Russia's new course had already been set. It intervened in China to serve its own national interests as conceived by the ruling caste in the Kremlin, to strike a blow at the British foe, and to achieve, if possible, the emergence of a strong bourgeois ally in the form of a nationalist China.

At the same time, again, the new oligarchy had by no means as yet consolidated itself. Revolutionary ideas and revolutionary influence constituted the only outer rim of Russia's self-defense; it was still weak and without powerful military strength or the means to achieve it. The Stalinist leadership was still confronted by an internal opposition within the Communist party, headed by the principal surviving leaders of the October Revolution. The vast problems of economic transformation still lay ahead of it. The new molds had not yet hardened, the new directions had not yet been irretrievably taken.

It is difficult to speculate how these circumstances might have been affected by a revolutionary victory in China. Trotsky has suggested that a different outcome in 1927 might have revived the fading hopes of the Russian workers, ended their sagging disillusionment and political fatigue, and stimulated their active re-entry in the political arena. Trotsky believed that the weakness of the Opposition was due primarily to the apathy of the Russian people. It is not easy to say how a revolutionary victory in China might have affected the bitter struggle for leadership in the summits of the Bolshevik party. But it is certain that such a victory would have changed the political face of Asia and the rest of the world. The great revision in relations between the Western powers and China and their colonies in Asia would have taken place then, in the 1920's, instead of waiting for a generation on the outcome of a second World War. The imperialist strategy of Japan would have been drastically altered, and so would the whole timetable of wars and revolutions that we have since experienced in these decades. The whole balance of world forces would have been tipped in different directions, profoundly affecting both the internal and external positions of Bolshevik Russia and changing all the terms of contemporary world history.

But the facts moved otherwise. The revolution in China ended in 1927, as we have seen, in a debacle both for the Chinese people and for the Russians. This result dispersed the last lingering hopes among Russians for the extension of the international revolution on which Lenin had so heavily counted. It drove the Soviet bureaucracy deeper into the refuge of national isolation. It drove Russia into a frenetic drive for self-sufficiency and sped it on its way toward becoming a full-blown police state.

The defeat in China goaded Stalin into completing the liquidation of the Opposition in his own party. Trotsky had been annoyingly right in the debate over China. He and his fellow Oppositionists had mortally affronted, among other things, the pretensions of infallibility assumed by Stalin and his group. The period in which open debate was possible even within the limits of the single-party regime was drawing to a close. This was the time when meetings of international Communist bodies, hitherto always open and fully reported in the press, became quasi-conspiratorial gatherings whose documents were hidden from publication and even from the participating delegates. This was the time when the last remnants of democratic practices within the Bolshevik structure were stamped out. Piecemeal repression of Oppositionists during the rest of that year was climaxed, at the Fifteenth Congress of the Communist party in December 1927, by the wholesale expulsion of all dissenters, followed by their arrest, imprisonment, or exile.

At the same time, the bureaucracy lurched into programs for the development of Russian economic power at a fearfully forced pace. This was the beginning of the Five-Year Plans, the "liquidation of the kulaks as a class," mass deportations, forced collectivization, armed grain-collections, the man-made famine in the Ukraine, and the beginning of the use of forced labor on a vast and systematic basis as an integral part of Soviet economy. There soon followed the bizarre frame-up trials, the mass purges and liquidations that in the mid-thirties periodically decimated the party, the army, and the government apparatus and tied the whole machinery of the state and the society to the ruling clique by bonds of silent terror. The oligarchy assumed total power in every sphere of life, ruling with periodic plebiscitary endorsements from a cowed electorate and with the entire economic machine and the omnipotent police as the weapons of its power. The result was a monolithic superstate from whose methods Hitler borrowed but which even he could never approximate. Having achieved complete and undivided control of the economy and the state, the bureaucracy concentrated on building up the economic and military power of the Russian state.

To this end, it also subordinated the Communist movements abroad. The Communist International, already Russified, became more and more openly and more cynically an agency of Soviet foreign policy. Its only criterion became the advantage, the safety, the aggrandizement of the power of the Russian state. Its function through the 1930's was to preserve the status quo in which Russia could remain undisturbed while it built up its strength and, in addition, to serve, by whatever other useful means, the further purposes of Russian policy. These were the years of the wild zigzags in international Communist behavior, the crucial historic tragedy of Hitler's Fascist victory in Germany, the People's Fronts, the mutual defense pacts, the aborted French general strike and the Spanish civil war, the pacts with Hitler and Japan, the war against Finland, and the partition of Poland following the outbreak of the second World War. These events consumed barely more than a decade of time. That decade swallowed up the remnants of the Russia that had been so embryonically and so briefly a workers' state heralding the rise of international socialism. In its place, when the fog of the second World War began partially to clear away, stood a triumphant nationalist Russia, one of the two surviving major powers of the globe, bent upon the spoils of victory and upon its own aggrandizement. Its army spilled across eastern and southeastern Europe and brought into being a group of puppet states, moving the western strategic boundaries of the new Russian empire to the Adriatic and to the heart of the fallen Reich. In East Asia, the plans of this resurgent Russian imperialism were clearly foreshadowed at the Yalta Conference, in February 1945, where Stalin extracted terms for Russian entry into the war against Japan, a move which President Roosevelt quite mistakenly believed necessary to bring the war to a close. Stalin's terms included acknowledgment of Russia's "pre-eminent position" in Manchuria, control of Port Arthur as a Russian base and of Dairen as an "international" port, control of the Manchurian railway system, and acquisition of southern Sakhalin and of the Kurile Islands. These terms were written into an old-style secret imperialist horse-trading pact, made binding upon China without consultation. These Russian accessions were duly formalized in a treaty imposed on China and signed in Moscow on August 14, 1945. They were confirmed by seizure that same week by Russia's six-day "war" against collapsing Japan. By these moves, Stalin's Russia regained the positions won and lost by the Czar a half-century before, stepping back into the place from which Japan had driven it and swiftly assuming a territorial and political position vis-à-vis China far stronger than any Japan had ever held. Its controlled periphery now ran around the far edges of Manchuria and of all the great continental space occupied by the border regions of Inner and Outer Mongolia and Sinkiang. This periphery was soon extended in a manner of which the Czars might have dreamed but which they could never achieve. The victories of the Chinese Communists brought Western influence in China to an end and automatically moved the entire country into the new Eurasian empire ruled by Russia.

The speed of the Chinese Communist conquest of power apparently ran ahead of the Kremlin's immediate expectations. In Manchuria the Russians had ruthlessly stripped down the major industrial plants, moving critical machinery into Russia and leaving hollowed shells of factories to which, ironically, the Communists soon fell heir. Russia's direct contribution to the Communist victory was small. During its nine-month occupation of Manchuria in 1945–46, it had made available to the infiltrating Communist armies the captured stores and weapons of the defeated Japanese. Later it used its control of the key port of Dairen in a manner that favored local Communist military strategy. But these contributions were minor. They may have affected in some degree the course of the civil war in Manchuria, but they by no means decisively influenced the outcome in China as a whole. They came to far less, indeed, than the involuntary contribution of the United States, for large stocks of American war equipment supplied to the Kuomintang armies eventually fell into Communist hands. But these were not decisive either. The Chinese Communists won power by being strong enough to move into the vacuum created in Chinese affairs by the Japanese surrender and by the disintegration of the Kuomintang regime.

These circumstances reflected the relative independence of the Chinese Communists, who unmistakably came to power by their own momentum. Unlike those installed in eastern Europe, the Chinese Communist leadership was self-made and its triumph was home-grown. The contrast between the Russian-made debacle of 1927 and the Chinese-engineered victory of 1949 may very well have been lost on the younger generation of Chinese Communists and the great mass of their followers. But it is difficult to imagine that it was absent from the minds of the older Chinese Communist leaders or that it did not help to shape and color some of the psychological underpinnings of the new Russian-Chinese relationship inside the new world Communist empire. But even without these ghosts of the past, the new Chinese-Russian relations were already shaped by a whole cluster of actual and potential conflicts between Russian and Chinese national interest: the power relations in Manchuria—cockpit for generations of the Russian drive for power in Asia—and in the other major border areas of Mongolia and Sinkiang; the terms of trade and the speed and scope of Russian capital aid to Chinese development; the Chinese Communist relationship to the Communist movements in other parts of Asia and elsewhere in the world. Some of these issues rose almost at once; others cast visible shadows even in the first years of this great new Eurasian alliance. Given the overwhelming preponderance of Russian power in the context of the world struggle, it was clear that China would have to remain for a considerable time the junior partner. But it was also clear from the outset—as shown by the conflicts over Manchuria and over the Russian-mounted war in Korea—that these mutual relations would be a complex pattern of pressure and counterpressure and that internal conflict was going to plague the builders of the new totalitarian Eurasian empire for a long time to come. Meanwhile, in China itself, the new regime embarked upon a massive effort to make over that great land and to restore it to its ancient place as the center of the world.

In this way the elements that had come together and then split apart a quarter of a century before now came together again, each one different and consequently forming a new compound. The Kuomintang, which had risen to the top in 1927, disappeared as a major ingredient. The Chinese Communist party, having smothered whatever chance there might have been for the emergence of a new Chinese urban democracy, shaped itself through hardening years of war in the remoteness of rural China into an instrument for winning and wielding power by the absolute use of force. Stalin's leadership in Russia transformed that country into a vast prison camp and over mountains of dead and living bodies created the super-power which he bequeathed to his successors. The Chinese Communists seized power in China and yoked themselves to the Russian drive to win power in the world. Together they plunged on down the dark road of totalitarianism.

APPENDIX

Appendix

ᕾᕿᕾᕿᕾᕿᕾᕿᕾᕿᕾᕿᕾᕿᕾᕿᕾᕿᕾᕿᕾᕿᕾᕿᕾᕿᕾᕿᕾᕿᕾᕿᕾᕿᕾᕿᕾᕿ

THE RISE AND FALL OF "SOVIET CHINA"

[This account of the abortive Kiangsi "Soviet Republic" and the Red Army movement in Central China between 1927 and 1934 is reprinted here without change from the text of the original (1938) edition of this book. It was dropped from the first revised edition in 1951 and is reinstated here for its reference value for students of the history of the Chinese Communist movement.—H. R. I.]

Partisan warfare has a tradition in China as long almost as history itself. In great waves rising and lapsing through twenty centuries peasant wars repeatedly convulsed the country and toppled dynasties, only to exhaust themselves while economic relationships were restored and renewed in the ancient grooves of static Chinese society. In times of upheaval peasant armies aroused millions across whole provinces of the Empire. In the intervening periods of the rise and decline of new ruling houses, partisan bands continued in tens and hundreds in a thousand scattered localities to reject the new yokes offered for the old. Chinese economy and the society erected over it were indeed historically static. Yet Chinese history is by no means a placid saga of changelessly unrolling centuries. It has been a history filled with violence and bloodshed, with recurring revolts against the very self-renewing forms of servitude which condemned China to stagnate while the Western world grew.

These were the traditions stirred again to life in South and Central China by the revolution of 1925–27. The millions who unbent from their toil in a new effort to take the land for themselves were less than a century removed from those who had marched with the Long-Haired Taipings. Yet the peasants who rose in 1926–27 could for the first time hope to succeed where their insurgent forebears had invariably failed. Out of the society dissolving under the impact of imperialist penetration the elements of a new solution had taken form and awaited only to be compounded. By themselves the peasants,

scattered, stratified, and backward, could play no independent role.
The Chinese bourgeoisie, itself bound to the system of exploitation
on the land, could not lead the struggle to smash it. But the new class
of urban workers sought in its own interests a fundamental revision
of property relations at the base of society, and by linking their fortunes to those of the workers the peasants could now hope for the first
time to break through the vicious historical circle to which they had
for so long been bound.

It was precisely the failure of the Communist party to solder the
links between the oppressed classes of town and country and to unite
them under a bold revolutionary program that had opened the path
to the bourgeois counterrevolution. When the proletarian movement
was checked, the agrarian revolt was left headless. It lost thousands
of its leaders to the terror that scourged the countryside. What was
more costly still, it lost the leadership of the city workers who alone
could give the peasant revolt the coherence and economic-political
framework within which the peasants could regain the land and hold
on to it while new productive forms were developed with their help.

As a result, the movement that had for a brief time united ten
million peasants was beaten down and its best militants dispersed.
Scattered peasant detachments fled to the hills and resumed the role
of partisan bands. They joined hands with companies and regiments
of Kuomintang soldiers who had mutinied and taken refuge in the
mountains. From the towns and cities, fleeing the headsmen of Chiang
Kai-shek and his allies, Communists—some workers, mostly intellectuals—came to the villages and in many places assumed leadership of
the peasant-soldier partisan bands. From a fusion of these elements
there emerged in 1928 "Red Armies" which acknowledged the leadership of the Chinese Communist party, although in many places the
peasant revolt continued to flare quite independently of the party's
participation.

The first and most important of these armies was formed at Chingkangshan, a mountain on the Hunan-Kiangsi border where many
veterans of the abortive Autumn Harvest uprisings of 1927 made
their way. Here came the German-educated Communist officer Chu
Tê, at the head of less than two thousand men, mainly the remnants
of the army of Yeh T'ing and Ho Lung. The Yeh-Ho army, it will
be recalled, had revolted at Nanchang in August 1927 and had
marched south through Kiangsi to Kwangtung. There it was smashed

in October in its attempt to take Swatow. With Chu Tê, many of the soldiers went to Hailufeng, the eastern Kwangtung districts where the peasants had risen in revolt, seized the land, and organized themselves into village soviets. Yeh T'ing went to Canton and after the insurrection disappeared from the political scene. Ho Lung set out with a small force and re-emerged later at the head of a partisan army in Hupeh province. After Hailufeng was reconquered by the Canton militarists, Chu Tê led a handful of men first to the northern districts of the province and then into Hunan. He recruited some peasants along the line of march and arrived in April 1928 at Chingkangshan.

Here he found peasant detachments from southern Hunan, several companies of insurgent soldiers who had come from Wuhan and other Yangtze cities, and a peasant force from eastern Hunan led by the Communist Mao Tsê-tung. In Wuhan Mao had served as head of the Peasant Department of the Kuomintang and there had carried out the policy of keeping the peasants in check while the counterrevolution advanced upon them. When the crash came he had fled to the districts of Pingkiang and Liuyang, in eastern Hunan. There he led the uprisings of the Autumn Harvest. When they failed, he led what was left of his little band to Chingkangshan. They joined there with a local bandit force headed by Yüan and Wang. After Chu Tê's arrival, all the forces were merged and took the name of Fourth Red Army, with Chu as commander-in-chief and Mao Tsê-tung as political leader. The official party record describes it as an army of ten thousand men of whom two thousand had rifles.[1]

This Red force did not spring from any large-scale spontaneous peasant movement. On the contrary, it was for a long time isolated from the peasantry in the surrounding countryside. Peasant committees set up by the guerrilla bands invariably collapsed and disappeared as soon as the armed Red forces passed on. During its months on Chingkangshan the army suffered repeated defections and endured dire hardships because of its isolation. Defeats often caused the peasant partisans to scatter back to their villages. The Hunanese detachments in particular repeatedly drifted away to revisit their homes. Only the most dogged perseverance on the part of the leaders and the harsh lash of necessity managed to keep the partisan force together, especially when winter set in and the strength of surrounding enemies made it impossible to forage for supplies. After nearly a year of aimless guerrilla raids, sorties, and retreats in the vicinity of Chingkangshan, it was decided to march southward in search of a better base. A small force under P'eng Tê-huai, a Communist officer who had marched his men from Hunan to Chingkangshan in the fall, was left behind to stand off approaching provincial troops. In January 1929, Chu Tê and Mao Tsê-tung led the way down the mountain passes at the head of a starving, freezing, ill-armed, straggling column of a few thousand men.

Out in the countryside they were confronted by the apathy and even the hostility of the peasants. "The masses completely failed to understand what the Red Army was," said a party report. "In many places it was even attacked, like a bandit gang."[2] After nearly meeting disaster in an unexpected clash with Kuomintang provincials near Tayu, the Reds circled toward the Kwangtung border. They marched among peasants who had been cruelly deceived not once but three times by armies that arrived flying revolutionary banners and promising them relief from their burdens. "The Red Army had no support from the masses. There were great difficulties in finding encampments, carrying on military operations, and securing information. . . . We marched across snow-covered and icy mountains, closely pursued by the enemy. We sometimes covered ninety li [thirty miles] in a single day. Our sufferings increased. We were defeated in battle four times."[3]

On Chinese New Year's Day in mid-February, 1929, the exhausted Red force suddenly came upon a division of Kiangsi troops in a valley lying between Juichin and Ningtu in southern Kiangsi. The Reds attacked with desperate fury. When their ammunition gave out, they used their empty rifles, stones, and the limbs of trees. The enemy fled. With that victory the Chu-Mao force won a badly needed rest. In these remote mountain districts they established a new base, where they were joined in March by P'eng Tê-huai. Only the hardiest had survived. The whole force totaled 2,800 men. They went to work among the peasants, and when they began driving out the landlords and destroying land deeds, their ranks soon swelled. The territory they occupied they called the "Central Soviet district."

Simultaneously other Red pockets were being similarly formed with even smaller forces in northeastern Kiangsi, where the Communist Fang Chih-min headed a partisan band; in Hupeh near Hung Lake where Ho Lung was already making the lightning-like attacks and forced marches that made him a legendary figure. On the Honan-

Anhwei and Hunan-Kiangsi borders and in other scattered mountain districts, small Red forces made their headquarters. These were the component parts, widely separated geographically, of what became known as "Soviet China."

It was upon these partisan forces called Red armies that the Communist party, impregnated with adventurist moods on the morrow of the defeat of the revolution, based itself and its activity and its belief in the arrival of the "new revolutionary wave." The party leadership glimpsed the danger of the shift to the countryside and for a time tried to resist it. "If the danger of peasant psychology is not vigorously corrected, the revolution will be liquidated entirely and the party will die," prophetically warned a circular of the Central Committee in November 1928.[4] But these warnings grew more and more feeble as the party's base in the cities narrowed and its proletarian membership and following dwindled and almost entirely disappeared. In October 1929, the Executive Committee of the Communist International described the peasant war as "the peculiarity of the Chinese national crisis and the revolutionary wave." It was still, formally, a "side-current," but a side-current "along which the powerful high wave of the revolutionary movement will grow in the entire country."[5] Admitting the impotence of the Communist party in the cities,* the E.C.C.I. nevertheless proclaimed the arrival of the "initial point of the new revolutionary wave" and laid down a program of insurrection for the Chinese Communists to carry out. While in the cities the revolutionary labor movement was receding and the influence of the Communist party was being wiped out, the partisan armies in the interior had already come to be regarded as the "determining factor"[6] or the "driving force"[7] of the "revolutionary upsurge." Before long, all reservations were dropped. The "revolutionary upsurge" was "manifested not only in the rising labor movement, but *essentially and basically* in the agrarian movement. The agrarian revolution is the source spring of the new revolutionary wave."[8]

Yet the so-called Red armies as they emerged in 1928 and 1929

---

* ". . . The ideological and political influence of the Communist party as well as the state of organization of the working class is still backward in comparison with the growth of mass discontent . . . The majority of the Red unions are not yet mass organizations . . . The Communist party has not yet gathered around itself the leading revolutionary workers in the factories. Still less has it solved the task of capturing the majority of the working class." Letter of the E.C.C.I. to the C.C.P., October 26, 1929, *Red Flag* (Shanghai), February 15, 1930.

in scattered mountain districts of the central provinces were not even primarily peasant forces. It was only much later that they were able to rally around them sections of the peasantry in the districts they occupied. They were composed in the main of dispossessed peasants, jobless agricultural laborers, mutinous soldiers, local bandits, all declassed elements, playing no direct role even in agricultural production. Their activity for nearly three years consisted exclusively of guerrilla fighting and dart-like raids. They were unable to establish any fixed base. When in 1930 Ch'ên Tu-hsiu, the deposed and expelled leader of the party,* published an article[9] in which he warned the Communist party that the revolution could not be advanced by abandoning the workers and engaging in military adventures at the head of an army of lumpen-proletarians, he was viciously denounced as making common cause with the counterrevolution. Ch'ên borrowed Engels' definition of lumpen-proletariat, "the scum of the decaying elements of all classes,"[10] to describe some of the elements that dominated many of the partisan forces. Yet it is not at all difficult to find in the records of the Communist party ample corroboration of Ch'ên's analysis of the Red armies of that period. The party had to fight a long and only partially successful struggle to transform these armies into authentic organs of peasant revolt.

The Sixth Congress of the Communist party in 1928 deplored the tendency of the partisans to engage in "aimless plundering and burning" and described these activities as "the reflection of lumpen-

* After the Conference of August 7, 1927, deposed him from leadership, Ch'ên Tu-hsiu withdrew into retirement while the Comintern laid at his door exclusive responsibility for the disasters that had befallen the revolution. During the period of adventurism that followed, Ch'ên wrote several letters to the Central Committee opposing the policy of staging futile and costly uprisings. In August 1929, he addressed a letter to the Central Committee expressing his opposition to the party's course and demanding a re-examination of its policies. A few months later he and nearly one hundred others were expelled en masse as Oppositionists. In February 1930, the Comintern asked him to come to Moscow. He refused, demanding that the issues of the revolution be thrown open instead to full discussion within the party. Subsequently he solidarized himself with the Trotskyist Left Opposition that had been formed and was a leading figure in that organization until his arrest by the Kuomintang in 1932. He was sentenced to thirteen years' imprisonment, but was released in the fall of 1937. [He died in 1943.] See Ch'ên Tu-hsiu, "A Letter to the Central Committee of the Chinese Communist Party on the Questions of the Chinese Revolution," August 5, 1929, in *The Chinese Revolution and Opportunism* (Shanghai), October 1929; *Letter to All the Comrades of the Chinese Communist Party* (Shanghai), December 10, 1929; Ch'ên Tu-hsiu and eighty others, *Our Political Statement* (Shanghai), December 15, 1929; "Letter of Ch'ên Tu-hsiu to the Communist International," *Le Prolétaire* (Shanghai), July 1, 1930; Ch'ên Tu-hsiu, *Protest to the Kiangsu High Court*, February 20, 1933.

proletarian psychology."[11] Another party report spoke of "bandit psychology, degeneration into a bandit existence of killing and plundering," and even borrowed phrases far stronger than any used by Engels or Ch'ên Tu-hsiu to characterize some of the partisans as "Red bandits, burning, killing, and robbing."[12] A reporter for the Central Committee complained early in 1930 that "in many of the partisan bands, lumpen-proletarian ideas persist . . . often expressing themselves in unorganized burning, plundering, and killing."[13] Even publicly in the columns of no less a paper than *Pravda*, Mif wrote of the "very large percentage of . . . lumpen-proletarian elements" in some of the Chinese Red armies.[14]

The question, however, did not lie in the precise percentage of lumpen-proletarian elements in the Red armies then or even later. These armies did become the spearhead of a peasant revolt over considerable, if scattered, territories. Such armies had often been known in Chinese history. The important factor was that the Communist party was tending more and more to look upon these armies as the legitimate basis of its activity and to rationalize through them its growing isolation from the workers in the urban centers. It was the view of the Trotskyist Opposition that the party's lip service to "proletarian hegemony" over the peasant movement was a fraud so long as the party was itself divorced from the proletariat. This hegemony became all the more mythical when the putschist policies in the cities, the attempts to force strikes, to convert them artificially into armed political demonstrations, were stifling at birth the incipient revival of defensive struggles by the workers.

"Proletarian leadership" of the peasant-partisan movement had to be exercised through a living movement and not through a fictional slogan paraded through the party press. It was on this basis that the International Left (Trotskyist) Opposition demanded that the Communist party keep its roots in the cities and proposed a program of democratic struggle and the slogan of a National Assembly, elected by universal suffrage, as a point of departure for making the Communist party the truly authentic spokesman and leader of the Chinese workers. Revival of the labor movement under the impetus of a democratic program, declared the Opposition in 1930, could alone provide the peasant revolt with the indispensable leadership of the city workers and lay the basis for worker-peasant collaboration in the march toward the third Chinese Revolution.[15] The Trotskyist Opposition, however, was too weak to make its influence felt. The Communist party, throwing its main efforts and its best forces into the villages and replacing its disappearing worker-members with peasants, drifted farther and farther away from its work in the cities and finally practically abandoned it altogether. The militarist rivalries that split the Kuomintang camp and the constant economic difficulties which the regime could not surmount were regarded as sufficient symptoms of a ripe revolutionary crisis, and the Red armies in fact came to be regarded as a sufficient instrument for bringing that crisis to a head.

Having discovered the "initial point of the new revolutionary wave" in October 1929, the Comintern in July 1930 declared that "the new upsurge of the Chinese revolutionary movement has become an indisputable fact." Hence: "The immediate task of the Chinese Communist party is to prepare and concentrate all forces in the process of struggle to meet decisive battles in the nearest future."

"It is the peculiarity in the new upsurge," the resolution went on, ". . . that in the initial stage there is a certain [!] weakness, namely, the fighting masses cannot at the very beginning occupy the industrial centers. . . . Only in the process of the further development of the revolutionary struggles can the peasant war, led by the proletariat, expand to new territory. Then the mutual correlation can improve to better advantage." To this end attention had to be focused on strengthening the Red Army so that "in the future, according to political and military circumstances, one or several political or industrial centers can be occupied."[16]

While the Comintern, to be sure, surrounded itself with carefully worded injunctions about the need, in general, for organizing the workers and peasants, it laid the basis for all the fatal misconceptions which achieved their most grotesque form in the politics of Li Li-san, who had now become leader of the Communist party.

Dazzled by the Comintern's commission to him to "overthrow the power of the landlord-bourgeois bloc, to establish a worker-peasant dictatorship . . . to unfold mass political strikes and demonstrations, to expand the partisan warfare . . . and to turn the militarist war into class civil war,"[17] Li Li-san began to perceive on all sides the shadows of coming upheavals. When Chiang Kai-shek and a northern coalition headed by Fêng Yü-hsiang began a long and bitter civil war in 1930, Li was certain that the earth was ready to swallow up the Kuomintang and all its generals. "Prepare for the establishment of the revolutionary power!" he cried in March.[18] In June his Political Bureau adopted a resolution which saw the masses "marching in seven-league boots toward the revolutionary high wave" and called for active preparation of a country-wide uprising. Taking the Comintern's prattle about the "third period" of the final crisis of world capitalism quite seriously, Li envisaged the Russian Red Army marching in from Mongolia to support the resurgent Chinese Revolution.[19]

Quite in passing, Li deplored the depression of the labor movement, but he was naïvely confident that the workers were only awaiting the party's call to rise. He was sure that a single puncture in the Kuomintang dam would be enough to precipitate a revolutionary flood. "When the revolutionary high wave arrives," he was later quoted as saying, "90,000,000 can be organized in three days."[20] In the June resolution he wrote: "Long ago the masses said: 'When there is an uprising let us know and we shall surely come.' Now is the time when the Party must bravely call upon the masses: 'The time for insurrection has come! Organize yourselves!'"[21] He created what he called a General Council of Action into which he merged the party, the Young Communist League, and the "Red" trade unions. In Shanghai he formed a "Red Guard" composed of exactly one hundred and seventy-six workers to prepare for the "fourth uprising."[22] He plotted an insurrection in Nanking with a handful of soldiers. To the Red armies he gave orders to march on the cities. "The aim of the local uprisings is to capture local cities. . . . The perspective must inevitably be to converge with the central cities to accomplish the victory of the insurrection in the whole country."[23]

In words, both the Comintern and Li Li-san recognized that the proletariat had to lead the peasantry. Many long and even eloquent passages were devoted in all documents to this necessity under the heading "proletarian hegemony." Unfortunately, the proletariat had yet to re-marshal its own ranks and collect its own forces, scattered and crushed by the defeat of the revolution and the reign of Kuomintang terror that followed it. The Communist party tried to substitute itself for the proletariat as a class. In the process, however, it was transformed into a peasant party. Since the revolution could not radiate from the cities to the country, it was necessary to mobilize the country to close in on the cities.

It was with this in view that the Fifth Red Army under P'eng

Tê-huai marched westward from Kiangsi and on July 28, 1930, succeeded in occupying Changsha, capital of Hunan province. Li Li-san firmly counted on this as the signal for a spontaneous country-wide uprising with its center at Wuhan, where he expected to establish the capital of a "Central Soviet Government." Unfortunately, the Communist party had at its disposal in Wuhan only two hundred party members and one hundred fifty "Red" trade unionists.[24] Contrary to Li's expectations, there was no echo anywhere. There was no insurrection in the rest of the country. The ninety million remained passive. American, British, Japanese, and Italian gunboats, having evacuated frightened foreigners, steamed up the Siang River and mercilessly bombarded the occupied city.[25] The Red Army withdrew. Ho Chien, Governor of Hunan, returned with fresh divisions and began a slaughter of the helpless city population that did not pause until more than five thousand corpses choked open graves and until even the Changsha Chamber of Commerce appealed to Nanking to make him stop. Reinforced by the Chu-Mao Fourth Army, the Reds made another attempt early in September to hammer their way back into the city, but this time they failed and retreated once more toward the mountains of southern Kiangsi.

The Changsha episode bared at a stroke the fatal weakness of the whole Red Army course. The partisan forces had no connection with the workers in the city. When the Red Army marched in and "proclaimed the Soviet power, the power of the workers, peasants, and soldiers,"[26] the great mass of the city's five hundred thousand people remained inert, frightened, or just curious. The proclamation of "Soviet power" was the gift of a conquering army. It was not the product of mass action in the city itself. "There was insufficient connection between the attack of the Red Army and the mass struggles in Changsha," it was later admitted.[27] The result was a repetition on a different plane of the Canton fiasco. "In Changsha there was no mass Soviet elected by factories or streets."[28] Red flags were broken out all over the city and a mass meeting was called, but only three thousand people appeared. Another effort two days later was only slightly more successful.[29] The army, impregnated with the fundamental strategy of the peasant partisan—to strike, seize, destroy, and run—did not regard its occupation of Changsha as a permanent thing. "Its position was not consolidated. No city power was organized."[30] Instead it taxed the Chamber of Commerce for $400,000, which was

:ollected from the people by the merchants, and when the imperialist
)ombardment began it resisted briefly and withdrew.

When it left, three thousand workers recruited in the city went
with it. In other words, the most advanced of Changsha's workers,
:he possible nucleus of a revived labor movement, were withdrawn
:rom their factories and shops and converted into partisan-soldiers
:ompletely divorced from the town. The job of decapitating the
Changsha labor movement, begun in this way by the Red Army, was
:ompleted by Ho Chien's executioners. This was the net result of
:he Changsha adventure.

Sporadic attempts continued through the summer to encircle Wuhan and to take other cities, without result. In October the Red Army
:aptured Kian, in Kiangsi, but here again it confined itself to "recruiting new soldiers" and sent off its best forces in an effort to capture
Nanchang and Kiukiang. "Organization of the masses was completely ignored."[31] Kian had to be evacuated a few weeks later.

The strategists in Moscow, however, had already begun to realize
that the Red armies could not successfully attack the large cities. At
the Third Plenum of the Central Committee in September, Chou Ên-
lai, freshly back from Moscow, cautiously counseled retreat. "The
Central Committee," he said, "has had some mechanical conceptions,
thinking that the Central (Soviet) Government had to be established
in Wuhan, or at least in Changsha or Nanchang. . . . Of course it
would be better to get established in the bigger cities than in the
smaller ones, but this is a secondary question." He reminded the
Committee that the Comintern had fixed as the "primary task" the
consolidation of the Red armies and the broadening of the mass base
underlying them. "We must consolidate the present scattered Soviet
districts," he reported, "weld them together, strengthen and centralize the leadership of the Red armies, set broader peasant masses in
motion, and establish a Central Soviet Government to develop toward
the industrial cities."

Chou sharply denied that this meant retreat or that there was any
contradiction between the advice of the Comintern and the policies
of Li Li-san. For the cities, he repeated, the central task was still "to
prepare actively for armed uprising." Li had merely "overestimated
the tempo," made some "isolated tactical mistakes," and had a few
"mechanical conceptions," but was otherwise in "complete harmony
with the Comintern."[32]

But Li Li-san's "overexaggeration" of the Comintern's line ha‹ practically destroyed the party and demoralized its members. It wa‹ no longer possible to preserve in Li Li-san the myth of an infallibl‹ leadership. Accordingly all the heavy artillery was trundled out an‹ turned on the hapless Li. All the hyphenated invective he had em‹ ployed against his predecessors was now applied to him. A lette‹ from Moscow on November 16 ordered open warfare against hin‹ in the party. Under the personal supervision of Mif, Li Li-san wa‹ brusquely deposed. What was called the Fourth Plenum of the Cen‹ tral Committee met on January 7, 1931, and Mif's own protégé, Ch'ê‹ Shao-yü, was elevated into the leadership of the party on a progran‹ of "unconditional devotion to the line of the Communist Interna‹ tional."

The young men so abruptly enthroned as leaders of the Commu‹ nist party had all been students in Moscow during the years of th‹ revolution and had won their spurs conducting witch-hunts agains‹ Trotskyist sympathizers among the students at Sun Yat-sen Univer‹ sity. To give them control Mif shouldered aside the group of ol‹ militants who had served, not without opposition,[33] under the leader‹ ship of Li Li-san. A group of these older party members and trade‹ unionists, and some younger men, led by the veteran Ho Mêng-hsiung‹ met at a Shanghai hotel on the night of January 17 to consider th‹ new situation with which they were confronted. In circumstance‹ which are still a whispered scandal in the party ranks, that meeting‹ was betrayed to the British police of the International Settlement‹ Ho Mêng-hsiung and twenty-four others were arrested, handed ove‹ to the Kuomintang authorities, and executed at Lunghua on February‹ 7. Mif's docile young men became the undisputed leaders of the party‹

Other leaders of the party won the right to remain in its ranks‹ only by degrading themselves, by making the self-denying recanta‹ tions that had already become a fixed feature of Stalinist party meth‹ ods and which a few years later flowered into the "confessions" of old‹ Bolshevik leaders put on trial for their lives in Moscow. Ch'ü Ch'iu‹ po was compelled to denounce his own "cowardly rotten opportun‹ ism." Chou Ên-lai flagellated himself. "I call upon the whole Party‹ to condemn my mistakes," he cried.[34] Li Li-san had already left for‹ Moscow and once arrived there had hastily recanted of his sins. Even‹ the hardened cynics in the Comintern apparatus were a little shocked‹ by his eager self-repudiation. At a discussion held by the presidium‹

of the Executive Committee of the Comintern in December, Manuilsky expressed his astonishment: "If Li Li-san here defended his own
ideas and disputed with us one article after another," he said, "then
I would be easier in my mind. But Li-san so quickly abandoned his
views. This alarms me!"[35] Ch'ü Ch'iu-po, Chou Ên-lai, Han Yin, the
trade union leader, and others were sent to obscure posts in Kiangsi.
Li Li-san himself disappeared from view.*

The new leadership had the task of retreating from the disastrous
ultra-adventurism of Li Li-san to a more modest adventurist policy
that took the party's real strength more soberly into account. There
was no intention of making any more fundamental change. The main
features of the shift had already been indicated by the Comintern in
its November letter. "The military and technical weakness of the Red
Army must not be forgotten, the poverty of armament and ammunition, lack of artillery, etc. Such conditions make it impossible to occupy big cities, to attack the modern armies of imperialism, and to conquer the main centers. The experience of the occupation of Changsha
and the attack on Wuhan has already shown that such tasks cannot
be carried out by the present Red Army." It was necessary now "to
concentrate the best forces of the Party" to build a "real workers-
peasants Red Army" and to establish a Central Soviet Government
in one of the existing Soviet districts as a basis for future expansion.
"Only those who have nothing in common with Bolshevism can interpret this as a line of retreat," the letter said. "It is not a retreat but
an offensive. The line of insurrection is fixed."[36]

But a retreat it was, a retreat from the grandiose dreams of Li
Li-san. The new party leadership dropped the slogan of "local uprisings" and denounced as "Blanquist" the attempt to organize isolated mutinies in the armies of the Kuomintang.[37] The concentration
of the "best forces" of the party for the "primary task" of strengthening the Red Army and creating a central government also signalized
the completion of the shift from city to country, from proletariat to
peasantry. It was now not so much a question of bringing the urban

---

* Ch'ü was captured in Fukien in 1935 and shot by direct order of Chiang Kai-
shek. Han Yin was captured and apparently suffered the same fate. Many other
leaders were also shot or imprisoned. Teng Chung-hsia and Lo Tung-hsien, leaders
of the Hong Kong strike of 1925, were executed at Nanking in 1933, words of loyalty
to the proletarian cause on their lips to the last. See *China Forum* (Shanghai), November 7, 30, 1933. Li Li-san re-emerged in 1937 at Yenan, Shensi, the new Communist
party center, where he was introduced to a *New Masses* writer as "an old associate
of Dr. Sun Yat-sen." *New Masses*, October 12, 1937.

laborer abreast of the peasant revolt in order to lead it. Instead: "Every strike is a rear support for the Soviet districts."[38] Instructions issued to the party in June and again in September, 1931, dealt almost exclusively with the problems of the Red Army and the Soviet districts. Where they dealt briefly with the urban labor movement, it was to urge more intensive work in the cities in order "to create powerful support for our worker-peasant Red Army." It was the main task in the "non-Soviet" districts "to intensify support for the great victories of the Red Armies . . . to recruit soldiers for the Red Armies."[39]

Shanghai, Wuhan, Tientsin, Canton, and all other centers of industrial and proletarian concentration had become, in effect, the "rear" of the mountains of southern Kiangsi. In September 1930, when he was trying to justify his plans for capturing Wuhan and making it the "Soviet capital," Li Li-san had said: "I thought it would be a joke if we established the capital in the mountains."[40] But it was precisely to the mountains that they had to go and stay. Deep in the hills of south Kiangsi in the village of Juichin the Red armies established their capital and there, on November 7, 1931, they proclaimed the creation of the "Chinese Soviet Republic" and set up a Provisional Soviet Government.

The "Chinese Soviet Republic" consisted in 1932–33, the years of its maximum development, of six widely separated areas scattered along the border regions of the Central China provinces. Wang Ming (Ch'ên Shao-yü) boasted at the end of 1933 that the territory of Soviet China occupied "one-fourth of the vast territory of China proper." One-sixth, or one-fifth—both fractions were cited in the same speech—he described as "stable" Soviet domain.[41] Around the world the press of the Communist International boasted that the flag of the Soviets ruled fifty million, seventy-five million, eighty million of the Chinese people.[42] In a book that had the misfortune to hail the dawn of "Soviet China" just as twilight descended upon it, one Comintern writer put the population at ninety million.[43] The figures never agreed but were all enormous and all enormously exaggerated. The reality was far more modest, and the men on the spot who had to deal with realities and not propagandist myths were more soberly truthful.

Because the Red armies and partisan forces were for the most part, to use a favorite Chinese phrase, "like flowing water and moving clouds," the territory they occupied expanded and contracted according to the fortunes of war. At various times the Red Army, led by

Chu Tê, undoubtedly crossed or temporarily occupied at least sixty or seventy of Kiangsi's eighty-one hsien (counties); but there is ample authority for the statement that the most important and most stable Red Army area, the so-called "central Soviet district," held more or less permanently from 1930 to the end of 1934, comprised about seventeen hsien astride the Kiangsi-Fukien border, with a total population of three million. This fact was frequently cited by Mao Tsê-tung, president of the "Soviet Republic," and other Communist party spokesmen, although it was conveniently ignored by the Comintern press abroad.[44] The other Soviet districts, along the Hupeh-Hunan, Hunan-Kiangsi, northeastern Kiangsi, Honan-Hupeh-Anhwei, and Hupeh-Hunan-Kiangsi borders, were all smaller, less stable, and more frequently compelled to dissolve under the pressure of repeated attacks.

The Red armies themselves varied no less in size and strength, both in their more or less regular formations and in the auxiliary corps of peasant Red Guards who functioned with them in the incessant civil war against Chiang Kai-shek's Kuomintang forces. In 1932 one quite carefully checked estimate based on Communist records put the grand total of all armies operating in all districts at 151,000, of whom only 97,500 had rifles.[45] The same creative spirit who from his observation post in Moscow saw one-quarter of China under Soviet rule also expanded the Red Army to a force of 350,000 at the end of 1933.[46] Unfortunately again, a civil war could not be fought with soldiers represented only by digits scratched on Comintern copy paper. Chu Tê, certainly one of the most remarkable military leaders in all history, led a force in 1932 that numbered no more than 40,000 and which, according to the most sober estimates of responsible Communist representatives in Shanghai, never in its best Kiangsi days exceeded 70,000. Ho Lung's wraith-like force never exceeded 10,000. The other scattered forces were even smaller. All of them, of course, were aided by peasant auxiliaries whose number varied greatly from time to time and whose chief uses were in scouting and raids for supplies and creating diversions in the conduct of guerrilla operations.

That these forces and the territory they permanently occupied were in reality so small sharpens into all the bolder relief the quality of their achievements. No more brilliant pages have ever been written in the history of peasant wars than those which must record the exploits of the Chinese Red armies engaged in a civil war against enemies five, six, and seven times their number and a thousand times their superior in armaments. For more than five years, the Red armies outmaneuvered and defeated five successive Kuomintang campaigns against them. Because of the incomparable advantage of the support of the population, their superior mobility and generalship, their knowledge of the terrain, the Reds cut off and defeated division after division of Chiang Kai-shek's best troops and armed themselves exclusively with the weapons they captured. The slogans of land to the peasants and freedom from the rapacity of the Kuomintang regime plowed like tanks through the columns of Chiang's hired soldiers.[47]

Marveling at the many-sided aid given the Reds by the local peasants, a missionary correspondent of the *North China Daily News* found it "a strange thing that so many people are willing to undertake what they know means death."[48] Almost everywhere they went the Red armies expelled landlords, destroyed land deeds, debt bonds, and contracts. The peasants still suffered from many disabilities, but they understood that the Kuomintang campaigns were waged to restore to the landlord his land and his power. All the pompous "rehabilitation" plans announced by the Nanking government with each campaign were designed for this purpose only.[49] Resisting this, the peasants gladly fought and died. This was the heroism, the grandeur, too simple, too elemental for the missionary mind to grasp. It gave its blessing instead to the slaughter, rapine, and wanton destruction with which Chiang Kai-shek scourged the province in his effort to stamp out the peasant revolt.

Ho Ying-ch'in, Chiang's Minister of War, complained in 1931 that the peasants supported the Reds and made it difficult for the invading armies to secure food or transport.[50] Chiang Kai-shek told a Japanese interviewer in 1933 that the punitive forces found it "impossible to draw any line between a good citizen and a Red partisan" and were assailed by the feeling that "the enemy is lurking everywhere."[51] The story of the five anti-Red campaigns is a story of angry and frustrated complaints by Kuomintang generals, of mass desertions by companies and whole regiments, of shrill threats and reproaches from the missionaries and the treaty port foreign press. In the end Chiang Kai-shek had to put more than half a million men in the field and send aloft a fleet of more than three hundred American British, and Italian bombing planes to lay waste whole districts and to exterminate whole sections of the insurgent peasantry.

The remoteness of the Soviet areas, the mountainous terrain, the absence of roads or rails were all of great advantage in the military struggle of the Reds against the external enemy. These same factors, when raised from the military to the political and economic plane, became the source of insuperable internal obstacles. Not only was "Soviet China" remote from the main urban centers and the principal arteries of communications which are the life lines of a rural hinterland, but even within its own territory it ruled no cities or sizable towns. The chief cities of the province of Kiangsi, Kiukiang, Nanchang, and even Kanchow, deep in the heart of the Red area, remained in the hands of the Kuomintang, as did the links between them, the Kiukiang-Nanchang railway and the Kian River. Kiukiang was never seriously threatened. Nanchang was approached on several occasions but only for the purpose of creating military diversions. Kian, after the brief occupation of 1930, was never again conquered. Kanchow was repeatedly besieged but never taken. Even the hsien towns or county seats constantly changed hands with the shifting fortunes of the civil war. It was still theoretically the aim to capture at least "one or two central or secondary cities,"[52] but this was never achieved. Except for one sortie into Fukien, resulting in the occupation of Changchow for a few days in April 1932, the Red armies never again took or held any town of consequence. Instead, the increasing pressure of the Kuomintang attacks and the gradual tightening of the economic blockade held them ever more closely confined to their mountain fastnesses along the Kiangsi-Fukien border and along the fringes of other Central China provinces. The "Soviet movement" remained a movement of the villages alone.

The economic self-sufficiency of these villages had long since disappeared. They produced only rice and small quantities of bamboo, paper, and wood oil, which they had to exchange for the most elementary necessities that had to come from the outside, such as salt, cloth, kerosene, farming implements, and matches. This trade was conducted by merchants who preserved contact with the external market. Within the Red areas the merchants were at the same time owners of land, lenders of money, and employers of labor. The peasants themselves were divided into strata with conflicting economic interests. The struggle among them only assumed new forms after the largest and most powerful of the landlords had been driven out. Still dominant in the villages were the rich peasants, who were semi-landlords, employers of agricultural labor, and often merchants and moneylenders as well. After them came the middle peasants, who owned barely enough land to satisfy their meager needs and only occasionally hired hands to work in their fields. Finally there were the poor peasants, possessing inadequate land or no land at all and compelled to rent small plots or join the ranks of the agricultural laborers who possessed nothing but their labor power. The poor peasants and agricultural laborers were subjected economically to the rich peasants, while the middle peasants, in various gradations, fluctuated between them.

To these peasant classes, with their complex internal divisions and conflicts, the Communist party claimed that it brought "proletarian leadership." It based its claims sometimes on the purely abstract view that the Communist party was by definition the "party of the proletariat" and that consequently its mere presence guaranteed working-class hegemony in the peasant revolt. To strengthen this illusion, the party brought occasional workers in from the cities and gave them leading positions in the Red army and in some of the governing committees that were established. The effect of this practice, however, was to deprive the workers in the cities of their most advanced representatives. If the vigilant terror of the Kuomintang did not cut them away from the labor movement, the Communist party did. Once torn from their proletarian environment, these workers ceased to be proletarians and fell inevitably instead under the overwhelming influence of their peasant milieu. Divorced from the productive process, they could become neither the leaders of the proletariat nor the representatives of its leadership over the insurgent peasants.

Only real proletarian leadership of the agrarian revolt could save it from disintegration and dispersal. It alone could knit the poor and middle peasants and rural workers together for a common struggle against the village bourgeoisie. It alone could make this struggle effective by undertaking the complete reorganization of the national economy. But such leadership could be exercised only through the urban labor movement as a whole and through the establishment of its control over the centers of production and distribution on which rural economy so completely depended. In other words, the agrarian revolt had to fuse with a proletarian revolution to have successful issue.

Even under most favorable conditions, the general backwardness of the country meant that great obstacles would be encountered in reorganizing rural life and bringing industry to the direct aid of agriculture in a planned and systematic manner. In this the working classes of the more advanced countries would have to play an important and indispensable role. The scope and complexity of this problem was more than amply demonstrated in Russia, where the proletariat holds power but where factors of national isolation and economic backwardness have placed the most severe difficulties in the way of establishing a harmonious balance between urban and rural economy. Reduced to the comparatively microscopic scale of "Soviet China," scattered insurgent villages and mountain communities in a country still dominated as a whole by imperialist and native finance capital, the problem was proportionately more acute and the effort to solve it without a proletarian revolution was utterly hopeless.

The Communist party had never accepted the perspective of a proletarian revolution in China. It still insisted, after the experience of 1925–27, on the "bourgeois-democratic character of the Chinese Revolution." The theory of the "democratic dictatorship" which had been so thoroughly tested in Russia in 1917 and again in China ten years later remained the chief weapon in the ideological arsenal of the Chinese Communist party. In 1925–27 it had led them to dependence on the bourgeoisie, with disastrous results. Now it provided justification for depending upon a purely peasant movement, for relying, as before, on class interests which collided with those of the proletariat instead of fusing with them. The 1927 defeat had physically divorced the party from the working class. The adventurist course after 1927 converted it into a peasant party without roots or influence among the workers. It had become the Chinese equivalent not of the Russian Bolshevik party but of the Social Revolutionary party, whose example it followed in proposing to carry out an agrarian transformation on the basis of bourgeois property relations. Isolated in purely rural and economically limited pockets, the Communist party could not even begin to improve the status of the scattered semi-proletarians and agricultural workers in the districts under Red Army control, let alone to base a consistent and workable economic policy and political regime upon them. Despite all its pious resolutions and exhortations to the contrary, the Communists had to lean upon the rich peasants and merchants whose contact with the external market was indispensable to the maintenance of even a minimum existence for the Soviet areas. Despite itself, the party became the instrument of the dominant groupings in the villages.

The rich peasants came forward as leaders of the peasant revolt, bent on annexing some of the landlords' wealth and retaining their own. In many places they kept the movement limited to nonpayment of rent and taxes. When the peasants drove beyond this to the division of the land, they acquired the best land for themselves and retained their implements and draught animals. The influence of their position in the village clans and the superficial conflict between rich peasant and landlord made it easy for the former to dominate the lower strata of the peasant population. So long as the village remained subject to the operations of commercial capital and the external market, the village bourgeoisie, the rich peasants, and the merchants had to remain the dominant village classes, and they took every possible advantage of their strategic position.

The Communists fostered rather than resisted this development. The Sixth Congress of the party in 1928 adopted a conciliatory attitude toward the village bourgeoisie under the slogan of "not deliberately forcing the struggle against the rich peasants because to do so would be to confuse the fundamental contradiction between the peasant and landlord classes."[53] Accordingly, rich peasant land was to be left intact. "Confiscate landlord's land" was to be the principal slogan of the agrarian movement. In other words, the Communists now assumed the same antagonism between rich peasant and landlord as they had formerly assumed between the national bourgeois and compradore-landlord. They sought now to conciliate the rich peasants in the villages just as formerly they had tried, with such disastrous results, to adapt themselves to the national bourgeoisie in the cities. Even the familiar predictions about the "inevitable defection" of the rich peasants to the counterrevolution were dusted off and brought out,[54] and although in words some kind of limited or "secondary"[55] struggle was to be waged against these inevitable counterrevolutionists, in practice, as before, practical leadership was surrendered to them and their economic interests defended. The party found itself compelled to call upon the peasant poor, the rural workers, the artisans, and handicraftsmen to sacrifice their own immediate interests in order not to alienate the rich peasants and the merchants.

"Owing to the alliance with the rich peasants," admitted the Central Committee in 1929, "the interests of the agricultural laborers were sacrificed. . . . We feared the counterrevolutionary turn of the rich peasants and consequently asked the agricultural laborers to lower their demands."[56] In western Fukien in 1930 the Communists leading the partisan bands had "to compromise with the merchants in order to solve the difficulty of the import and export of supplies. They not only proclaimed protection of the merchants, but exempted them from taxation while the peasants still paid a 15 per cent land tax. . . . They had no means of curbing the raising of prices by the merchants . . . and sometimes they went so far as to limit the economic struggles of the shop employees and workers."[57]

In May 1930, a secret "Soviet Delegates' Conference" in Shanghai adopted a policy of frank conciliation toward the rich peasants and merchants.[58] The anti-proletarian consequences of this policy not only were pointed out in a brilliant analysis by a young Oppositionist, O Fong,[59] but were dimly realized by some in the party itself. Ch'ên Shao-yü criticized comrades in the Soviet districts who excused their failure to organize the agricultural laborers by declaring that "the peasants oppose it." He asked:

Shall we fail to organize the agricultural laborers for fear of the rich peasants? Then we are absolutely not the party of the proletariat. . . . In many Soviet villages rich peasant psychology dominates. Rich peasants occupy no small position in the mass organizations and in the party. They are aware of rich peasant interests only. This means that we have come to regard rich peasant psychology as the basic psychology of the peasant masses. . . . For the same reasons they do not organize shop employees, handicraft, and small enterprise workers. In Hupeh-Honan, for example, the slogan "For the interests of the middle and small merchants" was openly proclaimed and as a result not a single demand of the shop employees and handicraft workers was put forward.[60]

At the end of 1930, the Comintern described the situation in the following terms:

The agrarian revolution's most important tasks have not been solved. Not only rich peasants but even small landlords make their way into the Soviets, into the organs of the new power, into the Red army. The rich peasants seek to steal the fruits of the agrarian revolution. The rich peasant slogan— to distribute land according to productive implements—has not met with adequate resistance. In some places it was proposed to confiscate only the land of landlords holding more than fifty mou. Elsewhere there was a slogan for payment of debts to landlord-usurers owning less than fifty mou. . . . Equal division of land is the most important task of the agrarian revolution, but it has been carried out in very few places. The organization of the poor peasants has not even begun. . . . Coolies and agricultural laborers have not been organized into unions.[61]

After Li Li-san was held duly responsible for this state of affairs and Ch'ên Shao-yü put in his place, the situation not only failed to improve but grew steadily worse. "Two-thirds of the government is in the hands of the rich peasants," wrote a correspondent from one of the Soviet districts in 1931.[62] "Rich peasants are in all the party posts," wrote another in August that same year.[63] In 1933, at Juichin, the Soviet capital, a leading spokesman wrote:

The land was divided, but the landlords and rich peasants also received land and better land at that. A number of landlord and rich peasant elements still retain their authority and position in the villages. . . . Not a few of them are in control of party and government institutions and use them to carry out their own class interests. . . . In many places the land problem seems to be fully solved, but upon close scrutiny it appears that even landlords are found to have received land and the rich peasants still retain their superior land.[64]

Mao Tsê-tung, president of the "Soviet Republic," wrote:

Many landlords and rich peasants put on a revolutionary coloration. They say they are for the revolution and for the division of the land. . . . They are very active and rely on their historical advantages—"they can speak well and write well"—and consequently in the first period they steal the fruits of the agrarian revolution. Facts from innumerable places prove that they have usurped the provisional power, filtered into the armed forces, controlled the revolutionary organizations, and received more and better land than the poor peasants.

Mao estimated that this was the case in "80 per cent of the area of the central district, affecting a population of more than 2,000,000."[65] In his report to the Second "Soviet Congress" held at Juichin in January 1934, Mao revealed the striking fact that during a land-inspection movement conducted in the summer of 1933, "in the central Soviet district 6,988 landlord families and 6,638 rich peasant families owning a huge excess of land were discovered and their land seized and money taken from them to the total of $606,916."[66] Facts proved harsher and more compelling than party resolutions. Even the attempts made to redivide the land for the greater benefit of the poor peasants had to be abandoned in order not to unsettle crop production. At the end of the year a decree was announced prohibiting further redivision of the land because this practice had become "one of the most serious obstacles to an improvement in peasant agriculture."[67]

The demands of the agricultural laborers, artisans, and other rural workers were no less of a menace to the feeble and limited economic structure in the Soviet districts. In the central district this class was estimated to number about two hundred thousand.[68] Working singly or in twos or threes, scattered on the land, in the villages, or itinerant, these workers occupied a subsidiary position in the peasant economy. The capitalist cannot exist without the factory worker, but the peasant can get along without a hired hand. In the sense that they were divorced from the means of production and sold their labor power for wages, these workers were proletarians. The fact that they were scattered and played no independent role in production meant, however, that they tended to form part of the general petty bourgeois mass of the peasantry. They could not, in any case, play an independent political role. It was impossible to base any consistent policy upon their interests. A proletariat in power will find the means of marshaling rural labor and providing them with the economic means which will raise their level of existence, but here they stood alone, and when they tried to shorten their hours or increase their wages, the peasants resisted sharply or simply discharged them. Operating on the slimmest of all margins, the peasant could not double his workers' wages or the number of hands hired without utterly ruining himself. Similarly, in the shops and small enterprises, the merchants countered employees' demands by the simple threat to suspend activity altogether. This meant slow suffocation of trade, and the merchants knew they held the whip hand.

Shortly after it was established in November 1931, the "Provisional Soviet Government" adopted an admirable labor law even more sweeping in its provisions than the labor legislation of the Kuomintang in its early days. It called for a universal eight-hour day for adults, a six-hour day for youths of sixteen to eighteen, and a four-hour day for younger workers, for increased wages and generally improved working conditions. For propaganda purposes outside the Soviet districts and especially abroad, the word was taken for the deed. In "Soviet China" itself, however, it was soon realized that a law "passed for big cities and large-scale production cannot be completely and mechanically applied in the economically backward Soviet districts."[69] Attempts to enforce it had early been abandoned in the face of merchant-peasant opposition. "The comrades consider the labor law impracticable or else purely for propaganda purposes," reported the Hunan-Kiangsi party committee. "The Provincial Committee has combatted this tendency, but without much effect."[70] Many excuses were devised for the failure to apply the law. One of the most frequent was the plea that the new working hours could not be put into effect because "there are no clocks to reckon time by!"[71] After berating the functionaries of the lower rank for their stubborn "disregard" of the law, the leaders of the top were finally compelled to admit also that it was "impractical."

Lo Fu, a leading spokesman, described the unhappy result of attempts made to double the wages (from eight to sixteen dollars annually!) and cut the hours of farmhands. The workers were simply discharged. "The result was that the peasants were dissatisfied and the laborers were skeptical about our leadership." It was necessary, of course, to improve working conditions for the farm hands, "but such improvements must also be regarded by the peasants as necessary and practicable." The same applied to the apprentices in the shops and to the boatmen engaged in the river trade. "I have here the petitions of many merchants and employers from which we can see that the mechanical application of the labor law will inevitably be the decline of industry and commerce." It was necessary, of course, to improve the living standards and working conditions of the apprentices, "but we must make the employment of apprentices profitable, not unprofitable, for the master."[72] The workers were asked to understand that while they were the "masters of the State" they had to consent to remain the "exploited class" at the same time and refrain from making "excessive demands" or conducting strikes whose only effect was "to wreck the worker-peasant alliance."[73] This was the real essence of the "democratic dictatorship" in "Soviet China."

The attempt to organize the rural workers into unions produced in these circumstances either no organizations at all or alleged trade unions which functioned in reality against the interests of the workers. Figures on the "trade unions" in the Soviet dictricts varied widely. Within the space of a single year different published versions ranged from 14,000 to 30,000, to 150,000, to 229,000, and even to 2,200,-000![74] But the character of these unions, whatever their number, was so dubious that even the trade union center of the party at Shanghai had to complain. In its report for 1931 it spoke of the presence of "shopkeepers and rich peasants" in the unions.[75] The next year it addressed a scorching letter to the trade union officials in Kiangsi in which it accused them of admitting "peasants, priests, shop-owners, foremen, rich peasants, and landlords," while "on the other hand considerable sections of the agricultural laborers, coolies, employees, and artisans are on various pretexts barred from membership." The party comrades engaged in this work were accused of being "contemptuous of the workers and insolent toward them." The letter described the unions as "anti-proletarian in character, representing more the interests of the landlords, rich peasants, and employers."[76]

"The party in the Soviet districts, generally speaking, ignores proletarian hegemony," wrote one party leader in Juichin. ". . . Everywhere we see the serious phenomenon of the continual ignoring of the trade union movement. . . . The Committees never even discuss it. . . . Proletarian leadership exists still for the most part in words in party documents."[77]

This was the hard fact on which the Soviet experiment in Kiangsi broke its back. By driving out the landlords and sponsoring the division of the land, the Red armies had aroused the enthusiasm of considerable masses of the peasantry. In the absence of effective economic control, however, and in the absence of an effective proletarian mass movement, not only in the great cities, but in the towns nearest the Soviet districts,[78] the rich peasants re-emerged as landlords and the merchants re-emerged as the dominant class. The poor peasants and rural workers could win and hold not even the smallest material gains. Prices of the simplest necessities rose to unreachable levels. Unemployment became widespread. Peasants and rural workers alike began to wonder why they were fighting and to wish for any kind of peace so long as there was peace. Mass enthusiasm lapsed. Desertions from the Red Army grew in number.[79] A creeping paralysis began at the fringes of the Soviet districts and soon spread toward the center. Passivity corroded mass initiative. Pessimism gripped the leaders. This became known in party parlance as the "Lo Min line" because Lo Min, Fukien party leader, was one of the first to capitulate to these moods. "Even if our best leaders were to come, or to bring Stalin himself, or even resurrect Lenin from his tomb, and were to speak all together to the masses for three days and three nights, I do not think it would help change the moods of the masses," said Lo Min.[80]

Through 1933, the "Lo Min line" spread like a virus through the veins of "Soviet China." From Fukien it communicated itself to the Hwei-Hsen-An districts of south Kiangsi, where party functionaries, led by Têng Shao-pin, simply fled from their posts.[81] A Red Army enlistment campaign failed dismally and there was talk of conscription. Whole detachments of the Youth Guard Auxiliaries deserted and actually clashed with pursuing detachments of the Red Army.[82] Peasants often fled to the mountains to avoid transport work for the embattled army.[83]

The partisan bands not only rarely grow but are shrinking daily, as in Hwei-Hsen-An in the past and I-Chung and Nanfeng now. Desertions with rifles and betrayals are constantly occurring. . . . Corruption and degeneration constantly appear. Some partisan bands showed tendencies to banditry. . . . These are the conditions not only in the partisan bands but in the independent battalions, as in refusal to take orders, raids for money, etc. . . . The phenomenon of "soaking the tuhao" [raiding the hoards of the richer peasants] is very widespread. . . . Party workers going into the districts with small-size baggage soon increase it to large-size baggage. If they go with large-size baggage it soon grows into two loads for a carrying pole.[84]

New Lo Mins cropped up everywhere, even in the Red Army command, and finally in departments of the central government at Juichin. Ho So-hen of the workers-peasants inspection bureau was ejected for declaring that of the three million people in the Central Soviet district, two million were oppressed by rich peasants and landlords, and that "the Soviet governments of various grades have become instruments of the landlords and rich peasants for oppressing the masses."[85]

Chou Ên-lai appealed for "struggle against all kinds of wavering, pessimism, passivity, despair, weariness, and capitulation before difficulties."[86] Other leaders complained that the high turnover in party officials and the frequent changes in the districts were destroying mass enthusiasm, that the approach of any forces sent the peasants fleeing to the mountains. "They do not care if they are Red or White."[87]

The truly heroic effort made by the Red Army in the face of these moods defeated Chiang Kai-shek's drives in the summer of 1933, but the "victories" of those months were the beginning of the end. It was only a question of time before the superior strength of the Kuomintang, unassailed in the centers of its power, prevailed. It was only a question of time before the might of the Kuomintang military machine on land and in the air and the rigid tightening of the economic blockade produced their inevitable results. Chiang's bombers devastated whole districts and his troops inched down the province building fortifications as they advanced. Chiang abandoned the old strategy of sending long columns deep into Red territory, where they were cut off and annihilated. His army of more than 500,000 men, schooled by the German General von Seeckt and armed with weapons of the latest design from the munitions factories of Europe and the United States, closed in on the tiny Soviet districts like a fine-meshed steel net. There were ghastly massacres, violent and swift by bomb, gun, and torch, slow and agonizing by calculated starvation.[88]

In August 1934, one Red force of about ten thousand men, led by Hsiao K'ê, broke through the cordon and escaped westward. They were followed in November by the main force under Chu Tê and Mao Tsê-tung. On November 10, 1934, almost exactly three years after the proclamation of the Chinese "Soviet Republic," Chiang Kai-shek's troops triumphantly entered Juichin, the Soviet capital. Chiang had failed to exterminate all the Reds as he had promised, but he had succeeded in winning Kiangsi back for the landlords.

The Red forces marched and countermarched across Hunan, Kweichow, Yunnan, and Szechwan into Shensi, suffering incredible hardships, performing more incredible feats of valor and cunning. That "long trek" will be recorded as one of the most remarkable military exploits of all time, but it carried the Red Army still farther from the political and economic centers of the country. The defeat in Kiangsi could not terminate the peasant war, but it did deal a stunning blow to the organized insurgent peasant movement and consequently to the labor movement in the cities, then at its lowest ebb. New waves of terror, of capitulation and betrayals, destroyed most of what remained of the Communist party apparatus in the principal cities. Events had laid the ghosts of a thousand propagandist myths. Into the sparse desert land of the Chinese northwest the Communists marched toward a new impasse.

NOTES

Chapter 1 : THE ROOTS

[1] Cf. Karl A. Wittfogel, *Wirtschaft und Gesellschaft Chinas* (Leipzig, 1931) ; *Foundations and Stages of Chinese Economic History* (Zeitschrift fur Sozialforschung, Paris, 1935) ; "The Theory of Oriental Society," unpublished abstract.

[2] C. F. Remer, *The Foreign Trade of China* (Shanghai, 1926), p. 26. For tables on the opium trade see Joshua Rowntree, *The Imperial Drug Trade* (London, 1908), p. 344; H. B. Morse, *International Relations of the Chinese Empire* (London, 1910–18), I, 209–10.

[3] Cf. Rowntree, *op. cit.*, p. 242; and Wen-tsao Wu, *The Chinese Opium Question in British Opinion and Action* (New York: 1928), pp. 59–60.

[4] The population rose, according to one estimate, by 237,000,000, or about 190 percent, between 1712 and 1822 (S. Wells Williams, *The Middle Kingdom* [New York, 1882], p. 283). Another estimate for 1741–1851 showed a rise from 143,000,000 to 432,000,000, or about 200 percent (E. H. Parker, *China, Her History, Diplomacy, and Commerce* [London, 1901], p. 190). Dynastic records for 1661–1833 indicated an increase of cultivable land of only about 35 percent from 549,357,000 mow to 742,000,000 mow (Chen Shao-kwan, *System of Taxation in the Ch'ing Dynasty* [New York, 1914], p. 51).

[5] "Memorial of Lin Tse-hsu to the Emperor," 1838, trans. in P. C. Kuo, *A Critical Study of the First Anglo-Chinese War* (Shanghai, 1935), pp. 82–84.

[6] Prices rose 200 percent from 1830 to 1848 and 470 percent between 1849 and 1851, according to a Russian study published in *Problemi Kitai*, No. 1 (Moscow, 1929).

[7] H. D. Fong, "Cotton Industry and Trade in China," *Chinese Social and Political Science Review* (Peiping), October 1932, p. 97.

[8] H. B. Morse claims that $500,000,000 in silver was brought to China prior to 1830 ("The Foreign Trade of China" in G. H. Blakeslee [ed.], *China and the Far East* [New York, 1910], p. 97).

[9] G. E. Taylor, "The Taiping Rebellion," *Chinese Social and Political Science Review* (Peiping), January 1933, pp. 555–58.

[10] T. T. Meadows, *The Chinese and Their Rebellions* (London, 1856), p. 33.

[11] Taylor, *op. cit.*, pp. 597–99.

[12] K. Latourette, *The Chinese, Their History and Culture* (New York, 1934), I, 379.

[13] It is of interest to note that foreign firms dealing in commodities other than opium continued to favor the Taipings against the Manchus. They were still too weak, however, to influence the policies of the Powers. Cf. A. Lindley (Lin-Li), *Ti Ping Tien Kwoh* (London, 1866).

[14] J. K. Fairbank, "The Provisional System at Shanghai in 1853–4," *Chinese Social and Political Science Review* (Peiping), October 1934 and

April 1935, gives an account based on self-justifying British records of how this control was assumed.

[15] Taylor, *op. cit.*, p. 612.

[16] H. D. Fong, *China's Industrialization, A Statistical Survey* (Shanghai 1933), p. 2.

[17] Fong, "Cotton Industry and Trade in China," Tables 26, 30, 34.

[18] For useful documents of this period see M. E. Cameron, *The Reform Movement in China, 1898–1912* (Stanford, Calif., 1931).

[19] Brief summary in Latourette, *op. cit.*, I, 404 ff.

[20] Cf. R. Wilhelm, *The Soul of China* (New York, 1928), p. 26.

[21] A Peking dispatch to the *London Times*, November 10, 1905, spoke, for example, of "the events in Russia and the alarmist telegrams of the Chinese minister in St. Petersburg."

[22] For accounts of these boycotts, see C. F. Remer, *A Study of Chinese Boycotts* (Baltimore, 1933), chaps. iv–v.

[23] For a picture of these societies at work, see the early chapters of S. Tretiakov, *A Chinese Testament* (New York, 1934).

[24] In Shantung, property and literacy qualifications allowed votes to only 119,549 persons in a population of about 38,000,000. In Hupeh, 113,233 out of 34,000,000 voted. See *North China Herald*, February 18, 1910.

[25] Fong, *China's Industrialization*, Tables 1a and 1b.

[26] Lowe, *Facing Labor Issues in China*, Tables 6, 7, 8, 10.

Chapter 2: CHINA'S CRISIS: THE CLASS PATTERN

[1] Chen Han-seng, *Present Agrarian Problem in China*; also Buck, *Chinese Farm Economy*; Tawney, *Land and Labor in China*.

[2] "Report of the Land Committee of the Kuomintang," *Chinese Correspondence* (Hankow), May 8, 1927.

[3] Chen Han-seng, *Present Agrarian Problem*, pp. 2–5.

[4] Chen Han-seng, *Agrarian Problems in Southernmost China*.

[5] Cf. Annexes 6 and 7, *Annexes to the Report of the Council of the League of Nations* (Nanking, April 1934); also briefer summary and bibliographical notes in Tawney, *op. cit.*, pp. 50–54.

[6] Wong Yin-seng, *Requisitions and the Peasantry in North China*; Chen Han-seng, *Present Agrarian Problem*, pp. 15–18; Chen Han-seng, *Agrarian Problems in Southernmost China*, chap. v; "Kuomintang vs. Peasants," in H. R. Isaacs (ed.), *Five Years of Kuomintang Reaction*.

[7] Cf. *Chinese Maritime Customs, Annual Report for 1932*, pp. 48 ff.; Chen Han-seng, "Economic Disintegration of China," *Pacific Affairs*, April–May 1933; Lowe, *Facing Labor Issues*, Table 1; Dr. Friedrich Otto, "Harvests and Imports of Cereals," *Chinese Economic Journal*, October 1934; Beale and Pelham, *Trade and Economic Conditions in China, 1931–33*, pp. 7 and 149 ff. Food imports were 5 percent of the total in 1918 and 20 percent in 1932. In the latter year it took 43 percent of the total exports to pay for imports of food alone.

[8] Fong, "Cotton Industry and Trade," Table 2b; Remer, *Foreign Investments in China*, pp. 69, 86–91, 135; *China Year Book, 1926*, p. 822; Fang Fu-an, "Communications, the Extent of Foreign Control," *The Chinese Nation*

(Shanghai), September 10, 1930; Tao and Lin, *Industry and Labor in China*, pp. 12, 16–17.

[9] Chen Han-seng, *Present Agrarian Problem*, p. 18.

[10] Lowe, *Facing Labor Issues*, pp. 54–55. For a summary of studies made of the industrial population, see Fang Fu-an, *Chinese Labour*, chap. ii.

Chapter 3: WORLD CRISIS: THE RUSSIAN IMPACT

[1] The precise nature of the regime that has emerged in Russia is being redefined in terms that range from "degenerated workers' state" to "state capitalism." Karl Wittfogel, who has made such exhaustive studies of the "bureaucratic state" of old China, has in preparation a study provocatively titled "Russia's Asiatic Restoration."

[2] "Theses on the National and Colonial Question," *Theses and Statutes of the Third (Communist) International*, adopted by the Second Congress (1920), p. 70. Cf. Lenin, "Preliminary Draft of Some Theses on the National and Colonial Questions," *Communist International*, June–July 1920.

[3] Commenting on the Russian terminology and Russian spirit of the organizational resolution of the congress, Lenin said: "I have the impression that we made a big mistake with this resolution, namely, that we ourselves have blocked our road to further success" (quoted by Ruth Fischer, *Stalin and German Communism* [Cambridge, 1948], p. 186). See Lenin, *Collected Works*, English translation, X, 320–33.

[4] Ruth Fischer, *op. cit.*, chaps. xiv–xvi.

[5] "Theses on the National and Colonial Question," p. 70.

[6] For an exposition of these ideas and the polemics that raged around them, see Trotsky, *The Permanent Revolution; History of the Russian Revolution*, Vol. III, Appendix 3.

[7] *Protokoll des II Weltcongresses der Kommunistischen Internationale*, pp. 140–42.

[8] "Theses on the National and Colonial Question," p. 70.

[9] "Supplementary Theses," *Theses and Statutes*, pp. 72–75; cf. "Theses on the Eastern Question," *Resolutions and Theses of the Fourth Congress of the Communist International* (1922), pp. 53 ff. Cf. Safarov, "Report on the National-Colonial Question and the Communist Attitude Thereto," *Proceedings of the First Congress of the Toilers of the Far East* (1922), pp. 166 ff.

[10] "Minutes of the March, 1917, Party Conference," Appendix to Trotsky, *Stalin School of Falsification*, p. 239; Lenin, *Collected Works*, XX, 98, 107, 120.

Chapter 4: THE NEW AWAKENING

[1] Wang, *Youth Movement in China*, p. 100.

[2] Cf. Wong [sic] Ching-wei, *China and the Nations*, pp. 91–98.

[3] Tyau, *China Awakened*, pp. 237, 240.

[4] Tsui, "Influence of Canton-Moscow Entente, etc.," p. 113.

[5] Sun Yat-sen, *International Development*, p. xi; *Memoirs*, pp. 179–83.

[6] Sun Yat-sen, *San Min Chu I*, pp. 431–34.

354   THE TRAGEDY OF THE CHINESE REVOLUTION

⁷ For useful expositions of Sun's political doctrines and his efforts to reconcile them with Communist ideas, see Tsui, "Influence of Canton-Moscow Entente, etc.," and Woo, *Kuomintang and the Future of the Chinese Revolution*, chap. iii.

⁸ Ch'ên Tu-hsiu, *Letter to the Comrades* (December 10, 1929).

⁹ Ch'ên Tu-hsiu, "The Bourgeois Revolution and the Revolutionary Bourgeoisie," *Essays on the Chinese Revolution*, p. 60.

¹⁰ Speech of Liu Jên-chin, Fourth Congress, Communist International, November 23, 1922, *Inprecor* (French ed.), January 12, 1923.

¹¹ Sun Yat-sen, *International Development*, pp. 251–65.

¹² Wong [*sic*] Ching-wei, *op. cit.*, pp. 108–9.

¹³ See appendixes to V. A. Yakhontoff, *Russia and the Soviet Union in the Far East* (New York, 1931). Also, *China Year Book, 1924*.

¹⁴ *Izvestia* (Moscow), October 9, 1920, quoted by Pasvolsky, *Russia in the Far East*, p. 87.

¹⁵ H. Maring, "Die Revolutionar-Nationalistische Bewegung in Sud-China," *Die Kommunistische Internationale*, September 13, 1922.

¹⁶ Louis Fischer, *Soviets in World Affairs*, II, 540.

¹⁷ Mif, *Heroic China*, pp. 21–22.

¹⁸ Quoted by Hua Kang, *Great Chinese Revolution*, chap. vi, sec. 1.

¹⁹ *Program of the Kuomintang* (First National Congress [Canton] 1924).

²⁰ For surveys of working-class conditions see Bibliography in Lowe, *Facing Labor Issues in China*, pp. 189 ff.; also "Kuomintang vs. Labor," in *Five Years of Kuomintang Reaction*.

²¹ Cf. S. Wong and W. L., "La Chine Ouvrière," *Inprecor*, September 26, 1923.

²² Lowe, *Facing Labor Issues*, p. 40.

²³ "Proclamation of the National Conference of Railway Workers, February 14, 1924," trans. by Wieger, *Chine Moderne*, V, 263–64. For 1923 events see Lo Ch'ang-lung, *Massacre of the Peking-Hankow Railway Workers*.

²⁴ Chen Ta, *Analysis of Strikes*, p. 5.

²⁵ Wieger, *op. cit.*, V, 266, 269–70.

²⁶ Tsui, "Influence of Canton-Moscow Entente, etc.," p. 120.

²⁷ G. Voitinsky, "First Conference of Transport Workers of the Pacific," *Inprecor*, September 11, 1924.

²⁸ P'êng Pai, *Haifeng Peasant Movement*.

²⁹ Chang, *Farmer's Movement*, p. 2.

³⁰ "Manifesto of Sun Yat-sen, September 1, 1924." Wieger, *Chine Moderne*, V, 230; Wong [*sic*] Ching-wei, *op. cit.*, pp. 111–12; *Inprecor*, September 11, 18 and October 2, 1924; *North China Herald*, September 6, 1924.

³¹ Chang, *op. cit.*, p. 31.

³² Lowe, *op. cit.*, p. 36; Hua Kang gives 281 delegates, 166 unions, 540,000 workers (*Great Chinese Revolution*, chap. iv. sec. 1).

³³ Chang, *op. cit.*, p. 8.

³⁴ *Ibid.*, p. 32.

³⁵ *China Weekly Review*, June 13, 1925.

³⁶ Chen Ta, *op. cit.*, p. 27. Chen recorded for 1925 as a whole 318 strikes involving a known total of 784,821 workers, with the number unrecorded or unknown for one-third of the listed strikes, bringing the probable total to about 1,000,000.

³⁷ Chapman, *Chinese Revolution*, pp. 14–15.

38 Chen Ta, *op. cit.*, p. 28.
39 Têng Chung-hsia, *Survey of the Hongkong Strike.* Têng was one of the organizers and leaders of the general strike. He was shot by order of Chiang Kai-shek in the summer of 1933. Lo Teng-hsien, one of his principal lieutenants, was executed in Nanking in August the same year.
40 *China Year Book, 1926,* pp. 969–70.
41 Têng Chung-hsia, *op. cit.*
42 Quoted by Lowe, *op. cit.*, p. 44; see also *Administrative Reports of the Hongkong Government* (1925).
43 *China Year Book, 1926,* pp. 974–75.

Chapter 5: Canton: To Whom the Power?

1 Quoted by Hua Kang, *Great Chinese Revolution,* chap. iv, sec. 1.
2 Chapman, *Chinese Revolution,* p. 210.
3 *North China Herald,* June 6, 1925.
4 A recent study of American policy in China in this period is Dorothy Borg's *American Policy and the Chinese Revolution, 1925–28* (New York, 1947).
5 Chen Ta, "Labor's Part in the New Nationalism," *China Weekly Review,* March 6, 1926.
6 Samuel H. Chang, "An Analysis of Canton Bolshevism," *China Weekly Review,* March 20 and April 3, 1926.
7 *North China Herald,* March 20, 1926.
8 For Taku ultimatum, see *China Year Book, 1926,* pp. 1031–32; for a graphic description of the massacre, see Oskar Erdberg, "March Eighteenth," *Tales of Modern China.*
9 *China Weekly Review,* March 27, 1926.
10 *North China Herald,* March 20, 1926.
11 *China Year Book, 1926,* p. 1011.
12 Li Chih-lung, *Resignation of Wang Ching-wei.*
13 Tang Leang-li, *Inner History,* p. 234.
14 Louis Fischer, *Soviets in World Affairs,* II, 646.
15 *The Peasant Movement in Kwangtung* (Kuomintang Peasant Department Report) (Canton, October 1925).
16 *Inprecor,* January 7, 1926.
17 Stalin, *Marxism and the National and Colonial Question,* p. 216. Cf. Trotsky, *Third International After Lenin,* pp. 212–22.
18 "Resolution on the Chinese Question" (VI Plenum E.C.C.I.), *Inprecor,* May 13, 1926.
19 *Inprecor,* March 18, 1926.
20 Fuse, *Soviet Policy in the Orient,* p. 304. A photograph of Hu Han-min seated with his Krestintern colleagues will be found on page 305.
21 "Detailed Report of the Session of the Enlarged E.C.C.I." (VI Plenum), opening session, February 17, 1926, *Inprecor,* March 4, 1926.
22 "Resolution on the Chinese Question," *Inprecor,* May 13, 1926.
23 Tang Leang-li, *op. cit.*, p. 233.
24 Louis Fischer, *op. cit.*, II, 647.
25 *Ibid.*

[26] Trotsky, *Problems*, p. 254. An illuminating picture, in novel form, of Borodin's role in Canton is given by André Malraux in *Les Conquérants* (Paris, 1928), (*The Conquerors* [New York, 1929]). See also Trotsky's comments on this book in "The Strangled Revolution" and "A Strangled Revolution and Its Stranglers," in *Problems*, pp. 244–66.

Chapter 6: CANTON: THE COUP OF MARCH 20, 1926

[1] Tang Leang-li, *Inner History*, p. 231.
[2] *Whampoa Year Book* (December 1925).
[3] *Inprecor*, March 18, 1926.
[4] Li Chih-lung, *The Resignation*.
[5] *Inprecor* (French ed.), February 17, 1926.
[6] *China Weekly Review*, April 10, 1926.
[7] Hua Kang, *Great Chinese Revolution*, chap. iv, sec. 5.
[8] Li Chih-lung, *op. cit.*
[9] Tang Leang-li, *op. cit.*, p. 246.
[10] Li Chih-lung, *op. cit.*
[11] Têng Chung-hsia, *Survey of Hongkong Strike*.
[12] Sokolsky, *Tinder Box of Asia*, p. 336.
[13] Têng Chung-hsia, *op. cit.*
[14] Full text of resolution in Woo, *Kuomintang and the Future of the Chinese Revolution*, pp. 176–78; references and extracts in Hua Kang, *op. cit.*, chap. iv, sec. 5, and in Fuse, *Soviet Policy*, pp. 251–56.
[15] See chap. iii, n. 2.
[16] "The putsch of Chiang Kai-shek on March 20, 1926, when the Russian Communists were arrested in China, was not mentioned by a single word in our press" (Zinoviev, "Theses on the Chinese Revolution," in Appendixes to Trotsky, *Problems*, p. 347). "For a whole year, the Stalin-Bukharin group concealed the first coup of Chiang Kai-shek in March, 1926" (Albert Treint, "Déclaration du Camarade Treint," *Documents de l'Opposition*, p. 76).
[17] *Inprecor*, April 8, 1926.
[18] *Daily Worker*, April 21, 1926.
[19] G. Voitinsky, "The Situation in China and the Plans of the Imperialists," *Inprecor*, May 6, 1926.
[20] Sokolsky, *op. cit.*, p. 336.
[21] Tang Leang-li, *op. cit.*, p. 247.
[22] A. M. Kotenev, *New Lamps for Old* (Shanghai, 1931), p. 237.
[23] Tang Leang-li, *op. cit.*, p. 249.
[24] Louis Fischer, *Soviets in World Affairs*, II, 651–53.
[25] *Guide Weekly*, end of March 1926, reprinted with other articles and documents in *Our Party and the Canton Events*.
[26] "Open Letter of Ch'ên Tu-hsiu to Chiang Kai-shek," June 4, 1926, in *Our Party and the Canton Events*.
[27] "Open Letter of Kao Yu-han to Chiang Kai-shek," in *Our Party and the Canton Events*.
[28] "Letter of the Central Committee of the Communist Party to the Kuomintang," June 4, 1926, in *Our Party and the Canton Events*.
[29] Quoted by Li Li-san, in Preface to *The Chinese Revolution*.

[30] Ch'ên Tu-hsiu, *Letter to the Comrades.*

[31] "The Fifth Congress of the Communist Party of China and the Kuomintang," *Communist International,* April 15, 1927.

[32] Ch'ên Tu-hsiu, *op. cit.*

[33] Hua Kang, *op. cit.,* chap. iv, sec. 3.

[34] Quoted by Yüen Tai-ying, *Kuomintang and the Labor Movement.*

[35] "News from South China," *China Weekly Review,* July 31 and August 7, 14, 21, and 28, 1926.

[36] "Report of the Kwangtung Provincial Peasant Union" (February 1927), *Chinese Correspondence,* May 8, 1927.

[37] *China Year Book, 1926,* p. 982.

[38] Têng Chung-hsia, *op. cit.; China Weekly Review,* April 24, 1926.

[39] "Canton Boycott Negotiations," *China Year Book, 1926,* p. 989.

[40] *Ibid.,* p. 998.

[41] *China Weekly Review,* August 7, 1926.

[42] *Ibid.,* July 31, 1926.

[43] *China Year Book, 1928,* p. 976.

[44] *Ibid.,* pp. 977–78.

[45] Quoted in Louis Fischer, *op. cit.,* II, 645.

[46] *China Year Book, 1928,* p. 978.

[47] "Strike Regulations in Canton," *Chinese Economic Journal* (March 1927); "Labor Suppression in Canton," *North China Herald,* December 31, 1926; *August 7 Letter;* P. Mif, *Kitaiskaya Revolutsia,* pp. 97–98.

[48] Sydor Stoler, "The Trade Union Movement in Canton," *Pan-Pacific Worker* (Hankow), September 15, 1927.

[49] Browder, *Civil War in Nationalist China,* p. 12.

[50] "The International Delegation in China," *Inprecor,* April 28, 1927.

[51] Tom Mann, *What I Saw in China,* p. 8.

[52] Stoler, *op. cit.*

Chapter 7: FROM CANTON TO THE YANGTZE

[1] Chapman, *Chinese Revolution,* p. 20.

[2] Changsha correspondence to the *Guide Weekly,* quoted by Hua Kang, *Great Chinese Revolution,* chap. iv, sec. 4.

[3] Chen Ta, *Analysis of Strikes,* pp. 40–41.

[4] Folcine, Nassonov, and Albrecht, *La Lettre de Shanghai,* pp. 13–18.

[5] Trotsky, *Problems,* p. 271.

[6] Trotsky, "Speech of August 1, 1927," *Stalin School of Falsification,* pp. 165, 173.

[7] Stalin, "Speech of August 1, 1927," *Marxism and the National and Colonial Question,* p. 237.

[8] "Thèses sur la Situation en Chine" (adopted by the VII Plenum, E.C.C.I., November-December 1926), *Inprecor* (French ed.), February 20, 1927.

[9] "Report of T'an P'ing-shan" (VII Plenum), *Inprecor,* December 30, 1926.

[10] Stalin, "Prospects of the Revolution in China" (speech to Chinese Commission of the VII Plenum, November 30, 1926), *Inprecor,* December 23, 1926.

[11] "Detailed Report of the VII Plenum" (First Session, November 22, 1926), *Inprecor*, December 1, 1926.

[12] Albert Treint, "La Vérité Qu'on Cache sur la Chine, etc.," *Documents de l'Opposition et la Réponse du Parti*, pp. 77–78.

[13] Stalin, "Prospects of the Revolution in China."

[14] "Thèses sur la Situation en Chine" (VII Plenum).

[15] Stalin, "Prospects of the Revolution in China."

[16] "Speech of Shao Li-tzŭ (Kuomintang)" (VII Plenum, Session of November 30, 1926), *Inprecor*, December 30, 1926.

[17] Bukharin, "Speech to the 24th Conference of Leningrad District, C.P.S.U.," *Inprecor* (French ed.), February 12, 1927.

[18] "Speech of T'an P'ing-shan" (VII Plenum, Session of November 26, 1926), *Inprecor*, December 23, 1926.

[19] Stalin, "Prospects of the Revolution in China." See also "Speech of Petroff (C.P.S.U.)," *Inprecor*, December 30, 1926.

[20] Chen Ta, *op. cit.*, p. 43.

[21] *Hankow Herald*, January 5, 1927.

[22] Chapman, *op. cit.*, p. 35.

[23] Ransome, *Chinese Puzzle*, pp. 106, 113. One of Ransome's British informants at Kiukiang subsequently complained that his account was "insufficiently lurid."

[24] *Lettre de Shanghai*, p. 4.

[25] For texts and related citations, see *China Year Book, 1928*, pp. 739, 756 ff, 761, 764, 983, 1353.

[26] *Lettre de Shanghai*, p. 5.

[27] *August 7 Letter* (See Bibliography, *Letter to all the Comrades of the Communist Party*).

[28] *Lettre de Shanghai*, pp. 7–8. In later years Borodin never wearied of citing this banquet as evidence that he had actually struggled against Chiang Kai-shek. For Chiang's own account of the incident, see Wieger, *Chine Moderne*, VII, 140–42.

[29] Wieger, *op. cit.*, VIII, 23–24.

[30] *North China Herald*, April 2, 1927.

[31] *People's Tribune*, March 15, 1927; Woo, *Kuomintang and the Future of the Chinese Revolution*, p. 180.

[32] *People's Tribune*, March 16, 1927.

[33] *Ibid.*

[34] *Ibid.*, March 19, 1927.

[35] *Ibid.*

[36] *Lettre de Shanghai*, pp. 6–7.

[37] *Guide Weekly*, March 18, 1927, trans. in *North China Herald*, April 9, 1927.

Chapter 8: THE SHANGHAI INSURRECTION

[1] *Chinese Economic Journal* (March 1927); *Strikes and Lockouts in Shanghai Since 1918*.

[2] "The Fight for Shanghai," *Inprecor*, January 13, 1927.

[3] Sources differ on the exact figure. Official foreign reports, which as a rule understated strike figures, gave 106,000 (*China Year Book, 1928*, p. 996).

Lettre de Shanghai gives 300,000. Hua Kang's *Great Chinese Revolution* gives 360,000 with a supporting list of factories and shops. Hostile Chinese sources quote much higher totals. The Shanghai Bureau of Social Affairs lists 425,795 (*Strikes and Lockouts*, p. 62). Ho Shên, *Materials of Modern History*, III, gives 500,000.

[4] Hua Kang, *op. cit.*, chap. v, sec. 2.

[5] Ch'ü Ch'iu-po, *Controversial Questions in the Chinese Revolution*, Appendix 1.

[6] *New York Herald Tribune*, February 21, 1927.

[7] Ho Shên, "The Three Chinese Uprisings," *Materials for Modern History*, III, 170.

[8] *China Weekly Review*, March 12, 1927.

[9] *North China Herald*, April 16, 1927.

[10] *New York Herald Tribune*, February 21, 1927.

[11] *Lettre de Shanghai*, pp. 10–11.

[12] *China Year Book, 1928*, p. 1266.

[13] Hua Kang, *op. cit.*, chap. v, sec. 2.

[14] For striking vignettes of the Shanghai insurrection, see Malraux, *La Condition Humaine* (English translation, *Man's Fate*).

[15] Hua Kang and other Communist sources usually give 800,000 as the total involved. *Strikes and Lockouts* gives the number of actual strikers as 329,000.

[16] A. Neuberg (Heinz Neumann), *Insurrection Armée*, p. 141.

[17] Hua Kang, *op. cit.*, chap. v, sec. 3.

[18] Ho Shên, *Materials*, III.

[19] Hua Kang, *op. cit.*, chap. v, sec. 3.

Chapter 9: THE PRODIGAL'S RETURN

[1] Chinese say Chiang belonged to the *tung* layer, or twenty-second generation of the Green Society, which is organized along elaborate patriarchal lines. Referring to Chiang's "connection with the Green and Red societies," George Sokolsky added: "He may even be a member of one or both of these powerful underground groups, but that no outsider can know" (*China Year Book, 1928*, p. 1361).

[2] "Shanghai Workers' Delegates' Report," *Sen Pao* (Hunan), May 19–20, 1927; hereafter referred to as "Workers' Delegates' Report." See also Kuo Mi-lieh's account in the *People's Tribune*, April 16, 1927; *Inprecor*, June 23, 1927. For a description of the Green Society and its later development, see "Gang Rule in Shanghai" in *Five Years of Kuomintang Reaction*.

[3] Li Chih-lung, *Resignation of Wang Ching-wei*; Kiukiang correspondence, dated March 23, 1927, in *North China Herald*, April 2, 1927.

[4] Chapman, *Chinese Revolution*, p. 32.

[5] See report of G. A. Kennedy, *People's Tribune*, April 5 and 16, 1927. Most of Kennedy's findings were incorporated in a dispatch by William Prohme to *The Nation* (New York), April 13, 1927. For absence of proof of rape charges, see *China Weekly Review*, May 28, 1927. For material on the "Nanking Outrages" in the mood and spirit of the Shanghai foreign community, see *China Year Book, 1928*, chap. xvi.

[6] George Sokolsky, in *China Year Book, 1928*, p. 1361.

[7] "Workers' Delegates' Report"; Chen Fo-ta, one of the Shanghai delegates to the Pan-Pacific Trade Union Conference at Hankow, reported that the Shanghai pickets numbered 3,000, and had 2,800 rifles, 30 machine guns, 200 pistols, and 16 pieces of light artillery (*People's Tribune*, May 26, 1927).

[8] "There are not more than 3,000 Nationalist troops in Shanghai, according to reliable estimates from Chinese sources. General Ho Ying-ch'in has only 10,000 troops to hold Hangchow. The military forces of Chiang Kai-shek are now so scattered over so vast an area as not to be very valuable . . . for the suppression of the laborers" (*North China Herald*, April 2, 1927). "Chiang had only 3,000 troops in Shanghai. . . . None of the material elements were in Chiang's favor" (Sokolsky, in *China Year Book, 1928*, p. 1361). "Troops sympathetic to the revolution still outnumbered the counterrevolutionary troops. The troops under the direct command of Chiang Kai-shek were also vacillating" (Li Li-san, *Chinese Revolution*, p. 33).

[9] A. DeC. Sowerby, *North China Herald*, April 2, 1927.

[10] *Municipal Gazette*, April 2, 1927.

[11] Cf. Arthur Ransome's chapter on "The Shanghai Mind," in *Chinese Puzzle*.

[12] Rodney Gilbert, *North China Herald*, April 2, 1927. For a reply to this common argument see "That Model Settlement," *People's Tribune*, July 18, 1927.

[13] "Thoughts on Evacuation" ("by A Missionary Refugee"), *North China Herald*, April 16, 1927.

[14] *Ibid.* Of 8,000 missionaries, only 500 were still at their posts, according to the *Shanghai Times*, June 24, 1927. Some 5,000 fled the country; 1,500 took refuge in Shanghai and 1,000 in other ports.

[15] "The Real Issue in China," *Constitutionalist* (Shanghai), February 1927, pp. 321–23.

[16] E. E. Strothers, *A Bolshevised China—The World's Greatest Peril, and other Reprints* (Shanghai, June 1927), p. 6.

[17] *Ibid.*, p. 18. This report, a crude falsification, was widely current at the time. For categoric refutation of it by a British resident of Hankow, see Chapman, *op. cit.*, p. 87. It was typical, however, of the fantastic notions of developments in Hankow disseminated by the foreign press.

[18] Gen. Smedley D. Butler, commander of United States Marines in China, *North China Herald*, April 9, 1927.

[19] *Constitutionalist*, January 1927, p. 291.

[20] *China Weekly Review*, April 9, 1927.

[21] *North China Daily News*, April 7, 1927.

[22] *Far Eastern Review*, March 1927.

[23] *North China Daily News*, March 28, 1927.

[24] *North China Herald*, April 2, 1927.

[25] *Sin Wen Pao*, April 7, 1927.

[26] *North China Daily News*, March 30, 1927.

[27] *China Weekly Review*, April 9, 1927; *New York Times*, April 15, 1927. The sum of $15,000,000 is also mentioned by the "Workers' Delegates' Report," which divides it into $12,000,000 for Chiang; $1,500,000 for Pai Ch'ung-hsi; $1,000,000 for Chou Fêng-ch'i; and $500,000 for the gangsters. There is no record of the extent of foreign participation in these "loans" but a picture of how foreigners co-operated through Chinese intermediaries is given, in fictional form, in Malraux's *Man's Fate*.

[28] *Chen Pao* (Peking), April 3, 1927; *Sin Wen Pao*, April 5, 1927.

[29] *China Weekly Review*, April 9, 1927.

[30] *North China Daily News*, March 28, 1927.

[31] Quoted from *Pravda*, in Moscow dispatch to *New York Times*, April 1, 1927.

[32] *North China Herald*, April 9, 1927.

[33] Tang, *Inner History*, pp. 266–68. Cf. *Ta Kung Pao* (Tientsin), April 7, 1927.

Chapter 10: THE CONSPIRACY OF SILENCE

[1] *Shanghai Times*, March 25, 1927; *North China Daily News*, March 28, 1927.

[2] *Rote Fahne* (Berlin), March 17, 1927; *L'Humanité* (Paris), March 23, 1927; "The confusion created by Stalin-Bukharin . . . led the leadership of our party on March 23, 1927 to salute telegraphically Chiang Kai-shek, entering Shanghai, as the representative of the Chinese Commune. . . . [They] led the leadership of the French party astray to the point of confusing Gallifet with the Commune, the butcher with the victim" (Treint, "Déclaration Addressée au C.E. de l'I.C., le 22 Juillet, 1927, sur la Question Chinoise," *Documents de l'Opposition*, p. 67).

[3] Cf. "Theses on the Situation in China" (VII Plenum), *Inprecor* (French ed.), February 20, 1927; editorial in *Communist International*, February 28, 1927; article by Martynov, *ibid.*, March 15, 1927; "The Chinese Revolution and the Kuomintang," *ibid.*, March 30, 1927; and many others.

[4] Doriot, "A Travers la Révolution Chinoise," *L'Humanité*, July 8 and 12, 1927; Browder, *Civil War*, p. 15.

[5] See *Labour Monthly* (London), July 1927. Actually, the only people who tried to carry on a campaign against Chiang Kai-shek were a few individual Communists in Hankow, acting on their own initiative. Cf. *Lettre de Shanghai*, p. 8.

[6] *People's Tribune*, April 9, 1927.

[7] *People's Tribune*, April 22, 1927; Tom Mann, *What I Saw*, p. 11.

[8] *Inprecor* (French ed.), March 23 and 30, 1927.

[9] *L'Humanité*, March 23, 1927.

[10] Translation from original unpublished manuscript.

[11] Reproduced in *Inprecor* (French ed.), March 26, 1927, and in *Communist International*, March 30, 1927. See also Martynov, "The Regrouping of Forces in the Chinese Revolution," *Communist International*, March 15, 1927.

[12] This speech by Stalin was never published. Stalin was confronted with these passages by Vuyovitch at the Eighth Plenum of the E.C.C.I. in May in the form of Vuyovitch's own shorthand notes. "Comrade Stalin will always have the opportunity of rectifying unintentional inaccuracies by laying his stenogram before us," he challenged (cf. Trotsky, *Problems*, Appendixes, pp. 388–90). But Stalin offered no corrections and produced no stenogram because, as Trotsky remarked at the same meeting, "a few days later the squeezed-out lemon seized power and the army. . . . As a member of the Central Committee I had the right to get the stenogram of this speech, but my pains and attempts

were in vain. Attempt it now, comrades, perhaps you will have better luck. I doubt it" (*ibid.*, p. 91). The speech and its suppression are confirmed by Treint, a Stalin lieutenant: "A speech by Stalin himself at the Communist Academy in the presence of 3,000 officials of the party was never published . . . because the coup d'état of Chiang Kai-shek ten days later brought to his words the shattering refutation of events" (*Documents de l'Opposition*, pp. 36, 64). For a projection of Stalin's views on the Chinese scene, read the conversation between Kyo and "Vologin" in Hankow in Malraux's *Man's Fate*, pp. 146–55.

[13] Stalin, "Speech to the Youth Federation" (March 29, 1927), *Inprecor* (French ed.) April 9, 1927.

[14] T. Mandalyan, "Why Did the Leadership of the Chinese Communist Party Fail to Fulfill Its Task?" *Inprecor* (French ed.) July 23 and 30, 1927; Ch'ên Tu-hsiu, *Letter to the Comrades*; N. Bukharin, *Les Problèmes de la Révolution Chinoise*, p. 56. Cf. Malraux, *op. cit.*, pp. 209–10.

[15] *Communist International*, Russian edition, March 18, 1927; German edition, March 22, 1927; English edition, April 15, 1927.

[16] Quoted in *North China Daily News*, April 1, 1927.

[17] Translated from original as it appeared in *Sin Wen Pao* and other Shanghai newspapers, April 5, 1927. An extremely inaccurate translation appeared in the *People's Tribune*, April 10, 1927. Essential passages were published the same week, without comment, in the international Communist press (e.g., *Inprecor* [French ed.], April 13, 1927) and were included by Browder in his pamphlet (*Civil War*, p. 30), likewise without comment. Not until many months later did it become the target of violent attack.

[18] Between March 21 and April 12, unions in Shanghai swelled from a membership of 350,000 to 850,000, according to Chen Fo-ta's report. See *People's Tribune*, May 26, 1927.

[19] *Inprecor* (French ed.), March 26, 1927.

[20] *Sin Wen Pao*, April 8, 1927.

[21] *Ibid.*, April 3 and 5, 1927.

[22] *Ibid.*, April 2, 1927.

[23] *North China Herald*, April 2, 1927.

[24] P. Mif, *Kitaiskaya Revolutsia*, p. 98.

[25] Yang Tsao-cheng, *Events in Shanghai, Spring 1927* ("Materials on the Chinese Question," No. 13 [Moscow: Sun Yat-sen University]), p. 20. "Hsüeh Yüeh proposed to the Central Committee . . . to agree that he should not submit to Chiang's order. He was ready to remain in Shanghai and fight together with the Shanghai workers against the military overthrow that was in preparation"—Chitarov (a Comintern representative in Shanghai at the time), at the December 11, 1927, session of the 15th Congress, Communist party of the Soviet Union. This passage was deleted from the minutes and is quoted by Trotsky from the original stenographic record (Trotsky, *Problems*, p. 276). Mif confirms the incident, although in garbled form, in *Kitaiskaya Revolutsia*, p. 99.

[26] Malraux, *op. cit.*, p. 207.

[27] *Sin Wen Pao*, April 7, 1927.

[28] Reuters from Peking, *North China Daily News*, April 12, 1927.

[29] Cf. *Inprecor* (French ed.), April 20, 1927.

[30] *New York Times*, April 9, 1927.

[31] *Sin Wen Pao*, April 6, 1927.

[32] *Ibid.*, April 6, 1927.
[33] Cf. *People's Tribune*, May 7, 1927.
[34] Malraux, *op. cit.*, pp. 266–67.

Chapter *11*: THE COUP OF APRIL 12, 1927

[1] *China Press*, April 13, 1927.
[2] *North China Daily News*, April 13, 1927.
[3] *China Year Book, 1928*, p. 1362.
[4] *Shun Pao*, April 13, 1927.
[5] Cf. "Workers' Delegates' Report," *Hunan Sen Pao*, May 19–20, 1927. Corroborative accounts appeared in the *Sin Wen Pao* and other Shanghai papers.

[6] "Police Report for April," *Municipal Gazette*, May 21, 1927. Shanghai delegates to the Fourth All-China Trade Union Conference at Hankow reported that 140 known union leaders and 500 workers lost their lives resisting Chiang's coup (*People's Tribune*, June 30, 1927).

[7] *Sin Wen Pao*, April 13, 1927. For picture of "reorganization" see "Chiang Kai-shek's Fascist Trade Unions," *People's Tribune*, June 17, 1927.

[8] *Sin Wen Pao*, April 13, 1927.
[9] *North China Herald*, April 16, 1927.
[10] *Sin Wen Pao*, April 13, 1927; *China Press*, April 13, 1927.

[11] "90,000 workers were out"(*China Press*, April 14, 1927); "An appeal by the Communist Party for a general strike as a protest against the anti-Communist coup was obeyed at noon on April 13 by no less than 111,800 workers" (*Shanghai Municipal Police Annual Report for 1927*).

[12] *China Press*, April 14, 1927; Hua Kang, *Great Chinese Revolution*, chap. v, sec. 2; "Workers' Delegates' Report."

[13] *North China Herald*, April 16, 1927.

[14] *Peking Morning Post*, April 15, 1927, said official reports mentioned 1,000 arrests.

[15] Karl Marx, *The Eighteenth Brumaire of Louis Bonaparte* (New York, 1926), pp. 127–28.

[16] *China Year Book, 1928*, p. 1374.

[17] *New York Times*, May 4 and 19, 1927.

[18] *China Weekly Review*, June 25, 1927.

[19] *People's Tribune*, May 6 and 19, 1927.

[20] Released by the official (Wuhan) *Nationalist News Agency*, and published in *China Press*, April 14, 1927.

[21] *New York Times*, April 23, 1927.

[22] *New York Times*, April 14, 1927.

[23] E. Thaelmann, "La Révolution Chinoise et les Tâches du Prolétariat," *Inprecor* (French ed.), April 16, 1927.

[24] *Inprecor* (French ed.), No. 43, April 20, 1927; No. 44, April 20, 1927.

[25] Liau Han-sin, "Le Traître au Peuple, Chiang Kai-shek," *Inprecor* (French ed.), April 23, 1927.

[26] Stalin, "The Questions of the Chinese Revolution," *Inprecor*, April 28, 1927.

364 THE TRAGEDY OF THE CHINESE REVOLUTION

Chapter 12: MOSCOW: "THE REVOLUTIONARY CENTER"

[1] *North China Daily News,* April 26, 1927.

[2] Cf. speech of Chiang Kai-shek at Nanking, April 18, 1927, trans. by Wieger, *Chine Moderne,* VII, 142; James H. Dolsen, "Chiang Kai-shek's Plight," *People's Tribune,* May 25 and 26, 1927.

[3] All quotations from Stalin in this chapter are taken from the official English translation of his thesis, "The Questions of the Chinese Revolution," *Inprecor,* April 28, 1927.

[4] Trotsky, "The Chinese Revolution and the Theses of Comrade Stalin," (May 7, 1927), *Problems,* pp. 23 ff. All quotations from Trotsky in this chapter, unless otherwise noted, are from this document.

[5] N. Lenzner, "La Question Chinoise," *Inprecor* (French ed.), June 25 and 29, 1927; A. Stetski, "Un Tournant de la Révolution Chinoise," *ibid.,* April 27, 1927; Stetski, "La Dialectique de la Lutte en Chine," *ibid.,* May 7, 1927; L. Heller, "Après la Rupture du Front National Révolutionnaire en Chine," *ibid.,* May 7, 1927; J. Pepper, "L'Alliance de Chamberlain et de Tchang Kai-chek," *ibid.,* May 21, 1927, etc.

[6] N. Lenzner, "La Question Chinoise." (Emphasis in original.)

[7] Bukharin, *Problèmes de la Révolution Chinoise,* pp. 56, 59; Bukharin, "Report to the Plenum of the Moscow Committee of the Communist Party of the Soviet Union" (June 4, 1927), *Inprecor* (French ed.), July 2, 1927; also: "When is it necessary to conclude a compromise and when must one pass over to the offensive? That depends on concrete conditions. In particular, the E.C.C.I. considers that the tactic proposed by some comrades at Shanghai at the time of Chiang Kai-shek's coup d'état was absurd. This tactic consisted in arousing in advance an insurrection against the imperialists and against Chiang Kai-shek, and offering them battle on a broad front . . . In a broad armed action, the workers of Shanghai would have been exterminated by the bloc of the armed forces of Chiang Kai-shek and the imperialists, and the elite of the Chinese proletariat would have perished in a battle in which it had absolutely no chance of success" ("Résolution sur la Question Chinoise," *Inprecor* [French ed.], June 15, 1927).

[8] E. Eichenwald, "The Tactical Line of the Comintern in China," *Inprecor,* June 2, 1927.

[9] Bukharin, *Problèmes de la Révolution Chinoise,* p. 59.

[10] Tang Shin-she, "The Play of Forces of Chiang Kai-shek and the Hankow Government," *Inprecor* (French ed.), June 6, 1927.

[11] Trotsky, *Problems,* p. 285.

[12] Trotsky, "Second Speech on the Chinese Question," *Problems,* p. 103.

[13] Strong, *China's Millions,* pp. 38–39.

[14] Doriot, "À Travers la Révolution Chinoise," *L'Humanité,* June 25, 1927.

[15] Quoted by Trotsky, *Problems,* p. 280. This and other passages were deleted from minutes of the Congress.

[16] Louis Fischer, *Soviets in World Affairs,* II, 667.

[17] Mif, *Kitaiskaya Revolutsia,* p. 100.

[18] "Manifesto of the Fifth Congress of the Chinese Communist Party," *Min Kuo Jih Pao* (Wuhan), May 23–26, 1927.

[19] Official translation, *Inprecor,* July 28, 1927.

[20] "Declaration of the Pan-Pacific Trade Union Secretariat" (Hankow, July 25, 1927), *Inprecor,* September 2, 1927.

[21] Mif, *op. cit.*, p. 100.

[22] Hua Kang, *Great Chinese Revolution*, chap. v, sec. 2. This is a rephrasing of an idea more cautiously expressed by Ch'ü Ch'iu-po at the Sixth Congress of the Chinese Communist party in July 1928. Stalin's "revolutionary center" was too fresh in the memory of all concerned to allow bolder words at that time. Cf. Ch'ü Ch'iu-po, *Chinese Revolution*, chap. i.

Chapter 13: WUHAN: "THE REVOLUTIONARY CENTER"

[1] "Manifesto of the Central Executive Committee of the Kuomintang," *People's Tribune*, April 24, 1927; "Declaration of the Central Executive Committee of the Kuomintang," *People's Tribune*, April 19, 1927.

[2] "Declaration of the Delegation of the Communist International," *Chinese Correspondence*, May 1, 1927.

[3] *People's Tribune*, April 17, 1927.

[4] Ch'ü Ch'iu-po, *Chinese Revolution*, p. 114.

[5] *People's Tribune*, May 6, 1927.

[6] "Interview of Mr. Borodin with a Representative of the Rengo News Agency," *Chinese Correspondence*, May 8, 1927.

[7] Louis Fischer, *Soviets in World Affairs*, II, 667–68.

[8] *New York Times*, April 14, 23, and May 5, 1927.

[9] Chapman, *Chinese Revolution*, p. 136.

[10] *People's Tribune*, April 24 and 29, 1927.

[11] "Communiqué of the Waichiaopu [Foreign Office]," *Chinese Correspondence*, May 1, 1927.

[12] *People's Tribune*, April 27, 1927.

[13] *Chinese Correspondence*, May 1, 1927.

[14] *Reuters*, May 9, 1927, in *China Year Book, 1928*, pp. 735–36.

[15] M. N. Roy, "Imperialist Intervention in China," *Chinese Correspondence*, May 1, 1927.

[16] *People's Tribune*, May 14, 1927.

[17] Silver had been flowing to the coast throughout the preceding year. Acknowledged silver stocks in Shanghai rose from about 102,000,000 taels at the beginning of 1926 to 138,600,000 taels in April, 1927. Private hoards were presumably larger. Cf. *Capital and Trade* (Shanghai), March 18, 1926, and *China Weekly Review*, April 2, 1927. Cf. "Finance Situation Due to Panic and Sabotage," *People's Tribune*, May 21, 1927.

[18] Cf. "Reports to the Fourth National Labor Conference," *People's Tribune*, June 30, 1927, *et seq.*

[19] *People's Tribune*, March 12, 1927.

[20] Ch'ü Ch'iu-po, *op. cit.*, p. 58; Tang, *Inner History*, p. 271.

[21] *People's Tribune*, April 24, 1927.

[22] Text in *Chinese Correspondence*, May 8, 1927.

[23] "Manifesto of the All-Class Nature of the Revolution," *People's Tribune*, May 21, 1927.

[24] "Regulations of the Central Executive Committee of the Hupeh General Labor Union," *People's Tribune*, May 25, 1927.

[25] *August 7 Letter*.

[26] "Remarks of Earl Browder to a Meeting of Trade Union Leaders," *Chinese Correspondence*, May 8, 1927.

[27] Quoted by Mif, *Kitaiskaya Revolutsia*, p. 101.

[28] "Declaration to the Peasants," of the Third Plenary Session of the Kuomintang Central Executive Committee, *Chinese Correspondence*, May 8, 1927

[29] "Kuomintang Platform for Workers and Peasants" (October 1926) *Chinese Correspondence*, May 8, 1927; "Declaration to the Peasants."

[30] Details of the proceedings of the Land Commission were culled and combined from the following accounts: Ch'ü Ch'iu-po, *op. cit.*; Mif, *op. cit.* *August 7 Letter*. All direct quotations used are taken textually from these sources. A highly stylized account will be found under the title "The Night of August the Fourth," in Erdberg, *Tales of Modern China*.

[31] Ch'ü Ch'iu-po, *op. cit.*, p. 112.

[32] *People's Tribune*, May 19, 1927.

[33] Mif, *op. cit.*, p. 118.

[34] M. N. Roy, "Le Vᵉ Congrès du Parti Communiste de Chine," *Inprecor* (French ed.), July 13, 1927.

[35] *Ibid.* For Roy's *post factum* account, see his *Revolution und Konterrevolution*. For a comment on this book see Bibliography.

[36] Ch'ü Chiu-po, *op. cit.*, pp. 100 ff.

[37] Ch'ên Tu-hsiu, "Rapport au Vᵉ Congrès du P.C. de Chine," *Inprecor* (French ed.), June 4, 1927.

[38] Quoted by Mif, *op. cit.*, pp. 120 ff. Text also in Asiaticus, *Von Kanton bis Changhai*, p. 265.

[39] Ch'ü Ch'iu-po, *op. cit.*, pp. 104–5.

[40] "Manifesto of the Fifth Congress of the Chinese Communist Party," *Min Kuo Jih Pao*, May 23–26, 1927.

Chapter 14: THE STRUGGLE FOR THE LAND

[1] Ch'ü Ch'iu-po, *Chinese Revolution*, p. 53.

[2] Tsai Yi-tsen, "Report of the Delegate of the Hupeh Provincial Peasant Association," *Min Kuo Jih Pao*, May 20–21, 1927; hereafter referred to as "Hupeh Report."

[3] "Report of the Delegate of the Hunan Provincial Peasant Association," *Min Kuo Jih Pao*, June 12, 1927; hereafter referred to as "Hunan Report."

[4] "Hunan Report." See also "Resolution of the Hupeh Provincial Peasant Association," *People's Tribune*, July 2, 1927.

[5] Tsai Yi-tsen, "Difficulties and Recent Tactics of the Hupeh Peasant Movement," *Min Kuo Jih Pao*, June 12–13, 1927.

[6] *People's Tribune*, July 7, 1927.

[7] "Report of Kuomintang Work in Hupeh," *People's Tribune*, June 24–25, 1927; cf. "Speech of Tung Pi-wu to the Hupeh Party Conference," *People's Tribune*, July 1, 1927; "Reports to the Conference of Hupeh Kuomintang Representatives," *People's Tribune*, June 26, 1927, *et seq.*

[8] Sydor Stoler, "The International Workers' Delegation in Hunan," *Chinese Correspondence*, May 8, 1927.

[9] "Hupeh Report."

[10] Stoler, *op. cit.*

[11] "The measures for suppression of counterrevolutionary factions were not carried out sufficiently rapidly or carefully. Also it was impossible to induce the government to begin the immediate trial of the corrupt country gentry,

local bullies, and other counterrevolutionaries who were under arrest" ("Report of Kuomintang Work in Hupeh"). See also *People's Tribune*, May 12 and July 8, 1927.

[12] "Manifesto of the C.E.C.," May 20, 1927, *People's Tribune*, May 22, 1927.

[13] Strong, *China's Millions*, p. 166.

[14] "Report of the Hupeh Provincial Delegates' Conference, Wuchang, June 25," *People's Tribune*, July 12, 1927.

[15] "Hupeh Report"; "Report of the Kuomintang Work in Hupeh."

[16] Strong, *op. cit.*, pp. 166–69.

[17] "Report of Hupeh Provincial Delegates' Conference."

[18] Tsai Yi-tsen, *op. cit.*

[19] Earl Browder, "The Chinese Revolution Turns Left," *Labour Monthly* (London), July 1927.

[20] Ransome, *Chinese Puzzle*, p. 92.

[21] *August 7 Letter.*

[22] *People's Tribune*, May 21, 1927.

[23] *August 7 Letter.*

[24] "Manifesto of T'an P'ing-shan," *People's Tribune*, May 29, 1927.

[25] *People's Tribune*, June 9 and 11, 1927.

[26] Tang, *Inner History*, p. 273.

[27] *August 7 Letter.*

[28] Cf. *Min Kuo Jih Pao*, June 18–22, 1927; *People's Tribune*, June 4, 1927.

[29] *August 7 Letter.*

[30] *People's Tribune*, May 28, 1927.

[31] Cf. *August 7 Letter*; Ch'ü Ch'iu-po, *op. cit.*, p. 112; Chitarov, "Speech to XV Congress, C.P.S.U.," quoted in Trotsky, *Problems*, pp. 289–90; Mif, *Kitaiskaya Revolutsia*, pp. 139–40.

[32] Ch'ü Ch'iu-po, *op. cit.*, pp. 112–13; Cf. *People's Tribune*, May 27, 1927; Roy, *Revolution und Konterrevolution*, pp. 422–23. According to Treint: "T'an P'ing-shan . . . accepted at the beginning of June the command of an armed expedition against the agrarian revolution" ("Déclaration du Camarade Treint," *Documents*, p. 63). This statement also occurs in Max Shachtman, *Ten Years, History and Principles of the Left Opposition* (New York, 1933), p. 50. Queried by the author on this point, Treint insisted that his informant was Bukharin himself. The statement, however, is definitely erroneous.

Chapter 15: MOSCOW: THE "SUFFICIENT AUTHORITY" OF STALIN

[1] See *La Platforme de l'Opposition*, pp. 9–24; Trotsky, *Real Situation in Russia*, chaps. iii and iv, and *The Revolution Betrayed*, pp. 25–32.

[2] Trotsky, *Problems*, pp. 61–67, and *Third International After Lenin*, pp. 128–34.

[3] *Inprecor* (French ed.), May 25, 1927.

[4] "Déclaration du Camarade Treint," *Documents*, p. 65.

[5] "Communiqué de Secrétariat de C.E. de l'I.C. sur les Travaux de la Séance Plénière de Comité Exécutif," *Inprecor* (French ed.), June 8, 1927; Stalin, "The Revolution in China and the Tasks of the Communist International," *Communist International*, June 30, 1927; N. Bukharin, "Les Résul-

tats du Plenum de Comité Exécutif de l'I.C.," *Inprecor* (French ed.), June 29 and July 2, 1927; *Die Chinesische Frage auf dem 8 Plenum der Kommunistische Internationale.*

[6] Stalin, "Revolution in China."

[7] Trotsky, "First Speech on the Chinese Question," *Problems*, p. 100.

[8] Trotsky, "Second Speech on the Chinese Question," *Problems*, pp. 102–4.

[9] "Résolution sur la Question Chinoise," *Inprecor* (French ed.), June 11 and 15, 1927.

[10] Ch'ên Tu-hsiu, *Letter to the Comrades*; cf. Tang, *Inner History*, p. 280; Stalin, Speech of August 1, 1927, in *Marxism and the National and Colonial Question*, p. 249. As translated here, this speech Stalin quoted from a directive "relating to May 1927," that was apparently a draft or the text of the June 1 telegram. It listed all the points substantially as given by Ch'ên Tu-hsiu, omitting only the qualification concerning officers' land. According to Stalin's version, the directive began: "Without an agrarian revolution, victory is impossible." Then it went on: "Excesses must be combated not, however, with troops but through the peasant unions."

[11] Tang, *op. cit.*, p. 273.

[12] Ch'ên Tu-hsiu, *op. cit.*

[13] Trotsky, "Speech at the Joint Plenary Session of the Central Committee and Central Control Commission, August 1, 1927," *Stalin School of Falsification*, p. 165.

[14] Ch'ü Ch'iu-po, *Chinese Revolution*, p. 90.

[15] Ch'ên Tu-hsiu, *op. cit.*

[16] Tang, *op. cit.*, p. 280. Ch'ên, in *Letter to the Comrades*, confirms the incident of Roy's showing the wire to Wang Ching-wei. In the German edition of his book *Revolution und Konterrevolution*, published in 1930, Roy blurs the details of all the events in which he participated, but in the English edition, published in India in 1946, he adds this story in considerable confused detail. See his footnote, p. 520.

[17] Trotsky, *Problems*, pp. 121–22.

[18] Résolution sur les Interventions de Trotsky et Vuyovitch au Plenum de C.E. de l'I.C.," *Inprecor* (French ed.), June 8, 1927; "Communiqué de Secrétariat," *ibid.*; *Pravda*, May 31, 1927, reprinted in *Inprecor* (French ed.), June 11, 1927.

[19] *People's Tribune*, June 2, 1927.

[20] Tang, *op. cit.*, p. 274.

[21] *August 7 Letter.*

[22] *People's Tribune*, June 12 and 21, 1927.

[23] *Inprecor*, June 30, 1927.

[24] *People's Tribune*, June 29, 1927.

[25] E. Zeitlin, "La Nouvelle Étape de la Révolution Chinoise," *Inprecor* (French ed.), June 29, 1927.

[26] *August 7 Letter*; Mif, *Kitaiskaya Revolutsia*, p. 141.

[27] *Min Kuo Jih Pao*, June 13, 1927.

[28] Sia Ting, "The Peasant Movement in China," *Inprecor*, June 23, 1927; *People's Tribune*, June 30, 1927.

[29] Mif, *op. cit.*, p. 139.

[30] Louis Fischer, *Soviets in World Affairs*, II, 672.

Chapter 16: WUHAN: THE DEBACLE

[1] *Daily Worker*, New York, April 6, 1926.

[2] Fuse, *Soviet Policy in the Orient*, pp. 322–26, 327, 329.

[3] *Inprecor* (French ed.), June 8, 1927; Trotsky, *Problems*, pp. 123–24.

[4] Cf. "Detailed Story of Decisive Campaign in Honan," *People's Tribune*, June 19, 1927.

[5] Strong, *China's Millions*, pp. 62 ff.; M. N. Roy, *Revolution und Konterrevolution in China*, pp. 363–64; Louis Fischer, *Soviets in World Affairs*, II, 669; *People's Tribune*, June 1, 1927.

[6] *Chinese News Service* (Canton), June 23, 1927.

[7] "Marshal Fêng Yü-hsiang's Telegram to Hankow, June 21, 1927," *Nationalist China*, issued by the Kuomintang Secretariat, Canton, May 1927; cf. *China Weekly Review*, July 2, 1927.

[8] Tang, *Inner History*, pp. 283–85.

[9] *People's Tribune*, June 29, 1927.

[10] Wang Ching-wei, "The Party Must Lead the Mass Movement," *People's Tribune*, July 8, 1927.

[11] Sun Fo, "The Revolution and the Masses," *Chung Yang Jih Pao* (Hankow), July 14, 1927.

[12] N. Lenzer, "La Question Chinoise," *Inprecor* (French ed.), June 29, 1927.

[13] "Report of the Special Kiangsi Commission (Kuomintang)," *People's Tribune*, July 13–15, 1927.

[14] *People's Tribune*, June 15, 1927.

[15] Ch'ü Ch'iu-po, *Chinese Revolution*, pp. 114–15.

[16] Cf. *People's Tribune*, July 9, 1927.

[17] *August 7 Letter*; Ch'ü Ch'iu-po, *op. cit.*, pp. 115 ff.

[18] "Manifesto of the Fourth Labor Conference," *People's Tribune*, June 29, 1927. See also *People's Tribune*, June 23, 1927; Sz Toh-li, "The IV All-China Trade Union Congress," *Pan-Pacific Worker* (Hankow), July 1, 1927; "Speech of Lozofsky," *Pan-Pacific Worker*, July 15, 1927.

[19] Strong, *op. cit.*, p. 88.

[20] *People's Tribune*, June 30, 1927.

[21] *Ibid.*, July 1, 1927.

[22] *Ibid.*, June 30, 1927.

[23] Ch'ên Tu-hsiu, *Letter to the Comrades*.

[24] *Inprecor*, July 28, 1927.

[25] N. Bukharin, "The Position of the Chinese Revolution," *Inprecor*, July 6, 1927.

[26] N. Bukharin, "An Abrupt Turn in the Chinese Revolution," *Inprecor*, July 14, 1927.

[27] "Resolution of the E.C.C.I. on the Present Situation of the Chinese Revolution," *Inprecor*, July 28, 1927.

[28] "Declaration of the Communist Party of China," *Inprecor*, August 4, 1927.

[29] *People's Tribune*, July 20 and 26, 1927.

[30] Ch'ên Tu-hsiu, *op. cit.*

[31] Tang, *op. cit.*, p. 291.

[32] *Chung Yang Jih Pao*, July 6, 1927.

[33] *People's Tribune*, July 14, 1927.

[34] *People's Tribune*, July 18, 1927. Text of Soong Ching-ling's statement also in Woo, *Kuomintang and the Future of the Chinese Revolution*, pp. 270–73.

Chapter 17: AUTUMN HARVEST AND THE CANTON COMMUNE

[1] Jui Fu-san, "What Has Happened to the Seething Revolution?" *China Weekly Review*, August 20, 1927.

[2] "The Immediate Tasks of the Chinese Trade Unions in the Present Situation,"*Pan-Pacific Worker*, September 15, 1927.

[3] *People's Tribune*, July 29, 1927.

[4] "Organizational Report of Ch'ên Tu-hsiu to the Fifth Congress, Chinese Communist Party," quoted by Mif, *Kitaiskaya Revolutsia*, p. 117.

[5] "Circular of the Central Committee, Chinese Communist Party, Nov. 8, 1928," *Political Work of the Chinese Communist Party after the Sixth Congress*; Chou Ên-lai, *Organizational Questions in the Party at the Present Time*.

[6] Stalin, "On Current Questions," *Inprecor*, August 4, 1927.

[7] Strong, *China's Millions*, pp. 242, 251–52.

[8] M. N. Roy, "The Lessons of the Chinese Revolution," *Labour Monthly*, November 1927.

[9] Roy, *Revolution und Konterrevolution in China*, p. 405.

[10] "Resolution on the International Situation," by the Joint Plenum of the Central Committee and Central Control Commission (C.P.S.U.), after hearing Bukharin's Report [August 9, 1927], *Inprecor*, August 18, 1927.

[11] Ch'ü Ch'iu-po, *Chinese Revolution*, p. 122.

[12] *Pravda*, July 25, 1927 (trans. in *Inprecor* [French ed.], August 3, 1927).

[13] *August 7 Letter*.

[14] "Resolution on the International Situation."

[15] *Inprecor*, August 18, 1927.

[16] Ch'ü Ch'iu-po, *op. cit.*, pp. 124–45.

[17] "Circular No. 8 of the Kiangsu Provincial Committee," quoted in Hua Kang, *Great Chinese Revolution*, chap. vi, sec. 7.

[18] Ch'ü Ch'iu-po, *op. cit.*, pp. 134 ff.

[19] *Pravda*, September 30, 1927 (trans. in *Inprecor* [French ed.], October 8, 1927).

[20] "Political Resolution of the November Plenum of the C.C., Chinese Communist Party," *Inprecor*, January 26, 1928. For a discussion of the theory of the "uninterrupted ascent" see Trotsky, *Problems*, pp. 163 ff, and *Third International After Lenin*, pp. 187 ff.

[21] The account given of the events in Canton is based mainly on Heinz Neumann's report in A. Neuberg (pseud.), *L'Insurrection Armée,* and *The Canton Commune*, a collection published by the Chinese Communist party in 1930. The most important items cited or otherwise used in this collection include: Huang P'ing, "The Canton Commune and Its Preparation"; Têng Chung-hsia, "The Canton Commune and the Tactics of the Communist Party"; Lozofsky, "Lessons of the Canton Commune"; Lominadze, "The Anniversary of the Canton Commune"; Ch'en Shao-yü, "The Story of the Canton Commune." All quotations are from these articles unless otherwise indicated.

[22] For a discussion of the significance of the "soviet" in the Canton upris-

ing, see Trotsky, *Problems*, pp. 151–57, 203–6, and *Third International After Lenin*, pp. 201–12; cf. "When and Under What Conditions Soviets of Workers' Deputies Should Be Formed," *Theses and Statutes of the Communist International* (Second Congress), pp. 62–65.

23 *Peking Morning Post*, December 14, 1927; *Ta Kung Pao* (Tientsin), December 13, 1927; *Yi Shih Pao* (Peking), December 14, 1927.

24 *China Weekly Review*, December 31, 1927.

25 *Ta Kung Pao*, December 17 and 19, 1927.

26 *China Weekly Review*, December 31, 1927; for photos see *Five Years of Kuomintang Reaction*.

27 "The Significance and Lessons of the Canton Uprising," Resolution of the Central Committee, C.C.P., January 3, 1928, in Ch'ü Ch'iu-po, *op. cit.*, Appendixes, p. 247; "Résolution sur la Question Chinoise," *Résolutions Adoptées à la IXᵉ Session Plénière du C.E. de l'I.C.* (février 1928), pp. 53–54.

28 *Resolutions of the Sixth Congress of the Chinese Communist Party* (July 1928), p. 31; *The Revolutionary Movement in the Colonies*, Thesis adopted by the Sixth World Congress of the Communist International (July–August 1928), pp. 39–40.

Chapter 18: THE IMPRINT OF THE CHINESE REVOLUTION OF 1925–27

1 H. R. Isaacs (ed.), *Five Years of Kuomintang Reaction*, pp. 3–5.

2 For detailed reports on suppression of the anti-Japanese movement, see issues of the *China Forum* (Shanghai), 1932–34.

3 For listings of the extensive literature on this period, see *China: A Select List of References on Contemporary China*, compiled by Helen Conover, Library of Congress (rev. ed.: Washington, D.C., 1946; mimeographed); also, *Recent Books on China*, by Knight Biggerstaff, American Institute of Pacific Relations (New York, 1947; mimeographed). A particularly graphic picture of the Kuomintang regime during the war will be found in Graham Peck, *Two Kinds of Time* (Boston, 1950). For Chinese Communist materials covering the decade of 1937–47, see John K. Fairbank and Sun Zen E-tu (eds.), *Chinese Communist Publications: An Annotated Bibliography* (Cambridge, Mass.: Russian Research Center, Harvard University, 1949).

4 Chen Yung-wen, "Democratic Management in Public Enterprises," *People's China* (Peking), May 1, 1950. (In English.)

5 For an extended analysis of the new patterns of power created in the Pacific area by the war of 1941–45, see Harold R. Isaacs, *No Peace for Asia* (New York, 1947).

Appendix: THE RISE AND FALL OF "SOVIET CHINA"

1 Tung Li, "Report on the History and Present Condition of the Chu-Mao Red Army, September 1, 1929," *Military Bulletin of the Central Committee* (Shanghai), January 15, 1930.

2 *Ibid.*

3 *Ibid.*

[4] "Letter to All the Comrades, November 11, 1928," *Political Work After the Sixth Congress*.

[5] "Letter of E.C.C.I. to C.C.P., October 26, 1929."

[6] *Political Resolution of the Second Plenum, Central Committee, C.C.P.*, June 1929.

[7] *Circular No. 68*, Central Committee, C.C.P.

[8] M. James and R. Doonping, *Soviet China* (New York, 1932), p. 10.

[9] Ch'ên Tu-hsiu, "Concerning the Question of the So-called Red Armies," *Le Prolétaire* (Shanghai), July 1, 1930.

[10] Engels, *Peasant War in Germany* (New York, 1926), p. 18.

[11] "Resolution on the Peasant Question," *Sixth Congress*.

[12] Chien Sung, *Report of the Kiangsu Provincial Committee*.

[13] "A Discussion on the Peasant-Partisan War," *Military Bulletin of the Central Committee*, January 15, 1930.

[14] P. Mif, "Toward the Storm of the Chinese Revolution," *Pravda*, April 28, 1930, tr. in *Red Flag*, June 25, 1930.

[15] Cf. L. Trotsky, "The Chinese Political Situation and the Tasks of the Chinese Bolshevik-Leninists, June 1929," *Le Prolétaire*, July 1, 1930; "On the Chinese Revolution," *Militant* (New York), January 25, 1930; "The Slogan of the National Assembly in China," *Militant*, June 14, 1930; "Perspectives and Tasks of the Chinese Revolution, Manifesto of the International Left Opposition," *Militant*, October 1, 1930.

[16] "Resolution on the Chinese Question, by the Political Secretariat of the E.C.C.I., July 23, 1930," *Truth*, October 23, 1930.

[17] "Letter of the E.C.C.I. to C.C.P., October 26, 1929."

[18] *Red Flag*, March 26, 1930.

[19] "The New Revolutionary Wave and the Victory in One or Several Provinces, adopted by the Political Bureau, June 11, 1930," *Red Flag*, July 19, 1930.

[20] *Truth*, December 9, 1930.

[21] "New Revolutionary Wave, etc."

[22] Lo Mai, *Speech before Shanghai Activists* (Shanghai), December 3, 1930.

[23] "New Revolutionary Wave, etc."

[24] "Letter of E.C.C.I. to C.C.P., received November 16, 1930," *Truth*, December 14, 1930.

[25] *China Weekly Review*, September 6, 1930.

[26] *International Press Correspondence*, August 7, 1930.

[27] "The Political Situation and the Tasks of the Communist Party, Resolution of the Third Plenum, Central Committee, C.C.P. (September 1930)," *Truth*, October 30, 1930.

[28] Speech of Kuchiumov, "Discussion on the Li Li-san Line, by the Presidium of the E.C.C.I., December 1930," *Bolshevik* (Shanghai), May 10, 1931.

[29] *Ibid.*

[30] *Ibid.*

[31] Ch'ü Ch'iu-po, "Capture and Loss of Kian," *Truth*, December 9, 1930.

[32] Chou Ên-lai, "Report to the Third Plenum on Transmitting the Resolution of the E.C.C.I., September 24, 1930," *Materials of the Third Plenum*, No. 9.

[33] Ho Mêng-hsiung, *Statements to the Central Committee* [September 8, October 2, 9, 1930] (Shanghai, January 6, 1931).

34 "Statement of Comrade Ch'ü Ch'iu-po, January 17, 1931," *Materials of the Fourth Plenum; Statement of Comrade Chou Ên-lai*, January 3, 1931 (Prefatory Note to leaflet containing text of Chou's report to the Third Plenum).

35 *Bolshevik*, May 10, 1931.

36 "Letter of E.C.C.I. to C.C.P., received November 16, 1930."

37 "The Present Political Situation and the Central Tasks of the Party," *Truth*, February 2, 1931.

38 "Letter of E.C.C.I. to C.C.P., received November 16, 1930."

39 "Instructions to the Red Armies and All Party Organizations, June 10, 1931"; "Resolution of the Central Committee on Urgent Tasks," *Bolshevik*, November 10, 1931.

40 "Speech of Li Li-san to the Third Plenum," *Materials of the Third Plenum*, No. 10.

41 Wang Min and Kang Sin, *Revolutionary China Today* [Speeches at the XIII Plenum of the E.C.C.I., December 1933, in English] (New York, 1934), pp. 8, 28.

42 *International Press Correspondence*, September 8, 1933, April 20, 1934; *New Masses* (New York), March 13, 1934.

43 Agnes Smedley, *China's Red Army Marches* (New York, 1934), p. xx.

44 Cf. Liang Pin, "May 1 and Several Important Questions of Red Army Building," *Struggle* (Juichin), May 1, 1933; "Summary of Conference of Kiangsi Party Organizations," *Struggle*, May 20, 1933; Lo Fu, "Fire Against Right Opportunism," *Struggle*, July 5, 1933; Liang Pin, "The Question of Cash in the Soviet Districts," *Struggle*, August 5, 1933; Mao Tsê-tung, "Smashing the Fifth Campaign and Tasks of Economic Construction," *Red Flag*, November 20, 1933.

45 Isaacs (ed.), *Five Years of Kuomintang Reaction*, p. 129.

46 Wang Min and Kang Sin, *Revolutionary China Today*, p. 9.

47 *China Forum* (Shanghai), January 20, 1932.

48 *North China Daily News*, August 19, 1931.

49 Cf. "Survey of Certain Localities in Kiangsi," *Annexes* to the Rajchmann Report.

50 *Shanghai Evening Post*, November 10, 1931.

51 Chung Yang Kung Lien, June 1933, quoted in *Revolutionary China Today*, p. 40.

52 "Resolution on Urgent Tasks," *Bolshevik*, November 10, 1931.

53 "Political Resolution," *Sixth Congress*.

54 *Political Resolution of the Second Plenum*, June 1929.

55 *Letter of the E.C.C.I. to the C.C.P. on the Peasant Question*, June 7, 1929.

56 *Resolution of the Central Committee on Accepting the Directives of the E.C.C.I. on the Peasant Question*, August 1929.

57 Yuen Tai-ying, "Past and Future of the West Fukien Soviet," *Red Flag*, March 26, 1930.

58 Cf. Special Issue of the *Red Flag*, June 4, 1930, on the Soviet Districts Delegates' Conference; "Propaganda Thesis on the First Delegates' Conference," *Red Flag*, June 21, 1930.

59 O Fong, "Results of the Soviet Districts Delegates' Conference," *Our Word* (Shanghai), August 30, 1930.

60 Ch'ên Shao-yü, "Why Not Organize Agricultural Laborers' Unions?" *Red Flag*, May 17, 1930.

374   THE TRAGEDY OF THE CHINESE REVOLUTION

[61] "Letter of E.C.C.I. to C.C.P., received November 16, 1930."

[62] *Party Construction* (Shanghai), March 8, 1931.

[63] "Correspondence from the Hunan-Hupeh Soviet District, August 14, 1931," *Workers' and Peasants' Correspondence* (Shanghai), March 1932.

[64] Lo Fu, "Class Struggles under the Soviet Power," *Struggle* (Juichin), June 5, 1933.

[65] Mao Tsê-tung, "Re-examination of Land Distribution in the Soviet Districts is the Central Task," *Red Flag*, August 31, 1933.

[66] Mao Tsê-tung, *Red China* (London, 1934), p. 22.

[67] Wang Min and Kang Sin, *Revolutionary China Today*, p. 10.

[68] *Struggle* (Juichin), May 10, 1933.

[69] Lo Fu, "May 1 and the Examination of the Execution of the Labor Laws," *Struggle*, May 1, 1933.

[70] "Report of the Hunan-Kiangsi Party to the Central Committee," *Red Flag*, March 11, 1932.

[71] *Red Flag*, March 11, 1932; *Struggle*, February 4, 1933.

[72] Lo Fu, "May 1 and the Labor Laws."

[73] Lo Fu, "Class Struggles under the Soviet Power."

[74] *Red Flag*, March 11, July 10, 1932; *Struggle*, February 4, 1933; Mao Tsê-tung, *Red China*, p. 20; *Communist International*, September 15, 1933.

[75] *Red Flag*, March 11, 1932.

[76] "Letter to the Labor Unions in the Soviet Districts on the Question of Labor Union Membership, from the Standing Committee of the All-China Trade Union Federation," *Red Flag*, November 15, 1932.

[77] Têng Yen-tsao, "Examination of the Struggle for Strengthening the Proletariat," *Struggle*, February 4, 1933.

[78] "The Political Situation in China and the Tasks of the Chinese Communist Party," *Communist International*, September 15, 1933.

[79] *Struggle*, April 5, 25, 1933.

[80] Quoted by Po Ku, "For a Bolshevik Line in the Party," *Struggle*, February 23, 1933.

[81] Lo Fu, "The Lo Min Line in Kiangsi," *Struggle*, April 15, 1933.

[82] *Struggle*, May 1, 1933.

[83] *Ibid.*, August 29, 1933.

[84] Lo Mai, "For a Bolshevik Turn," *Struggle*, August 22, 1933.

[85] Lo Fu, "Fire Against Right Opportunism," *Struggle*, July 5, 1933.

[86] Chou Ên–lai, "Smash the Fifth Campaign," *Struggle*, August 29, 1933.

[87] *Struggle*, October 21, 1933.

[88] For a detailed description of the blockade in Kiangsi, see the report of its special correspondent with the Kuomintang armies, *Ta Kung Pao* (Tientsin), September 2, 3, 4, 1934.

BIBLIOGRAPHY

THE FOLLOWING is a selected list of the most important sources cited or otherwise consulted in the preparation of this study. More general reading lists can be found in numerous recent bibliographies. References used in the opening sketch of the more remote Chinese historical background are not included here but will be found in the Notes to Chapter 1. No attempt has been made to list separately the large number of special reports and articles, particularly from Comintern and Chinese Communist sources, which will be found in specific citations in the notes to the various chapters. A collection of Chinese documents, pamphlets, articles, and reports on the Chinese Communist movement is now available at the Hoover Institute and Library (Stanford, California), which in 1948 issued a list of these materials under the title, *Draft Survey of Materials Relating to Communism in China, 1927–34, Collected by Harold R. Isaacs.*

COMINTERN SOURCES

DOCUMENTS

"Theses on the National and Colonial Question," *Theses and Statutes of the Third (Communist) International* (Adopted by the Second Congress, July 17–August 7, 1920), Moscow, 1920.

LENIN, N., "Preliminary Draft of Some Theses on the National and Colonial Question," *Communist International* (Moscow, June–July, 1920).

Protokoll des II Weltcongresses der Kommunistischen Internationale. Hamburg, 1921.

Proceedings of the First Congress of the Toilers of the Far East, January 21– February 1, 1922. Petrograd, 1922.

"Theses on the Eastern Question," *Resolutions and Theses of the Fourth Congress of the Communist International, November 7–December 3, 1922.* London, n.d.

"Resolution on the Chinese Question" (VI Enlarged Executive Plenum, Executive Committee of the Communist International, March 13, 1926), *International Press Correspondence*, May 13, 1926.

"Thèses sur la Situation en Chine" (VII Plenum, Comité Exécutif, l'Internationale Communiste, novembre-décembre 1926), *La Corréspondance Internationale*, February 20, 1927.

"Résolution sur la Question Chinoise" (VII Plenum, Comité Exécutif, l'Internationale Communiste, mai, 1927), *La Corréspondance Internationale*, June 15, 1927.

Die Chinesische Frage auf dem 8 Plenum des Executive der Kommunistische Internationale. Hamburg–Berlin, 1928.

"Resolution of the E.C.C.I. on the Present Situation of the Chinese Revolution" (July 14, 1927), *International Press Correspondence*, July 28, 1927.

"Resolution on the International Situation" (Joint Plenum, Central Committee and Central Control Commission, Communist Party of the Soviet Union, August 9, 1927), *International Press Correspondence*, August 18, 1927.

"Résolution sur la Question Chinoise," *Résolutions Adoptées à la IXe Session Plénière du C.E. de l'I.C.* (février 1928), Paris, 1928.

The Revolutionary Movement in the Colonies. Thesis adopted by the Sixth Congress of the Communist International (July–August 1928). New York, 1929.

BOOKS, PAMPHLETS, ARTICLES, AND SPEECHES

Arbeiterbewegung und Revolution in China. Speeches and articles by Karl Radek, Leo Heller, T. Mandalayan, and others. Berlin, 1925.

ASIATICUS. *Von Kanton bis Changhai.* Berlin, 1927.

BENNET, A., *Die Kriegsgefahr die Chinesische Revolution und die Kommunistische Internationale.* Hamburg-Berlin, 1927.

BROWDER, EARL. *Civil War in Nationalist China.* Chicago, 1927.

BUKHARIN, N. "Speech to 24th Conference of Leningrad District, Communist Party of the Soviet Union," *La Corréspondance Internationale*, February 12, 1927.

———. "Les Résultats du Plenum du Comité Exécutif de l'I.C.," *La Corréspondance Internationale*, June 29 and July 2, 1927.

———. *Les Problèmes de la Révolution Chinoise.* Paris, n.d. (*circa* May 1927).

———. "Report to the Plenum of the Moscow Committee, C.P.S.U.," *La Corréspondance Internationale*, July 2, 1927.

———. "The Position of the Chinese Revolution," *International Press Correspondence*, July 6, 1927.

———. "An Abrupt Turn in the Chinese Revolution," *International Press Correspondence*, July 14, 1927.

China in Revolt. With speeches by J. Stalin, T'an P'ing-shan, D. Manuilsky, and N. Bukharin. Chicago, n.d. (*circa* 1926).

Die Arbiter Chinas im Kampf gegen den Imperialismus. Berlin, 1927.

DOLSEN, JAMES H. *The Awakening of China.* Chicago, 1926.

DORIOT, JACQUES "*A Travers la Révolution Chinoise,*" *L'Humanité*, Paris, serially, June–August 1927.

ERDBERG, OSKAR. *Tales of Modern China.* Moscow, 1932.

FISCHER, LOUIS. *The Soviets in World Affairs.* 2 vols. New York, 1930.
This title is included because Fisher's chapter on China gives strong internal evidence of being based almost exclusively on conversations with Borodin and is used in the present text as a source on Borodin's own views and versions of events.

FOKINE, N., NASSONOV, N., and ALBRECHT, A. *La Lettre de Shanghai*. Paris, 1927.
  A communication to Moscow by three Comintern representatives in Shanghai. Suppressed by Stalin and Bukharin, the letter was published in Paris by Albert Treint after he broke with the Comintern. An English translation will be found in the Appendixes to Trotsky, *Problems of the Chinese Revolution*, pp. 397 ff.

LENIN, N. *Collected Works*. English translation, New York, 1927, 1929, 1930.

LENINE, STALINE, et BOUKHARINE. *Le Communisme et la Question Nationale et Coloniale*. Paris, n.d. (*circa* 1926).

LENZER, N. *Die Chinesische Revolution und die Opposition in der KPSU*. Hamburg-Berlin, 1927.

MANN, TOM. *What I Saw in China*. London, 1927.

Materials on the Chinese Question. Sun Yat-sen University, Moscow, 1929. (In Russian.)

MIF, P. *Heroic China*. New York, 1937.
———. *Kitaiskaya Revolutsia*, Moscow, 1932.

NEUBERG, A. [pseud. of Neumann, Heinz] *L'Insurrection Armée*. Paris, 1931.

Resolutions and Decisions of the Pan-Pacific Trade Union Secretariat. Hankow, May 1927.

ROY, M. N. *Revolution und Konterrevolution in China*. Berlin, 1930.
  This is a rambling and diffuse account, full of contradictory passages and suffering from a marked paucity of precise details. In an English edition, published under the same title at Calcutta in 1946, the author has embellished his work with footnotes and additions drawn in part from an earlier book, *My Experiences in China*, and has made free and unacknowledged use of numerous citations and quotations which first appeared in the original edition of *The Tragedy of the Chinese Revolution*. Some of Roy's *post factum* claims about his own role in China in 1927 have to be checked closely against the record of his own published writings that year. They do not generally correspond.

SENG SIN FU. *China*. London, 1927.

STALIN, JOSEPH V. "Prospects of the Revolution in China" (Speech before the VII Plenum of the E.C.C.I., November 30, 1926), *International Press Correspondence*, December 23, 1926.

———. "Speech to the Youth Federation," *La Corréspondance Internationale*, April 9, 1927.

———. "The Questions of the Chinese Revolution" (Theses for the VIII Plenum of the E.C.C.I., May 1927), *International Press Correspondence*, April 28, 1927.

———. "The Revolution in China and the Tasks of the Communist International" (Speech to the VIII Plenum, May 1927), *Communist International*, June 30, 1927.

———. "The International Situation and the Defence of the U.S.S.R." (Speech at Joint Plenum of the Central Committee and Central Control Commission, C.P.S.U., August 1, 1927). [Partial English text in STALIN, JOSEPH V., *Marxism and the National and Colonial Question*, New York, n.d.

STRONG, ANNA LOUISE. *China's Millions*. New York, 1928.

T'AN P'ING-SHAN. "Report to the VII Plenum," *International Press Correspondence*, December 30, 1926.

TREINT, ALBERT. "Compte Rendu Analytique de la Petite Commission Chinoise," May 1927. [English translation in *New Militant*, New York, February 8, 1936.]

———. *Documents de l'Opposition et la Réponse du Parti*. Paris, November 1927.

TROTSKY, LEON. "Class Relations in the Chinese Revolution." Unpublished manuscript, dated April 3, 1927.

———. *History of the Russian Revolution*. New York, 1931.

———. *The Permanent Revolution*. New York, 1931.

———. *Platforme de l'Opposition*. Paris, 1927.

———. *Problems of the Chinese Revolution*. New York, 1931.
    This is the principal source of Trotsky's position on the Chinese events. It contains his 1927 theses, speeches to the VIII Plenum of the E.C.C.I., and several subsequent essays. The Appendixes include Zinoviev's 1927 theses and other documents.

———. *The Real Situation in Russia*. New York, 1928.

———. *The Revolution Betrayed*. New York, 1937.

———. *The Stalin School of Falsification*. New York, 1937.

———. *The Third International After Lenin*. New York, 1936.

    Also files of *International Press Correspondence*, published variously in Moscow, Berlin, and London, generally known and referred to in notes as *Inprecor*; *La Corréspondance Internationale*, French edition of *Inprecor*; *Communist International*, published variously in Moscow, Berlin, and London— also in German and French editions; *Problemi Kitai* (Moscow); *L'Humanité* (Paris); *Rote Fahne* (Berlin); *Daily Worker* (New York); *Labour Monthly* (London)—all official Communist publications.

CHINESE COMMUNIST PARTY SOURCES
(All in Chinese)

Canton Commune, a Collection. Shanghai, 1930.
    Contains articles and reports by Huang P'ing, Deng Cheng-tsah, A. Lozofsky, Lominadze, Ch'ên Shao-yü, and others.

CH'ÊN TU-HSIU. "Open Letter to Chiang Kai-shek, June 4, 1926," in *Our Party and the Canton Events*.

———. *Essays on the Chinese Revolution*. Shanghai, 1927.

———. *The Chinese Revolution and Opportunism*. Shanghai, 1929.
    A collection of letters exchanged between Ch'ên Tu-hsiu and the Communist Party Central Committee.

———. "Letter to the Central Committee of the Chinese Communist Party on the Questions of the Chinese Revolution" (August 5, 1929), in *The Chinese Revolution and Opportunism*.

———. *Letter to the Comrades of the Chinese Communist Party*, Shanghai, December 10, 1929. [English translation in *Militant*, New York, November 15, 1930, to January 15, 1931.]

———. "Letter to the Communist International" in *Le Prolétaire* [*Wu Chan Chih*], July 1, 1930.

———. *Protest to the Kiangsu High Court.* Shanghai, February 20, 1933.

CH'ÊN TU-HSIU and EIGHTY OTHERS. *Our Political Statements.* Shanghai, December 15, 1929.

CHOU ÊN-LAI. *Organizational Problems of the Communist Party at the Present Time.* Shanghai, 1929.

CH'Ü CH'IU-PO. *The Chinese Revolution and the Chinese Communist Party.* Shanghai (?), 1928.

———. *The Peasantry.* Wuhan (?), 1927.

———. *Some Controversial Questions in the Chinese Revolution.* Wuhan, 1927.

TÊNG CHUNG-HSIA. *Survey of the Hongkong Strike.* Canton, August 1926.

HO SHÊN. *Materials of Modern History.* 3 vols. Shanghai, 1933.

HUA KANG. *The Great Chinese Revolution of 1925–27.* 2 vols. Shanghai, 1931.

Letter to All the Comrades of the Communist Party. Issued by the Conference of August 7, 1927.
> This document is reprinted in the Appendix to Li Li-san, *The Chinese Revolution.* Referred to in the notes as *August 7 Letter.*

LI CHIH-LUNG. *The Resignation of Chairman Wang Ching-wei.* Wuhan, 1927.

LI LI-SAN. *The Chinese Revolution* [a collection of documents]. Shanghai, 1930.

LI LI-SAN, with STALIN, JOSEPH V., and OTHERS. *The Chinese Revolution and the Opposition.* Shanghai, 1929.

LO CH'ANG-LUNG. *The Massacre of the Peking-Hankow Railway Workers.* Peking, March 1923.

"Manifesto of the Fifth Congress of the Chinese Communist Party," *Min Kuo Jih Pao* (Wuhan), May 23–26, 1927.

Our Party and the Canton Events [a collection of documents and reports], Peking, July 1926.

P'ENG PAI. *The Haifeng Peasant Movement.* Canton, 1926. [Partial English translation in *International Literature*, Nos. 2–3. Moscow, 1932.]

P'ENG SHU-CHIH. *Fundamental Problems of the Chinese Revolution.* Shanghai, 1928.

"Political Resolution of the November [1927] Plenum of the Central Committee of the Chinese Communist Party," *International Press Correspondence*, January 26, 1928. [In English.]

Political Work of the Chinese Communist Party After the Sixth Congress, Shanghai, 1929.

"Report on the History and Conditions of the Chu-Mao Army," *Military Bulletin of the Central Committee*, January 1930.

Resolutions of the Second National Labor Conference. Canton, 1925.

Resolutions of the Sixth Congress of the Chinese Communist Party. Shanghai, 1928.

Resolutions of the Third National Labor Conference. Canton, 1926.

Resolutions of the Fourth National Labor Conference. Wuhan, 1927.

"Significance and Lessons of the Canton Uprising" [resolution of the Central Committee of the Chinese Communist Party, January 3, 1928]. In Appendixes to Ch'ü Ch'iu-po, *The Chinese Revolution.*

YÜEN TAI-YING. *The Kuomintang and the Labor Movement.* Wuhan, April 1927.

Also files of the *Guide Weekly* (Chinese Communist organ) and the *Pan-Pacific Worker* (published in English at Hankow).

OTHER SOURCES

Administrative Reports of the Hongkong Government, 1925.

BEALE, LOUIS, and PELHAM, G. CLINTON. *Trade and Economic Conditions in China, 1931–33.* London, 1933.

BUCK, J. LOSSING. *Chinese Farm Economy.* Shanghai, 1930.

CHANG, T. C. *The Farmers Movement in Kwangtung.* Shanghai, 1928.

CHAPMAN, H. O. *The Chinese Revolution of 1926–27.* London, 1928.
    Valuable eyewitness material.

CHEN HAN-SENG. *Agrarian Problems in Southernmost China.* Shanghai, 1936.

———. *The Present Agrarian Problem in China.* Shanghai, 1933.

CHEN TA. *Analysis of Strikes in China from 1918 to 1926.* Shanghai, n.d.

CLARK, GROVER. *China in 1927.* Peking, 1928.

FANG FU-AN. *Chinese Labour.* Shanghai, 1931.

FONG, H. D. *China's Industrialization, a Statistical Survey.* Shanghai, 1933.

FUSE, KATSUJI. *Soviet Policy in the Orient.* Peking, 1927.

GANNETT, LEWIS S. *Young China.* (Reprints from *The Nation,* New York, 1926–27.)

HOLCOMBE, ARTHUR N. *The Spirit of the Chinese Revolution.* New York, 1930.

HU SHIH. *The Chinese Renaissance.* Chicago, 1933.

ISAACS, HAROLD R. (ed.). *Five Years of Kuomintang Reaction.* Shanghai, 1932.

LOWE, C. H. *Facing Labor Issues in China.* Shanghai, 1933.

LYNN, J. C. *Political Parties in China.* Peking, 1930.

MALRAUX, ANDRÉ. *La Condition Humaine.* Paris, 1933. [Eng. trans., *Man's Fate.* New York, 1934.]

———. *Les Conquerants.* Paris, 1928. [Eng. trans., *The Conquerors,* New York, 1929.]

PASVOLSKY, L. *Russia in the Far East.* New York, 1922.

Peasant Movement in Kwangtung. Report of the Peasant Department of the Kuomintang. Canton, October 1925.

rogram of the Kuomintang. Issued by the First National Congress. Canton, 1924.

RANSOME, ARTHUR. *The Chinese Puzzle.* London, 1927.

REMER, C. F. *Foreign Investments in China.* New York, 1933.

——. *The Foreign Trade of China.* Shanghai, 1926.

Shanghai Municipal Police Annual Report, 1925, 1926, 1927.

SOKOLSKY, GEORGE. *Tinder Box of Asia.* New York, 1933.
    The author was connected with and at times employed by various Kuomintang factions. He also wrote for the British press in Shanghai and later for Japanese-sponsored publications.

Strikes and Lockouts in Shanghai Since 1918. Bureau of Social Affairs, Shanghai, 1933.

SUN YAT-SEN. *The International Development of China.* New York, 1922.

——. *Memoirs of a Chinese Revolutionary.* London, 1927.

——. *San Min Chu I.* Shanghai, 1927.

TANG LEANG-LI. *The Inner History of the Chinese Revolution.* London, 1930.
    A history of the period from the point of view of Wang Ching-wei, whom the author served as biographer and amanuensis.

TAO, L. K., and LIN, S. H. *Industry and Labor in China.* Peiping, 1931.

TAWNEY, R. H. *Land and Labor in China.* New York, 1932.
    Especially useful for lists of monographs and special studies.

TSUI SHU-CHIN. "The Influence of the Canton-Moscow Entente upon Sun Yat-sen's Political Philosophy," *Chinese Social and Political Science Review* (Peiping), April–October 1934.

TYAU, M. T. Z. *China Awakened.* New York, 1922.

WANG, TSI C. *The Youth Movement in China.* New York, 1928.
    Particularly useful for survey of student movement following World War I.

Whampoa Year Book. Canton, December 1925.

WIEGER, PÈRE LÉON. *Chine Moderne.* 8 vols. Siensien, Hopei, 1921–32.
    Immensely valuable, although often highly miscellaneous, collection of translated excerpts from the contemporary Chinese daily and periodical press.

WITTFOGEL, KARL. "The Theory of Oriental Society." Unpublished abstract. Filed at Far Eastern and Russian Institute, University of Washington, Seattle.

——. *Wirtschaft und Gesellschaft Chinas.* Leipzig, 1931.

WONG [*sic*] CHING-WEI. *China and the Nations.* New York, 1927.

WONG YIN-SENG. *Requisitions and the Peasantry in North China.* Shanghai, 1931. (In Chinese.)

WOO, T. C. *The Kuomintang and the Future of the Chinese Revolution.* London, 1928.

    Also files of Chinese daily newspapers, including *Shun Pao* and *Sin Wen Pao* (Shanghai); *Chen Pao* (Peking); *Ta Kung Pao* (Tientsin); *Min Kuo Jih Pao* (Hankow). In English: *People's Tribune* (Hankow) and *Chinese Correspondence* (Hankow)—both official Kuomintang publications; *Hankow Herald*; *China Weekly Review* (Shanghai)—American-owned, and an excellent source of detailed contemporary reports; the British-owned *North China*

Herald, North China Daily News, Shanghai Times; the American-owned *China Press*; *Shanghai Municipal Gazette*, *Chinese Economic Journal*; *Chinese Social and Political Science Review* (Peking). The *China Year Book* (published in Shanghai under British auspices) contains useful although highly biased information in its issues for 1926 and 1927–28. Some useful correspondence occasionally found its way into the *New York Times* and the *New York Herald-Tribune*.

INDEX

Agrarian problems: Taipings and, 9–11; decline of production, 21; economy, 25 ff., 67–68; Sun Yat-sen and, 57; Stalin and, 119–21, 245–46; "officers' land," 219, 245; *see also* Agrarian revolt, Peasant movement

Agrarian revolt, 3, 6, 221–37, 301, 323–24, 340 ff.; Taiping rebellion, 7–9; "officers' land," 219, 245; Stalin's June 1 telegram to Hankow, 245; E.C.C.I. on, 327; *see also* Peasant movement, Taiping rebellion

All-China General Trade Union Federation, 236, 270

All-China Labor Federation, 264

All-China Peasant Association, 234, 236

All-China Trade Union Conference (Fourth), 263

Anarchism, 56

Andreyev Hall, 86

Anfu clique, 61

Anglo-Russian Trade Union Unity Committee, 206–7, 239

Annam, 12

Anti-Japanese movement, suppression of, 298

Arcos, Ltd., raid on, 207

Autumn Harvest Uprisings, 280–81, 324, 325

Blücher, Vassily, *see* Galen, General

Bolshevik party, 37–42, 50, 64, 295, 314, 334, 341

Borodin, Michael, 63–64, 82, 83, 84, 87, 88, 89, 90, 93, 98, 99, 102, 103, 113, 116, 122, 126, 127, 155, 184, 198, 202, 220, 236, 244, 246, 248, 251, 258, 265, 277; drafts Kuomintang program, 64; on end of Hongkong strike, 108; on Left leaders, 197; on peasant "excesses," 234; leaves Hankow, 269; summarizes experiences, 275–76; later career, 276 n.

Boxer Indemnity Funds, 77

Boxer Protocol of 1901, 16

Boxers (I Ho Ch'üan), 15–16, 18, 76, 147

Boycotts, Chinese, 17–18

Browder, Earl, 109, 157, 158, 159, 183, 212, 220, 228, 232

Bukharin, Nikolai, 50, 117, 121, 163, 195, 239 n., 243, 244, 252, 277; denounces Wuhan, 265

Burma, 12

Cambodia, 12

Canton, 64, 65, 68–72, 80–81; government, 74–88, 89 ff., *et passim*

Canton Commune, 282–92, 303; size of opposing forces, 284; selection of soviet in, 284–85; manifesto, 286–87; casualties, 290–91

Canton coup of March 20, 1926, 93 ff.; *see also* Chiang Kai-shek

Canton-Hankow railway, 18

Canton-Hongkong seamen's strike (1922), 62, 84

Canton-Hongkong Strike Committee, 88

Canton insurrection, 282–92

Canton soviet, 284 ff.

Canton Workers' Delegates' Council, 88

Capitalism in China, 2, 4; early development, 12–13; and World War I, 21–22, 35–52; Sun Yat-sen's views on, 57, 66; and strikes, 77–78, 84; *see also* Imperialism, Industrialization

Central Committee of the Chinese Communist party, *see* Chinese Communist party

Central Executive Committee, *see* Kuomintang

"Central soviet district," 302, 326, 337; *see also* Chinese Soviet Republic

Chamberlain, Sir Austen, 206, 208

Chang Chi, 131

Chang Ching-chiang, 81, 92, 93, 95, 145, 164

Chang Chun, General, 158

Chang Fa-k'uei, General, 261, 262, 280, 284, 289, 290; and Canton insurrection, 282 ff.

Chang Fao-cheng, 280

Chang Hsiao-lin, 131, 142, 145, 152, 177

Chang Hsüeh-liang, 254

Chang Kuo-t'ao, 59, 269, 278

Chang Lien-shen, 227

Chang T'ai-lei, 278, 291

Chang Tso-lin, 76, 126, 131, 170, 172, 208, 254, 271

Chang Tsung-ch'ang, 131–32, 136, 139

Ch'anghsintien, railroad workers' union at, 57

Changsha coup (May 21, 1927), 234–37, 247–48, 250–51, 279; investigated by Tang Shêng-chi, 248–49; comment by Comintern, 250

Ch'ên, Eugene, 107, 108, 197, 205, 206, 208, 265, 271, 280

383